# AMERICA'S JOAN OF ARC

*J. Matthew Gallman*

# AMERICA'S JOAN OF ARC:

## THE LIFE OF ANNA ELIZABETH DICKINSON

OXFORD

UNIVERSITY PRESS

2006

# OXFORD
UNIVERSITY PRESS

Oxford University Press, Inc., publishes works that further
Oxford University's objective of excellence
in research, scholarship, and education.

Oxford   New York
Auckland   Cape Town   Dar es Salaam   Hong Kong   Karachi
Kuala Lumpur   Madrid   Melbourne   Mexico City   Nairobi
New Delhi   Shanghai   Taipei   Toronto

With offices in
Argentina   Austria   Brazil   Chile   Czech Republic   France   Greece
Guatemala   Hungary   Italy   Japan   Poland   Portugal   Singapore
South Korea   Switzerland   Thailand   Turkey   Ukraine   Vietnam

Published by Oxford University Press, Inc.
198 Madison Avenue, New York, New York 10016
www.oup.com

Oxford is a registered trademark of Oxford University Press

Library of Congress Cataloging-in-Publication Data
Gallman, J. Matthew (James Matthew)
America's Joan of Arc : the life of Anna Elizabeth Dickinson / J. Matthew Gallman.
p. cm.
ISBN-13: 978-0-19-516145-8 (0195161459 : alk. paper)   1. Dickinson, Anna E.
(Anna Elizabeth), 1842–1932.   2. Women abolitionists—Pennsylvania—
Biography.   3. Abolitionists—Pennsylvania—Biography.
4. Women orators—United States—Biography.   5. Orators—
United States—Biography.   6. Feminists—Pennsylvania—Biography.
7. Antislavery movements—United States—History—19th century.
8. Women's rights—United States—History—19th century.   I. Title.
E449.D544G35 2006
973.7′114092—dc22
2006000888

1 3 5 7 9 8 6 4 2

Printed in the United States of America
on acid-free paper

# ACKNOWLEDGMENTS

One pleasure in reaching the end of a project is that it affords the opportunity to acknowledge a long list of accumulated debts. I first encountered Anna Dickinson while reading Civil War newspapers over two decades ago. She has been the focus of my scholarly attention for much of the last eight years. In that time I have worked in several institutions and enjoyed the advice and friendship of many wonderful colleagues.

I would like to thank my friends at Loyola College in Maryland, Gettysburg College, Occidental College, and the University of Florida for providing stimulating environments and good companionship. Particular thanks to Tom Pegram, Patricia Ingram, Barbara Vann, Christina Ericson Hansen, Bill Bowman, Magdalena Sanchez, Scott Hancock, Tim Shannon, Teresa Amott, Deborah Barnes, Melanie Conroy-Goldman, Jennifer Hanson, Eleanor Hogan, Lynn Dumenil, Doug Smith, Marla Stone, Arthe Anthony, Elizabeth Dale, Jack Davis, and Bill Link, who all endured conversations about the life and times of Anna Dickinson. I owe a particular debt to my UF colleagues Jeff Adler and Louise Newman, who both read the entire manuscript and offered valuable suggestions both large and small. If I could have followed all their advice this would be a much stronger book.

When I began this project the National Endowment for the Humanities provided funding for a summer of research. I have turned to the NEH for assistance on several occasions, and I cannot imagine where the profession would be without the continued support from this vital institution. The librarians at both Loyola College and Gettysburg College purchased complete copies of the Anna Dickinson Papers on microfilm, without which my research would have been impossible. The librarians, archivists, and interlibrary loan staffs at Loyola, Gettysburg, Occidental, and the University of Florida all provided excellent professionalism and assistance. A special thanks to Karen Drickamer, Director of Special Collections at Gettysburg College. As the Henry R. Luce Professor at Gettysburg College I had additional research assistance. My thanks to both the Luce Foundation and Provost Dan DeNicola for their support. Thanks also to Holly Fisher, University of Florida, for her research assistance.

In 2002–2003 I served as the Ray Billington Professor of History at Occidental College and the Huntington Library. In addition to the companionship I found at Occidental, I had the marvelous opportunity to spend a year enjoying the library, archives, and gardens at the Huntington. Thanks to Robert Ritchie and his wonderful staff for all their patience and support. Many of my best moments at the Huntington were spent discussing history with my fellow researchers. The list of colleagues who joined me for lunch or coffee is long, but I owe a special thanks to Zachary Leader, Daniel Walker Howe, Elliott West, Karen Lystra, Josh Piker, and Lara Kriegel for their words of counsel and their lively collegiality. One of the great pleasures of my year in Southern California was that it gave me the opportunity to spend many evenings with my old friend Joan Waugh. I thank Joan for her wonderful hospitality and for dozens of conversations about Anna Dickinson, the Civil War era, and the special challenges in writing biography.

As I have worked my way through Dickinson's life, I have had the opportunity to try out my ideas before a variety of audiences. Thanks go to Lloyd Benson and Furman University, Margaret Creighton and Bates College, Brooks Simpson and his students at Arizona State University, Gary Gallagher and his students at the University of Virginia, the Gettysburg National Military Park, the Maryland Historical Society, the Huntington Library, the participants at the 2000 "Women's Private Writing Conference" at the University of New England, several Gettysburg College Alumni groups, and my colleagues at both Gettysburg and Occidental, for arranging and attending various lectures and seminars. I always came away from these events with valuable insights and renewed enthusiasm for the project. I was particularly honored to deliver the 2002 Klement Lecture at Marquette University. Thanks to James Marten for inviting me, giving me a guided tour of Milwaukee, and making valuable suggestions as I revised the lecture for publication. I have also been fortunate to publish portions of this research in quite a few edited collections. I list these publications in the bibliographic essay, but here I would like to acknowledge this extraordinary group of editors, whose comments often forced me to rethink the themes and interpretations that shape this book. Thanks to Steven Woodworth, Joan Cashin, Wendy Gamber, Michael Grossberg, Henrik Hartog, Alice Fahs, Joan Waugh, and Ann O'Hear.

Many other people made contributions—both small and large—to this project. James Harvey Young, who worked on Anna Dickinson more than 60 years ago, met with me in Atlanta, looked over some early chapters, and graciously granted me access to his research notes and an unpublished Dickinson biography. Stanley Engerman read an early essay and offered his characteristically cogent comments.

I had the privilege to write one essay on Dickinson in honor of my mentor, Morton Keller. He responded with a few words of wisdom, but in a larger sense all that I write bears his mark. LeeAnn Whites commented on a large portion of the manuscript, and she has discussed Dickinson with me in hundreds of e-mails over the last several years. I have come to admire LeeAnn's nuanced understanding of the importance of gender in nineteenth-century America and I only wish that my analysis of Dickinson was up to her high standards. Cheryl Greenberg and Dan Lloyd offered their hospitality when I visited Hartford. Howard Wach and I appeared together on a panel in 2000 and shared several conversations about writing the lives of public women. Jean Baker shared her thoughts on Dickinson's relationship with Susan B. Anthony, and she generously sent me early drafts from her book, *Sisters: The Lives of America's Suffragists* (New York: Hill and Wang, 2005). David G. Smith sent me transcripts of antebellum petitions signed by the young Anna Dickinson. I look forward to seeing the fruits of his research. Douglas Wilson shared several Illinois newspaper stories about Dickinson. Bill Welge, of Goshen, N.Y., sent me clippings describing the new plaques honoring Dickinson's memory.

When I embarked upon this project I hoped to join several scholarly conversations that had fascinated me for many years. Along the way I have had many conversations and e-mail exchanges with scholars who have helped shape our understanding of nineteenth-century American women. In addition to the scholars noted above, I thank Catherine Clinton, Ann Douglas, Carol Faulkner, Judy Giesberg, Melanie Gustafson, Amanda Holmes, Mary Kelley, Laura Skandera-Trombley, Lisa Tetrault, Elizabeth Varon, and Wendy Hamand Venet for bits of information or words of advice and encouragement. And a special thanks to actress and playwright Carolyn Gage, who inspired me on two occasions.

Although most of Dickinson's papers are in the Library of Congress and available on microfilm, I have hounded scores of librarians and archivists—either in person or by mail—for assistance. I cannot possibly thank every archivist who has helped me along the way, but—in addition to those noted above—I would like to acknowledge Barbara Bair, Library of Congress, Washington, D.C.; Linda Matthews and Victoria Hesford, Special Collections, Robert W. Woodruff Library, Emory University, Atlanta, Georgia; Jackie McKiernan and Margaret Mair, Harriet Beecher Stowe Center and library, Hartford, Connecticut; John D. Stinson, Manuscripts and Archives Division, New York Public Library; Christopher Densmore, Friends Historical Library, Swarthmore College, Swarthmore, Pennsylvania; Nan Card, Rutherford B. Hayes Presidential Center, Fremont, Ohio; Elizabeth Oldham, Nantucket Historical Association, Nantucket, Massachusetts; Amy Leigh, Duke University, Durham, N.C.; Susan Crowe, Indiana Historical Society; Ann Roche, Goshen, New York, Public Library; Leslie Fields, The Gilder Lehrman Collection, Pierpont Morgan Library, New York City; and the staffs at the Greeley, Colorado public library, the Connecticut Historical Society, and the University of Illinois library.

When this book neared the writing stage I sent a proposal to Susan Ferber at Oxford University Press because many friends had told me that she is one of the best in the business. This turned out to be some of the best advice I received in the course of this project. Susan has been everything I could ask for in an editor, offering both broad suggestions on the shape of the book and careful readings of several drafts. I would also like to thank two anonymous readers who provided excellent feedback on an earlier version. Certainly this would be a better book had I been able to meet all the suggestions.

As always, I thank my family, Jane Gallman, Eve Potgieter, Kurt Potgieter, Anita Cotuna, and Theo Cotuna, for their support. And a special welcome to the family to Hannah and Joshua Cotuna!

# TABLE OF CONTENTS

# INTRODUCTION

WHEN six men broke down her bedroom door on a blustery February day in 1891, they found Anna Elizabeth Dickinson sitting on the floor surrounded by leather-bound scrapbooks, newspaper clippings, and stacks of correspondence. Throughout her celebrated life, the famed orator, author, and actress had kept her scrapbooks with painstaking care, filling page after page with accounts of her lectures, reviews of her books and plays, and assorted published rumors about her personal and public affairs. Scathing critiques and fawning praise sat side by side on the page, testament to her belief in the power of a balanced story, and perhaps in her conviction that history would judge her favorably so long as the record was complete. Dickinson's scrapbooks and clippings comprised the narrative of a distinctly public life, or—to be more precise—they represented her life story as told by the men and women of the press.

And what a life it had been. By the time she was in her early twenties Anna Dickinson was among America's most famous women, having established herself as one of the nation's leading orators. Dubbed "America's Joan of Arc" for her youth and fiery passion in the midst of war, Dickinson successfully stormed the male-dominated bastion of partisan politics, becoming a leading stump speaker for the Republican Party even while maintaining a radical critique of the relatively moderate Lincoln administration. After the Civil War she became a star of the lyceum circuit and one of the country's most widely recognized and oft-photographed celebrities. While other public speakers turned to light fare, Dickinson remained a powerful radical voice, challenging popular attitudes on gender, race, and class, while rubbing shoulders with the nation's celebrated suffragists and reformers. When she could no longer earn a living on the platform, Dickinson turned to the stage as both playwright and actress, eventually trying her hand at a series of male roles. Even when her theatrical career floundered, Dickinson commanded tremendous popular attention, as the leading newspapers debated her strengths and deficiencies. In the course of a 30-year career, this extraordinary woman appeared in the public arena under a variety of guises. She joined a distinguished group of congressmen and luminaries on the first transcontinental railroad trip to California; she toured the postwar South and faced down unreconstructed Southerners; she climbed Pike's Peak and neighboring summits; she authored a controversial novel and two other volumes; and never one to back down from a fight, she sued one of America's leading actresses and the Republican National Committee.

All of these exploits appeared in the scrapbooks that surrounded Dickinson on that fateful day. As subsequent volumes would document, on February 25, 1891, Anna Elizabeth Dickinson was forcibly removed from the home she shared with her sister, Susan, in the sleepy town of West Pittston, Pennsylvania. The kidnappers, as Dickinson would later characterize them, were an unlikely group: two local doctors; the county overseer of the poor; the Dickinsons' landlord; and two kindly neighbors, who were apparently there to provide additional muscle in subduing the diminutive 48-year-old. Mrs. Griffith, an elderly neighbor and confidant of Susan Dickinson, was there to provide a female presence. Susan, who had arranged the entire affair, was nowhere to be seen. The group hustled the irate orator into a waiting carriage, bound for the local railway station. Ignoring her protests and denying her efforts to communicate with friends or lawyers, they took her by train to Pennsylvania's State Hospital for the Insane at Danville, where she was confined against her will.

Dickinson would eventually fight back, suing those responsible for her incarceration and the newspapers that had trumpeted her insanity, and lashing out at old friends who had come to her aid, but not to her defense. Ironically, the woman who had spent so much of her life speaking for the oppressed found herself recast as the victim in her final round of public performances. And with each new battle she would fill fresh scrapbook pages with clippings, sometimes scribbling "lies" or "untrue!!" in the margins as her public humiliation mounted.

It is tempting to speculate about how Dickinson spent those final few days locked in her room before the intruders took her to the asylum. They said she had refused to open her door, even to accept food. There is little question that Dickinson was deeply unhappy and that her behavior had grown erratic by early 1891, though it is less clear that she was really insane. Was she cutting, and gluing, and organizing, catching up on the story of a life that had finally slowed down enough to allow for such pleasures? Or was she mustering material for her upcoming trial against the Republicans? Perhaps she was poring over stories of her past triumphs and failures, using the time to reflect on her amazing public life.

Consider one clipping from the January 18, 1864, issue of the *Cincinnati Gazette*. The headline reads: "A Girl in the Capitol." "Washington has witnessed strange scenes, betokening stranger changes, in the last two years" the author—who used the pen name "Agate"—began. "But," he continued,

> I can recall none so strange as that witnessed in the Hall of the House of Representatives last Saturday night.
> The largest audience ever assembled there had gathered—the Statesmen, the Politicians, the Soldiers, the leaders of Public Opinion . . . The President of the Nation was present, with Cabinet officers, Heads of Bureaus . . . There came upon the platform before the imposing audience the Vice-President of the Nation and the Speaker of the House of Representatives, and between them a young Quaker girl, eighteen months ago an humble *employee* in the mint, to-night the bravest advocate for the integrity of the Republic and the demand for universal liberty throughout it.

Feeling unable to do proper justice to Dickinson's appearance, Agate quoted extensively from the *Washington Chronicle*:

> . . . a young, red-lipped, slim-waisted girl, with curls cut short, as if for school, with eyes black with the mirthfulness of a child, save when they blaze with the passions of a prophetess, holding spell bound in the capital of the nation for an hour and ten minutes, two thousand politicians, statesmen and soldiers, while she talked to them of politics, statesmanship, and war! It was a wonderful sight, and it was a wonderful success.

"Her success," Agate concluded, "has been the most remarkable ever won at the Capital, and all who love the cause of the People, of the Soldiers, and of Liberty, will follow her with their prayers and benedictions."[1]

When she spoke before this august assembly Anna Dickinson was barely 21 years old. In a few short years she had achieved such fame and public importance that nearly a hundred Republican officeholders had signed the letter inviting her to address them in Washington.[2] The event took on an additional dramatic dimension when President Abraham Lincoln and Mary Todd Lincoln joined the audience halfway through the speech, just as the young orator was assailing the administration for its approach to civil rights and the president's seeming conciliatory stance toward the rebel states. A clipping from the *Independent*, an organ of radical Republicanism, picks up the narrative. "Mr. Lincoln sat with his head bowed, rarely looking Miss Dickinson in the face, but evidently catching every word, and, I have not a doubt, admiring her courage and honesty. When she had criticized the terms of the last proclamation, Miss Dickinson as boldly avowed her belief that the people would insist that Mr. Lincoln should retain his office for another term. The careworn face of the President dropped lower still at this, but the galleries sent up a tremendous shout."[3] Clearly the speaker was not merely an interesting female oddity, invited for the amusement of Washington's most powerful men. Anna Dickinson's endorsement of Abraham Lincoln's reelection appeared to have true political significance. No matter that Dickinson herself would be barred from the vote for another 56 years.

Had Anna Dickinson—sitting alone in her room more than a quarter century later—yielded to the temptation to bask in her past glories, these stories might well have engendered a flood of mixed emotions and complex memories. No doubt she enjoyed revisiting the printed praise echoing from her youth. She would also have recalled the many stories behind these clippings. The appearance only came after extended wrangling over details and admission prices, and nearly cost her several powerful friends. The glowing account signed by Agate was penned by young journalist Whitelaw Reid. Reid would go on to become editor of the New York Tribune and a major figure in the Republican Party, but in January 1864 he was still a young reporter who had recently met Anna Dickinson and was thoroughly smitten. In the decades to come, as their professional stars both rose, Reid and Dickinson developed a strong, sometimes quite intimate, relationship. But eventually the two powerful personalities would clash, and profound affection would turn to hostility, almost certainly making Agate's enthusiastic words bittersweet in 1891.

Given her impressive public life, why is it that Anna Dickinson has been largely forgotten by history? For many decades the narrative of American women's history, and particularly the history of women in public life, was defined by the major movements, namely the battle for suffrage and women's rights. Susan B. Anthony, Elizabeth Cady Stanton, and Lucy Stone occupied the positions of honor, and much of the historical emphasis was put on annual meetings, political strategies, and dueling organizations. Other formal institutions, including the American Anti-Slavery Society, the United States Sanitary Commission, the Woman's Loyal National League, and the Women's Christian Temperance Union, became the focus of historical studies. Naturally enough, much of the traditional narrative revolved around the correspondence, speeches, resolutions, annual reports, and newspapers of those women who devoted their lives to these organizations. And many of those principle figures published their own memoirs and histories of these crucial events, further shaping how we recall the past. Never much of a joiner, Dickinson received little more than a minor notice in these institutional narratives.

There is irony in this relative absence from the collective memory. At the height of her fame Dickinson was an invaluable asset to the cause of women's rights, both because of the stands she took and because of her own example as an immensely successful public woman. During the Civil War the Republican Party, the Union League, and the Sanitary Commission all profited from Dickinson's rhetorical power. Every Northern organization dedicated to abolition or woman suffrage sought her formal endorsement, and most would have gladly offered her an elected position just to yoke her name to their cause. She consistently supported woman suffrage with her public rhetoric and her appearances at various meetings. But by declining opportunities to take on formal roles in the institutions that would frame the canonical narrative, Dickinson inadvertently consigned herself to a minor place in the published memory. Worse, Dickinson disappointed—and even alienated—several of those women who would chronicle these crucial years when she failed to attend meetings, declined to accept offices, refused to embrace temperance, and—most disturbingly—threw her considerable political weight behind black male suffrage even at the expense of woman suffrage.

As the scholarship on American women's history has evolved, Dickinson's life in a sense slipped between two stools. The more traditional narratives that concentrated on famous women commonly paid less attention to the arenas of public life where Dickinson distinguished herself, and undervalued the causes—the plights of working women, prostitutes, Mormon women—that she embraced. In more recent decades the field of American women's history has exploded, as waves of new scholars have explored hitherto neglected topics, often emphasizing the diverse experiences of ordinary women as opposed to the exploits of distinctive public figures. These historians have mined diaries, letters, court records, popular magazines, and a host of new sources to uncover the lives of anonymous New England women, planters' wives, mill workers, enslaved women, urban laborers, prostitutes, immigrant women, and frontier women. As these new historians widened the net beyond the famous and unusual, Anna Dickinson's life was too extraordinary to attract much attention.[4]

Dickinson's later life also damaged her place in public memory. Some may still have remembered her as the brave young girl who stirred wartime crowds into patriotic frenzies while standing up for the rights of women and blacks, but for others that powerful recollection eventually gave way to images of a failed actress who complained bitterly about her critics and later fell into the abyss of alcoholism and insanity. Those authors intent on celebrating a glorious past may have thought better about hitching their historic memories to Dickinson's fallen star.

For all the history stored away in her scrapbooks, those pages missed much of Anna Dickinson's life story. They were her most treasured story because it was that public identity—some combination of reputation, influence, and fame—which mattered most in determining how Dickinson would live from year to year, and how she could engage in public discourse. But like every other public figure, Dickinson's life had numerous narratives that rarely found their way into the newspapers. At the most basic level, Dickinson's private concerns and motivations were the same as those of most other people, whether famous or anonymous: family, friends, loves, leisure, health, and finances all occupied her thoughts and attentions. A few persistent strands ran through the 30 years of Dickinson's career, creating a private backdrop to her public life. From her first months on the road Dickinson played the role of family breadwinner, supporting herself, her mother, and her older sister, and often assisting her three older brothers. This responsibility, coupled with her own expensive tastes, frequently left Dickinson weighed down by financial concerns, even when she was earning tremendous amounts of money. Various dramas surrounding Dickinson's diverse array of friends and suitors represented a second thread running through these years. A dynamic, charismatic woman, Dickinson always seemed to be surrounded by admirers—both men and women —who vied for her attentions. Although she had many male suitors, Dickinson never married and few of these men seemed to tempt her romantically. Meanwhile, she developed a series of close relationships with several women, some of which included physical intimacies. Although the precise dimensions of Dickinson's sexual life and identity remain in the shadows, the accumulation of experiences over time with various women suggest clear patterns and occasional complexities. A third thread concerned Dickinson's often troublesome health. Although she was an energetic woman, who enjoyed hiking, mountain climbing, and horseback riding, the rigors of the road at times took their toll, forcing her to cancel appointments and recuperate in hotels or with friends. And with the passage of time she developed a variety of nagging ailments, including both digestive and liver problems. The latter may have been related to prolonged alcohol abuse, although until her late forties Dickinson's alcohol consumption attracted little comment. Finally, and perhaps interwoven with all the other public and private threads that defined her life, in 1891 Anna Dickinson became tarred with the brush of insanity.

This book brings together these various personal and professional threads into a single life. It is axiomatic that when we remember history and historic figures we tend to read events backwards. We examine celebrated lives in the context of the significant episodes to come, seeking to uncover the seeds of success or failure before they are fully germinated. But of course actual lives unfold in their own chaotic, unpredictable ways, with the mundane and the momentous commonly intertwined, and the events around the corner rarely predictable. The chapters that follow attempt to place Anna Dickinson's dramatic life within the context of a larger society in flux, while also contemplating how her grand public triumphs often occurred against a backdrop of private joys and disappointments. It was indeed an extraordinary life.

# Part I

# ANNA DICKINSON'S
# CIVIL WAR

# Chapter 1

# EARLY LIFE AND CAREER

Born in Philadelphia on October 28, 1842, Anna Dickinson was the youngest of five children. Her parents were both from old Quaker families, and, like many of their brethren, John and Mary Dickinson were adamant abolitionists who occasionally opened their Arch Street home to fugitive slaves.[1] John Dickinson, a dry-goods merchant, had been an active member of the local branch of the American Anti-Slavery Society until his untimely death in 1845, when Anna was only two years old. Mary Edmundson Dickinson raised her children—three sons and two daughters—in a household full of books, journals, and newspapers, and with strict attention to the teachings of the Society of Friends. As was often the case in mid-nineteenth-century America, the death of the family's male breadwinner had a major impact on the Dickinsons' financial well-being, forcing Mary Dickinson to turn to a variety of economic strategies. For a time she ran a small school out of her home. Periodically she took in boarders. And she probably received occasional assistance from fellow Quakers. Although some later chroniclers tried to paint Anna Dickinson as a heroine born in poverty, it is more accurate to say that she grew up comfortably, but without material excess and certainly with the clear expectation that she would have to find some occupation, at least until she married.[2]

When many of her peers were entering female academies, Dickinson initially stayed home and studied with her mother. Thanks to financial support from a Philadelphia philanthropic trust, the precocious Quaker girl was able to spend

several years at the Friends Select School of Philadelphia and at the nearby
Westtown Boarding School, before ending her formal education at age 15. Many
fairly affluent young women in the urban Northeast enjoyed more education,
but in this age before the development of substantial public school systems or the
advent of compulsory education laws, Dickinson's limited formal education was not
really out of the ordinary for girls of her social class.[3] More importantly, Dickinson's
classroom experiences were supplemented by her ongoing informal education in
a crowded household full of politically aware older siblings and a steady stream of
reform-minded visitors. Among these guests in the Dickinson parlor were some of
the most celebrated African Americans of the day, including family friends Frederick
Douglass and Robert Purvis.

In later life, Dickinson would often speak out against the institution of marriage,
arguing that the traditional relationship robbed wives of the opportunity to grow
to their true potential, leaving daughters with a distorted sense of their own
possibilities. In contrast, she claimed, "in nine cases out of ten the children of
widowed mothers have a profounder respect for womanhood and motherhood
than where both parents are living."[4] Even though the loss of her father left a void
in her life and forced her family into reduced financial circumstances, Dickinson
concluded that her own strength as a highly successful, independent woman owed
much to the example she learned by watching Mary Dickinson raise her family. It
was also significant that Dickinson was the youngest of the five. Susan was nine years
older than Anna, and their brothers, John Jr., Edwin, and Samuel were seven,
four, and two years older, respectively.[5] John, the most academically inclined of
the brothers, eventually entered the Methodist ministry and also had stints as a
professor of mathematics and religion in California. Both Edwin and Samuel were
sickly in later life, and neither demonstrated much professional ambition, but
their periodic letters to their younger sister revealed inquisitive minds and strong
political sensibilities. Susan, the eldest, shared Anna's passion for politics and
public discourse, although she never matched her younger sister's charisma or
aggressive nature. As the eldest daughter, Susan assisted her mother in running the
Dickinson household. By the happenstance of birth order and gender, Susan would
be her mother's principal caregiver for the next 30 years, allowing her younger sister
the freedom to pursue other dreams. It requires no great imagination to picture
young Anna Dickinson joining her family in spirited debates about abolitionism,
the emerging sectional crisis, the status of women, and a host of topics that would
shape her future oratory. But before long her mother and all four siblings would
become to some degree dependent on Dickinson's earnings or connections,
producing an awkward inversion of these familial roles.

When she was only 13 years old, Dickinson made her first excursion into the
public arena, providing a fascinating glimpse into the inner workings of her young
mind. In January 1856 she came across a startling newspaper story describing how

a Kentucky schoolteacher had been brutally tarred and feathered for publishing an antislavery letter. The story so enraged the young abolitionist that she fired off a long letter to William Lloyd Garrison's antislavery newspaper, the *Liberator*. Rather than emphasizing the horrors of slavery, Dickinson's letter adopted a technical constitutional argument emphasizing freedom of the press. "It is an established truth," she wrote, "that where the press is free, the people are free, and that, where freedom of the press is not known, the people are the slaves of despotism." To find such behavior in Kentucky, ostensibly one of the more liberal slave states, illustrated the folly in adopting a policy of patience, Dickinson insisted. "How long will Northern men watch this struggle between Freedom or Slavery" she asked. "How long will they see their rights trampled on, their liberty sacrificed, their highest and most lofty sentiments crushed beneath the iron heel of oppression!"[6]

It was a powerful letter, one that gave no indication of the author's youth. By signing her name "Anna E. D." Dickinson openly acknowledged that a woman had written the letter, but nothing in her argument suggested a gendered analysis, nor did she follow a common path by asserting that being female afforded her a special perspective on the moral issue of slavery. It was an argument based upon the Constitution and the Bill of Rights, not the sort of moral suasion that characterized much abolitionist rhetoric, particularly that written by those midcentury Northern women whose reform impulse emerged from a commitment to domesticity.[7]

In many senses, mid-nineteenth-century America was a world of clearly defined gender roles and distinctions, particularly for Northern women and men raised in middle-class households.[8] To read the popular periodical and advice literature was to discover a society of quite explicitly delineated gender spheres. Young women learned the guidelines that defined what has been called a "Cult of True Womanhood," while young men were equally conscious of how social expectations shaped distinct roles for them. For Dickinson's contemporaries, the cultural message was quite clear: Young women were to cultivate a range of domestic skills in preparation for their futures as wives and mothers. And, as an adjunct to this celebration of domesticity, they were to exhibit purity, piety, and a willing submissiveness to patriarchal authority.[9]

Even within the confines of the domestic sphere—defined either by physical space or ideology—Northern women were not mute observers of public events, however. The same assumptions that defined them as the more gentle, pious, and pure sex also opened the door for reform-minded women to critique society's immorality and injustices. In this sense, domesticity became the entrée for many women to engage in public conversations about alcohol, prostitution, poverty, and chattel slavery. Moreover, an increased emphasis on the educational role of mothers, particularly in molding the characters of their sons, became powerful leverage for expanding educational opportunities for young women.

While the limitations and assumptions of bourgeois domesticity produced some unanticipated, and empowering, ironies—keeping women in bondage while forging powerful bonds among them, as one historian has phrased it[10]—some antebellum women challenged the very premise that a nation established on the basis of political equality was living up to its ideals as long as it remained culturally, legally, and economically committed to gender difference and inequality. The first major moment in the American women's rights movement occurred in 1848, when about 300 women and men gathered for two days in July at Seneca Falls, New York. Their discussions ranged widely, touching on a wealth of concerns and grievances. In the end, a hundred of the participants signed the famed Declaration of Sentiments and accompanying Resolutions, penned by Elizabeth Cady Stanton. This historic document anticipated the movement's agenda for the rest of the nineteenth century and beyond, and it outlined the realities Anna Dickinson would face, and fight, as she grew into adulthood.

Stanton began the Declaration of Sentiments with language modeled on the Declaration of Independence, but the "self-evident" truth at the core of this new Declaration was that "all men and women are created equal." Building upon this central assertion, Stanton catalogued the myriad ways in which American women were barred—by law and by culture—from full participation in public life. Women were not allowed to vote; were denied full political participation; were robbed of property rights within marriage; were denied equal access to work, education, or the pulpit; and were subject to a variety of unjust laws over whose terms they had no legal say. Moreover, those assumptions that seemingly elevated women to a special moral plane actually disadvantaged them as well, producing a double standard in which men and women were held to different rules of behavior. It was, in short, a world that denied women their inalienable rights as equal citizens.[11]

Even while daily life in her Philadelphia home encouraged young Anna Dickinson to develop her considerable talents, she soon learned that the world beyond those walls was shaped by a multitude of laws and social prescriptions conspiring to limit the options open to a young woman of modest circumstances. If an unmarried woman hoped to support herself, remaining at least temporarily outside the bonds of matrimony, she had few available career paths. During the decades before the Civil War some young women migrated to factory towns, where for a short while rapid industrialization and paternalistic housing arrangements offered the possibility of earning good wages while remaining within the bounds of social respectability. A far greater number found domestic work in the homes of more wealthy families. But neither of those options would have suited someone from Dickinson's social world. Even though the death of John Dickinson had left the family in reduced circumstances, they still saw themselves as part of Philadelphia's broad middle class.[12] Susan Dickinson worked as a teacher prior to the Civil War, but her wartime letters reveal a persistent dissatisfaction with that career. For a while she toyed with becoming a governess, and later she spoke of coloring photographs for a living or perhaps developing her musical talents. Eventually Susan turned to journalism, initially eking out a meager income on piece work until she managed to fashion a successful career in later life.[13] When she left school, Anna worked for a time as a copyist before following her mother and sister into teaching, first as an assistant teacher in nearby Beaver County and then for brief stints in Berks County and Bucks County. Much later she recalled these experiences without fondness: "Nature may have intended me for a preacher, but I doubt she ever meant me for a teacher unless, perhaps in the matter of discipline."[14]

It is impossible to know if, as a teenager, Dickinson aspired to a career in the public arena. She would have been fully aware of the cultural and legal constraints on many public ventures by women, and there is no doubt that the devout Quaker Mary Dickinson communicated a conservative religious vision of proper feminine behavior, even while she taught Anna the value of moral reform.[15] The signers of the Seneca Falls Declaration eloquently mapped out profound inequities, but their bold public statement—and the annual women's rights meetings that followed —suggested a radical critique of contemporary mores that also found its way into the Dickinson parlor. An enthusiastic reader, young Anna Dickinson would have been well aware of the emerging debate on women's rights and of women who were entering public discussions through the abolitionist movement, the temperance campaign, moral reform crusades, and diverse charitable work. Many of these reformers toiled in relative anonymity, attending meetings, distributing pamphlets, volunteering at fundraisers, and filling halls to hear celebrated speakers. But the commitment to reform led some women into unfamiliar public roles, such as chairing large gatherings or addressing mixed audiences of women and men.[16]

In the antebellum decades oratory played a major role in American public life, particularly in Northern cities. Colleges trained young men in the art of classical rhetoric; ministers instructed their flocks from the pulpit; patriotic holidays were the occasion for spirited ceremonial addresses. The nation's leading politicians —including Henry Clay, Daniel Webster, and Charles Sumner—earned acclaim for their oratorical brilliance. Public rhetoric was used for pedagogy, political discourse, and popular entertainment. The great orators attracted grand crowds and became national celebrities. And as the century progressed it became increasingly commonplace for ordinary citizens to gather in small halls to discuss—and sometimes debate—the public issues of the day.

At midcentury public oratory was still largely dominated by white men of the more privileged classes, and that male-dominated world of rhetoric and ritual underscored the fundamentally patriarchal nature of public life. But by the eve of the Civil War it was no longer a complete oddity to see women speaking before supportive mixed audiences at women's rights and abolitionist gatherings, and a handful of female orators had strayed beyond the friendly confines of such radical reform gatherings. America's first female public speaker was probably the Scottish-born Frances Wright, who migrated to New York in 1818 and soon became active in various reform movements. She delivered her first public lecture in 1828, and before long she was a celebrated orator, traveling across the country to spread her own brand of social reform. Her popularity did not last long. The flamboyant Wright—who was already morally suspect because of her public appearances—soon became linked to "free love" and sexual immorality, undermining her career. Other women followed her footsteps onto the lecture platform. Maria W. Miller Stewart, an African American orator, delivered a well-publicized abolitionist lecture in Boston in 1832. Later that decade Sarah and Angelina Grimké, sisters from a slaveholding South Carolina family, attracted substantial attention and controversy as they toured the North speaking against the peculiar institution. The sisters became a flashpoint for the debates over women in public when a Congregational clergyman attacked them for their public appearances. Sojourner Truth—the captivating African American preacher who had been born in slavery in New York state—was already known for her distinctive oratorical style when she accepted an invitation from William Lloyd Garrison to share a speaking tour with him and English abolitionist George Thompson in 1851. Frances Harper, an African American woman born to free black parents, also toured as a popular antislavery speaker.[17]

These touring lecturers, and dozens of others of less national celebrity, helped ensure that by 1860 female orators would not have to face the sort of hostility that the Grimkés had encountered. But that is not to say that the appearance of women on public platforms was either common or universally embraced. While only a handful of antebellum women had the temerity to go on the platform, thousands used their pens to weigh in on the social, cultural, and even partisan political issues of the day, thus engaging in public discussions without physically standing before an audience. The most celebrated of these writers was Harriet Beecher Stowe, whose best selling novel *Uncle Tom's Cabin* amounted to an extended critique of slavery and the particular sins accompanying the Fugitive Slave Act of 1850. In addition to dozens of popular novelists, antebellum women edited journals and newspapers, published pamphlets, penned newspaper columns, or—like the young Anna E. D.—wrote the occasional letter to the editor. Certainly some of these authors saw their writings as an extension of, or even a celebration of, their distinctive domestic roles, rather than as a conscious assertion of a new public voice. Others put their words into the public arena, but used pseudonyms or initials to obscure their sex. Still, journals and newspapers included ample evidence of women who were actively engaged with the issues of the day and thus asserting an expanded public role.[18]

A more rigidly drawn line kept most women out of the rough and tumble world of partisan electoral politics. Female political stump speakers were almost completely unheard of in the antebellum decades. This explicitly male domain was commonly understood as no place for feminine virtues. But even when they were not on the stump, Northern women found other ways to engage in this discourse. A handful of antebellum women published partisan political pamphlets or editorials; others adopted different strategies for influencing policymakers, ranging from petitioning to lobbying. Studies of diaries and letters reveal that many other women were not only deeply interested in the political issues of the day, but also had strong stakes in the intricacies of electoral conflicts. In several elections in the early 1840s Virginia's Whig and Democratic parties openly vied for public support from the state's politically active women, underscoring the value of their public endorsement.[19]

In the 1850s the nation's political culture was in flux, producing fertile conditions for the emergence of a political sensation like Anna Dickinson. Early in the decade the Second Party System—which had pitted Democrats against Whigs for more than a generation—collapsed, and the new, exclusively Northern, Republican Party emerged out of the ashes of the old Whig Party. Dedicated to blocking the expansion of slavery into the territories, the new party forced debates about the South's peculiar institution into party politics. Some strong-minded abolitionists —including the great William Lloyd Garrison—declined to sully their hands in the world of partisan politics and political compromise, but others joined the ranks of the Radical Republicans, pushing a reform agenda through the new party.[20] Partly because of these reform sensibilities, the new party became a particularly hospitable home for activist women intent on engaging in partisan discourse. In the presidential campaign of 1856, Jessie Benton Frémont—the daughter of Missouri senator Thomas Hart Benton and the wife of Republican candidate John C. Frémont—emerged as an important political voice in her own right. Abolitionist journalist Jane Grey Swisshelm maintained her political independence, but she regularly endorsed Republican candidates in the pages of the *St. Cloud (Minnesota) Visiter* and, later, the *St. Cloud Democrat*. Several veterans of the women's rights and abolitionist movements, including Lydia Maria Child and Elizabeth Cady Stanton, authored campaign literature and lobbied for the party. A few women, including Swisshelm and popular temperance orator Clarina Howard Nichols, spoke at Republican rallies, while others entered the public arena in other guises.[21] Meanwhile, party regulars on both sides perfected new techniques for luring voters to the polls, often blurring the lines between public entertainment and political campaigning. As one pair of historians has characterized it, many ordinary voters were not so much rabid party loyalists as engaged citizens, who responded to political campaigns as a consumer responded to the marketplace. In such an environment, carefully packaged political spectacles were critical to electoral victory.[22]

Even while Anna Dickinson's eastern, urban world placed substantial constraints on what young middle-class women could—and should—do, the moment held out tantalizing possibilities for the adventuresome few. Within her own social circle it was perfectly acceptable for a young woman to think and talk about public issues, and to weigh in when discussions turned to partisan politics. Before long, and almost certainly with no particular goal of blazing a new trail for women, Anna Dickinson would find herself moving onto unfamiliar public terrain as she moved from the parlor to the platform. And as her popular appeal grew, it would not be long before the party regulars took notice. How she handled that fame, and how audiences responded, would dictate both her own public career and her larger legacy.

Dickinson got her first taste of public speaking in January 1860, when she was barely 17 years old. Three decades later she recalled the occasion with relish. One Saturday afternoon she read an advertisement from the "Friends of Progress" announcing a public debate on "Woman's Rights and Wrongs" to be held the next day. Without consulting her pious mother, Dickinson ventured into a crowded Clarkson Hall on the Sabbath, expecting only to listen from the audience. But soon she became outraged by a "bristling dictatorial man" who announced that although his daughters were the equal of any man's, they were destined to lives of domesticity and were unsuited to careers as doctors, lawyers, preachers, bankers, or the like. Enraged, Dickinson recalled, she leapt to her feet, shook her "slim finger in his face," and declared "in Heaven's name, sir, what else is to be expected of such a father?" With no regard for debating protocol, the young Quaker launched a furious attack, driving the man from the hall with her invective. The audience's response must have been electric or, at the very least, startled. No one expected such strong remarks from a diminutive young woman.[23]

Dickinson enjoyed the adrenalin rush that accompanied her brief impromptu appearance, and the ensuing attention and praise.[24] In the following months she delivered similar short remarks at other gatherings, developing a reputation in the greater Philadelphia area. That October, on the eve of the national elections, Dickinson accepted an invitation to attend the 23rd annual meeting of the Pennsylvania Anti-Slavery Society at Kennett Square, outside of Philadelphia. This time her appearance was not a spontaneous response from the floor or a few brief remarks. Instead, she shared a platform with famed abolitionists Lucretia and James Mott, Oliver Johnson, James McKim, and Robert Purvis. Even in this company, Dickinson distinguished herself for her radical beliefs. While others argued that slavery was an evil not sanctioned by the Constitution, Dickinson insisted that "even if the word slave is not in the Constitution the idea is," in the form of the Fugitive Slave Act and various legal restrictions on the movements and actions of enslaved peoples. Thus, she reasoned, constitutional change must be at the heart of the abolitionist movement. This argument produced an extended parry with some of the meeting's elder statesmen. According to the celebratory newspaper accounts, Dickinson more than held her own against some fierce challengers. "However erratic, enthusiastic, or impractical her sentiments," one reporter declared, "they were remarked with the closest attention."[25]

The published accounts of this early speech prefigured much of what was in store for the young orator. Journalists remarked on the physical contrast between the young, handsome, almost trembling, Quaker girl standing up to her older, far more polished, male adversaries. It is easy to conclude that Dickinson was welcomed at these meetings because she was such an appealing curiosity, whose passion tugged at the heartstrings of her audience. But, if the various layers of paternalistic condescension—introduced by both the reporters and her companions on the platform—are peeled back, Dickinson's speech, like her letter to the *Liberator* more than four years earlier, presented a distinctive ideological perspective that bespoke an almost dispassionate and legalistic logic, albeit wrapped in a powerfully passionate delivery.

These were certainly heady months for Dickinson. Success followed success as she accepted invitations to speak at gatherings throughout the region, occasionally earning modest speaking fees. Meanwhile, Dickinson managed to land a clerk's position at the United States Mint in Philadelphia, allowing her to escape the life of the teacher. That February, barely a year after she first spoke up at the Progressive Friends' meeting, Dickinson delivered her first major address. Returning to the themes of that first angry outburst, Dickinson selected "The Rights and Wrongs of Women" as her subject. Like many of her fellow abolitionists, Dickinson moved freely between critiques of slavery and gender inequality. Fittingly, she was introduced to the crowd at Philadelphia's famed Concert Hall by Lucretia Mott, a fellow Philadelphia Quaker and one of the nation's leading abolitionists and advocates for women. Following closely on the agenda set by Mott and the other women's rights pioneers, Dickinson—speaking without notes—insisted on the fundamental equality of the sexes and lampooned the inconsistencies embedded in the cultural and legal barriers that denied that reality.

The Philadelphia papers were split in their assessments of Dickinson's public performance. The *Press* dubbed the lecture "the words of mediocrity spoken through the lips of genius," and suggested that "the young lady in question cannot do better than exchange the harassing duties of public life for those serener and domestic walks so befitting her sex." The *Philadelphia Evening Bulletin* countered that Dickinson, after a rocky start, "made a speech that many a popular speaker might have been proud of." But after offering a generally positive summary of Dickinson's main themes, the *Bulletin* added a discouraging conclusion that seemed to miss her essential point: "We were sorry to hear the lady damaging her cause by claiming intellectual equality with men. She seems ignorant of the fact that although woman can be as great as man, the equality is not in kind but in degree—the equality of the noblest intuition with noblest intellect."[26]

At this point Dickinson's public oratory was already becoming a second occupation. She had earned small fees for several lectures, supplementing her wages at the mint, and the invitations were beginning to absorb her energies and enthusiasms. But shortly after the Concert Hall lecture, the national crisis temporarily sidetracked Dickinson's emerging career. In November the nation had elected Republican Abraham Lincoln as president in a contest that left the slave-owning South alienated and fearful for its future. Within months the deep South had abandoned the Union to form an independent Confederacy. Soon Philadelphia, with its strong commercial and cultural ties to the South, rang with calls for compromise. The president-elect himself had appeared in the City of Brotherly Love on February 22—only five days before Dickinson's Philadelphia debut—and did his best to reassure his listeners. But in mid-April all talk of sectional reconciliation vanished as Confederate forces fired on Fort Sumter, South Carolina.[27]

In retrospect it is easy to see how these events transformed Anna Dickinson from a radical reformer to a fervent patriot. As young men marched off to war, this fiery young woman was perfectly poised to strike a nerve in audiences left behind. Dickinson had already established her gift for public oratory among a regional following of kindred spirits and she had discovered her love for the platform. But at first, all thoughts turned to war fever and for a while there was little popular interest in attending public lectures.[28] In a few short months Anna Dickinson had made the abrupt, and unplanned, transition from anonymity to modest celebrity. It remained to be seen what would become of her budding fame in the midst of civil war.

# Chapter 2

# "THE NECESSITIES OF THE HOUR": ANNA DICKINSON'S CIVIL WAR

IMMEDIATELY after the firing on Fort Sumter, Dickinson still held her position in the United States Mint, but she longed for new public speaking opportunities. Like her fellow abolitionists, she disapproved of Abraham Lincoln's limited war aims, emphasizing the restoration of the Union and not the elimination of slavery, and she jumped at every opportunity to share her views. In the fall of 1861 Dickinson spoke at an abolitionist gathering in Avondale, Pennsylvania, with her hero William Lloyd Garrison in attendance. That October she shared a platform with Garrison at the annual meetings of the Pennsylvania Anti-Slavery Society, and the powerful editor of the *Liberator* was so taken with the young orator that he promised to help her career in any way he could.[1]

In late October the Army of the Potomac, commanded by Democratic General George McClellan, suffered a disastrous loss at Ball's Bluff. Shortly thereafter, Dickinson delivered a critique of the progress of the war and a scathing attack on the Union's Democratic commander. "Future history will show," she declared, "that this battle was lost not through ignorance and incompetence, but through the treason of the commanding general, George B. McClellan." These charges pleased her radical audience, but they cost Dickinson her position at the mint.[2] For several months Dickinson scraped together an income delivering lectures in the Philadelphia area. Sometimes she spoke on women's rights but more frequently she addressed "The National Crisis." Even as she developed her talents, Dickinson worried about the modest fees. Finally, following a particularly well-received appearance at Philadelphia's Concert Hall in early March, she mustered up the nerve to seek Garrison's assistance. Could he help her find engagements in Boston? Garrison responded with remarkable dispatch. On March 22 he wrote a long and thoughtful letter. It would be a bad idea for her to arrive in Boston as an unknown and attempt to fill halls with a political lecture, Garrison advised. Instead, he had arranged for Dickinson to speak on "The National Crisis" before the late Theodore Parker's old congregation at Boston's Music Hall. He had also convinced the Massachusetts Anti-Slavery Committee to offer Dickinson a month-long tour of smaller towns across the state and region.[3]

By early 1862 the teenage orator had already delivered dozens of public lectures, and she had been rubbing shoulders with the likes of Lucretia and James Mott for quite some time, but it was still thrilling to receive such attention from the great leader of the abolitionist movement. For the next several weeks Garrison played the role of attentive mentor to the abolitionist protégée, sending a series of gently pater-nalistic letters offering thoughts on her travel plans, and advice on speaking tech-niques. A scheduling error postponed her planned Boston debut for three weeks, enabling Dickinson to get her feet wet in a few smaller New England venues. As she completed her first of many tours of New England manufacturing towns, an

Anna Dickinson *carte de visite*. Produced by Wilson Brothers photographers, Hartford, Connecticut. Probably ca. 1863. Author's personal collection.

Wendell Phillips *carte de visite*. Produced by Napoleon Sarony. Author's personal collection.

enthusiastic Dickinson reported home that the crowds had been large, intelligent, and enthusiastic. Meanwhile Garrison and his colleagues made sure that she received positive notices in the abolitionist press.[4]

Dickinson arrived in Boston expecting to speak on the twenty-seventh, only to discover that Wendell Phillips had fallen ill and wanted Dickinson to speak in his stead on the twentieth. "[T]hink of that mum," a jubilant Dickinson wrote home, "this small snip,—acting as Wendell Philllipses substitute & at his own request at that. Well I had a great cram—4 or 5 thousand people,—Wendell Phillips himself & all the literary fragments about Boston floated up there to listen—& they all said it was a magnificent success—Mr Phillips called next day to say he had never been so gratified,—and so deeply moved—'actually my dear Anna brought tears

William Lloyd Garrison *carte de visite*. Photographer unknown. Author's personal collection.

into my eyes—they had almost forgotten the sensation.'—I see him almost every day—as well as a great many other splendid people—& indeed they have almost devoured me." Even in these exhilarating early days on the road, she had one eye on her financial future. "I do not expect to be very rich,—in pocket wealth this time" she reported, "but I am making my way & name now. —when I come again next winter Mrs. Dall says—'You can . . . demand your own price.'" 5

In the constellation of abolitionist stars, none shone brighter than William Lloyd Garrison and Wendell Phillips, and Dickinson clearly found their company exhilarating. During that first visit to Boston, Dickinson was Garrison's house guest, and—in a pattern that would be duplicated time and again—the entire family adopted the young orator. Young Fanny Garrison soon became a devoted friend and correspondent, while several of Garrison's sons quickly fell under her spell.[6] But it was lonely, and sometimes nerve-wracking, to be away from home with such expectations on her shoulders. Even as Dickinson was exuding enthusiasm, abolitionist Samuel May, Jr., was writing to Elizabeth Buffum Chace—Dickinson's Rhode Island host—sharing concerns about the young orator: "You are entirely right in all you say of the need of very judicious treatment, in Miss D's case. It must be a great trial and even danger, to so young a person, to be the object of so much interest, to receive so much public applause, and to possess so great and happy a talent for holding and swaying the minds of large audiences. In Boston, however, she seemed to be very much depressed, and appeared to need to be reassured. She had been under pretty high nervous pressure, in view of speaking to Theodore Parker's congregation, and had not slept a wink the whole night before, nor eaten a mouthful of breakfast that morning, as Mr. Garrison informed me." It was a delicate balance. Dickinson's abolitionist sponsors celebrated her talents and they quickly recognized her particular value to the cause. As Phillips later recalled, "she was the young elephant sent forth to try the bridges to see if they were safe for older ones to cross." But those closest to her already saw the potential dangers of too much early success, as well as the emotional fragility that seemed to lie beneath the surface.[7]

As she anticipated, it would be a few months before Dickinson would be able to command large fees. In the meantime, she built her reputation. Following her success at the Music Hall, she delivered several more addresses in the Boston area. In early May Garrison introduced Dickinson as a featured speaker at the American Anti-Slavery Society meetings at New York City's Cooper Institute. Addressing now familiar themes, Dickinson began by asking "Who or what is the cause of the war?" The obvious answer, she declared, was that slavery and racial prejudice were behind the conflict and it was merely a matter of time before the war must become a war of emancipation.[8]

That summer Dickinson went home, exhausted from her whirlwind tour of New England, energized by her engagement in public discourse, and with no clear means of employment. While she rested in Philadelphia, Dickinson established a work pattern that she would follow each summer for more than a decade. As she explained to Elizabeth Chace, her tour of New England had not only taught her a "fuller appreciation of the great cause" but also brought the conviction that she had much work to do.[9] Throughout several hot months, Dickinson gathered new evidence and reworked familiar material as she prepared a new lecture on women's rights and a rousing patriotic address on "The Nation's Peril." Meanwhile, Dickinson and her sister, like many other women in Philadelphia, incorporated visits to a local military hospital into their weekly routine. But unlike other women who volunteered in hospitals as an extension of their domestic role, the politically inclined Dickinson viewed her experiences and her patients' stories through a distinctly partisan lens. That fall she unveiled a new lecture on "Hospital Life." Rather than filling her talk with the romance and pathos of the hospital ward, Dickinson used the speech to push a broader political agenda, attacking the institution of slavery and critiquing the progress of the war.[10] In November she introduced "A Plea for Women" at Boston's Tremont Temple and in the weeks to come she delivered various versions of her lectures on women's rights, hospital life, and "The Nation's Peril" to audiences around New England.[11] On January 1, 1863, Dickinson returned to Tremont Temple to join fellow abolitionists—including Frederick Douglass—in celebrating Abraham Lincoln's Emancipation Proclamation.[12]

Throughout the winter of 1862–1863 Dickinson once again enjoyed the hospitality of various radical New England families. Although she managed to secure occasional lecture fees, her future remained uncertain. When she warned Susan that the immediate prospects were not very bright, her worried older sister answered that "I hope . . . both for thy sake and ours that thee will be pretty well paid . . . What a weight would be taken off if we were only fairly out of debt." Dickinson grew so concerned about her family's finances that she spoke of acting, a move discouraged by her sister and mother. Instead, Susan suggested that she deliver dramatic readings while the lecturing options remained so dismal.[13] But Dickinson's heart was in public discourse on national affairs.

Even as Dickinson and her sister were bemoaning lecturing prospects, the young orator's stock was rising in Republican circles, particularly among the party's radicals. When she delivered "A Plea for Women" in December, her host, Linus A. Gould, was apologetic that he could offer a mere $30, but promised that they would pay her much more the next season.[14] Meanwhile, New Bedford's Joseph Ricketson—another abolitionist who had entertained her in his home—sent Dickinson notes praising her charm, oratory, and political beliefs, while regretting that he had been unable to convince the local lyceum committee to engage a radical female.[15] Dickinson's big break came when Benjamin F. Prescott, the secretary of the New Hampshire Republican Committee, saw her lecture in Concord. Prescott concluded that Dickinson's passionate style would translate well to the partisan stump, and in early January he invited her to return to New Hampshire as a paid campaigner. With the controversial Emancipation Proclamation now on the books, the war dragging on, and enlistments dwindling, the Republican Party had ample reason to worry. The 1863 state elections promised to be an important test for Lincoln's reelection bid. Suddenly Dickinson was launched into a flurry of activity, delivering 20 paid lectures across the state in March. When the Republicans carried most of the state in the hotly contested election, Dickinson received her share of the credit, earning particular praise from the governor-elect. As the Republican *Granite State Free Press* declared, "we are confident that had Miss Dickinson spoken in every town in the State, the result would have been more gratifying." Her triumph was only enhanced by the news that one local Republican candidate, who had declared "don't send that damn woman down here to defeat my election," was among the party's few casualties.[16]

Lucretia Mott watched Dickinson's rapid political rise with special interest. "Anna E. Dickinson has 'found herself famous,'" the Pennsylvanian remarked to a cousin. "In New Eng[land] she has made a great sensat[ion]" and in Philadelphia "she drew a great throng, who were carried away with her eloquence," prompting the local Republicans to secure her services for the upcoming campaign. "She has more fight than I can go with," the soft-spoken Quaker admitted, "still her genius & rare gifts are admirable." Mott was particularly pleased to recall that her husband, James Mott, had taken Dickinson "under his wing in the [beginning] of her youthful career—& he is now much gratified with her success—as I am also—for some of her Critics saw her defects & were disposed to blame us for encourag[ing] her while so young."[17] Dickinson suddenly found her calendar packed with invitations from Republicans across the Northeast. She went directly from New Hampshire to Maine, before turning to the crucial campaign in Connecticut, where incumbent governor William Buckingham faced a strong challenge from Hartford Democrat Colonel Thomas Seymour. Despite her previous successes, some party regulars in Connecticut balked at putting a woman on the stump.[18] A sympathetic Samuel May acknowledged that "Connecticut is disgracefully pro-slavery—that is sure. It has a large population too mean to be called <u>men</u>."[19]

On March 24 Dickinson gave her first Connecticut lecture at Hartford's Tuoro Hall, earning her a handsome fee of $100. The following day she addressed the Loyal Woman's League of Hartford. By the time she began her tour of Connecticut's smaller towns, she had attracted substantial popular attention. A jubilant James G. Batterson telegraphed his Republican colleague Benjamin Prescott from Hartford that "Miss Dickinson spoke to a crowded house last night. She has no equal in Connecticut. People wild with enthusiasm." For several weeks Dickinson traveled the state, entertaining audiences in Middletown, New Britain, Meriden, Manchester, and Waterbury.[20] The Republican press paid particular attention to Dickinson's spirited exchanges with antiwar Democrats at Middletown's McDonough Hall. Soon after she began speaking, several of these "Copperheads" turned off the gas, leaving the hall in darkness and prompting the speaker to quip that "there are those here who evidently love darkness better than light, because their deeds are evil." Later, rowdies interrupted her with cries of "fire" and other distractions. But time and again the 20-year-old orator silenced her adversaries with her quick wit. "Yes there is a fire," she replied, "by God's grace we have kindled a fire, which these people by their acts are assisting, that will never go out, till naught is left of the principles they profess, or of their party—save ashes."[21] In Waterbury, Dickinson appealed to a predominantly Democratic, and heavily immigrant, audience, by claiming that President James Buchanan, a Democrat, had once declared that immigrant workers should be happy earning ten cents a day. When an Irishman in the audience yelled "that's all we get now," the quick-witted Dickinson won over the crowd by countering: "Then, my friend, you must be working for a Democrat!"[22]

As election day approached, Connecticut's party leadership invited the popular Dickinson to return to Hartford for an election-eve address for an exceptional fee of $400. Printed notices for her April 4 appearance placed Dickinson's name prominently above those of other Republican luminaries—all male—from across the state and the nation. And in a particular effort to pack the audience with eligible voters, the party made the unusual request that "ladies will cheerfully give way, and not attend to night" so that more male voters could hear the speech. Despite this, Dickinson arranged to have several boxes reserved for Hartford women and many more sat on the stage, while men packed the floor and galleries for the two-hour address. As had become her pattern, Dickinson's address was highly partisan, and often wickedly biting, emphasizing Democratic shortcomings even more than Republican strengths. And, in a deft adjustment to her audience, Dickinson drew particular applause by stressing the concerns of the working-class voters. "You have nothing to gain, laboring men, by voting for slavery," she declared. "Give the slaves their liberty at the South and they will stay there. Refuse it, and they will come to the North, and slave labor will be in competition with your own." As one reporter summarized: "Her facts were given with clearness and precision, her arguments were logical and convincing, her invective and sarcasm keen and cutting, her eloquence impassioned and irresistible." The lecture was a rousing success.[23]

As Dickinson became an increasingly important political player, the nation's journalists grew progressively more intent on explaining—or explaining away—her significance.[24] Even those accounts that did not expressly discuss the propriety of women speaking in public routinely included detailed, highly gendered, discussions of Dickinson's clothing, appearance, mannerisms, and rhetorical style. After her first appearance before the Pennsylvania Anti-Slavery Society, one Philadelphia paper had made much of the 17-year-old's youth and appearance, proclaiming that "the beauty and talent of the young woman exercised a talismanic effect upon even the rudest."[25] Later the examinations of Dickinson's appearance became more clinical, as observers seemed to look for clues to her great success. In March 1862 the Press reported that: "In person, she is rather under the medium height, with a fine, intellectual-looking countenance, large nose, with distended nostrils, which, as she spoke, moved with a sort of nervous twitching, Her mouth is rather large, with arching lips, which gives it an expression of firmness, and, although we cannot say that the general contour of her face is pretty, we must say that, in her general appearance, she is rather prepossessing." Another reporter concluded, "Miss Dickinson, unlike most ladies who speak in public, is young, and made a narrow escape from being pretty." The New York Herald attributed Dickinson's success to her "youth and good looks" as well as her oratorical skills, noting that "[s]he has a full, gracefully rounded figure, is of the medium size of women, has a well balanced, firmly set head, round oval face, a fresh, healthy complexion, inclining to the hue of the brunette, and wears her dark hair in full, heavy clusters about her neck." Such detailed physical descriptions, even when accompanied by glowing accounts of her rhetoric, established Dickinson as a physical object whose appeal was not purely about oratorical skill.[26]

While some dismissed Anna Dickinson as little more than a charmingly attractive curiosity, other reporters celebrated Dickinson as a serious public woman. As early as April 1862 the *Providence Press* applauded Dickinson as an orator in the abolitionist tradition of William Lloyd Garrison and Horace Greeley. Later that year a New Hampshire newspaper declared that "[t]here has been and still is great prejudice against female lecturers, but all reformers in all ages of the world have met with opposition. Fair minded men and women are willing to listen to all." Theodore Tilton's the *Independent* warned that "[t]hose who have prejudices against women who speak in public ought not to see Miss Anna E Dickinson of Philadelphia, if they mean to keep those prejudices."[27]

The efforts to place Dickinson into some existing gender paradigm periodically yielded contradictory results. One newspaper approved of Dickinson's public appearances, finding that "Miss Dickinson is preeminently a woman, with nothing but a woman's artillery to conduct and propel electric forces." A Philadelphia paper agreed that Dickinson's skills were distinctly feminine. She was, "A perfect mistress of her art, a modulated voice—no declamation, that's schoolboyish—no gesture, that's mannish—for the most part with clasped hands, clenched at times, pacing the stage when the words came too fast for her—with an occasional impatient tap of her foot—a most womanly way of rendering a speech, and, just because it is womanly, utterly incomprehensible to masculine critics." But other favorable accounts used distinctly masculine language to describe—and praise—her rhetorical powers. A correspondent to the *Philadelphia Press* reported that "[s]he handled her subject in a most masterly, and, I might add, statesmanlike manner, giving facts, figures and dates in such a compact and harmonious whole as to impress all with her wonderful power of memory, and intelligent comprehension of her subject." A New Hampshire paper added that "[t]o the true woman's natural wit and readiness, she adds a masculine vigor of thought and generalization." Such articles all shared the conviction that Anna Dickinson was an effective speaker who had every right to a public audience, and they all measured her strengths and shortcomings in gendered terms. But they shared no consensus about whether Dickinson was distinctly feminine, or a gender transgressor who had the ability to apply male logic and masculine oratorical skills to the political problems of the day.[28]

However they assessed her personal traits, Dickinson's supporters agreed that she was unique, perhaps even heaven-sent. Following a triumphal appearance in Hartford the *Daily Post* argued that she was "[n]ot a woman but a girl 20 years of age, a Joan of Arc that God sent into the field . . . to maintain the cause of the country at this dreadful and last crisis." The city's *Courant*, edited by Charles Dudley Warner, found that Dickinson was "using the great talents given her by God for the salvation of her country."[29] These themes persisted throughout the war. Many concluded that Dickinson was sent by God to attend to the nation's urgent needs. "When the country was in its darkest," one report began, "A Philadelphia woman, another maid of Orleans in youth, in chivalric daring and grave forecast, in sweet womanly grace and lambent genius . . . went forth . . . and stood among the people." In this fashion, some of Dickinson's supporters seemed to embrace her ideas while explaining away her larger significance as a woman in the public arena.[30]

Both her controversial words, and the fact that they were delivered by a woman, produced outrage among Northern Democrats. And the resulting battles in the press were only fueled by Dickinson's fondness for selecting targets in the local media and delivering clever barbs at their expense. The early Democratic responses to Dickinson were dismissive, but generally not too vicious. After she called General George McClellan "either a traitor or a doughface," one reporter acknowledged that "we have seldom heard a more eloquent speaker . . . even though she advanced the most unwelcome sentiments."[31] Others opted for the paternalistic assumption that Dickinson was merely a mouthpiece for the abolitionist male leadership, or— worse—that the Radical Republicans were shamelessly swept up by Dickinson's beauty and charm and thus unable to discern her true mediocrity. These early detractors commonly blamed the Republicans for leading the innocent Dickinson astray. Prior to her Hartford appearance the Democratic *Times* ran a sarcastic announcement, noting that "Miss Dickinson has been stumping New Hampshire, in company with that hoary and avowed old disunionist, Garrison, in behalf of the dying cause of Black Republicanism." Worse, the *Times* claimed, Miss Dickinson was not only an abolitionist and an advocate of women's rights, but also a known "spiritualist," part of a popular religious movement that featured spirit rappings, séances, and other communications with the dead. Warner's *Courant* lunged at the bait. Not only was Dickinson not a spiritualist, she was "a noble, patriotic woman—a woman who is using the great talents given her by God for the salvation of her country in its day of trial." Warner's newspaper deftly shifted the focus from the propriety of Dickinson's public appearance to the inappropriate behavior of the *Times*' editor, calling on him to have "the decency to retract, and make the apology due from a gentleman."[32]

At each of her previous stops in New England, Dickinson had stayed in private homes, leaving behind a growing list of devoted correspondents and thoroughly charmed men, women, and children. While in Hartford, Dickinson had her first introduction to the intellectually vibrant Nook Farm community, where she developed a web of friendships that would prove crucial in shaping her future. Charles Dudley Warner—a Nook Farm denizen—wrote so enthusiastically of Dickinson that a waggish competitor suggested that "Brother Warner writes of her as if he had been chained in his den for a thousand years without the slightest glimpse of calico till now." Whenever Dickinson returned to Hartford she would visit with Warner and his wife Susan, and during her travels she corresponded faithfully with the Warners and their relatives. Among their fashionable neighbors, Isabella Beecher Hooker and her husband John enjoyed a particular prominence. Isabella, whose siblings included Harriet Beecher Stowe and Henry Ward Beecher, was a leading figure in Hartford's Loyal Woman's League, which hosted Dickinson's second Hartford performance. That evening the Hookers invited Dickinson to their home, where Isabella and Anna stayed up late into the night discussing politics and women's rights. Hooker would become a major figure in the women's rights movement, and she often recalled those early conversations as crucial in shaping her world view.[33]

The Connecticut election went well for the Republicans. Buckingham won by just over 2,600 votes and the party added another congressman to Connecticut's Washington contingent. Party leaders singled out Dickinson for particular praise, catapulting the Philadelphian to a new tier of fame. William Lloyd Garrison, puffed up with pride by her successes, celebrated Dickinson's success in the *Liberator*: "Called in an hour of need to New Hampshire and Connecticut to assist in stemming the tide of treason which threaten to overwhelm Republicanism, it is said that the salvation of both states is largely due to her." Meanwhile, Dickinson had done extraordinarily well financially, earning 100 dollars for each of her routine stump speeches and 400 dollars for the election-eve speech at Allyn Hall, much of which went to cover household expenses including the rental of a new home.[34]

Her Connecticut success thrust Dickinson fully into the national limelight, as the New York press began to examine this surprising political phenomenon. Before she debuted in Gotham, Dickinson returned to Massachusetts for another round of handsomely paid addresses. By then the hectic schedule had begun to take its toll. "I have been in N.E. for five months," she wrote to a friend, "for 8 weeks, closing with the Conn. Election, I spoke every night, with one or two exceptions—My voice is almost ruined, . . . the Dr. says—it must have <u>rest</u>."[35] Rest, however, would prove elusive. In late April, Dickinson hurried to New York where she spoke on "The Day— The Cause" to a large and distinguished audience at New York's Cooper Institute. Henry Ward Beecher, the nation's most famous minister, introduced the orator, while Horace Greeley of the *Tribune* and the *Independent*'s Theodore Tilton were among the luminaries on the platform.[36] It was another rousing success. While other radicals steered clear of partisan political rhetoric, Dickinson seemed equally comfortable supporting the administration's war effort and excoriating antiwar traitors. As usual, Republican papers sang her praises while the Democratic press attacked both the message and the messenger. Elizabeth Cady Stanton was in the audience and declared she "felt fully repaid for all the years of odium through which we have passed in order to make it possible for women to speak on the political topics of the day." Years later she recalled that "On no two occasions of my life have I been so deeply moved, so exalted, so lost in overflowing gratitude, that woman had revealed her power in oratory."[37]

In a young career already full of important benchmarks, Dickinson's first lecture at New York City's Cooper Institute merited special notice. In addition to the extensive press coverage, Dickinson reportedly earned nearly a thousand dollars for that single appearance, establishing her as one of the nation's most popular drawing cards.[38] The following day a group of New York gentleman invited her to repeat her lecture at the Cooper Institute, and two days later she received a similar invitation from 20 members of Philadelphia's Union League, including Republican Congressman William D. Kelley.[39]

While Dickinson made her own professional decisions and framed her own political beliefs, she routinely turned to various radical advisors and Republican operatives—Garrison and May in Boston, Prescott in New Hampshire, Batterson in Connecticut—who arranged her lectures and helped shape her early career. In Philadelphia, Judge Kelley not only set up her Academy of Music presentations, he also used his influence to lobby Philadelphia newspapers covering her appearances. In this fashion Dickinson's public identity developed through a combination of her own gifts and energies and the meticulous support of an impressive coterie of male political wire pullers, most of whom, like Kelley, quickly developed a paternalistic affection for the charismatic Quaker.[40]

By the summer of 1863 the Union was at a military and political crossroads. On May 2—the day Dickinson delivered her second Cooper Institute Address—the Union forces under General Joe Hooker were defeated by Robert E. Lee's Army of Northern Virginia at Chancellorsville. The following month the audacious Lee led an invasion into Pennsylvania, culminating in the bloody battle of Gettysburg on the first three days of July. In the meantime, the Lincoln administration struggled under the combined weight of military misfortune, controversial conscription, and internal divisions over emancipation. Against this disturbing backdrop, Anna Dickinson's passionate patriotism and fiery style, coupled with her unabashed abolitionism and sharp critiques of traitorous Copperheads, struck a nerve with audiences.

But the burdens of fame and the pressures of family responsibility had begun to leave their marks. In April, Susan Dickinson sent Anna a gushing letter about how friends and neighbors had been particularly attentive now that her younger sibling had become a celebrity. In the same long letter Susan worried about Dickinson's chronically sore throat, described her own failed efforts to secure a new job, and reported on the search for a new family home in Philadelphia. How must such a letter, so full of mixed messages, have affected Anna Dickinson? On the one hand, her sister and mother were perpetually concerned about her fragile health, worrying that she was pushing her body too hard. On the other hand, Susan's note underscored for Dickinson that her family depended on her continued success. Meanwhile, Susan's letter reinforced the ancillary benefits of fame. While she was enjoying triumphs from Maine to New York, Dickinson's mother—to whom she was deeply devoted—basked in the reflected glory of her youngest child.[41] This glory, in turn, gave Dickinson additional leeway with her conservative mother. That summer an old family friend asked Dickinson if her family had "become reconciled to thy public work?" "Oh yes!" Dickinson answered, "What I am doing was all wrong at first. It is all right now. Success, like charity, covers a multitude of sins."[42]

In early June Dickinson sent an unusually reflective letter to James Beecher, whom she had befriended in Boston. "I am tired, &—low be it spoken—cross," she wrote. "I get nothing done,—all sorts of people come to me on all sorts of trivial business . . . letters pour in upon me, till I cry out in despair, remembering they are to be read & <u>answered</u>—meantime my work, actual work—study, thought, preparation, suffers . . . People tell me I have done thus & so . . . flatter, praise, caress me . . . then beg my heart not to be spoiled—There is too great a need of work, . . . And when one thinks of great hearts, & noble souls, the brave men,—fighting, suffering, dying for the cause . . . what an inspiration to work."[43] In one sense this letter reveals a young woman committed to her patriotic labors, annoyed to the point of distraction by all the trappings of that fame. On the other hand, one wonders if she did not protest too much. This letter suggests that perhaps the attention was going to her head, leaving Dickinson in danger of believing the most celebratory letters and editorials about her importance. Certainly her friends and relatives, even while heaping on more praise, worried that the attention would spoil her. That same afternoon Dickinson sent a similar letter to Charles Dudley Warner. Again she complained—with no sense of irony—about the unceasing press of correspondence. Although worn out, Dickinson was ebullient. We live in "A time so jolly," she wrote. "Ah, my friend, the necessities of the hour,—the fearful danger, —the necessity of <u>unselfish</u> work,—of laboring with one's whole heart for the dear cause;—these shut out all minor or personal feelings—I can only pray, that it may always be so."[44] It was certainly not lost on Dickinson that the nation's crisis had provided her with an unusual opportunity to enter the public arena.

It was this rising celebrity that led journalist Whitelaw Reid to make a pilgrimage to the Dickinsons' new Philadelphia home later that June. Reid, who had been covering eastern politics and the war for the *Cincinnati Gazette*, was about five years older than Dickinson and a rising star in his own right. A Washington insider, he was accustomed to hobnobbing with leading Republicans. Through Judge Kelley he secured a private interview with Philadelphia's oratorical sensation. Reid and Kelley met Dickinson in her modest Locust Street home, which he described as one of Philadelphia's typical "brick fronted, white-shuttered, marble stepped abominations." As soon as Dickinson joined them in the parlor, Reid was struck by her "voice so rich, so deep, so mellow, that you cannot help envying the possessor." As she spoke, Reid inspected Dickinson's physical appearance:

To begin with, this is no scrawny featured, sallow-faced, pantalooned female of forty, of the woman's rights persuasion, but a girl—a few months over twenty. ... Plump, round, supple figure, of about medium height, with graceful outlines half concealed by the neatly fitting dress, glossy black hair, cut tolerably short and falling in luxuriant profusion about the neck and curling away from a low, broad forehead; deep eyes, of a dark hue you can hardly define, contracting and dilating in the excitement of the animated talk; a broad, rich mouth, with ripe lips that curve into a score of expressions in an instant; a square, not masculine, but still firmly set chin, that gives a hint of the persistent purpose that has brought this girl up through all manner of difficulties to a position almost as proud in its way as that of Mrs. Stowe . . .

The two spent a pleasant June afternoon chatting before Kelley whisked Reid away to other appointments, well before the captivated journalist was ready to leave his host.

That evening they ran into each other at a party in the Philadelphia suburbs, and Reid found himself studying Dickinson in this public setting "rather in the light of a rare specimen of natural history than as a well-bred and accomplished young lady." He found it hard to imagine that "this merry and (if I must confess it) bewitching young damsel was the stirring orator whom Henry Ward Beecher and other not less worthy critics had covered with such unbounded eulogy." Reid quickly dismissed the rumor that more mature reformers must be writing Dickinson's speeches. She was far too quick-witted and strong-willed to yield to such controls. Still, the patriarchal journalist concluded that Dickinson, "like all other women . . . sometimes jumps to illogical conclusions without any bother of reasoning on the road" and that sometimes her moments of inflamed anger on the platform were more amusing than the stuff of serious rhetoric. "But enough!" he declared. "This young girl, so brilliant, so magnetic, so wonderfully gifted, is a real genius. And God gives us so few of these, we may be pardoned the rudeness of talking about them in the newspapers."[45] Reid's extensive portrait marked an important milestone in Dickinson's public career, as thousands of interested readers now had a window into her world. The orator, no doubt pleased with the account, carefully cut out the article and placed it in her scrapbook.

For the next six months Dickinson juggled a host of offers and obligations. On July 6, as the North celebrated the Union's victory at Gettysburg, Dickinson shared a platform with Judge Kelley and Frederick Douglass at a recruiting rally for Philadelphia's Supervisory Committee for Recruiting Colored Regiments. It was a festive occasion, in which Dickinson and her colleagues celebrated both successes in the field and the gains accompanying emancipation and black military service. But while she opened her remarks with patriotic enthusiasm, Dickinson frankly acknowledged the awkwardness of the moment. Here she was, a white woman, saying "Anglo-Africans, we need you," knowing full well that the men before her stood to receive unequal bounties and pay for serving their country. "My cheeks would crimson with shame," to make such a request for her race alone, she admitted. But if the current conditions were unjust, the future was bright and the alternatives clear. "You hold the hammer which, upheld or falling, decides your destiny," she declared. "You have not homes!—gain them. You have not liberty!—gain it. You have not a flag!—gain it. You have not a country!—be written down in history as the race who made one for themselves, and saved one for another" she concluded, as her audience broke into rousing cheers.[46] That September she attended a review of the newly enlisted 8th Regiment of the United States Colored Troops training at Philadelphia's Camp William Penn, where she delivered a few impromptu remarks to a group of new recruits, many of whom had heard her dramatic words only a few months earlier.[47]

Soon Dickinson returned to the political platform, speaking for the Republicans in Pennsylvania followed by a brief campaign visit to Buffalo, New York. In her native state, party organizers sent Dickinson into Democratic strongholds in southeastern Pennsylvania where they apparently reasoned that she might succeed in melting the hearts of hostile voters. Although she once again earned praise from local party organizers, this campaign was not the unmitigated success of her earlier ventures. The veteran campaigner chafed at the state committee's poor organization, and was disappointed at the modest compensation she received for her 15 to 20 appearances.[48]

The Pennsylvania campaign added a colorful chapter to Dickinson's growing lore. Prior to her excursion into a particularly hostile mining region, a Philadelphia Republican warned that "apprehensions are expressed that you will meet with a rough reception at Shamokin and I have been asked to urge you to avoid that place." Nonetheless, Dickinson appeared there on October 5, and according to one popular story an irate miner fired a shot at the pugnacious orator as she spoke, perhaps even clipping off a portion of her celebrated short hair. But even in such hostile surroundings Dickinson enjoyed some success, as another Shamokin miner later wrote that "I am proud to acknowledge myself as *one of her converts.*"[49]

In November Dickinson took a break from campaigning long enough to visit Chicago's Northwestern Sanitary Fair. Throughout the Civil War the United States Sanitary Commission raised money, prepared packages, and sent agents and materials to the soldiers at the front. But the U.S.S.C. was perhaps equally valuable in promoting patriotism on the home front and offering an outlet for the North's substantial voluntaristic energies. Although a national organization with its main offices in New York City, the U.S.S.C. functioned largely as an immense network of local voluntary organizations. As the war entered its third year, the flow of contributions had begun to wane and organizers turned to elaborate citywide fundraising fairs to fill coffers and reinvigorate local enthusiasm for the war.[50] Since December 1862 the Chicago branch of the Sanitary Commission had been under the direction of associate managers Mary Livermore and Jane Hoge. With their supplies depleted, Livermore and Hoge resolved to stage a fair. Livermore approached Dickinson about attending the event, which she promised, would provide a "great moral demonstration" supporting the war while "bring[ing] together the noblest women of the country." Although Dickinson had only lectured in the East, Livermore assured her that "western women mention your name with pride." After extensive negotiations Dickinson finally agreed to attend the Chicago fair and deliver two lectures for a fee of $600.[51]

Dickinson turned out to be the great star of the Northwestern Sanitary Fair. The public lectures were vintage Dickinson oratory. She spoke on "The Duties of the Present Hour," calling on patriotic Northerners to continue battling the traitorous, slaveholding South. And, as had become her pattern, she included a series of anecdotes celebrating the bravery of the Union's African American soldiers. She also delivered a few remarks at a dinner honoring soldiers in the local hospital. On that informal occasion Dickinson spoke not as a celebrated political orator, "but simply as an American woman, out of a full heart, and with trembling lips, to thank you. . . . Should your life ebb on some distant battle-field, where no woman's hand can smooth your dying pillow, and no friendly ear receive your parting sigh —still even there our love and affection shall follow you," she promised. In this emotional setting Dickinson adopted a much more traditionally feminine voice than she employed in her characteristic stump speeches.[52]

Dickinson's Chicago visit was not without controversy. Local Copperheads seized upon the published news that Dickinson had demanded enormous fees, questioning how one "so pretentious in her patriotism" could demand such a large compensation from such an important charity? But the *Chicago Tribune* rose to the orator's defense, explaining that by agreeing to speak for $600 Dickinson had actually sacrificed $1,000 in lost earnings, while covering her own travel costs.[53] As the Chicago press bickered over her visit, Dickinson had already moved on, returning to the campaign grind in New York and Pennsylvania.[54]

As her Chicago trip illustrated, by the middle of 1863 Dickinson's fiercest Copperhead critics were ready to take the gloves off. "Mirrors, it is said, are unlike women, inasmuch as they reflect without speaking, while women are apt to speak without reflecting," quipped the Democratic *New York World* following her Cooper Institute appearance. "But Miss Dickinson in speaking mirrored her audience. Divested of the grace of her sex, as they of the humanity of theirs, stripped of the gentleness and charity and pure mindedness of woman as they of the dignity and sobriety and wisdom of men, she unsexed and they without sense, the exhibition was one which no woman of refinement and no man of good sense could witness without blushing for her kind." Shortly after she returned East, Rochester's Copperhead *Courier and Union* published a virulent attack on "Short Haired Anna." Dickinson, the editorial claimed, spoke in the "style of the strong-minded, brazen-faced sex who eschew womanly dignity, and make the rostrum take the place of the cradle and baby-jumper, that is just now in great favor with the admirers of the unsexed; and, as a natural consequence, she flutters her plumage of feathers in the face of the community, and in this way makes a very pitiable effort to bedaub a certain class whom she is hired to abuse, with the slime from her unclean nest." The account condemned Dickinson's "slime," "filth-throwing," and general vulgarity, explaining that "We are not ordinarily in the habit of criticizing women; but when leaving the sanctity of their home retirement and the privacy of womanly pursuits, they assume manhood's tasks and enter the political arena" where rough and tumble debate was the norm.[55]

In barely two years Anna Dickinson had made the rapid transition from her early war status as a captivating young Philadelphia radical with a gift for oratory, to her role as a successful abolitionist speaker in New England, to her new identity as a national celebrity. During her long weeks and months on the road, Dickinson had developed a new personal and professional relationship with her sister Susan. With no obvious prior planning, and presumably with no real contemplation of the larger significance of their evolving roles, Susan gradually became the manager of the Locust Street home, companion for their mother, and occasional administrative assistant for her younger sister. Susan's letters from home combined concern for Anna's well-being, reports on Dickinson's professional correspondence and scheduling, and detailed accounts of family bills. Even at this early stage the relationship must have occasionally felt awkward. "Thank thee for the money and for what thee so kindly says about money matters in general," Susan wrote in December 1863. "Thee's a dear, good, kind sister—and thee knows I think it none the less that I don't often put my feelings into words."[56] A few months later Dickinson's mother sent her an uncharacteristically long and contemplative letter. On the one hand, she worried that her youngest child spent so much time on the road that she had no true home. On the other hand, she acknowledged that "thou art the chief burden bearer for us all and nobly have thou born it."[57]

Meanwhile, Dickinson's political identity had also taken on new dimensions. Somewhere along the line she made the subtle transition from an eloquent youthful advocate to a powerful political voice in her own right. In the early days some of the elder statesmen of the abolitionist movement and the Republican Party seemed most interested in shaping her emerging public career, rather than soliciting her political opinions. But even then Dickinson understood her task as far more than speaking *for* others. She assembled, digested, and interpreted information at a voracious rate, applying her own personal stamp to her public performances.[58] Before long, national political leaders began turning to Anna Dickinson for her political endorsement. As early as May 1863, Kansas senator Samuel C. Pomeroy asked Dickinson to lend her name to a "Vigilance Committee" he chaired, which aimed to block Secretary of State William H. Seward's reported efforts to negotiate a "dishonorable peace" with the Confederacy. In fact, Pomeroy invited her to join a proposed "Executive Vigilance Committee" of seven or eight members. In February 1864, when Pomeroy orchestrated a failed movement to replace Abraham Lincoln with Radical Republican Salmon P. Chase as the party's presidential nominee, he included Dickinson on the short list of recipients of his "strictly private" "Pomeroy Circular" calling for Lincoln's ouster.[59] If Chase's supporters were going to unseat the moderate Lincoln, they wanted Anna Dickinson in their corner. But by then Dickinson had already made important strides toward the Republican center and was unwilling to cast her lot with her radical friend.

The crucial moment in the evolution of Dickinson's political status came in December 1863, when Judge Kelley delivered a momentous invitation to the Dickinson home. "Miss Dickinson," the short note read, "Heartily appreciating the value of your services in the campaigns in New Hampshire, Connecticut, Pennsylvania & New York, & the qualities that have combined to give you the deservedly high reputation you enjoy; & desiring as well to testify that appreciation as to secure ourselves the pleasures of hearing you, we write in cordially inviting you to deliver one or more addresses this winter, at the Capital, at some time suited to your own convenience." It was signed by Vice President Hannibal Hamlin, 23 senators, and 78 congressmen. Almost every Republican officeholder in Washington, including such luminaries as Charles Sumner, Henry Wilson, Schuyler Colfax, and Thaddeus Stephens, had joined forces in asking Dickinson to speak to them in the nation's capital. The invitation had been in the works for several weeks, thanks largely to the efforts of Congressman Kelley and Whitelaw Reid. After extensive discussions of logistics Dickinson suggested January 16, 1864, as a date for her appearance, requesting that the proceeds of the lecture be devoted to the needs of "the suffering freedmen."[60]

The Washington lecture was not merely a great honor, it was also a wonderful opportunity and an interesting political challenge as recent events presented a complex political landscape. Like most abolitionists, Dickinson had been disappointed at the Lincoln administration's gradual approach to emancipation and its unequal treatment of African American soldiers. Moreover, on December 8 Lincoln had issued his Proclamation of Amnesty and Reconstruction, which promised surprisingly generous terms to Southern whites whose states returned to the Union, while providing almost no protection for African Americans beyond emancipation itself. As Dickinson prepared for her address, advice and support poured in from various friends and advisors. Even her brother, Samuel, sent an uncharacteristically long and political letter, urging his younger sister to use the opportunity to call for a federal bureau to protect the freedpeople crowding into Washington.[61]

Dickinson's Washington lecture was witnessed by nearly all of Republican officialdom—including the president and first lady—and reported by many of the nation's leading newspapers. New Hampshire diarist Annie G. Dudley was among those in the audience, and was pleased with what she saw: "Went to the House of Representatives to hear 'Anna E. Dickinson' who spoke on the 'Perils of the Hour.' She had a very distinguished audience: The President, one or two members of the Cabinet, Senators & Members & yet she was perfectly self-possessed and spoke equal to any man I ever [seen]; her language was perfect, and subject well connected, used no notes except a few [words] on a slip of paper which she rolled around her fingers."[62] On the grand political stage, the 21-year-old Dickinson navigated a careful path between Republican extremes. On the one hand, she itemized a long list of radical grievances against the moderate Republican president, sparing no strong words although Lincoln sat in the audience. On the other hand, Dickinson cleverly built her oratory to the conclusion that "the Hour" required continued support for the nation's leader.[63] The good-natured Lincoln appeared to enjoy the event, even though he received a serious tongue-lashing. Dickinson's eventual endorsement of the president prompted tremendous applause from the partisan audience, and when the president and first lady rose to leave, the audience clamored for a few words. Lincoln declined the invitation, but provoked more laughter and applause when he relayed—through Vice President Hamlin—that he was too embarrassed to speak.[64] Afterwards, the Lincolns reportedly received Dickinson in the office of the speaker of the house.[65]

Dickinson's friends were effusive in their praise of her performance. Whitelaw Reid authored a celebratory account for the *Cincinnati Gazette*, and basked in the glow of her triumph. As an outspoken critic of Lincoln, Samuel Pomeroy kept his distance after the lecture but sent a note praising it as "an entire and complete success!" From Nook Farm, Charles Dudley Warner congratulated Dickinson for conquering Washington, wishing only that Richmond would fall so easily.[66] Invitations arrived from across the country asking Dickinson to reprise her "Words for the Hour."[67] On the twenty-seventh she journeyed home to Philadelphia to speak at the Academy of Music; the following week she enjoyed a grand return to New York's Cooper Institute. From there she headed north and then west, with stops in Connecticut, western New York, western Pennsylvania, Ohio, Indiana, and Illinois. Meanwhile, her sister and mother reported a new family crisis: brother Edwin's health was failing and he needed money to return East from California. Dickinson ended up sending home nearly $1,200 to cover the cost of Ed's trip.[68]

In the meantime, Dickinson's triumphant appearance before Congress pushed some of her most dedicated critics to new heights of outrage. The *World's* response was particularly inflamed: "She attracts crowds when she speaks, by appealing to the same love of the marvelous and monstrous which Barnum has made his fortune in exhibiting woolly horses, dwarfs, Feejee mermaids, and other queer fish. Yet this silly young person was allowed the use of the hall of Representatives last Saturday to make one of her unwomanly displays." Shortly thereafter, the *Geneva (NY) Gazette* ran a long essay attacking "Anna E. Dickinson and the

Gynaekokracy." Applying a fascinating variant on familiar anatomical metaphors for political life, the *Gazette* argued that periodically "idiosyncrasies . . . originate and throw to the surface certain manifestations of disease more or less loathsome and distressing; just as in a morbid state of the human body, boils and carbuncles are produced upon the surface by insidious causes seated perhaps in the vital forces of the system." "Among the excrescences upon the body politic," the article continued, "is one which may be best described by its Greek name Gynaekokracy, which manifests itself in the absurd endeavors of women to usurp the places and execute the functions of the male sex. It is a moral and social monstrosity—an inversion . . . of the laws of nature."[69]

While the profession of itinerant orator had not changed much since the previous year, the political context of Dickinson's 1864 appearances had evolved alongside her political role. Although she had endorsed Lincoln's renomination in Washington, Dickinson remained critical of the president and unsure if she would actively work for his reelection, particularly if the party could muster a viable alternative. As one Rochester paper put it, "Miss Dickinson is not lecturing for the Republican party, and much less for the elevation of any particular man. She speaks only what she believes to be true, regardless of the consequences, or whom it may hit; and it is only the good fortune of Republicans and the Administration that they are generally pretty much right, and are not hit oftener and harder. To say that she should be guarded or muzzled so that she shall only hit the malignant copperheads, would not be fair. It would transfer her into a mere party hack, going around making stump speeches for the benefit of the party."[70] A year earlier Dickinson had been engaged in exactly what the paper was now belittling: attacking Copperheads as a paid Republican stump speaker, perhaps even as a "party hack." This time around she was filling halls on the basis of her own fame, and was not politically beholden to any party sponsors. Meanwhile, the 21-year-old had gradually begun to dispense with her staid Quaker garb, adopting the fashionable clothing of a rising celebrity. The transition was at first subtle enough to be lost on William Lloyd Garrison, Jr. "I thought she was plainly dressed," her old friend wrote after an 1864 appearance, "but walking home with Mrs Jarvis & Mellie, those two ladies spoke of her display. I asked in what. Point lace & diamonds they said." A few months later a dismayed Martha Coffin Wright commented that she could "not admire her prancing up & down the stage, rustling a silk train after her—Her simpler ways, when she spoke a few years ago, suited me much better." Perhaps it was unavoidable that as she matured and grew in popularity, Dickinson would disappoint some who knew her in her youth.[71]

In the months before the Republican convention it was still possible to be a patriotic party member while contemplating alternative candidates. For the time being Dickinson's "Words for the Hour" lecture remained largely unchanged: she attacked Democrats, praised the sacrifices of Union soldiers, devoted special attention to the heroism and unfair treatment of African American soldiers, and highlighted the plight of freedpeople in the North. But after the Washington appearance Dickinson seems to have omitted the explicit—and dramatic—endorsement of Lincoln's renomination that had previously accompanied her harsh criticisms of the president.[72] As she traveled, Dickinson's political friends weighed in with divergent political perspectives. Reid, an active Lincoln adversary, tweaked Dickinson for her "wickedness about the renomination," while the practical Prescott pointed out that Salmon P. Chase's campaign had collapsed and Lincoln was really the only option.[73] Privately, Dickinson mulled over the alternatives with little enthusiasm. She feared that Lincoln promised little concrete assistance for African Americans and she acknowledged to Reid that it had been a mistake to publicly endorse him. But Chase's political stock had plummeted after Pomeroy's circular became known, and Dickinson was personally unimpressed with John C. Frémont, a favorite of many abolitionists. Still, she remained convinced that the nation was ready to elect a true abolitionist if the right candidate could be brought forward.[74]

Sometime that spring, Judge Kelley arranged for Dickinson to join him for a personal meeting with Abraham Lincoln. No official record of the encounter exists, and for Lincoln it may have been little more than a routine visit with a celebrated citizen. The conversation focused on developments in Union-occupied Louisiana, and particularly the actions of Lincoln's military governor, General Nathaniel Banks. After the fact, Kelley and Dickinson had very different versions of the encounter. Judge Kelley privately described the meeting as a positive exchange, in which Lincoln clarified his position toward Banks, Reconstruction, and the future of the freedpeople, while Dickinson—according to Kelley—said relatively little. When she returned to the platform Dickinson told audiences a different tale about the meeting, declaring that she used the opportunity to give the president a piece of her mind about his unacceptable Southern policies. Some of the more hostile newspaper accounts portrayed the lecturer as openly mocking the president's demeanor during their meeting, a charge that Dickinson later denied. One loyal Republican heard the speech in Boston and found that Dickinson's critique of Banks and wartime Reconstruction hit the mark, but her sarcastic and personal attack of Lincoln was "in the worst possible taste," undercutting her message. Whatever the true character of this meeting, a few things about the event are clear. First, the fact that it occurred at all suggests something of Dickinson's political importance. Second, whatever Lincoln said in the meeting failed to win over the abolitionist orator: her criticisms grew more biting in the weeks to come. And, third, by telling her version of the meeting on the lecture platform, Dickinson did tremendous damage to her relationship with her old mentor and friend, William D. Kelley.[75]

As the presidential campaign of 1864 approached, the Union's political landscape grew increasingly complex.[76] The movement to thrust Salmon P. Chase into the presidency had failed miserably in February, but the president faced challenges from across the political spectrum. Prior to the Baltimore convention, party dissidents, following the lead of Wendell Phillips, met in Cleveland, where they nominated John C. Frémont, demanded black suffrage and Southern land distribution, and bitterly denounced the president.[77] Other anti-Lincoln abolitionists lobbied to postpone the party convention. But the Republicans gathered as planned in early June, renamed themselves the National Union Party for the election, renominated Lincoln unanimously, and replaced Vice President Hannibal Hamlin on the ticket with former Tennessee Democrat Andrew Johnson. Despite the enthusiasm of the moment, the road ahead was rocky. Reports from the front seemed to be dominated by the painfully slow progress of Ulysses S. Grant against Robert E. Lee in Virginia, punctuated by unprecedented death counts from places like the Wilderness (May 5–7), Spotsylvania (May 8–20), and Cold Harbor (June 2–3) before the Union army settled into a long and frustrating siege of Petersburg. Meanwhile, in Washington the president alienated congressional radicals by pocket vetoing the Wade-Davis Bill, which had countered the president's Proclamation of Amnesty and Reconstruction by proposing much more stringent conditions on Southern states seeking readmission to the Union. Across the political aisle, Democrats of various stripes responded to unpopular policies and general war weariness by mustering their forces for a challenge in November.

For Dickinson, the situation presented particular challenges. Her more centrist Republican friends were enthusiastic about the president and unhappy with her persistent criticisms, and even some of the abolitionist leaders Dickinson most admired—such as Garrison, Oliver Johnson, and Charles Sumner—were openly backing his campaign. But Wendell Phillips was unwilling to compromise his principles and others had joined him in rallying around Frémont. The savvy Whitelaw Reid advised her to avoid excessive criticisms of the president. "It can do no good now for you to get tangled in the stripes of personal politics, & it may do much harm," he warned.[78] In June, Theodore Tilton confided in Dickinson that he could not support the movement to elect Frémont, much as it pained him to break with Phillips, because he feared that such a campaign was effectively supporting the Copperheads against the Union. Susan B. Anthony, who had recently befriended Dickinson, wondered what had become of "the good old doctrine 'of two evils choose neither.'" She acknowledged that Frémont might be a poor choice, but "to profess confidence in Lincoln would be a lie in me" and she would have none of it. Instead, the leader of the women's movement and of the wartime Woman's Loyal National League floated a grand idea for a series of mass meetings, featuring Dickinson, Wendell Phillips, and perhaps Frederick Douglass, calling for "entire freedom & political rights for the black man."[79]

By mid-July it seemed that Dickinson was leaning toward sitting out the campaign. She told Elizabeth Cady Stanton that she thought Lincoln was "the wisest scoundrel in the country, & I would rather lose all the reputation I possess

& sell apples & peanuts on the street than say aught—that would gain a vote for him." On the other hand, she acknowledged that "I cannot work for Fremont, as matters <u>now stand</u>, I cannot see into the future. I stand & wait—if there is no way open for work I will keep quiet for a while."[80] Meanwhile, Judge Kelley responded to a conciliatory note from Dickinson by assuring her that she remained in his affections. The Philadelphia congressman had long since concluded Dickinson should not be blamed for "misstep[s]" she had made "at the instigation of those, who, practicing upon your earnest nature, impel you to work from which they shrink." In fact, in early August Congressman Kelley passed on one of Dickinson's notes to the president, offering Lincoln the prediction that "the writer though dissatisfied with 'Baltimore & Lincoln' is not prepared to support 'Cleveland & Fremont' " and will eventually choose Lincoln as the lesser of two evils.[81]

Despite Kelley's confidence, Dickinson remained befuddled, and shared her uncertainty with her old friend Frederick Douglass. Douglass confided in a mutual friend that Dickinson was so anxious to jump into the fray that he feared she would throw her weight behind Frémont, although he had recommended that her best strategy was to wait and see what the Democrats did at their convention.[82] But Dickinson insisted that she had never endorsed Frémont and that her public criticisms of the president should not be misunderstood as a rejection of his candidacy.[83] Meanwhile, a growing group of radicals discussed plans for staging a new Republican convention in September in Cincinnati to settle on some alternative to Lincoln.[84] As he assessed the Union's military situation and political climate the president wrote an astonishing private memorandum on August 23, 1864, acknowledging that it was "exceedingly probable that the Administration will not be re-elected," and announcing his commitment to working with his successor to bring the war to a speedy end prior to inauguration day.[85] The following week the Democrats clarified the political situation somewhat when they met in Chicago and nominated General George McClellan, but even then their message was mixed: the party's platform—dominated by its peace faction—called for a negotiated peace, whereas candidate McClellan promised to win the war and preserve the Union. Still, the Democrats agreed in rejecting emancipation and insisting that Lincoln must be dethroned, and it appeared that a growing portion of the Northern public concurred.[86]

Dickinson finally concluded that some public statement was in order. On September 3 she sent an open letter to Tilton at the *Independent* entitled "The Duty of the Hour." In this extraordinary public letter, Dickinson explained that she had received numerous inquiries about her plans for the campaign and complaints about her criticisms of the Lincoln administration. She insisted that she remained first and foremost a patriot, not beholden to any particular party. The previous winter, when options seemed open, she had indeed supported efforts to identify "better men" to replace Lincoln on the ticket, but Dickinson declared that she had never endorsed the Cleveland convention or its nominee and she remained loyal to the Republican—or Union Party—ticket. In her most crucial statement, Dickinson announced that "I shall not work for Abraham Lincoln; I shall work for the salvation of my country's life, that stands at stake."[87]

Various Northern newspapers reprinted Dickinson's letter and numerous correspondents praised her stance. General Benjamin Butler dropped her a quick note of praise from the War Department. Philadelphian Edwin Hawkins, a stranger to Dickinson, read the letter in the *Philadelphia Press* and told tell her that "[a]ny man that can read it & vote for the Democratic nominee is unworthy to be called a man." Whitelaw Reid congratulated Dickinson on her highly successful "advent into newspaperdom," but insisted that he would only vote for Lincoln as if he were swallowing bitter pills.[88] Amidst all of this praise, one of the few criticisms Dickinson received came from Lillie Chace, a young—and rabid—abolitionist Quaker from Rhode Island. "I suppose thee would rather I should say frankly what I think about thy position, because it has grieved me a little," Lillie wrote. "Of course, thee must do what seem to thee best, but it seems to me as if after thee had tried —nobly tried to lift the Republican Party up to thy level, and failing, thee was going down to theirs." In late October Tilton introduced Dickinson to a Cooper Institute audience in New York where she attacked George McClellan and the Democrats, rather than praising Lincoln. She adopted the same approach for several more preelection lectures, following the path she had mapped out in her letter to the *Independent*. In the midst of the bloody war, she insisted, a patriotic nation must stick with the current administration.[89]

Events moved quickly between early September and election day in November. Despite his best efforts to distance himself from the Democratic platform, McClellan found his candidacy tainted by the party's peace wing. In early September Atlanta fell to Union troops under William Tecumseh Sherman, providing Lincoln with a much needed military victory. A few weeks later Frémont officially withdrew from the race, and most Republican radicals grudgingly supported the Lincoln-Johnson ticket. On election day Lincoln won a comfortable victory, aided by the ballots of more than a quarter million Union soldiers, the vast majority of whom voted for their commander in chief rather than the ex-general McClellan.[90]

After Lincoln's victory, Dickinson's oratorical dilemmas continued in a slightly altered form. How should she interpret the election when she remained dissatisfied with Lincoln? "I appreciate your quandary," Charles Dudley Warner assured her. His advice was to speak to the larger issues and the true meaning of the election, rather than getting bogged down in celebrating Lincoln.[91] In December Dickinson delivered a prowar lecture on "The Meaning of the Election" in Philadelphia. Anticipating the peace to come, she also introduced a new talk on "A Plea for Labor."[92] After a brief hiatus, Dickinson returned to Boston's Music Hall to unveil a lecture on Reconstruction she called "A Glance at Our Future." With the war in its final stages, she called for stern treatment of the rebels and aggressive protection of the rights of freedpeople.[93] Over the next few months she continued to speak on Reconstruction and the rights of African Americans, but she also spoke regularly on "A Plea for Labor" and "Woman's Work and Wages."[94] In so doing, Dickinson was returning to her earlier themes while also laying the groundwork for a peacetime speaking career.

By early April it was clear that peace would arrive in a matter of weeks. Besieged Petersburg finally succumbed to the Army of the Potomac, under Ulysses S. Grant; the following week Richmond fell, and jubilant Northern readers read descriptions of Abraham Lincoln walking the streets of the deserted Confederate capital. But the celebrations did not last long. A week later the president fell to an assassin's bullet, and festive red, white, and blue bunting gave way to black crepe. For Anna Dickinson, this was a particularly difficult turn of events. As a public speaker, she felt moved to speak. But as one of the martyred president's more persistent critics, perhaps silence would be most judicious. Oliver Johnson, who had arranged many of Dickinson's New York appearances, admitted that he did not know what was best. Perhaps a lecture at the Cooper Institute would strike just the right note, but maybe the very notion would alienate emotionally drained audiences. At least one correspondent expressed outrage that Dickinson would even consider speaking about the man she had so often attacked. The always blunt Lillie Chace told Dickinson that "Of course I cannot feel that sorrow which his admirers do, but I have little trust in Johnson."[95]

Finally, Dickinson could not resist the urge to speak. In early May she visited New York to speak on "Our Martyred President" at Cooper Institute. With Theodore Tilton presiding, and 3,000 in attendance, Dickinson paid homage to the fallen president's numerous virtues. Dickinson openly acknowledged that she had often criticized Lincoln and his policies, and although she eulogized his memory she said that she retracted none of her earlier critiques. Turning from one beloved leader to another, Dickinson called for a vigorous prosecution of the Rebel leaders, including Robert E. Lee, whom she called "the leading spirit of the rebellion." The nation's traitors, she insisted, deserved stern punishment. Even to the very end, Dickinson and Abraham Lincoln had different paths in response to the nation's greatest crisis.[96]

## Chapter 3

# "BELOVED OF SO MANY": THE MANY FACES OF A WOMAN IN PUBLIC

PERHAPS more than any woman of her day, Anna Dickinson came of age in the public eye. Between her first public appearance at age 17 and her tribute to the martyred president a few months before her twenty-third birthday, she had been on the road as much as she had been at home. In those five crucial years Dickinson's life and the nation's history had become intertwined, as each was shaped and redefined in the midst of the Civil War. For the young orator these were years when she learned to present different faces to different audiences while complete strangers and intimate friends constructed their own versions of her true identity. Those men and women who personally encountered Dickinson in her travels discovered at once a charming, almost frail, young woman, and a captivating dynamo. She was a figure who engendered profound emotions, even love, in almost complete strangers, while also earning the quasi-official sobriquet "America's Joan of Arc" for her public role. For those who saw her on the platform, or read of her exploits, Dickinson became an adored—and sometimes despised—celebrity.

By the middle of the Civil War Dickinson had established herself as a highly successful professional orator and a political voice to be reckoned with. Time and again, her Republican colleagues had demonstrated that they valued her political support. And if her adversaries initially dismissed her as mere entertainment, or as a popularizer of other people's ideas, before long those who knew her career best understood that Anna Dickinson was no political puppet. As she established this unique professional and political niche, her labors—and the reactions of others—were shaped by her age and gender, as well as her roots within Quaker abolitionism. Although Dickinson encountered some of the leading public women of Civil War–era America, among them Lucretia Mott, Susan B. Anthony, and Elizabeth Cady Stanton, the most important people in her early wartime career were almost exclusively powerful public men: dedicated abolitionists; Republican wire pullers and officeholders; and reporters and editors. Many of her early mentors adopted a sort of kindly paternalism, providing contacts and guidance while also worrying about her health and happiness, and eventually passing the young phenomenon on to the next stage in her travels. As Dickinson grew more experienced and her circle of advisors widened, she developed patterns that would serve her well for decades to come. When faced with a political conundrum—such as the election of 1864—she weighed often contradictory opinions before settling on her own path. Numerous influential men and women had her ear, but all eventually discovered that she made up her own mind.

Surprisingly, Dickinson's closest correspondents and political advisors rarely addressed the significance of her position as a *woman* speaking in so many political venues. Dickinson's own wartime letters spoke of the importance of the work, and her personal call to engage in it, but not of the particular importance of a woman's voice entering into the national conversation. With the exception of her informal talk at the soldiers' dinner following the Northwestern Sanitary Fair, she generally declined to assert a distinctive gendered perspective on the national crisis. Hers was a political perspective, offered in the spirit of patriotism and not out of a notion of separate gender spheres or any sense of a woman's distinctive moral voice.

But even if Dickinson saw herself as a creature of politics, or perhaps as a valiant Joan of Arc who went into battle because her causes were just, *not* because she was young and a woman, her public identity was certainly shaped by her uniquely transgressive characteristics. Wherever she traveled, journalists made much of her sex, her youth, and her appearance. Highly gendered debates—pitting "unmanly" Democratic critics against chivalric Republican editors—followed in her wake. Ironically, Dickinson's wartime successes were owing to both her gender and the fact that she defied gender norms in how she spoke in public. The emphasis on dramatic spectacle that had characterized political campaigns in the 1850s continued into the war years, but with the lines between entertainment, patriotism, and politics hopelessly blurred. Wise party advocates recognized Anna Dickinson as the ideal melding of the popular and the political. Meanwhile, with the Civil War as a bloody backdrop Northern political discourse became even more fierce. As a political orator, Dickinson built her reputation on bellicose rhetoric, not demure feminine calls for protecting home and hearth. She was at her best when on the attack, exchanging barbs with hecklers, belittling Copperhead editors, or charging adversaries with treason. She also grew adept at navigating the politics of social difference, crafting special appeals to factory workers or facing down angry Pennsylvania miners. Her critics may have mocked the fact that she was a woman entering a man's world, but they were equally upset with her strong, combative rhetoric. Although criticized for her unladylike "filth-throwing," Dickinson's youth and gender may have afforded her a bit more latitude, particularly in a historic moment when the stakes seemed so high and the campaigning so vicious. When Dickinson walked onto the platform she displayed an iron fist, but commonly draped in a velvet dress.[1]

In early 1864 Mary Dickinson wrote her youngest child a long note wrestling with how hard it was to "think of thy not having a home of thy own to rest" in her travels.[2] For weeks and months on end Anna Dickinson routinely was a guest in someone else's home. This life on the road quickly became a wearing grind. The lectures themselves took a physical toll. She routinely spoke for two hours, without notes, pacing her platform while straining to project her unamplified voice to fill large halls. As a celebrity, Dickinson grew accustomed to being pampered by enthusiastic hosts, but she paid the price by entertaining them with lively conversation during endless meals and receptions. In later life she would learn to love the autonomy of hotels, but in her youth it was more common for Dickinson to be passed from host to host.

As her career progressed, Dickinson's private world became crowded with a long list of sometimes quite intense friendships born of these brief visits, maintained by enthusiastic—although sometimes one-sided—correspondence, and cultivated in return visits the following season. In Boston, the Garrisons embraced Dickinson when she was fresh from Philadelphia. Later, young Fanny Garrison became one of her most dedicated correspondents. In Rhode Island, Elizabeth Chace took charge of Dickinson's welfare and her young daughter—Lillie Chace—wrote to Dickinson as if Anna were her older sister, sharing ideas on politics and reform. When Dickinson first visited Connecticut, she came under the guidance of W. J. Burton, but before long she had become adopted by the lively, intellectual group she found at Hartford's Nook Farm community. And, much like her relationships with Fanny Garrison and Lillie Chace, something in Dickinson's bold and charismatic manner struck a nerve with several younger Nook Farm women, including Alice and Mary Beecher and Lilly Gillette.

The relationships that Dickinson developed with these young women illustrate both her unique position as an itinerant celebrity and the broader patterns of friendship among nineteenth-century women. At many stops in her travels Dickinson shared a bed with a young woman of the household, forming intimate bonds during late-night conversations. In Boston, Dickinson slept alongside Fanny Garrison, who later declared that "I missed my soft pillow so many times, and have wished some how or other I might wake up and find a pair of some body's dear arms around me." In early 1864 Lilly Gillette—who had met Dickinson while visiting her aunt in Hartford—asked the orator to visit her family in Cincinnati. "When you come you will sleep with me, & when you sleep with me we will have a splendid talk" she promised. The following year Lilly—who had married Charles Dudley Warner's brother—urged Dickinson to visit Hartford. "We'll sleep together & I promise not to make you talk all night," Lilly vowed.[3] This sort of intimacy—including shared beds, physical caresses, and loving kisses—was a common component in friendships between nineteenth-century women, and was certainly not at odds with a hetero-sexual identity or the prospect of marriage to a man. Of course Anna Dickinson put her own unique stamp on these otherwise common relationships among young women. Whereas other women created bonds that endured for many years, producing a sort of emotional monogamy between kindred spirits, the charismatic Dickinson provoked an intensity of reaction from young women she had barely met. And because she spent so much of her time as a perpetual houseguest, she simultaneously developed these ties with women scattered across the Northeast.[4]

As an attractive, vibrant young woman, it is no surprise that Dickinson also attracted the romantic attention of several men. During one visit to Nook Farm, she went horseback riding with Republican judge Joseph P. Allyn. In May 1863, the judge sent Dickinson a distinctly flirtatious letter. For a man in his arid political world it was, "like an oasis in the desert to enjoy the luxury of addressing an intelligent woman," he declared. Two weeks letter he wrote again, this time asking Dickinson for a copy of her latest photograph, and proclaiming that "I would give much for one real breakneck canter with you." Over the next few months the two corresponded regularly and Allyn reaffirmed his particular admiration for Dickinson's oratory and beauty. But for some reason the relationship soured. On July 21 Judge Allyn sent Dickinson a long heartbroken letter. "God spare you from the pain you have inflicted on me these last few days and in those cruel lines," the letter began. "I beg you to retract those cruel, unjust, undeserved words. You may reject my love, I must bear that as a brave man should, but your friendship I have a right to else the past is a black unmitigated lie." For several pages the poor judge alternately assailed Dickinson for her unjust cruelty and flailed himself for his despair.[5]

This short, passionate correspondence ended abruptly with this letter. Dickinson must have shared some details of the relationship with her sister. A few weeks later Susan wrote, "Ah, the poor Judge! Mother says thee'll be like other women, settle sometime, and she don't believe thee'll ever have a better offer than the one thee's been putting by." This suggests that Judge Allyn had proposed marriage and Dickinson had declined. Perhaps she cut off all contact with him.[6] Meanwhile, in March 1863 Abraham Lincoln named Allyn an associate justice to the supreme court of the new Arizona territory and that August he set out for the West. When the party reached Santa Fe, Allyn wrote longingly of "her 'whom to have loved was a liberal education.'" There is no evidence that Dickinson reciprocated Allyn's affections, although they apparently spent some pleasant moments together. Such was the powerful effect she had on those she encountered in her travels.[7]

In late 1864 Dickinson made a campaign stop in Pittsburgh where she stayed at the home of the Irishes, a local Republican family. She left behind a household of devoted fans. Less than a week after she left, Elias H. Irish, a lawyer and state legislator, sent Dickinson a long letter describing "the world of sighing about this house since you went away." Over the next year or so the two exchanged letters, and saw each other briefly in Washington, but their relationship truly blossomed shortly after the war when Dickinson returned to western Pennsylvania in August, 1865. Now thoroughly and openly in love, Irish sent Dickinson a long letter recalling wondrous moments hiking in the mountains. The devoted attorney had clearly felt the brunt of Dickinson's biting tongue and sarcastic wit in their moments together, and remarked "how kind we grow—on paper—yet if thou were here thou shoulds't not have one pleasant word." Still, he concluded, "[w]rite thy worst and I will press it to my lips. Strike & I will kiss the rod. Again, greatest, dearest & best of girls. Receive my blessing & believe me ever and always."[8]

For the next several months the two struggled with assorted illnesses as Dickinson tried to arrange another visit. They apparently saw each other in early 1866, and shortly thereafter Irish sent Dickinson an extraordinary 16-page letter, which he claimed represented 200 pages of discarded drafts. The sadly smitten suitor wrote eloquently of precious afternoons wandering the Alleghenies picking blackberries and riding horseback alongside the "matchless black-haired Gipsey," and glorious evenings listening "while my silver tongued enchantress builded castles in the air, and beguiled, enthralled my fancy, enthralled my heart . . . through many a golden hour." But Irish realized that Dickinson did not share his passion, and he wrote of cruel words from her and how he had foolishly allowed his "feelings to be so easily played upon."[9]

The tragic subtext to this long letter was that Elias Irish was deathly ill, perhaps from the aftereffects of malaria, and his family had decided to send him to the South for his health. Dickinson visited Irish at least once that summer, and on two occasions arranged to send him shipments of grapes. His death in November 1866 deeply affected her.[10] Given the tragedy of the story, and the passion of Irish's long letters, it is tempting to cast the Pittsburgh attorney as the tragic lost love of Dickinson's youth. And there is probably some truth to that. A few clues hint that Dickinson never really shared Irish's passion, however. Several months before Irish died, Dickinson's mother wrote asking, "Why daughter Anna, what is Elias's attraction to Phila? Can't give up the chase? What is to be done?"[11] This suggests that Dickinson had described Irish to her mother as a failed suitor. As Irish lay on his death bed, Dickinson confided her sadness to one friend who responded that "the sad condition of your friend Mr. Irish must indeed have been trying; you must not blame yourself; love does not always come when asked for . . . He will pass away & according to my theory [you] will then be in a better condition to see how utterly impossible it was for you to give up your life for his." Apparently Dickinson had expressed guilt about not reciprocating the dying man's love, and perhaps she had also concluded that her public career would not allow her to lead a traditional life as the wife of a Pittsburgh lawyer.[12]

The ebbs and flows in her relationships with Allyn and Irish—separated by only a year or so—present some fascinating similarities. Both men met Dickinson through political connections, but soon the friendships grew social. Both wrote fondly of horseback rides, long walks, and conversations, and sharing fruit with the charming orator. Both seemed bedazzled by Dickinson's charm, but each quickly learned that her sarcasm was not reserved for the platform. And, most dramatically, each man's emotions eventually reached a boiling point, producing long melodramatic letters after Dickinson's rejection. Although Dickinson certainly seems to have enjoyed the company of Allyn and Irish, particularly the latter, it is hard to conclude that either really knew the object of their affections particularly well. For these men she seemed to have remained a dark-haired figure on a pedestal rather than a flesh-and-blood individual.

Among Dickinson's many Boston friends, Louise Brackett and her husband Walter, a well-regarded artist, stand out for their lengthy, close friendship. Lou Brackett first met Dickinson in early 1863 and shortly thereafter Brackett invited her to come to Boston "and live with me—and accept my hearts love—and humble home," an invitation that Dickinson accepted for short stints on numerous occasions.[13] Lou took particular joy in teasing Dickinson about a long list of suitors who expressed interest in the young orator. On several occasions she spoke of a judge—apparently not Allyn—who seemed quite taken with her young friend. "Seriously now you would not think of leaving me for that little Judge would you," Brackett teased.[14] When famed Union general Benjamin Butler visited the Bracketts, Lou entertained Dickinson with descriptions of one of Butler's young staff officers, who announced that he hoped to kiss Dickinson on sight. "God knows he would not have to ask me twice, if Walter was willing," Brackett chortled.[15]

Lou Brackett also served as an early intermediary between Dickinson and Colonel James Beecher, passing on notes from him in May 1863 and hinting that there was romance in the air. The following March, Colonel Beecher, who was with the United States Colored Troops, visited the Bracketts while on furlough. Lou found that he "seemed rather melancholy I thought; partly from his affection for you and partly from his anxiety about his regiment." According to Brackett, the poor colonel had tried to visit Dickinson in Philadelphia but had found her not at home. She added that he declared "he would forfeit a month's pay . . . for one kiss from you" but instead he had to settle for kissing Lou—with Walter's permission—with the promise that she would pass it on to Dickinson when they next met. Thus, Brackett promised, "when I next meet you . . . I'll give you a 'Beecher kiss.' "[16]

By early 1864 Beecher was already deeply in love with Nook Farm's Frankie Johnson. That January the colonel acknowledged that he loved Anna nearly as much as Frankie, and he wrote that with her "slender body and womanly gentleness" she had done more for the cause than he could accomplish in the field. But Beecher's chief concern was that Dickinson devoted too much of her emotional energy to others rather than finding sustenance for herself. "I wish you would come out of your seclusion & tell me of yourself," he wrote.

> You are sort of Mother Confessor to Frankie & march around dignifiedly among Hartford . . . as though you were neither loving nor loveable—when I know you are both. Say—Anna, who do you love—or are you beloved of so many that you are not content with any one? Where is your castle in the air? Where your household & fireside? & into whose eyes will those bright loving eyes of yours look trustingly—you see my friend I do not look at you or think of you as the 'eloquent & gifted oratress' . . . but rather as a true noble hearted loveable woman wonderfully endowed its true with the power to move hearts by words, but very, very powerful to win love & return the same when the right lover comes to claim it.[17]

The following October, James and Frankie were married and living in Florida with Beecher's regiment. "Do you suppose we shall ever meet again? & where," he mused. "Somehow you seem connected with my past life. Though only few days were we together. Frankie loves you dearly, which is fortunate. So do I, which is rational."[18]

The handful of letters between Dickinson and Beecher suggest that the orator and the colonel shared a special bond that Dickinson would enjoy with only a handful of people over the years. In their brief moments together, Dickinson must have been unusually revealing of her true nature. While Allyn and Irish wrote rhapsodically of mountain hikes and stolen moments sharing fruit with the enchanting Dickinson, Beecher had caught a glimpse of the "noble hearted loveable woman" beneath the more celebrated "eloquent & gifted oratress."

Amidst her persistent bantering about Dickinson's romantic life, Lou Brackett's letters were thick with seemingly erotic comments and jests about her own affections for her young friend. Not long after they first met, Brackett ended a note by giving Walter's love and adding "don't love anybody as you love me." A few months later, after characteristic teasing about Dickinson's murky love life, she demanded that "[w]hen you again write do write some love to me, dont waste it all on the men, I can appreciate it better than they can, believe me I can." Dickinson responded with affection that thrilled her friend, who effused: "your letter gave me such exquisite pleasure indeed; I will marry you—run off any where with you, for you are such a darling. I can feed your soul, if not your body sweet Anna—do I offend your delicacy?" In this last phrase Brackett almost seemed to suggest that only Dickinson's "delicacy" stood between them and a more intimate physical relationship.

Later in the same letter she asked: "How do you live without seeing Lou? Ah! I know, with your lovers, numerous as they are. I want to hear of all your love-affairs when I see you again will you tell me? I am at present fearfully bored with a young lady . . . she bores me to death—she cant remain away from me long enough for me to eat." Here Brackett seemed to be implying—at least in jest—that the 21-year-old Dickinson was juggling a variety of love affairs while the married Lou Brackett was losing interest in an affair with a less interesting young woman.[19]

The following month, with Dickinson about to arrive in Boston, an impatient Lou declared that "I scarce can wait to see you: the very thought of seeing your genial and magnetic face once more—makes my heart leap with pleasure—do you love me the same? Has no vile woman torn your heart from me? I fear no man." Dickinson ended up canceling her visit, but a few months later she wrote a letter that gave Lou tremendous joy. "Your last letter made me so very happy!" she proclaimed. "I read it twenty times, and kissed it twice as many, O you darling, how much I love you, my very heart-longings for you almost make me sick." The following March, Dickinson thrilled Brackett with another affectionate letter. Although it seemed that everyone loved Anna, Brackett insisted that "you are mine and belong to me, until you get married —say it is true? Have you wearied of my nonsense, of my love? . . . I have an irresistible desire all through this letter to make love to you in down right earnest."[20]

Taken in isolation, it is unclear what to make of the physical intimacies and desires Brackett described. Like Dickinson's wartime relationships with Fanny Garrison and Lilly Gillette Warner and several other younger women, her private moments with Lou Brackett did not indicate that either woman doubted that Dickinson—who was still in her early twenties—would eventually marry a man. Nonetheless, Brackett's enthusiasms may well have offended the younger woman's "delicacy," raising sexual issues she was not prepared to confront or at least fully embrace at that stage in her life.[21]

While various close friends and suitors were constructing versions of Anna Dickinson based on their personal interactions with the celebrated orator, legions of journalists and newspaper editors defined and categorized Dickinson based exclusively on what she presented to the public from the platform. Dickinson's appearances almost inevitably invited contentious commentary about the propriety of women speaking in public. Those political allies who wished to embrace her ideas had to contend with the fact that a woman was articulating them; her enemies had the challenge of selecting how best to marginalize the speaker and belittle her arguments. In short, Dickinson's performances became occasions for popular discourse about women in public, thus producing a new version of her identity that was crucial to her professional future while even further removed from her true character and experience. And even while the press coverage reflected Dickinson's growing fame and significance, many of their assessments—whether essentially supportive or explicitly hostile—seemed intent on minimizing Dickinson's larger significance and undercutting any transformative value of her distinctive public role.

Like other public figures, Dickinson adopted different guises in different settings. Reporters who attended her public lectures and individuals who chatted with her in person did not come away from the experience with identical perceptions, but most who encountered her were struck by Dickinson's powerful persona and striking appearance: her manner of speaking, her dark eyes and short curly hair, her overwhelming intensity. Somewhere beyond the version of Dickinson constructed by those who knew her personally and longed for her company, and the public version crafted by the public discourse of journalists, editors, and professional observers, lay a third face of Anna Dickinson that reflected a new aspect of fame in mid-nineteenth-century America. As a public celebrity in an evolving national market, Dickinson developed a distinctive relationship with scores of fans and admirers who only knew her from a distance, but who constructed their own version of the orator that was unfiltered by editorial opinions and unaffected by personal contact.

Beginning during the war years, and continuing for decades, Dickinson received hundreds of letters and notes from complete strangers, and hundreds more from people she barely knew. Taken together, these missives illustrate how fame was shaped and cultivated in Civil War–era America, and they also hint at how Dickinson was received by different segments of society. Many friends, acquaintances, and complete strangers sought a physical artifact, marking some concrete connection to the celebrated public figure. Often this meant writing a note asking for an autograph or perhaps a signed photograph. Early in the war, such requests commonly came from people Dickinson knew from her travels. New Bedford's Joseph Ricketson asked for a photograph as early as June 1862; a few months later Frank Garrison was thrilled to receive a copy of Dickinson's image in the mail; Louise Brackett had a picture of Dickinson on display in her parlor.[22]

Young Lillie Chace's relationship with the rising celebrity grew increasingly complex, sometimes blurring the lines between friend and fan. In early 1863 Lillie asked Dickinson for a photograph. Later in the war Chace met a young man who was a "true blue abolitionist" and she promised to secure Dickinson's autograph for him and his sisters. Other friends remarked on how Dickinson's fame made her signature a valuable commodity, occasionally asking her to send a scrap of paper for some autograph-hungry acquaintance. Shortly after the war, the *Independent*'s Theodore Tilton asked Dickinson to write some fundraising letters, pointing out that there were people who would gladly pay $50 simply for her signature. The following month New York abolitionist Oliver Johnson requested an autograph for one of his friends, adding that he had never before made such a request, "so pray be a good girl, and comply promptly."[23]

Dickinson's popularity dovetailed with the antebellum explosion in mass-produced photography. In the mid-1850s French photographer André Disdéri patented a process for producing multiple images from a single wet plate. By the end of the decade the production of these *cartes de visite*—small, inexpensive photographs mounted on cards—had become a booming business on both sides of the Atlantic. The emergence of professional portrait photographers made it possible for ordinary citizens to assemble albums of friends and loved ones. With the advent of the Civil War, thousands of soldiers visited photographers' studios to become memorialized in their uniforms before marching off to war. This changing technology also added a new dimension to the nature of fame, shifting the relationship between the celebrity and the fan. Photographic entrepreneurs marketed lists of images featuring politicians, writers, actors and actresses, and Civil War military leaders. In late 1862, the New York photography firm of Edward and H. T. Anthony advertised a catalogue featuring 2,000 portraits and another 300 war scenes photographed by Mathew Brady. Leading celebrities earned substantial sums to sit for studio portraits. For a decade or so the enthusiasm for collecting reached spectacular heights, as shops across the North advertised the latest images and enthusiasts filled specialized albums with their favorite celebrities.[24]

Anna Dickinson autographed *carte de visite*. Produced by F. Gutekunst photographer, Philadelphia, Pennsylvania. Probably wartime. Author's personal collection.

Anna Dickinson stereoview. Part of E. & H. T. Anthony's postwar series of "Prominent Portraits," this stereoview was based on a wartime photograph taken by Edward Anthony. Author's personal collection.

One can trace Anna Dickinson's gradual evolution from popular orator to full-fledged celebrity through her numerous photographs and other public images. Dickinson was no stranger to the photographer's studio even before she went on the platform. At least one photograph survives from her youth, and in the early stages of her public life Dickinson exchanged *cartes de visite* with friends and admirers. By as early as the fall of 1862, Dickinson's image had begun to circulate more broadly. That September, Frank Garrison reported that he had seen engravings of Dickinson in *Frank Leslie's Illustrated Newspaper.* In April 1863 Edward A. Anthony contacted Dickinson about adding her image to his firm's list, promising that the picture would be advertised to coincide with her upcoming Cooper Institute lecture. Two weeks later Anthony wrote again, asking Dickinson to sit for a portrait at Mathew Brady's studio. That fall Susan Dickinson reported some testy negotiations surrounding images taken by Philadelphia photographer Frederick Gutekunst. A shady acquaintance of Gutekunst had planned to sell pirated copies of Dickinson's *carte de visite.* Susan quickly put a stop to this. "The idea of having them hawked about the country by some irresponsible traveling agent, as if thee'd been so anxious to have them sold as to go to him and have them sold round in that style," she exclaimed. Gutekunst agreed to provide Dickinson with copies of three different images while arranging to sell them, in an appropriately discreet fashion, at his own counters. By the end of the Civil War, *cartes de visite* of Dickinson sporting the backmarks of many of the nation's most fashionable photographic studios circulated widely.[25]

For the devotee and collector, the photograph albums themselves became an interesting reconfiguration of the meaning and manifestation of fame. In place of the traditional autograph album, fans collected the seemingly more intimate images of the women and men they most admired. For the most fortunate, those treasured portraits also bore a personal autograph or slogan. Like some of her peers, Dickinson took to frequently signing her name with an inspirational motto: "The world belongs to those who take it."[26] While previously autograph collectors had reserved their albums for the signatures of celebrities, it was commonplace for these new collectors to put *cartes de visite* of famous people in photograph albums alongside family and friends. Thus, admirers placed Dickinson's image interspersed with pictures of the likes of Abraham Lincoln, Henry Ward Beecher, and Ulysses S. Grant, but also with anonymous aunts, uncles, and other relatives. In this fashion, the wartime celebrities became peculiarly integrated into the lives of those Americans who followed their exploits from a distance.

Not all of Dickinson's wartime followers were content with autographed pictures or similarly impersonal tokens. Shortly after the war, Emma Fisher of Roxbury, Massachusetts, wrote asking for a lock of Dickinson's hair. Dickinson sent Fisher an autograph but deflected the more personal request explaining that her hair had recently been shorn. Several months later the persistent Fisher wrote that she had recently seen Dickinson lecture and was pleased to discover that the orator's hair had grown long enough to spare a curl or two.[27]

Some male admirers were so enraptured that they penned lengthy love letters to the beguiling young Quaker. A man from Elmira, New York, sent a poem praising the "woman who stands brighter than her sex." Chicago's W. M. Boucher was so struck by a Dickinson lecture that he declared "My soul longs for a companion whom I can respect for her goodness & wisdom & whose body & spirit I can love with an absorbing emotion," adding that since Dickinson was single, he wondered if she would "permit a correspondence with the view of becoming acquaintances." These fans, and many others like them, saw something in Anna Dickinson on the platform that moved them to write words of deep affection and even passion to the young woman they had never met.[28]

While many responded to Dickinson's performances with passionate words or requests for physical artifacts, some of the most profound responses came from young women who found inspiration in the orator's public career. Lillie Atkinson was a dedicated abolitionist Quaker from Cherry Lawn, New Jersey. About a year younger than Dickinson, Atkinson and her family had known the Dickinsons long before Anna became a national figure. Before the war the two filled their correspondence with radical politics and abolitionist doctrine, and on several occasions Atkinson expressed her frustration when the older men in her world seemed uninterested in her opinions. In Dickinson's career Atkinson found one to model her own after. While preparing for a debate on women's rights, Atkinson wrote requesting a few pointers, vowing to take her older friend's ideas and "clothe them in my own language." Two years later Atkinson attended one of her old friend's lectures but had no opportunity to shake her hand after the performance. Instead, she sent a teasing, somewhat melancholy, note. "Please, dear Anna," she wrote, "I dont know how to write properly to persons who have become so great and famous, and find myself looking back with a sigh at those dear old days of years agone, when I could talk to thee without fear of thy *greatness*." Atkinson worried that her old friend would conclude that she had been "standing still" rather than developing her own talents. It was as if Atkinson were using Dickinson's public successes as a yardstick against which to measure her own endeavors.[29]

Fanny Garrison, who had numerous models for public activism, often shared a distinct gender sensibility in her letters with Dickinson. After attending Harvard's "Class day" Garrison noted that "it is so mean that we are only allowed there on that day, as though we were only dolls to help their enjoyment when they are pleased to want us." Later, anticipating an upcoming Dickinson lecture, Fanny Garrison declared that "It makes me so happy when a woman does something grand and noble. The act is so fine a plea for woman's rights."[30] Young Lillie Chace clearly looked up to Dickinson as an example of what women could accomplish. When New Hampshire Republicans invited Dickinson to speak, the 15-year-old Chace pointed out how ironic it was that state laws decreed that Dickinson—by virtue of her sex—should not be exposed to the public world of the ballot box but it was somehow appropriate for her to lecture in public. As Dickinson's successes mounted, Chace announced that "I am very glad of thy success, both because I love thee, and because I am a <u>woman</u>, and as much I thank thee from the bottom of my heart for the great work thee is doing for <u>us</u>." Like Atkinson and Garrison, Chace's relationship with Dickinson led her to look inward, openly wondering if she had the "necessary 'brass'" to be a public speaker like her friend. A year after the war, when she had drifted from Dickinson's inner circle, Chace wrote again, hoping "I may yet see thee again 'face to face,' and in thy presence feel how true it is that womanhood and womanhood's glory and charm are inherent in her nature, not the forced growth of her hot-house seclusion." The 17-year-old admitted that she lacked the strength "to break the bonds that hold me" and thus she depended on the strength of powerful advocates like Anna Dickinson.[31]

Young women who did not know Dickinson personally were similarly inspired by her trailblazing public activities. When Dickinson spoke in Chicago, Frances Willard, who was a few years older than the orator, was in the audience. Years later the great temperance advocate would recall that she spent a sleepless night reliving "the cadence of that wondrous voice." "Beyond all men and women to whom I have yet listened," she declared, "Anna Dickinson has been to me an inspiration."[32] One of Lillie Chace's boarding school roommates asked Lillie to "'Give [Anna] my love . . . and tell her I was so delighted because her first lecture was on

that question'—the Woman—'I dont ever expect to lecture myself, but I feel.'" Others
wrote to her directly. "Good bless you Anna Dickinson," a Massachusetts woman
wrote, and "thank you for every word you said [and] . . . for the good your lecture
did for me personally." Shortly after the war, Harriette Keyser, a 25-year-old New
York schoolteacher, sent Dickinson a long, autobiographical letter. "When God
calls me to any work, I shall step out of the ranks," she promised. In the meantime,
she wanted only to thank Dickinson for words that had served to "encourage and
strengthen" her. Another correspondent—the mother of eight daughters—was so
moved by a Dickinson lecture that she vowed to "rescue" two prostitutes by hiring
them as servants, explaining that she only had to figure out how to do so without
her husband learning of their background. Others wrote praising Dickinson as a
beacon for all womankind, or seeking advice on how to launch a career in public
speaking or on other routes into the public arena.[33] Although many journalists had
tried to minimize the larger significance of Dickinson's public role, for decades
to come American women would look to her as a challenging, heroic model of
how women could elbow their way into public discourse.

For the remainder of her career, Anna Elizabeth Dickinson's public identity would
be inextricably wrapped up with the national memory of the Civil War. Whatever
else she would accomplish in the decades to come, audiences and reporters invariably
recalled her wartime role as America's Joan of Arc. This popular link to the Maid
of Orleans, which Dickinson happily embraced, signified her passionate patriotism
and her fiery personality.[34] Long after the war, audiences recalled how Dickinson
stood up to treasonous Copperheads, exchanged barbs—and perhaps dodged bullets
—in Pennsylvania's mining districts, and did her part to support the Union troops
in the field and the Republicans on the stump. Fortunately for Dickinson, the national
memory stressed her patriotism, rather than her critiques of Abraham Lincoln.
In the same way that the national memory of the Civil War tended to eventually
obscure the internal divisions that had wracked the Northern states, Dickinson's
highly partisan wartime role soon became recalled for her patriotic nationalism and
not her occasionally vitriolic partisanship.

   Dickinson's role as a wartime political speaker was understood as quite distinct
from the thousands of other women who had entered the public arena during
the Civil War. Although praised for her patriotism, Dickinson was not linked in
the public mind with the legions of Sanitary and Christian Commission workers,
Ladies Aid Society volunteers, nurses, and other "noble women of the North"
who made their contributions within more familiar gender contexts. And while
she transgressed into traditionally male venues, the postwar hagiography did not
generally consider her alongside the war's celebrated women spies and female
soldiers. In the years immediately following the war, when Frank Moore wrote
*Women of the War: Their Heroism and Self Sacrifice* (1867) and Linus P. Brockett and
Mary Vaughan coauthored *Woman's Work in the Civil War: A Record of Heroism,*

*Patriotism and Patience* (1867), they failed to include Anna Dickinson's wartime exploits in their hefty tomes. These books were essentially dedicated to women who did "women's work" in the Union's interest, or those handful of women who became honorary males for the duration. Dickinson fit neither category, and thus these quasi-official celebrations of Civil War women omitted the great Anna Dickinson.[35]

In one sense Anna Dickinson's wartime labors actually coincided most closely with those anonymous women, in the North and the South, who adjusted their economic activities in response to wartime hardships. Unlike many other Civil War–era women, Dickinson's financial challenges were not directly caused by the conflict: her father died long before the war; her brothers did not go off to fight; no invading troops destroyed the family homestead. But, like many of her peers, the national crisis did open up unusual economic options for Dickinson. Ironically, the sectional conflict presented her with an opportunity to support her mother and sister as a political lecturer, much as the explosion of war contractors produced crucial wage work for working-class sewing women, and opened positions for middle-class women as clerks in various branches of the federal government.[36]

But if material obligations drove Dickinson to push her body to its physical limits during the war, it was her political passion and patriotism that lured her to the platform. Here Dickinson's public role was similar to, although also profoundly different from, the wartime activities of America's leading advocates for women's rights. Between the crucial 1848 meeting at Seneca Falls and the secession crisis 12 years later, the women's movement in the United States had slowly gathered momentum, assisted by annual conventions and shaped by leaders like Susan B. Anthony and Elizabeth Cady Stanton. The movement's initial broad agenda had been defined by the diverse principles articulated in the Declaration of Sentiments, but with the passage of time the emphasis had tilted increasingly toward woman suffrage as the chief objective. In the years immediately before the Civil War the leaders of the women's movement, based largely in New York, had begun to experiment with new strategies for engaging in public discourse. As part of a long and successful statewide effort to promote two crucial laws enhancing the legal rights of married women, Susan B. Anthony and her colleagues perfected their lobbying techniques in Albany while a half dozen lecturers traversed the state delivering speeches in 150 communities. But before long, the pull of national events would distract the leadership from women's issues. When the secession crisis erupted, both Anthony and Stanton toured the state speaking out against the slaveocracy, and urging disunion over compromise with the South. Their excursions became known as the "mob tour" because of the hostility the abolitionist women faced. With the outbreak of war, both Anthony and Stanton joined most of their abolitionist colleagues in supporting the war effort, and in 1862 Anthony in fact temporarily turned to the stump, delivering five speeches in New York's Schuyler County supporting Republican gubernatorial candidate James S. Wadsworth.

In early 1863 national policy debates and gender politics converged as Stanton and Anthony—acting in the political context created by the appearance of Union Leagues across the North—founded the Woman's Loyal National League (WLNL) in New York. Setting aside the agenda of the women's movement for the duration, the WLNL's leadership ostensibly set out to gather hundreds of thousands of signatures calling for immediate emancipation, but in the process they were also developing a huge political pressure group to lobby for women's issues. During the 1864 campaign Stanton and Anthony publicly supported the movement to replace Abraham Lincoln with abolitionist John C. Frémont, thus using their public positions to influence national politics. With the failure of the Frémont movement, both women opted to join their fellow radicals in sitting out the election rather than supporting the moderate Lincoln. Clearly the leaders of the women's movement were developing a variety of political strategies, including insider lobbying, massive petitioning, and public oratory. Anna Dickinson corresponded with Susan B. Anthony during the war about both the WLNL and the election of 1864, but while they shared the same political ideals, the two adopted different political paths, with Dickinson playing a much more partisan political role while declining to participate in the activities of the WLNL.[37]

Although Anthony and Stanton and a few of their colleagues did cross over from reform-based oratory to the occasional campaign address, as a partisan political speaker Anna Dickinson was unparalleled among wartime women. In response to her great successes, the Democratic Party experimented with female speakers of their own, trotting out actresses Emma Webb and Teresa Esmonde for occasional lectures countering the Republicans' Joan of Arc. And Cordelia Phillips, a Republican orator, gave at least a few lectures supporting Lincoln in 1864. The appearance of these imitators on the platform late in the war is strong testimony to Dickinson's tremendous popular appeal, but none remotely approached her success as a political force or a national celebrity.[38] Unlike those women who had responded to the Civil War within the context of their culturally defined roles, or those who had adjusted their economic or political behavior "for the duration," Anna Dickinson had constructed a unique public identity that meshed her own considerable passions and talents with the patriotic and political demands of a society in flux.

*Part II*

---

# AN ENDURING
# PUBLIC FIGURE

# Chapter 4

# "A WOMAN OF EARNEST CONVICTIONS": THE LYCEUM

WHEN the Civil War came to a close, the nation faced a battery of questions. Many concerned the fate of the conquered Southern states and the future of the newly liberated freedpeople. Should the rebels be welcomed back into the Union or punished for their treason? How should the Southern states incorporate African Americans into their economic, political, and social worlds? The war also opened a Pandora's box for the Northern states. As Radical Republicans moved to force racial transformations on the defeated Confederacy, abolitionists were quick to point out injustices embedded within Northern society. How could the Union accept the sacrifices of black soldiers while refusing to let African Americans share fully in the nation's political life? But the impulse to enfranchise adult black men invited the logical response: should the nation grant a political voice to African American men while continuing to exclude women, who had served so valiantly and sacrificed so freely to protect the Union?

These issues weighed heavily on Anna Dickinson. As an advocate for both women and African Americans, she would be forced to take a position on one of the crucial political debates of the day: which citizens should be granted suffrage in the postwar world? And as an outspoken wartime patriot, she could not resist weighing in on the South's future. In the postwar decades Dickinson would cast her net much more widely, critiquing economic inequalities, sexual inconsistencies, legal imbalances, and a host of impediments to a truly just society. The platform remained her preferred forum; each season she unveiled one or more new lectures commenting on the state of national affairs and particularly on the status of women and blacks. But Dickinson would also experiment with the written word, publishing a novel, an extended treatise on public policy, and a humorous little book about life on the road.

Dickinson engaged in this ongoing dissection of postwar America with concerns for her own economic and political future as a constant backdrop. After Appomattox she faced her own challenges. How could she maintain the political voice she had cultivated during the war? In a society that offered few opportunities for women to express their views, how would she find audiences that would meet both her compulsion to be heard and her thirst for fame? Meanwhile, she had also grown accustomed to a substantial income. Would she be able to maintain that lifestyle now that there was no longer a demand for her patriotic rhetoric? The months after the close of the Civil War were a time for Dickinson—like the nation—to take stock.

Perhaps it was this uncertainty about her future that prompted Dickinson to visit the offices of phrenologist John P. Jackson in June 1866. Whatever her intentions, Dickinson submitted to Jackson's thorough examination of her skull and features and he produced a detailed analysis, commenting on her physical traits, her emotional makeup, and her future. Dickinson, Jackson concluded, had such an unusually large brain that it was a testimony to the "toughness & compactness of your constitution" that she was able to give it the proper support. That constitution required substantial exercise and more sleep than ordinary citizens, and Jackson offered Dickinson extensive counsel on her diet and consumption patterns. (He was, in fact, quite on the mark about both Dickinson's love of exercise and fondness for sleep.) Jackson's assessment of Dickinson's character was extensive, and also impressively on target. She was, he reported, unusually "well developed in combativeness and destructiveness," making her well suited to battle evils of all sorts. He saw in Dickinson a strong sense of morality and a compulsion to fight injustice. But the orator was also unusually sensitive to public opinion, seeking repeated reassurance that she was doing well and occasionally—in apparent overcompensation for her lack of self-esteem—adopting excessively strong opinions that ran counter to her more agreeable nature. The report concluded that Dickinson "would be a good actor as well as a good orator" because she had both the capacity to live in the moment and to be highly reflective. Privately, Dickinson enjoyed "a philanthropy of friendship that can embody a large number." "You can," Jackson observed, "make every one of a hundred persons feel for the time being that they stand as high with you as anybody else." Looking to the future, he advised that "you are capable of living strongly as a wife, as a mother, as a friend, and as a patriot." The challenge would be to figure out how to juggle those various roles.[1]

During the war Dickinson had maintained a very full lecture calendar by cobbling together a variety of paid engagements, sometimes receiving flat fees and occasionally taking a percentage of ticket receipts. For weeks on end she toured Northern states as a hired Republican advocate. Between these campaign swings she contracted with local lecture committees or promoters to speak on the National Crisis and related matters. Even when she spoke in aid of a patriotic charity, Dickinson had rarely appeared without a fee.[2] With peace, Dickinson's immediate concern was not so much to come up with new subjects for her oratory—her interests were broad and her opinions seemingly boundless—but to adopt the right strategies to ensure a full professional schedule.

One thing was clear: the Union's military victory did nothing to ease her financial burdens. Although her three brothers occasionally pitched in to help with family finances, none earned much money and all three at one time or another turned to their younger sister for assistance. In early 1866, brother Samuel—who was living in Washington, D.C. with his new wife, Mary—sent the family a rather testy letter, explaining that although he had previously offered to assist with household expenses, he had been led to understand that Anna was covering the bills and thus he had allocated the funds to his own family. A few months later Dickinson sent Samuel and Mary (who was five months pregnant) a financial gift, prompting them to respond with worries that she was not taking care of her own future. "Save thy money dear sister," Samuel cautioned, "we are anxious thee should provide for thyself & then for Mother . . . for a rainy day may come." Later that year Dickinson's brother Ed, who had a long history of various illnesses, wrote from New York asking if "My Dear Little Wanderer" would be willing to lend him $3,000 to $4,000 so that he could buy his way into a secure position at the firm where he worked. And, as 1866 came to a close, Samuel pressed Anna about a promised loan of $150. In the meantime, Susan regularly reported on mounting bills and household expenses, making it quite clear that she and her mother still depended on Anna's earnings.[3]

The lure of public performance, the urge to participate in political discourse, and the ongoing financial pressure all flowed together, directing Dickinson toward the platform rather than some other professional endeavor. The Lyceum Movement originated in New England in the late 1820s. In its original embodiment the lyceum was distinctly local and pointedly educational. Community groups would arrange a series of lectures, commonly on scientific, historical, or philosophical topics, to be delivered by amateur orators, who were almost exclusively men. Occasionally such groups invited a celebrated literary or cultural figure to travel some distance for an engagement, and such speakers received modest honoraria for their troubles. By the 1850s the lyceum had evolved into what might best be termed highbrow entertainment. Lecture courses featured celebrated, polished professional speakers who often addressed the major reform issues of the day. In other cases committees gravitated toward speakers—generally artists, authors, or entertainers—whose fame in other arenas was sufficient to fill a paying house of the curious or star struck.

By the time Anna Dickinson came on the scene in the midst of the Civil War, the practice of public lecturing had become largely constricted to patriotic oratory. As her wartime career illustrated, the lines between partisan rhetoric and lyceum-like public speaking had blurred considerably, perhaps to her advantage. The lecturing field had been further limited by the decline in public enthusiasm for more mundane topics and the absence of some of the prominent antebellum speakers who either traveled abroad or joined the Union Army.[4] After the war, the lyceum regained its antebellum popularity, but with several important changes. The most dramatic was the sudden growth of a variety of highly successful lyceum bureaus. Although he was not the first in the field, James Redpath, a celebrated reformer and journalist, deserves credit as the father of the postwar lecturing boom. Having established the Boston Lyceum Bureau in 1868, James Redpath essentially served as an agent to the stars, taking over many of the bureaucratic headaches that plagued traveling orators. For 10 percent of their earnings, lecturers could hand the day-to-day details, like advertising, travel planning, and negotiations with local hosts, over to Redpath's Lyceum Bureau. Before long Redpath and his partner George Fall had managed to line up an impressive stable of famed speakers, including Henry Ward Beecher, Wendell Phillips, and John Gough, the trio of acknowledged princes of the platform; literary and journalistic giants such as Mark Twain, Horace Greeley, and Petroleum Nasby; and leading female reformers Mary Livermore, Julia Ward Howe, and Frances Willard. Competing bureaus emerged across the country, often arranging lecture courses for specific regional markets. These included T. B. Pugh's "Star Course," which orchestrated a popular annual lecture and entertainment series at Philadelphia's Academy of Music.[5]

The most popular and active postwar speakers did quite well financially. Compensation for individual appearances varied depending on the size of the hall. Prior to the war, lecture committees commonly paid established speakers between $50 and $100 an evening, with the larger urban halls sometimes paying several times that figure. Redpath and his competitors raised the stakes for their leading clients, negotiating fees that routinely fell in the $200 to $300 range and occasionally were much higher. In 1872 Henry Ward Beecher received $1,000 for a single lecture. John Gough, the lyceum's most active orator, reportedly earned $40,000 with the Redpath Bureau in 1871–72, and for years he received an annual income of around $30,000.[6]

For a decade after the war Anna Dickinson was one of the nation's most active and successful lyceum speakers. She followed a grueling schedule that varied only slightly from year to year. Each fall, usually in the last week of September, she would set out on a series of extended swings that would take her through the Northeast, the Midwest, and—some years—through the far West or the South. Certain annual stops became like second homes. In Chicago and Milwaukee she developed extended circles of friends, and she repeatedly returned to old haunts in Boston,

Hartford, and New York. Apart from a regular Christmas break in Philadelphia, Dickinson would remain on the road until the end of May or even into June. Sometimes she stayed with friends, but she came to prefer staying at hotels, safe from overbearing hosts. For eight months a year Anna Dickinson was the quintessential public woman. She spoke five or more times in a week, delivering lengthy lectures without the aid of amplification, often exhausted after traveling by rail from her previous engagement. During the 1870–71 season—for which her records are most complete—Dickinson delivered somewhere between 130 and 150 addresses across the nation. Only leading temperance advocate John Gough maintained a more active schedule.[7]

In the immediate postwar years Dickinson kept her own schedule, with the assistance of her sister Susan. Some of the preliminary arrangements were made during the summer months, as she rested, researched, and prepared lectures for the upcoming season. But often the final preparations were made while she was on the road. Invitations to speak or adjustments to arranged schedules generally went to Philadelphia, where Susan did her best to maintain a calendar while forwarding most planning decisions to Anna. Dickinson periodically sought professional assistance in arranging portions of her calendar. In July 1865 she asked John Gough what he thought of New Haven's John G. North as a prospective agent. The kindly Gough—who later recalled Dickinson as "a noble woman, of whose friendship I am proud"—replied that all agents were, at best, a necessary evil, and that his experiences with Mr. North had not been good. Despite his warnings, Dickinson made some arrangement with North that proved unsatisfactory; in February Susan wrote cryptically about " 'blackmail' " payments that he had demanded.[8] The following season Dickinson booked quite a few lectures through agent T. B. Pugh. When Pugh unveiled his "Star Course" series in 1869, Dickinson was one of his headline speakers and she continued to appear on his Philadelphia list for several years. But there were limits to how much control Dickinson was willing to yield. In the spring of 1868 she declined Pugh's offer to organize her entire tour, preferring to rely on her own managerial skills and her sister's administrative assistance.[9]

The fees Dickinson negotiated varied from location to location, but she was clearly one of the most handsomely compensated postwar speakers. From the middle of the war until 1867, her standard payment was $100 an evening, although she earned much more for major urban appearances. In 1868 she raised her regular fee to $150, and in 1872 it rose again, to $200 a night.[10]

In 1870, Dickinson signed on for a season with Redpath's Boston Lyceum Bureau. Redpath was drawn to Dickinson both as an important star and as a charismatic individual. "There is not a particle of forced modesty about her," he effused, "and every one feels as though they were sitting in the presence of a very chaste and pure-minded woman."[11] For her part, Dickinson found Redpath personally charming and was sufficiently impressed with his professionalism to give him a chance to arrange her schedule. The season with the Boston Lyceum Bureau was a busy and lucrative one. She netted in excess of $20,000 after commissions and expenses, rivaling Gough and Beecher.[12] But the schedule that Redpath's partner, George Fall, arranged proved particularly arduous. As Dickinson wended her way across the nation, she and Susan exchanged letters commiserating about the harsh calendar. "Geo Fall will be the end of me & my doings I'm afraid," Dickinson complained. "By his stupid arrangement I had to leave Rochester last night—at 10—ride till 10 this morning. . . . I have now lost $1,200 already this season by engagements actually dropped & shall think myself fortunate if I do not lose even more before the season is over." Having spent several years running their own operation, perhaps Susan and Anna were skeptical of any plans imposed by an outside agency. Whatever the case, Dickinson abandoned Redpath's bureau and returned to scheduling her own lectures. Unfortunately, the split was not entirely cordial. Dickinson and George Fall each claimed that the other owed substantial funds for unpaid expenses. Finally, a frustrated Dickinson turned the case over to her friend and admirer—and high-powered lawyer—Benjamin Butler, who happily squashed the hapless agent.[13]

As she prepared for the 1871–72 lecture season, a rumor circulated that Dickinson—having broken with the Redpath Bureau—had retired from public speaking altogether. She promptly arranged for a notice in the New York papers announcing that "Miss Dickinson has not refused to make engagements through lecture bureaus. She has managed her own course of lectures, preferring to do so, thus arranging directly with the party or society to be served, and avoiding any delays or misunderstandings."[14] She continued to arrange her own itinerary in 1872–73, but the following season she handed over part of the job to New Yorker O. G. Bernard and his "National Lecture Bureau." This arrangement worked fairly well for a time, but in December a muddled Boston engagement produced some friction that reappeared that spring, straining Dickinson's relationship with Bernard.[15]

In her 11 years on the road, Anna Dickinson had established herself as an adept, and sometimes demanding, businesswoman. For much of that time she and Susan juggled her calendar successfully, planning trips and negotiating fees with a wide assortment of committees, promoters, and local bureaus. In those seasons when she handed over a portion of the task to a professional agent, the benefits of managerial assistance were apparently outweighed by the added annoyances of unreasonable travel, botched schedules, and other frustrations. Or, perhaps Dickinson simply preferred to control her own movements and was destined to second guess any arrangements imposed upon her by an outsider. Although she fell out with Redpath, Fall, and Pugh, Dickinson maintained a professional relationship with O. G. Bernard, who would travel with her during her extended tour of the South in 1875.

During her public speaking career Dickinson wrote and delivered roughly 20 different lectures. Some reflected her response to a particular event or issue, others addressed broader social and political concerns. Although she usually spoke about contemporary issues, Dickinson's most popular lecture was a historical speech on the life of Joan of Arc. Dickinson unveiled "Jeanne D'Arc" in 1870 and reprised the performance hundreds of times over the next several decades, sometimes rotating the familiar text with a new lecture as she toured the nation.

As was her pattern, Dickinson grounded her version of the fifteenth-century French heroine's life in substantial research, but she also took pains to make the story her own. While other histories portrayed Joan as a pious, saintly worker of miracles who responded to divine voices, Dickinson described a more distinctly patriotic, political woman, tailored to her nineteenth-century audiences and in keeping with her own popular identification with the Maid of Orleans. In Dickinson's hands, the historic Joan of Arc became the "true woman" her audiences would most recognize and embrace, exhibiting piety and purity rather than unsettling masculine transgressive traits. But Dickinson's Joan also showed an independence and strength of character that anticipated the "new woman" of the late nineteenth century. In many senses Dickinson created a Joan who was most like herself, both in her true patriotic fervor and in her reputed otherworldly power. "I believe she was called to her work," Dickinson would announce. "Not by voices . . . [but] just as you and I are called" to do the "work appointed of God" and follow "the voice of conscience." And while others diminished Joan as "a mere blind tool in the hand of fate" Dickinson saw in her, much as her supporters saw in the orator, "a creature of genius, of power and patriotism." It was a portrayal full of drama and pathos that thrilled audiences for nearly a quarter century. Part of the power of the performance would always be in the enduring links between speaker and subject.[16]

Although her other lectures reflected national events and the need to attract and entertain a familiar pool of listeners from season to season, Dickinson consistently returned to the same themes, often reconsidered from new angles. She challenged her audiences to consider the rights and needs of the politically silent or socially mistreated, providing her own distinctive perspective on the nation's ills. She frequently spoke for women, mapping out a broad array of economic, legal, and political concerns that went well beyond the more limited agenda defined by the suffrage movement, which she also supported. "Woman's Work and Wages"—one of her first postwar lectures—argued that women should receive equal pay as men for the same work, and pointed out that even talented and ambitious women had few avenues for making a living. "Something to Do" mined the same themes while urging women to take the initiative in demanding equal pay for equal work. In "Idiots and Women" Dickinson mocked a legal system that granted women the same legal status as the mentally ill, barring both from the right to suffrage. "To the Rescue" addressed the legal rights of women, while "The Social Evil" opposed the legalization of prostitution.[17]

As the years passed, Dickinson was increasingly drawn toward broader social problems and themes. On several occasions her journeys inspired new topics. In 1869 she joined a select group of politicians and dignitaries on a western tour, riding the recently completed transcontinental railroad. When she visited San Francisco Dickinson grew so outraged at the poor conditions of Chinese laborers in the city that she challenged her hosts to improve the material circumstances and educational opportunities for immigrant workers. Her words did not go over well with the paying audiences, but they quickly endeared her to San Francisco's Chinese community who embraced her as a distinguished guest. But even as she spoke up for the weak and powerless, Dickinson suggested a tough-minded approach to suffrage and political inclusion. "Do I say," she asked " 'Put the ballot into the hands of the Chinaman' God forbid! We have enough stupid, ignorant, beastly voters already —and not Americans either!" The answer, she argued, was to educate immigrants so that they could be productive citizens.[18]

On that same trip the group stopped in Salt Lake City, Utah, which inspired Dickinson to write a spirited attack on Mormonism, Brigham Young, and the practice of polygamy. In this lecture, which she called "Whited Sepulchres," Dickinson spoke eloquently of the contrast between the beautiful Utah surroundings and the status of women in Mormon society. According to church doctrine, she claimed, "woman is sent into the world to smooth and soothe a man and to adorn his life. He is to spread, and glorify and magnify himself." More troublesome, the politicians with whom she toured implicitly endorsed the hateful system by pledging government aid in Utah's future prosperity while turning a blind eye to their treatment of women. Like many of her other lectures, Dickinson peppered "Whited Sepulchres" with the stories of individual women, some of whom seemed oddly content with their lot in life. But "how can they be contented, since they are women, and not fiends?" she asked. "Piercing through ignorance, and bigotry, and superstition, and false faith, every woman there is sad and sore and discontented to her heart's core."

While this world was foreign to her eastern audiences, Dickinson insisted that the subordinate legal and cultural status of Mormon women was no more than a dramatic example of larger social patterns. The "underlying theory in regard to the proper place, work, duty and office of women in the world, whereon this whole system of polygamy is reared and strengthened," she argued, "is precisely the same in Salt Lake as in every city in Christendom." Despite all the contemporary talk of women's rights and reform, Dickinson explained, most women would be perfectly happy with a life of domesticity. But "whilst it is natural for women to accept wifehood and motherhood for her portion, it is unnatural for her to accept such wifehood and motherhood, as in too many cases is offered her today." The answer, she concluded, was for all women to enjoy expanded educational and professional options, not necessarily to challenge the position of men in society but to fulfill their own potentials as "true women."[19]

A few months after Dickinson returned from California, the nation's newspaper readers turned to the sensational Richardson-McFarland murder trial. In November 1869 Daniel McFarland walked into the *New York Tribune* office and gunned down journalist Albert Richardson, who had been having an affair with his estranged wife, actress Abby McFarland. McFarland was an alcoholic, who had a history of beating his wife. The two had been separated for several years and Abby McFarland was in the process of pursuing a divorce in Indiana, with the intention of marrying Richardson. To make the case even more dramatic, as Richardson lay on his deathbed, Brooklyn minister Henry Ward Beecher agreed to marry the two lovers, although Abby's divorce was not legal in New York. In the subsequent trial the all-male jury, having heard the love letters between Richardson and Abby McFarland, found the defendant innocent by reason of insanity and—in a final unkind cut— they granted Daniel custody of the couple's only child. Dickinson, like many other leading advocates of women's rights, watched these events unfold with growing anger. In January she unveiled a new lecture, "Men's Rights," in New York City. Like "Whited Sepulchres," this new lecture built from a particular outrage to a broader indictment of patriarchy. The McFarland case, she argued, not only revealed flaws in the American legal system and divorce law but it also illustrated the double standards of morality that ensured the rights of men while consigning women— and especially married women—to second-class status.[20]

While she remained concerned with gender issues, in the early 1870s Dickinson turned to broader concerns. Even as she was touring the country she had already begun gathering facts and opinions on prison reform, compulsory education, and trade unions and labor, both in the United States and abroad.[21] In "Demagogues and Workingmen" Dickinson was at her iconoclastic best, critiquing both organized labor and entrenched corporate capital for standing in the way of progress. She expressed particular disappointment with labor unions, which trumpeted their defense of the working man while rejecting unskilled workers and turning their backs on Chinese laborers. After attending the "brave lecture" at New York City's Steinway Hall, her old friend Oliver Johnson declared, "You are now one of the accepted teachers of the nation, and your utterances have great influence upon the public mind. I must think it creditable to your courage that you ventured to challenge the principles . . . of the Labor Reformers, and to expose the demagogism of some of their leaders." Others, particularly those with labor sympathies, were less pleased. Another veteran abolitionist scolded Dickinson, declaring that "Demagogues showed you thoroughly ignorant of the subject; and ignorance in a person of your capacity and opportunities is inexcusable."[22]

Dickinson's correspondence provides only the vaguest sense of how she selected her topics and produced her lectures. A tireless reader, she pored over a wide assortment of newspapers and journals. When a complex subject attracted her interest, Dickinson took advantage of her vast circle of well-connected friends—in both journalism and government—to gather data. Although Dickinson routinely turned to friends for their political advice, there is almost no evidence of her seeking input on which lecture topics to tackle. Perhaps this distinction is instructive. While her peers on the lyceum circuit often chose lighter themes or the hottest topics, when drafting her lectures Dickinson seemed confident that her reputation and natural charisma would fill halls even when she swam against the mainstream. Throughout her lyceum career Dickinson walked a very fine line. On the one hand she carefully cultivated her public reputation, and on the other hand she used her powerful position on the platform to articulate her own political beliefs even when they were unpopular.

Once she had settled on topics, Dickinson devoted much of the summer months to writing complete scripts of the new lectures.[23] She generally followed certain stylistic patterns. A student of history and of the classics, Dickinson often grounded her analysis in anecdotes drawn from her studies, effectively giving her speeches a timeless character. After establishing this intellectual context, Dickinson built her case using a combination of facts and statistics and a series of poignant, evocative anecdotes. In her early lectures on women and work Dickinson commonly turned to her own youthful experiences as an underpaid schoolteacher. Later, she perfected the art of spinning sad tales about innocent young women who slid into lives of prostitution, or seamstresses who were unable to make ends meet. In this fashion, a typical Dickinson lecture appealed to both the brain and the heart.

Although her lectures often concerned women's issues, Dickinson almost never adopted a distinctly feminine rhetorical style or perspective. While some of her contemporaries claimed that women—by virtue of their sex—brought a special perspective to public debates, Dickinson did not expressly play that card. As her career progressed, Dickinson abandoned her staid Quaker garb in favor of more expensive, flashy dresses and jewels. Some observers remarked on this transformation, commenting on how the maturing Dickinson had donned the trappings of celebrity. But even as she had come to enjoy the material benefits of her fame, Dickinson, unlike many other female orators, never seemed to present herself to an audience as the picture of circumscribed femininity.

A few years after the Civil War, author Mark Twain, a celebrated public speaker in his own right, went to see Dickinson speak in New York and dispatched his observations to San Francisco's *Alta California*. An insightful, often caustic, observer of people, Twain offered a valuable portrait of his young rival on the lyceum circuit. Even before she began speaking, Dickinson already projected intriguing contradictions: "She had on a heavy cherry colored silk dress, cut very plainly, and lace cravat and cuffs. Her thick, straight hair is short—only just touches her collar behind. Her dress was suited to a middle-aged person, her hair to a girl, and her face to one sometimes, and sometimes to the other. I cannot possibly guess her age," Twain reported. Once Dickinson began to speak, Twain found himself taken with her distinctive style. "She talks fast, uses no notes what ever, never hesitates for a word, always gets the right word in the right place, and has the most perfect confidence in herself." And, although "she was born in Philadelphia" she "wanders into a brogue frequently that sounds very like Irish."

While some wartime critics had claimed that Dickinson was more style than substance, Twain came away pleased with the lecture as a piece of writing. She "reasons well," he wrote, "and makes every point without fail. Her prose poetry charms, her eloquence thrills, her pathos often moves to tears, her satire cuts to the quick." On this particular occasion, he noted, "the aim of her speech was to call the attention of the people to the meagre number of avenues to an honest livelihood that are permitted to women . . . and to demand, as simple justice to her sex that those avenues be multiplied till women may earn their bread elsewhere than in kitchens and factories without unsexing themselves." Although he was no great advocate for women, Twain found that "she did her work well. She made a speech worth listening to." He came away from the performance convinced that Dickinson was earning her high fees. Nonetheless, he warned that "her sarcasm bites" and while that "is her best card" on the platform, "she will make a right venomous old maid some day."[24]

In addition to the changing business arrangements pioneered by Redpath and his colleagues, the postwar lyceum also evolved from a male-dominated institution to a setting where women were much more extensively represented. While Dickinson had been quite distinctive as a female orator during the Civil War, she was now joined by a small cadre of female celebrities. Although the leading men claimed the status as the true stars, women like Livermore, Stone, Howe, Anthony, and Stanton all attracted large audiences and earned substantial fees. Like most of their male colleagues, these female orators owed their fame to their work as activists or writers, and their public rhetoric was commonly an extension of their other labors.[25] Dickinson's wartime successes had certainly helped open the door for these other women. Whereas she had endured endless wartime editorials questioning the propriety of women speaking in public, the postwar pundits largely shifted their focus to the next tier of questions, asking what women should properly say and under what circumstances.

In 1869 the *Nation* ran an editorial on "Woman in the Lyceum" inspired by a recent New York appearance by rising star Kate Field. Although other women had appeared on the platform, the author claimed that Field "is the first woman who has avowed her intention of becoming a professional speaker in public" as opposed to entering the public arena to support a larger cause. The challenge for those handful of women who chose to appear on the platform, he argued, was that the most influential members of their audiences would be men who—like it or not—had specific notions about what women should and should not do. And those men would be put off by the sight of any woman "standing and talking for an hour and a half at will." A woman in public, the article concluded, should distain "pantaloons, or purely 'sensible clothes' " and "she should sit down, as Miss Field does." But the larger message of the *Nation*'s essay was that Kate Field's lecture, which addressed the question of women speaking in public, had really missed the point. "People go to hear female orators, readers, and lecturers just as readily as males, if they are worth hearing," it explained, "and our advice to women would be to stop talking about their right to follow this and that calling, and follow it." Anna Dickinson's name never came up in the *Nation*'s essay, but it is impossible to miss her powerful presence hovering over the text. Dickinson declined to take a chair and demurely proclaim from her seat. She had the talent to draw an audience in the rough and tumble world of male-dominated oratory, and she never bothered to make her presence in public the subject of her speech.[26]

As a highly successful speaker, Dickinson served as a trailblazer, role model, and mentor for other young women who hoped to enter the public arena. In late 1866 Lizzie Powell asked Dickinson to appear before her New York literary society, explaining that "I want some among us to learn that a woman who has earnest convictions, is not less a woman when she stands before men and women to speak them."[27] A few years later Dickinson received a long letter from an Ohio mother of four who had grown tired of the drudgery of housework. "I get so tired of cooking and waiting on boys all the time," she revealed. "I would like to try [lecturing] but I thought it would be better to go away to commence and I thought it be better go with somebody and think it looks better for women to go together and as I never got up before a crowd it would be better I have some lectures written if you could write some for me and send them I could learn them and then I could go with you." Most of Dickinson's female admirers had a more realistic sense of the orator's true role, but this letter from a complete stranger illustrates how many perceived of her as a beacon of hope.[28] Those who objected to the emergence of public women also singled her out for comment. In 1870 the *Brooklyn Eagle* prefaced a negative review of a new female speaker by declaring that "Miss Anna Dickinson has much to answer for." Her "social philosophy" and occasional "virulence" were bad enough, "but responsibility for the numerous and varied company of imitators whom emulation of her success has imposed on the public cannot be so easily escaped."[29]

The life of the itinerant speaker was sometimes a peculiar one, which could only be fully understood by fellow orators. Although the lyceum schedules required that the paths of major speakers rarely crossed, Dickinson and her colleagues commonly exchanged notes about agents, hosts, and audiences, and occasionally arranged to meet on the road. Sometimes if one speaker was delayed in transit another would step in to fill the void.[30] Within the fraternity of orators, there was a much smaller sorority of female public speakers. If Dickinson was an idol to aspiring public women, she was an invaluable resource for those women who actually embarked on public careers. One of Dickinson's protégées was Olive Logan, the lovely and vivacious advocate for women's rights. The two famed speakers probably first met early in the 1868–69 season. That spring they got together in New York City, before Dickinson set off for the West. Shortly afterwards Logan sent Dickinson a long and affectionate letter. "I wish I had your logical power," she admitted. "However, we can't all have everything." Logan hoped that Dickinson would prove a valuable ally: "I feel as if you and I can be of great mutual benefit to each other, not so much in a merely business way . . . [but] in extending back to the other that affectionate sympathy which is so cheering, so soothing to woman placed in the light we are before the public." And almost to confirm this shared celebrity status, the two women exchanged their latest *cartes de visite*.[31]

For a while Logan and Dickinson enjoyed just the sort of professional friendship Logan had envisioned. Dickinson periodically recommended her to lecture committees or agents and used her prestige to assist her career.[32] Logan, who was a journalist as well as an orator, authored a glowing essay on Dickinson for the radical newspaper, the *Revolution*.[33] They also commiserated about life on the road. "You ask me if I do not sometimes get tired of 'people,'" Logan wrote. "Sick of them—sick of their talk, and their looks, and their platitudes and empty heads. I have lots of invitations from people to come and spend the summer with them; but I cannot make up my mind to do it." Only another public woman could fully grasp the petty annoyances that accompanied life on the road, and the two naturally gravitated toward each other. They also occasionally exchanged unflattering remarks about other public women. In October 1869 Logan wrote that "the most unheard of efforts are being made this year to foist upon the public every sort of feminine oratory from the lofty poetess to the little newspaper scribbler, from actresses to workingwomen, and from Washington lobbyists to women preachers." This newcomer to the platform was quick to dismiss those other women who were simultaneously pursuing their own careers.[34]

Like many of her other female friendships, Dickinson's letters from Olive Logan suggest a brief period in which they shared physical intimacies and certainly a distinctive affection. "I have often sighed for some true friend of my own sex," Logan admitted in an early letter, "whom I could thoroughly respect for her genius, and at the same time love for her loveliness; nothing in the shape of a man could be to me what a woman could—at least until you turn into a man; and if you ever do, remember you promised to make furious love to me, I shall make furious love in return, then we shall be married, and live happy forever more." It is unclear what to make of these powerful pronouncements and perhaps tempting to read too much into them. Logan's words are similar to Lou Brackett's earlier declaration that "you are mine and belong to me, until you get married" and that she "feared no man" would truly replace her in Dickinson's affections. Both women wrote letters to Dickinson that were charged with erotic tension, while at the same time they each presumed that Dickinson would eventually settle into a heterosexual marriage. A month later Logan once again wrote of both her professional admiration and her personal affection for her new friend. She felt devoted to Dickinson, she explained, "because I love and honor you, as, I truly believe, I never did woman. You are an honor, not only to the sex, but to these United States of ours . . . With all the love in my heart, and all the kisses on my lips, I am, O Sweet Anna . . . your loving friend . . ."[35]

Logan certainly admired Anna Dickinson and she was clever enough to heap words of flattery on her influential colleague. For a time Dickinson seemed equally fond of her enthusiastic imitator, but before long she lost patience with the ambitious Logan. In late 1870 Susan Dickinson reported chatting with Logan after a Philadelphia appearance, adding that the orator was characteristically enthusiastic in her praise of Dickinson, but warning her sister to take that "at its face value."[36] By the end of the year the relationship had soured, prompting Logan—who had recently become engaged to be married—to write a long, distraught, letter. "Some cloud has fallen between us—from what dark corner of the sky, you know, and I do not. But I tell you truly, Anna, I have never been disloyal to the friendship I have held for you since first I met you—never in heart, or by word. I do not make friends one day to quarrel with them the next. I hold them true till they prove to me they are false. I do not know why you are silent toward me. I have imagined some things, but have put them aside as unworthy of you—impossible to you. . . . Some unusually skillful mischief maker has been at work here." Here, again, the passionate Logan leaves tantalizing clues about a complex situation. Apparently Dickinson had stopped writing without explanation, leading Logan to suspect that unnamed acquaintances had spoken ill of her.[37]

If Olive Logan seemed for a time to model her career on Dickinson's successes, Kate Field—another young, vibrant woman who burst onto the postwar lyceum circuit in the late 1860s—was even more calculated in her professional aspirations.[38] Like Logan, Kate Field turned to Dickinson for professional advice, which Dickinson graciously provided. There is no evidence that the two ever became close friends or confidantes, although for a short time they corresponded.[39] While Field and Dickinson constructed a seemingly cordial, even friendly professional relationship, several members of Dickinson's personal circle viewed Field as little more than an attractive, and essentially shallow, interloper in a field pioneered by Dickinson. Susan Dickinson concluded that "I'm sorry for Kate Field as a woman—such a character is to be pitied as well as despised." When Field considered going onto the stage, Dickinson's friend Melinda Jones found the idea a strange one: "Women are queer—but perhaps I cant be just to Miss Kate, as I dont like her." And when Field's initial theatrical reviews were mediocre, Lou Brackett commented that "I am not one bit sorry that they were no better for her—for she is so ungracious."[40]

Dickinson's acquaintance with Field also eventually went off the rails. In the late 1870s, Susan hoped that Anna would write to Field about some matter, but Dickinson replied that there were "<u>reasons</u> why I don't care to write to her at present tho I am sure that a request from thee would meet a very cordial response."[41] The following year, after she had turned to the stage and was struggling with unfavorable theatrical reviews, a frustrated and slightly jealous Dickinson wrote to Susan about Field's professional successes: "She is a failure at everything, but she is a <u>newspaper</u> woman, so the journals of the day have more to say about her than if she were ten successes and an outsider," she complained.[42]

Olive Logan and Kate Field were Dickinson's most obvious imitators and competitors in the postwar decade, although both women tended toward lighter topics. While Olive Logan was amusing her audiences with her essay "A Word about Dress," which tackled the thorny issue of what women should wear in public, and Kate Field was speaking in public on the propriety of women as public speakers, Anna Dickinson was increasingly drawn to controversial topics, ranging from prostitution, to polygamy, to the McFarland murder trial.[43] Still, from a professional perspective Dickinson had to reckon with these emerging orators. In fact, when she considered touring England in 1871 the news that both Logan and Field had planned similar trips convinced her to set the plans aside.[44]

Several other women also emerged on the platform during these years, laying claim to the professional benefits that Anna Dickinson had been instrumental in creating, and often eventually earning the disdain of Dickinson and her friends. When popular English orator Emily Faithfull visited America, editor and author Laura Curtis Bullard made a tremendous fuss over the young celebrity, throwing a reception in her honor and urging Dickinson to make an appearance. A minor mishap kept Dickinson from attending Faithfull's reception, but she happily agreed to introduce her English colleague to an enthusiastic Philadelphia audience and assisted Bullard in navigating the American lecture bureaus for Faithfull.[45] It did not take long for Faithfull's American hosts to lose their enthusiasm. Even before she had begun touring, Sallie Austin wrote to Dickinson from Milwaukee, outraged at the publicity the Englishwoman had already garnered: "You and I know very well how easy it is for a woman with wealth, rank and influential connections to do things, such twaddle makes me so mad." Bullard's husband admitted that although he found Faithfull charming, she was not much of an orator. Barely a week later that charming veneer had chipped away, and he was reporting that Faithfull owed her limited successes to "the efforts of friends on her behalf" although, he sighed, "[n]othing can penetrate the thick hide of English conceit." Dickinson shared her own reservations about Faithfull with Sallie Austin shortly before the orator sailed for England that April, although the two had no public falling out.[46]

One of the more amusing episodes concerned conservative lecturer Lillian Edgarton who had also burst upon the scene in the late 1860s. According to Dickinson, Miss Edgarton had been "fond of saying . . . that when she left school an enthusiastic young girl, she was inspired to her work by the overwhelming admiration she had for me & had been greatly helped since then by the friendship which she had for me." Dickinson found this rather surprising since at the time she was only 28, whereas—she told her mother—if Edgarton "ever sees 35 again put me down for a false calculator." Moreover, the two had never met or communicated, which made for an awkward scene when Dickinson showed up at one of Edgarton's lectures in Grand Rapids, Michigan. Dickinson enjoyed the moment so much that she sent Susan and her mother a long, amusing description. The letter revealed quite a bit about how Dickinson observed her female competitors on the platform. Edgarton "was quite stunningly arranged with flowers & lace & ribbons, . . . hair like a mop (stinking, too, it is spoken) with some [?] perfume (the last proof of vulgarity) much rouge & powder & a great dab of India ink under each eye." Even more disturbing, "her manner is full of affectation—her voice is worse." Edgarton had built her reputation by appearing on the platform as the height of femininity, criticizing those women who were clamoring for an expanded public and political role. Dickinson had no patience "with this style of woman— a woman who really believes that her place is at home & who stays there is to be thoroughly respected—but a woman who makes speeches to demonstrate that a woman has no right to speak" was beneath contempt. It was bad enough that Edgarton had offended Dickinson's sensibilities with her flowers, ribbons, perfume, and rouge, but it was intolerable to see this pretender entering the public arena to criticize the sort of gender progress for which Dickinson stood.[47]

Perhaps this letter set Dickinson thinking more broadly about the new cohort of women who had appeared on the scene and who had, in many cases, co-opted popular discourse about women in the public arena. The following month Dickinson toyed with submitting an article to the *Atlantic* "protesting against the public accepting as the 'movement'—such women as are, by reason of thrusting themselves there, in the fore front of it." Although she named no names, Dickinson was very likely thinking of women such as Logan, Field, and Edgarton, who presumed to speak for women without any particular credentials within the larger women's rights movement. Although the idea for the essay had some appeal, Dickinson thought better of it, fearing that it would "bring a hornets nest about my ears."[48] Still, she and her friends frequently assessed these women against a political standard. Dickinson's brother Ed dismissed Edgarton as little more than "a fine figure, a voice better than any other woman on the platform except that owned by thee—a good deal of rhetorical flourish, and a <u>rather</u> pleasant way of saying commonplace things." Noah Brooks told Dickinson that "you know 1873 times more about the woman question than she does."[49]

For more than a decade Anna Dickinson had enjoyed a remarkably successful career as a public speaker. She had earned a substantial income, traveled in high style, and supported her mother and sister in Philadelphia. In the process she had left her mark on the lyceum movement and on the place of women in public. As an aggressive businesswoman and one of the circuit's most popular speakers, Dickinson helped make postwar oratory a hugely popular postwar phenomenon.

And as the leading woman on the platform, she became a model for female admirers and imitators. The fact that by the early 1870s the presence of women on the platform was no longer treated as a novelty owed much to Dickinson's successful labors during and after the war. And the very public, unapologetically transgressive nature of Dickinson's fame as a celebrated woman—and the respect and wealth she earned—served as a powerful example to countless other young women across the country who saw in her the possibilities for violating cultural boundaries and entering the public arena.

Dickinson's unusual fame and the political messages she delivered from the platform also gave her a distinctive role within the changing postwar world of public women. On the one hand, she came to the public arena because of her passion for abolitionism, women's rights, and the Union cause, which placed her squarely within the reforming sisterhood of Susan B. Anthony, Elizabeth Cady Stanton, Mary Livermore, Lucy Stone, and their associates. On the other hand, Dickinson supported herself and paid for her mother's home with her public speaking and she was clearly concerned with her celebrity and reputation, which seemed to locate her closer to female speakers like Field, Logan, and Faithfull. In fact, she was in both worlds—the reformers and the professionals—but of neither. Dickinson did her best to parlay her celebrity into a substantial income while simultaneously using the pulpit she had earned with her eloquence to make an array of radical political statements.

Dickinson sometimes paid a price for walking this fine line. In 1871 a testy Elizabeth Cady Stanton vented her frustration at those celebrated women who had declined to support the suffrage movement and its leadership. "Neither Anna Dickinson nor Kate Field ever tho't enough of our movement to make a speech on our platform," she complained.[50] Near the end of the decade Stanton responded to news that Dickinson had fallen upon hard times by admitting that although the news "makes my heart sad," the truth was that "she forgot her high calling and thought only of making money, thus she lost her power and inspiration. Gold is good in its place, but when it becomes the primal consideration, it turns the heart to stone." Stanton's comments must have cut Dickinson deeply, for years later—when Stanton's correspondence was published—she copied the entire letter into one of her many notebooks.[51]

Stanton's criticism would have stung because it both hit close to home and was still largely unfounded. Throughout the 1860s and 1870s Dickinson charted a difficult course, speaking up for her fundamental beliefs about the rights of women while guarding her earning potential, and her own sometimes tenuous health. Dickinson's relationship with the postwar woman suffrage movement was often quite troublesome, complicated by difficult personal relationships, thorny organizational divisions, and pressing economic demands. In the end, Dickinson chose her own path, even when it alienated the icons of the movement.

# Chapter 5

# WHAT ANSWER?:
## SUFFRAGE AND
## CITIZENSHIP IN THE
## POSTWAR WORLD

WITH the close of the Civil War, the newly reunited United States faced a series of debates about the structure of political participation and the nature of citizenship in the postwar world. Several different issues shaped these discussions, and Anna Dickinson found herself in the thick of each public conversation. Four years of bloody war had confirmed that the union formed by the Constitution could not be dissolved through secession, but that Constitution left few clues about how to reintegrate the defeated Southern states back into the Union, and particularly how to treat those Southern men who had served the Confederacy. More complicated still, by destroying the institution of slavery the Civil War left nearly 4 million freedpeople as its most powerful legacy. Now the nation would have to decide what role, if any, these recently enslaved Americans would have in shaping their own political futures. Meanwhile, the leaders of the woman suffrage movement were quick to point out that Northern women had made tremendous sacrifices in support of the cause. If the political deck was going to be reshuffled in the postwar world, why not finally remember the ladies?

The future of the freedmen, and broader debates over citizenship and suffrage, dominated postwar abolitionist discourse, producing painful antagonisms and debilitating divisions among old allies. William Lloyd Garrison, the founder of the American Anti-Slavery Society (AASS), argued that now that emancipation had been achieved the Society should disband. Wendell Phillips split with his old friend and urged that the AASS carry on the fight, shifting its emphasis to black suffrage. Despite her affection for Garrison, Dickinson sided with Phillips, agreeing that the AASS had not finished its work until freedom had been protected with the franchise.[1]

As events unfolded, the campaign for black suffrage produced a series of destructive conflicts between ideology and expediency. Leaders of the woman suffrage movement, who had thrown their substantial organizational might behind emancipation for the duration of the war, had every reason to suppose that the Union's victory and the rise to power of their Radical Republican allies would yield valuable returns in the postwar world.[2] But when push came to shove, the Radical Republicans in Congress supported the Fifteenth Amendment granting the franchise to black men while explicitly excluding women. For Dickinson, this decision would pit her loyalties—both political and personal—to the women's movement against her allegiances to the Republican Party.

It is striking how fast the political center shifted in the postwar years. Although true radicals like Dickinson and Phillips called for black suffrage, even the Wade-Davis Bill—which had set out the radical agenda for Reconstruction—made no provision for giving freedpeople a political voice. But by the end of 1865 Congress had sent the Fourteenth Amendment to the states for ratification. This amendment protected black citizenship and took major strides toward black male suffrage, by requiring that the states either enfranchise blacks or face proportional reductions in their congressional representation. This left radicals like Dickinson disillusioned with the moderate Republicans. Northern states with small African American populations could continue to exclude black men from the franchise even while Southern states underwent revolutionary—if only temporary—political transformations. The ratification of the Fifteenth Amendment in 1870 took the next step in providing that access to the vote would not be abridged "on account of race, color, or previous condition of servitude," but the nation's women, both black and white, would wait another half century to enjoy the same right. During the crucial five years from the end of the war to the close of the decade Dickinson—both through her lyceum lectures and through a range of other public activities—played a major role in shaping these events. In the process she broke ranks with many of her wartime allies.[3]

Immediately after the war, the Radical Republicans in Congress battled the new president Andrew Johnson for control over Reconstruction. Republicans like Charles Sumner, Wendell Phillips, and Ben Butler—all friends of Dickinson—lost patience with Johnson's limited civil rights agenda, his opposition to black suffrage, and his apparent generosity toward the defeated rebels. Dickinson shared this perspective, and while her male colleagues challenged the president in Congress and the Senate, she joined an array of abolitionist orators who toured the nation assailing the president. In "Flood Tide" Dickinson continued her wartime themes by attacking the Democratic Party, but now Johnson figured prominently in her litany of villains.[4] Although she was not alone in her critique of Johnson, Dickinson took a professional risk adopting such outspoken stances. Charles Dudley Warner sent Dickinson a whimsical note on her travels, imagining his friend "wandering up and down in the wilderness of the West . . . alone in the cars, stopping at hotels like a man, praised till your head is turned, and then sloshed by coarse beer . . . without a husband to your name, with all the bad world on your shoulders to reform, fighting Andy Johnson and the devil, saying what nobody else dare say." Back home, Philadelphia Congressman William Kelley warned Susan Dickinson about the political climate in the nation's capital and worried that her sister's anti-administration oratory might jeopardize the minor government positions her two brothers had secured.[5]

As 1866 came to a close, the off-year elections figured to be a referendum on the Fourteenth Amendment and on Johnson's narrow approach to Reconstruction. Various correspondents urged Dickinson to speak on national politics.[6] When Congressman Kelley asked Dickinson to campaign for him, she drove a hard bargain, demanding guaranteed fees and a substantial list of lecture dates.[7] But although these negotiations showed Dickinson as a businesswoman, she revealed her continuing political passion when she explained to Isabella Beecher Hooker why she must miss her daughter's wedding for the campaign. "Were it ordinary work I would not let a month of engagements stand in my way," she insisted, "but its the sort of fight in which every word has effect & every blow tells."[8]

Meanwhile, national political discourse focused on the ex-Confederate states. That spring and summer Northern voters recoiled in horror at reports of violence against freedpeople. In August conservative supporters of the president staged a National Union Convention in Philadelphia, featuring delegates from both the Northern states and the newly reconstituted Southern state governments. The convention passed resolutions praising the administration and affirming that the Constitution was thriving in the South.[9] Irate Republicans countered with their own Southern Loyalists' Convention in Philadelphia the following month. Technically a meeting of representatives from the Southern states, the Southern Loyalists' Convention included hundreds of prominent Northern Republicans —including Dickinson—who attended as nonvoting observers or honorary delegates. The convention faced the thorny debate over constitutionally enforced black enfranchisement. Although Southern Republicans embraced black suffrage, Northern party members split over the issue, which promised to be a political liability in their home states.

For several days the convention focused on attacking Andrew Johnson, but on the fourth day the delegates from the Southern states issued a report supporting black suffrage. Border-state Republicans tried to avoid the debate and, failing that, many Northern delegates walked out, inducing a state of confusion. Into the temporary void stepped Theodore Tilton, Frederick Douglass, and Dickinson. The three old friends jumped to the podium and convinced the remaining delegates to reconstitute themselves into an enthusiastic mass meeting. For several hours the convention listened to stirring oratory in favor of black suffrage, and biting attacks on the hypocrisy of Northern and border-state Republicans who had failed to support the resolution. The next day the convention voted to endorse the Southern delegates' proposal supporting black suffrage.[10]

It was a powerful and politically significant moment. Even if the arguments themselves were not entirely new, the timing was crucial. Afterward Douglass would credit Dickinson and Tilton with joining him in articulating the arguments that would yield the Fifteenth Amendment, ensuring black male suffrage. "[Thank-you for] rescuing the great convention of the unreconstructed states from moral and political destruction," he wrote to Dickinson.[11] The Southern delegates were particularly taken by Dickinson. Nashville's Henry Barr sent an effusive note, and George Marcy invited her to visit his model plantation in Georgia.[12]

But the Convention was not without its unpleasant aftereffects. Dickinson's performance probably led to the cancellation of her scheduled campaign appearances in Pennsylvania.[13] Moreover, shortly after the meetings a chagrined Henry Wilson wrote Dickinson two long letters complaining that she had unfairly singled him out as an opponent of black male suffrage, whereas the Massachusetts senator insisted that he had done nothing to resist the suffrage resolution and had only left the convention early to meet previous obligations. The 23-year-old Dickinson was having none of Senator Wilson's excuses. "I am most heartily sorry to have been compelled to speak of you as the Senator that belied New England," she wrote, and "doubly sorry that there should have been such truth in the assertion as to make it sting. Pardon the severity of the declaration, when I tell you that I was but the mouth-piece of every Radical in that convention." It was a tough letter. "I would rather speak pleasant things than unpleasant," she insisted, "but I am bound to speak the truth."[14]

The Radicals fared well in the 1866 elections, and even before the new Congress had been seated the Republicans grew increasingly emboldened in their criticisms of the president. Dickinson continued to be one of the administration's most vocal critics, calling for Johnson's impeachment. For a time she even entertained an invitation to travel through the South, organizing Republican voters and campaigning for Republican candidates.[15]

As her appearance at the Southern Loyalists' Convention illustrated, Dickinson's commitment to racial justice did not stop at the Mason-Dixon line. Throughout the postwar years the eloquent political gadfly lobbied for black suffrage in diverse arenas, while generally steering clear of the movement's organizational infighting. In mid-May 1866, when the American Anti-Slavery Society met in New York for its annual meetings, the women's rights leadership convened their first postwar convention, timed to coincide with the abolitionist gathering. Since Wendell Phillips had previously blocked efforts to combine the AASS with the women's movement into a single organization, Susan B. Anthony and her colleagues had stolen the march on their abolitionist brethren by forming the American Equal Rights Association (AERA), dedicated to "universal suffrage" without regard to race or gender.[16] Dickinson declined invitations to appear at the AASS's annual meetings, and although she agreed to attend the women's rights convention she balked at speaking. "I'm a great deal of a Quaker," she explained to Anthony. "I don't like to take up any work till I feel called to it. My personal interest is perhaps stronger in that of which thee writes me than in any other, but my hands are so full just now. I [will] see what I shall do in the future, and I hope the near future. Wait for me a little—forbear, and I honestly believe I'll do thee some good and faithful service." In this fashion, Dickinson managed to lend her support to the new organization while still holding Anthony and her colleagues at arm's length.[17]

Over the next several years the iconoclastic Dickinson would in turn thrill and disappoint the women's rights leadership with her powerful oratory and supportive gestures on the one hand, and her refusal to fully commit to their organizational goals and strategies on the other. For Dickinson, the dilemma involved navigating a path between her unflinching support for black male suffrage and her longstanding advocacy of women's rights. While the women and men of the AERA rejected the Fifteenth Amendment as an abandonment of women, Phillips and the AASS concluded that political and historical circumstances dictated that it was "the Negro's Hour" and they did their best to silence any discussion of woman suffrage at their meetings.[18] Dickinson maintained her ties with the AASS, but proved to be a periodic thorn in their side. When the Society gathered in New York in May 1867, Dickinson and fellow abolitionist Stephen Foster disrupted the meetings by demanding to know how the Society could support the vote for black men while ignoring the political future of black women.[19]

While Dickinson alternately embraced and sparred with Phillips and the AASS, she was being aggressively wooed by Susan B. Anthony and Elizabeth Cady Stanton. For years the two more experienced women's rights advocates had, like veteran anglers, done their best to reel Dickinson closer to the suffrage movement. In 1863 Anthony had tried unsuccessfully to induce Dickinson to deliver some choice "woman's words for the hour" at the inaugural meetings of the Woman's Loyal National League in New York City, but for the duration of the conflict Dickinson concentrated on partisan and patriotic themes and Anthony had to be content with offering her counsel on national politics.[20] After the war Anthony became a more persistent correspondent. Although Dickinson declined to speak at the first AERA meeting, Anthony remained confident that her young protégée would prove a valuable asset. In August 1866 Anthony urged Dickinson to attend the upcoming New York State Equal Rights Convention in Rochester, adding that "[i]f the women fail to speak the one word of the hour," she asked "who shall do it[?]"

Two months, and three more letters later, Anthony was still on the case: "I know you will do all you can and I know too the pressure to keep you from doing in the one direction—Still I mean always to keep beckoning you upward & onward till you speak right out in word the deep, rich, earnest love for your own sex that I know lies in the inner courts of your being . . . Anna, as I love you & you love me—and we both love the right—I ask you to examine the 'inner light' and [give] . . . your testimony for the enfranchisement of the whole people." When it became clear that Dickinson, who was still on the road with paid speaking engagements, would not appear at the convention, a disappointed Anthony sent a printed invitation through her sister Susan in Philadelphia, with the request that Anna at least send along a letter of support.[21]

As 1866 came to a close, the independent-minded orator was being pulled in all directions. While Anthony pressured her for words of support, Dickinson also entertained offers to campaign for William D. Kelley, and then threw herself into the thick of the Southern Loyalists' Convention. Meanwhile, Susan Dickinson and her brothers maintained a steady stream of requests for additional funds and—in the midst of it all—Dickinson endured reports of Elias Irish's slow decline and tragic death. In December, perhaps not coincidentally, Dickinson fell ill in Chicago and was forced to cancel a series of engagements as she recuperated.[22]

In 1867 the suffrage movement focused on an unlikely pair of states: Kansas and New York. In March the Kansas legislature voted to stage two separate referenda that November to consider removing the words "white" and "male" from the state Constitution, thus potentially establishing universal suffrage. Meanwhile, New Yorkers had planned a constitutional convention for June, and suffrage advocates intended to lobby the Empire State to remove restrictions on both women and blacks. Kansas became a crucial testing ground for the movement as intrepid women's rights orators traversed the state. Anthony implored Dickinson to join the crusade. "If the men of Kansas will only vote . . . to strike out 'white male'" from their constitution, Anthony effused, "then we shall have the first brick knocked down." But Dickinson was at home in Philadelphia recuperating from a lung ailment and canceled a planned excursion west.[23]

Throughout the spring and summer Susan B. Anthony continued to praise, flatter, and cajole in letter after letter. "Have the world & yourself see & know Anna Dick. didn't fall in line . . . but that she lead the way," Anthony pleaded. Meanwhile, in New York the Equal Rights Association had gathered 20,000 signatures calling for universal suffrage; but in late June the convention's suffrage committee, chaired by Horace Greeley, recommended in favor of removing the property qualification for black men and against woman suffrage. Anthony hoped that Dickinson would join her in Albany—it is "the golden moment for you" she insisted over and over—but Dickinson missed the convention, opting instead to take a brief vacation with her mother. When she read about the convention debates, Dickinson admitted to

Anthony that "my blood boiled, my nerves thrilled . . . [at] the exquisite care with which men guard their own rights." "Daily I pray for a tongue of flame and inspired lips to awaken the sleeping, arouse the careless, shake to trembling and overflow the insolence of opposition." With those words it seemed as if Dickinson was tempted to be just that powerful voice, but other demands continued to intervene.[24]

After the New York Republicans rejected the suffragists' efforts, the Kansas campaign took on added significance. Prominent male radicals, including Tilton, Phillips, Henry Ward Beecher, and Kansas Senator Samuel C. Pomeroy, signed an appeal calling on Kansas voters to support woman suffrage. Even Greeley agreed that such an experiment was worth trying. But the state Republican Party opposed the measure, and the odds of success in November seemed increasingly long. In August Stanton and Anthony set off to canvass the state, and once again Anthony hoped that Dickinson would join them. Before they left, Anthony tried yet another appeal to Dickinson's better nature, this time quoting from her old friend Frederick Douglass: "I must tell you Frederick Douglass who you know loves you—said to me—Anna did up the pathetic . . . wailing last winter—she must now go up to higher, more womanly, ground, or she will lose something from the reputation she now holds —I know you feel it, for we have talked it over & over—but I repeat it from those grand lips." The following month Anthony wrote from Lawrence, Kansas, detailing her progress and concluding, with admirable optimism, that "if only Anna E. Dickinson could make ten or 15 of the strong points—we should feel sure." But Susan Dickinson urged her sister to remain home and preserve her strength. Meanwhile their brother Samuel had fallen deathly ill and would not survive the year.[25]

In the meantime, Stanton and Anthony had made the controversial decision to join forces with the wealthy, flamboyant, and distinctly racist George Francis Train. Although a strong ally of women, the Democrat Train's presence on the road with the suffrage leaders damaged the campaign in the eyes of many observers and made an appearance by Dickinson even less likely. Longtime abolitionist and women's rights advocate Lucy Stone was pleased with Dickinson's decision. "I am glad that you are not compromised by the spectacle Miss Anthony is making of Woman's cause by parading through the country with such a man as Train," she wrote. "It seems to me she can be scarcely less crazy than he is." Later that winter Susan Dickinson reported that a letter had arrived from Anthony. "Dont let her coax thee into anything she can quote as endorsing in any way G. F. Train" Susan warned. "They're really unscrupulous in trying to get endorsements."[26]

Dickinson remained loyal to the Republican Party and that loyalty created a fissure between her and her suffrage friends. While they were losing the referenda in Kansas, Dickinson stayed East where she unveiled her new lecture, "Breakers Ahead," calling on the Republicans to support black male suffrage. This turn of events appalled Anthony. "But in earnest Anna," she wrote, "it was & is an 'awful' blunder—For I see your speech is not The New Republic—is not woman—but only

Elizabeth Cady Stanton and Susan B. Anthony (standing). Ca. 1880–1900. Library of Congress.

the black man—whom, as I told you they would—the republicans have thrown overboard—I tell you Anna rats—that is female rats ought to know enough to leave a sinking ship." As Anthony suffered through a bitter defeat in Kansas she was deeply disappointed in her young colleague. But she still hoped that Dickinson would see the error of her ways. Further complicating this already-complex political landscape, Anthony had grown increasingly attached to Dickinson personally, longing for her physical presence and reveling in their private moments together.[27]

The losses in 1867 forced Stanton and Anthony to contemplate their options. Abandoned by the Republicans, shushed by liberal men, and criticized by some of their longest allies, they had learned that "we might fight the battle again" and "standing alone we learned our power." Thus inspired, and assisted by Train's funds, they founded the *Revolution,* a weekly newspaper dedicated to women's rights, and began publication in January 1868.[28] The New York offices of the *Revolution* became a favorite meeting place for the nation's radicals and one of Dickinson's favorite haunts when she visited the city. That first spring Nellie Hutchinson, writing as a correspondent for the *Cincinnati Commercial,* toured the *Revolution*'s offices. Anna Dickinson happened by during Hutchinson's visit, and quickly became the focus of Hutchinson's portrait, offering a marvelous window into how Dickinson moved through this world:

> We hear a bustle in the outer room—rapid voices and laughing questions—then the door is suddenly thrown open and in steps a young Aurora, habited in a fur-trimmed cloak, with a jaunty black velvet cap and snow feather set upon her dark clustering curls. What sprite is this, whose eyes flash and sparkle with a thousand happy thoughts, whose dimples and rosy lips and white teeth make so charming a picture? "My dear Anna," says Susan, starting up, and there's a shower of kisses. Then follows an introduction to Anna Dickinson. As we clasp hands for a moment, I look into the great gray eyes that have flashed with indignation and grown moist with pity before thousands of audiences. They are radiant with mirth now, beaming as a child's, and with graceful abandon she throws herself into a chair and begins a ripple of gay talk. The two pretty assistants come in and look at her with loving eyes; we all cluster around while she wittily recounts her recent lecturing experience.[29]

This electric scene was reenacted whenever the itinerant orator dropped by the *Revolution*'s offices, and she routinely enjoyed a comparable reception from the men at the *New York Tribune.* In fact, Dickinson probably found some version of this exuberant greeting wherever she roamed in the postwar decade.

In the spring of 1868 Dickinson still declined invitations to woman suffrage meetings while swimming against the tide among her AASS companions. Lucy Stone asked Dickinson to attend the anniversary meetings of the American Equal Rights Association that May "if you find the internal prompting to do so," but she added that "[y]our work is so good all by itself that I am sure none of us will feel hurt if you think best to keep it so," particularly since Train had been added to the mix. A few weeks later Anthony reiterated the request and asked Dickinson to serve as a vice president of the Association. But like the previous year, Dickinson declined to attend the AERA's annual meetings. Instead she spoke for the rights of black women at the AASS meetings in New York's Steinway Hall, once again issuing a public challenge to Wendell Phillips.[30] Even while she kept the organized women's movement at arm's length, Dickinson was both central to the *Revolution*'s community of reformers and a mainstay on its printed pages. Only days after Nellie Hutchinson published her essay on Dickinson's visit, the *Revolution* ran a letter from a Jamestown,

New York man who had heard her latest lecture and came away a passionate suffragist and, better yet, a subscriber. In late April the newspaper printed a front page story on Dickinson's most recent visit to the office. A few weeks later it praised her "Idiots and Women" as "the ablest lecture she has ever delivered."[31]

During the fall of 1868, in the midst of these political and associational complexities, Dickinson turned to an entirely new form of public discourse: she wrote a novel, which she called *What Answer?*[32] Although she was well read and had been writing her own speeches for years, Dickinson had no experience with writing fiction. Surprisingly, her voluminous correspondence provides very few clues into her thoughts as she produced the novel.[33] The text itself suggests that Dickinson was inspired by Harriet Beecher Stowe's antebellum novels, with their artful combination of romantic pathos and pointed political commentary. Dickinson had probably met Stowe a few times during her visits to Hartford, where she often stayed with the novelist's sister, Isabella Beecher Hooker. As soon as *What Answer?* appeared in print, Dickinson sent Stowe a copy in search of her influential endorsement. Stowe consumed Dickinson's book with relish, and immediately dropped her young friend an enthusiastic note: "I lay on my sofa all alone on Saturday night & read your book all through & when I got through I rose up mentally . . . & said Well done good & faithful Anna—daughter of my soul—I thank you for this. Your poor old grandma in the work rejoices to find it in your brave young hands. . . . Don't mind what any body says about it as a work of art. Work of art be hanged!—You had a braver thought than that." The words must have thrilled Dickinson. Equally important was Mrs. Stowe's review in the *Hartford Courant*, which declared that "If anybody can read that book unmoved, we have only pity for him."[34]

In *What Answer?* Dickinson interwove a tragic interracial love story with a scathing commentary on race relations in the Civil War North.[35] The novel opens in New York City in the fall of 1860, as a handsome young man gazes out a window onto a bustling 5th Avenue. The young man is Willie Surrey, the bright, charming, privileged son of a wealthy foundry owner. As he watches the crowd below, Willie catches a glimpse of a beautiful woman and is immediately smitten. He will meet her soon enough, but first we meet another key character: Abram Franklin. Abe is a young African American man who works as a clerk for Willie's father. Lame from birth, Abe must limp the long walk home each day because the city streetcars are segregated. Much worse, the predominantly Irish factory workers have threatened to strike unless Mr. Surrey fires their black co-worker. Willie and Abe are boyhood friends but now our hero is powerless to stop the racist tide and can only do his best to find Abe another position. The following day Willie, still stewing over racial injustice, attends a school recital where he sees the woman from 5th Avenue— Miss Francesca Ercildoune—read an impassioned antislavery poem. The two begin a courtship and are on their way to falling in love, until Willie tells her the tale of Abe's firing. Francesca soon disappears without explanation, leaving Willie distraught and confused. As luck would have it, national events intercede with the firing on Fort Sumter. Willie enlists in the 7th New York volunteers, and goes off to war without hearing from his beloved Francesca.

Slowly the reader learns Francesca's secret. Although she looks white, Francesca's father is half black, the son of a Virginia slaveholder and an enslaved woman.[36] At a young age her father had been sent to England, where he had married Francesca's mother, an English woman who was long since deceased. Mr. Ercildoune had eventually moved his family to Philadelphia where they quickly discovered that Northern society was also thick with prejudice and injustice. Dedicated to racial justice, and disgusted by the fact that her fair skin enables her to move freely in white society, Francesca has mistakenly concluded that Willie was no different from the rest.

For two years the couple are apart. Willie's letters to Francesca are returned unopened. Meanwhile, Dickinson crafted a series of episodes with the Union army in the field, several of which demonstrate Willie's true commitment to racial justice. At Chancellorsville, Willie loses his arm and is sent home on furlough. While riding a Philadelphia streetcar he intercedes on behalf of a one-legged black soldier who is about to be thrown off the segregated car. Francesca witnesses this scene and agrees to let Willie call on her, and soon the two fall deeply in love and resolve to marry. Francesca's brother and father are initially skeptical, but they soon accept that Willie's intentions are honorable. Willie's family and friends are less understanding. When the Surreys learn Francesca's true racial identity the family disinherits the young war hero and his bride.

Their marital bliss is not to last long. In July 1863 Willie takes a break from his new position recruiting black soldiers and goes to visit his bedridden old friend Abe Franklin. While he is there, the New York City draft riots rip through the city. The rioters, targeting African American homes and institutions, break into the Franklins' house, knock Willie out, and drag poor Abe from his bed. Relying heavily on actual events, Dickinson described Abe's horrible death at the hands of the mob. Unable to spare Abe from torture and execution, Willie sets out to warn Francesca. But the mob sets upon the young officer, beating him to death. (This, too, was based on the actual death of a Union colonel.) Francesca learns of the killing and rushes to her dying husband's side, only to be brought down by a stray bullet. In a touch of heavy-handed irony, the two star-crossed lovers die on the street immediately in front of the Surreys' home.

While this interracial love story drives the novel's narrative, Dickinson packed her tale with an assortment of other characters, and balanced the home-front tragedies with more uplifting events on the battlefield. Time and again, Dickinson's African American characters behave bravely and honorably, and those whites who are most fully exposed to black men and women find their prejudices falling away. The novel closes on election day, 1865. Tom, Willy's oldest friend, and Robert, Francesca's wounded brother, ride a carriage to the polling place, where a mob accosts the black war hero. " 'Challenge the vote!' they cry, 'No niggers here!' " A melancholy Robert turns to Tom and asks, " '1860 or 1865?—is the war ended?' " This then, was the question that the book's title challenged readers to answer.

Dickinson's experiment with fiction provided her with a new platform for articulating some of her favorite themes. She wrote many of her most dramatic chapters close to the facts, relying on newspaper accounts and her own observations, perhaps combined with insights from several friends who had served as officers with the United States Colored Troops. Certainly the central message of *What Answer?*—and the themes that attracted both the greatest praise and the sternest criticism—concerned the transgressive romance between Francesca and Willie. On the one hand their interracial love suggested great possibilities for the future. And, on the other hand, their rejection by most of white society, followed by their tragic deaths, illustrated the destructive racism at the core of Northern society. Dickinson also used Francesca and her family to examine the essential incoherence of a social and cultural hierarchy built upon racial identity. Francesca moves freely in white society because she is light skinned and well educated, but when her friends learn her true racial identity their perceptions of her proper place change abruptly. Racial distinctions, Dickinson seemed to be saying, were not only immoral but essentially arbitrary and capricious.

The horrible deaths of Abe Franklin, Willie, and Francesca reminded readers that Southern society had no monopoly on racial violence and injustice. But Dickinson also hinted at a brighter future. Those white soldiers who fought alongside black men, or who had personal encounters with honest and brave enslaved men and women, returned home transformed by their experiences. With these plot lines Dickinson suggested that one path to racial justice would be through expanded personal interactions across the racial divide. But as the novel's final scene indicated, the North would only experience true racial equality when its black citizens—or at least the black men—enjoyed a political voice at the polling booth. It is significant that Dickinson did not end *What Answer?* with the tragic deaths of her two central characters, but instead with Robert Ercildoune being turned away from the polling booth. Here she underscored several points. The friendship between Tom Russell and Robert Erciloune demonstrated the potential for racial harmony. More importantly, Robert's personal integrity, physical sacrifice, and powerful stoicism made an eloquent case for the ratification of the Fifteenth Amendment, granting black men the franchise.

Dickinson's friends and fellow radicals joined Harriett Beecher Stowe in praising *What Answer?* Oliver Johnson called it a "powerful blow against the Satanic spirit of caste" and the *Independent*'s Theodore Tilton declared that Dickinson had "rendered a noble service to your day and generation." Charles Sumner, one of the author's great heroes, told Robert Purvis—the model for Francesca's father—that "of course, it is not what people call an artistic book, but it is full of <u>power</u>. <u>I don't cry</u>; but that book did make my eyes overflow."[37] Her most honest friends acknowledged that the novel was more brave than a well-crafted work of fiction. Lillie B. Chace admitted that "I shan't say it is the most wonderful book ever written . . . but it is such a <u>true brave</u> and spoken at the hour of need." Whitelaw Reid, never one for mincing words, told her that "[t]he literary character of the book is <u>not</u> bad. There are passages in it of wonderfully vivid force. But there are frequent phrases that offend a critical taste; & the construction of the story seems to me not altogether artistic." The moderate Reid added "that I am not quite sure that the specific aim of the book—if I correctly interpret it—is worthy of the prominence you give it." Some private assessments were even less charitable. Martha Coffin Wright read the novel with interest and acknowledged to a mutual friend that "[o]f course there is heroism in defending an abused race, & making her hero true to it . . . [but] her dialogue is miserably flat . . . I think it will fall very dead & am sorry she didn't keep to her lecturing & leave the field to Mrs Stowe."[38]

For a first novel, *What Answer?* did fairly well. Dickinson's Boston publishers, Ticknor and Fields, ran advertisements quoting from Stowe's enthusiastic review and similar praise from abolitionists Lydia Maria Child, Gerrit Smith, and Frederick Douglass. Later notices announced that the book had sold 10,000 copies, and in 1869 Fields, Osgood, and Company reprinted it.[39] The press afforded the novel substantial attention, befitting Dickinson's celebrity. Published reviews generally mirrored the private responses to the book. The *Springfield Republican* praised the novel's moral force but acknowledged that it had the technical flaws of a first literary effort. The *Philadelphia Press* found much to praise, but concluded that the book was "less a novel than a lecture." At the other end of the political spectrum, the Democratic *New York World* concluded that the radicals had finally "spoiled a nice little woman to make an unprofitable little political scold."[40] Among the major national journals, the *Nation* dismissed the book as little more than good intentions poorly executed. Dickinson's friend Isabella Beecher Hooker was so outraged that she sent an angry letter to the editor, but the journal responded that the true fault lay with those uncritical readers who praised Dickinson for her worthy goals and patriotic past without insisting that she perfect her craft.[41]

Although many readers focused on the unsettling interracial romance, others recognized the novel as a broader indictment of the nation's caste system, defined by race as well as class. And a few understood that the novel was really about politics, and particularly black male suffrage. The book was also, for Dickinson, a new excursion into the public arena. In the next decade she would publish two more books, but she never tried her hand at another novel. More than 40 years later Dickinson responded to a query by remarking that "I was never fond of Book-Making but I tried to do justice to the Black Troops—and others, in *What Answer?*"[42]

Among the more stern criticisms of *What Answer?* perhaps the most surprising came from Elizabeth Cady Stanton in the pages of the *Revolution*. The review began favorably enough, with praise for the novel's "high moral purpose" and "graphic descriptions." But while other radicals applauded Dickinson for her political idealism, Stanton found the novel's racial themes "thoroughly hackneyed," and "so ceaselessly sung in the ears of the American people for the last thirty years" that nothing new could be accomplished by another retelling. "Miss Dickinson would have given the world a better book," Stanton concluded, had she written closer to her own experiences as a young woman trying to make "an honest living in the world." Stanton's review clearly set the book into the context of the vigorous ongoing debate over the Fifteenth Amendment. By placing black suffrage at the center of the novel, Dickinson had thrown her weight in favor of the Radical Republican position, and counter to the stance taken by Anthony and Stanton and the woman suffrage leadership. Surprisingly, Dickinson explicitly omitted any reference to women who were home-front volunteers, sanitary commission workers, nurses at the front, or facing the loss of loved ones on the battlefield. For an author who had deep commitments to both women and African Americans (both men and women), Dickinson had opted to push one agenda over the other in her first work of fiction.[43]

A few days after the review, Anthony ran into Theodore Tilton, who "scolded" her about the *Revolution*'s unfair treatment of their young friend. In fact, the editor of the *Independent* sent Stanton a lengthy defense of *What Answer?* in which he praised the novel's racial themes while pointing out that the interracial marriage could be viewed as an affirmation of women's rights, particularly since in the past white Southern men had commonly taken slave mistresses without any thought of marriage. Stanton published Tilton's private letter and responded with some good-natured sparring of her own, including the ironic observation that with her marriage Francesca had—regardless of her race—essentially abandoned most of her civil and economic rights because she was a woman.[44]

There were all sorts of subtexts beneath this generally lighthearted exchange, and several years of complex history. Stanton and Anthony had long recognized Dickinson as a valuable ally. Among the most telling measures of Dickinson's importance was her prominent place in the new volume *Eminent Women of the Age: Being Narratives of the Lives and Deeds of the Most Prominent Women of the Present Generation*. Published in Hartford in early 1869, *Eminent Women* was comprised of 49 biographical sketches of some of the world's leading activists, authors, educators, actresses, and physicians. The handsome book was illustrated with engravings of 14 of the most celebrated subjects. Although Dickinson was one of the youngest women in the volume, her biography—penned by Stanton herself—was among the longest, and the book featured an image of the orator engraved by George E. Perine.[45] Prior to the book's publication, both Stanton and Anthony took pains to do Dickinson's career and likeness justice. Stanton labored at length on the 32-page

Engraving of Anna Dickinson. This engraving by George E. Perine appeared in James Parton et al., *Eminent Women of the Age: Being Narratives of the Lives and Deeds of the Most Prominent Women of the Present Generation* (Hartford, CT: S. M. Betts & Company, 1869). Susan B. Anthony and Elizabeth Cady Stanton distributed copies of this engraving to new subscribers to the *Revolution*. Author's personal collection.

essay, periodically taking a break to wax eloquent about her subject's wondrous wartime career, while Anthony personally dealt with Perine's studio.[46]

Before *Eminent Women* appeared in print, Stanton and Anthony used the *Revolution* to attract interest in the collection, often using Dickinson's inclusion as a selling point. In October the radical newspaper began running a serialized version of Stanton's essay on Dickinson. Meanwhile, readers were told that they could purchase copies of Perine's engraving of Dickinson at the *Revolution* offices. A few months later the novice newspaperwomen experimented with a creative marketing scheme, promising subscribers their choice of an engraving of Dickinson, Anthony, or Stanton if they introduced a new subscriber to the *Revolution*. In January they added that customers who delivered two new subscribers could select free copies of one of four new books, including *What Answer?*[47] None of the principals seems to have noted the irony that the *Revolution*, dedicated to the cause of woman suffrage and explicitly opposed to the Fifteenth Amendment, was rewarding subscribers with copies of a novel that was antithetical to these goals. Thus was the celebrity of Anna Dickinson.

As Lucy Stone had suggested, even when Dickinson was not attending conventions or touring with other suffragists she remained a powerful independent voice for women, and one largely in synch with the women's movement. In November 1868 Dickinson unveiled a new lecture at New York's Cooper Institute, delivered for the benefit of the newly formed Workingwoman's Association. The invitation had come from Anthony, who had been urging Dickinson to write something new about laboring women. Stanton, perhaps feeling sheepish after her harsh review of *What Answer?*, wrote an editorial announcing the upcoming lecture and defending Dickinson against critical comments in the *Nation*. "Let those dilletanti gentlemen" who had mocked the orator's skills try to imagine any 25-year-old young man matching her achievements without all the culturally determined economic and educational advantages that men enjoyed.[48]

In "A Struggle for Life" Dickinson continued her efforts to expand the public conversation about women beyond the suffrage debate. Like several of her earlier lectures, this new offering stressed the economic plight of working women and the moral decline that too often accompanied their poverty. Once again, Dickinson personalized her broader themes by building them around a poignant anecdote: the tragic case of Hester Vaughn. Vaughn, a 20-year-old English immigrant, had followed her husband to the United States only to discover that he had married another woman. Penniless, she found work as a domestic and then as a dairy maid, but she lost her job after she became pregnant following a sexual assault. Vaughn moved to Philadelphia where she apparently delivered her child alone in a freezing tenement house. The baby soon died under mysterious circumstances, leading to Vaughn's arrest and conviction for infanticide. For Dickinson, this tale of working-class poverty, sexual exploitation, and legal injustice illustrated the themes that she held most dear.

Vaughn's story had previously appeared in the Philadelphia press, and the *Revolution* had reprinted one letter describing her plight. After the Cooper Institute lecture, Stanton and Anthony threw themselves into Hester Vaughn's cause, echoing Dickinson's central argument that the young woman's story illustrated how society —and the legal system—conspired against poor, innocent women. Surprisingly, the *Revolution*'s unusually brief account of Dickinson's lecture made no mention of her focus on the Vaughn case, and two weeks later when Stanton wrote an editorial about Vaughn she made no mention of Dickinson's speech and in fact claimed that the case had been ignored by women. Soon the Workingwomen's Association rallied to Vaughn's cause, forming an organization and naming a visiting committee to inquire into the Philadelphia case. In December the committee—including Dr. Clemence S. Lozier, a well-respected female doctor—reported that Hester Vaughn was innocent of infanticide and had been horribly mistreated by her lawyer, and they presented a memorial to the governor of Pennsylvania calling for Vaughn's release. This time the reports in the *Revolution* and an editorial by Parker Pillsbury credited Anna

Dickinson with publicizing the case. Although, characteristically, Dickinson played no role in the subsequent committee activities, Vaughn's eventual release was in no small part due to "A Struggle for Life."[49]

In February 1869 Dickinson finally appeared on the platform at a suffrage convention when she attended meetings hosted by her old Chicago friend Mary Livermore. As Livermore's published account in the *Revolution* demonstrated, the occasion illustrated Dickinson's flair for the dramatic. "Everybody's heart gave a throb of gladness" on the morning of the second day when Dickinson finally strode into the hall, having ridden all night to make this "her *first* appearance on the platform of a Woman Suffrage Convention." Dickinson almost immediately found herself engaged in a heated debate with Rev. Robert Laird Collier, who had attended to denounce woman suffrage. Each speaker rose several times, exchanging blistering remarks about the nature of both men and women, and Livermore gleefully reported that "again and again the merciless little lady impaled him with her wit and satire." Not surprisingly, Dickinson reportedly won the support of most of the audience. At the end of the day she reappeared on the stage to close the convention by delivering "A Struggle for Life." According to Livermore, "many women wept" and "men were swayed with new emotions."[50]

Shortly after the convention ended in Chicago, the *Revolution* announced that the AERA anniversary meetings would be held in New York City that May, with Dickinson listed first among the expected speakers. In April the *Revolution* published a letter from Dickinson to Anthony, written from Ohio, promising to see her in New York for the convention. Yet the annual meetings came and went with no appearance from Dickinson.[51] It is difficult to weigh how the personal, the political, and the purely economic conspired to keep Dickinson away from the 1869 meetings. Several months earlier, Anthony had written to Dickinson addressing the orator's continuing objections to the racist George Train, and those concerns certainly remained an issue. Dickinson's mother had her own deep reservations about the leaders of the women's movement and had hoped that Dickinson would not speak at the meetings, and Susan Dickinson had urged her sister to steer clear of excessive entanglements. And the Fifteenth Amendment, which had been passed by Congress and sent to the states for ratification, remained a major point of disagreement. In fact, even as Dickinson was emphasizing the economic status of women in her own oratory, the *Revolution* had grown increasingly intent on stressing political equality as the central goal.[52]

In the meantime, as Dickinson maintained her distance from the organized movement, Anthony and Stanton embraced other young women orators who were closer to their political agendas. In late 1868 an effusive editorial praised Olive Logan as a strong advocate of woman suffrage, and throughout 1869 Logan's name cropped up more and more frequently in the pages of the *Revolution*. One measure of Logan's emerging status came in June 1869, when *Harper's Bazaar* included Logan's picture—alongside Dickinson's—in an engraving celebrating eight "Champions of Woman's Suffrage." Meanwhile, 20-year-old Phoebe Couzins, who was studying law in St. Louis, had earned the sobriquet the "Anna Dickinson of the West" for her prosuffrage oratory. Both Logan and Couzins spoke, to much acclaim, at the May meetings, in a sense filling the void created by Dickinson's absence.[53]

The New York meetings proved particularly important for the history of the woman suffrage movement. Stanton and Anthony had hoped to use the occasion to revitalize an organization that had been crippled since 1867, but they confronted a movement that had grown increasingly divided over strategy and personality. While the *Revolution* and its editors remained committed to resisting the Fifteenth Amendment and stressing a national suffrage agenda, New England suffragists— led by Lucy Stone, Abby Kelley Foster, Henry Blackwell, and Thomas Wentworth Higginson—had formed the New England Woman Suffrage Association, which supported the Fifteenth Amendment and remained loyal to the Republican Party. When the May meetings opened, it quickly became clear that the two groups could not happily coexist, as Stephen Foster and Frederick Douglass—two old Dickinson allies—charged Stanton and Anthony with racism for their rhetoric, their ties to Train, and their resistance to the Fifteenth Amendment. When the meetings broke up three days later, it was clear that the AERA had run its course as a viable organization.

If the acrimonious debates in New York were an occasion to stand up and be counted, it is easy to see why Dickinson chose to be elsewhere when her personal ties lay most strongly with Anthony and Stanton, but her political inclinations were more closely aligned with the New Englanders. Soon after the convention closed, the editors of the *Revolution* hosted a reception of delegates at the Women's Bureau (the newspaper's new home on 23rd Street), where they formed the National Woman Suffrage Association (NWSA), with Stanton as president. A few weeks later their New England adversaries set the wheels in motion to establish the competing American Woman Suffrage Association (AWSA), and the organizational divide within the movement was complete.[54] Perhaps unwilling to be entirely excluded from this new organizational world, Dickinson hesitantly agreed to be listed as one of the NWSA's vice presidents and to deliver the keynote address at its inaugural meetings in New York later that month. With the Fifteenth Amendment well on its way to ratification, Dickinson delivered a powerful lecture supporting the proposed Sixteenth Amendment, which would expand the franchise to women. Or, as Stanton put it with more than a touch of irony, "she stands ready to demand for herself what she has so long and faithfully urged for all men of the nation." Following Dickinson's triumphant presentation, Horace Greeley's *New York Tribune* ran a biting review of the lecture, mocking Dickinson's illogical arguments for woman suffrage. Dickinson was not amused, particularly because she assumed that the unsigned review was from the pen of her old friend Whitelaw Reid. The

*Revolution* published her lengthy rebuttal on its front page, under the heading "A Critic Criticized," and Stanton wrote an editorial chiding the *Tribune*'s hostile approach to suffrage under Reid's managing editorship.[55] Various friends and strangers rallied around Dickinson. Ralph Meeker, who was on the *Tribune* staff, dropped her a note praising her rebuttal, but added that he was pretty sure that neither Reid nor Greeley had authored the review.[56]

The embattled Reid felt moved to come to his own defense. He wrote Dickinson a short note that he signed "a miserable waif": "Fairly hit! But if you mean me . . . you've missed the mark you aimed at," he insisted. "For I didn't write the article in question—nor a line about you—whenever I am fortunate enough to see you again I'll tell you about it," he promised. Then he sent Stanton a letter marked "personal" telling her that "You punish me so genially, & good humoredly that I ought to be very grateful," but in fact "the joke of it is that I didn't write the article reviewing her speech" although of course he did agree to publish it. Months later the tensions had yet to thaw and Reid found himself pleading his case to Susan Dickinson in hopes that Anna would drop the issue.[57]

Only months after the launching of the NWSA, the *Revolution* ran into serious financial difficulties. Despite a subscription list that had reached 3,000, the paper was failing to meet expenses and remained dependent on donations, and Susan B. Anthony—who celebrated her fiftieth birthday in a gala celebration that February —had grown weary of the poorly compensated labors of running the radical paper. Isabella Beecher Hooker and her sister Harriet Beecher Stowe offered to throw their influence and writing talents behind the newspaper, but only on the condition that it change its name to something more politically palatable. Stanton and Anthony balked at the idea and Hooker eventually thought better of it herself. Meanwhile, Mary Livermore, Lucy Stone, and Harry Blackwell had founded the *Woman's Journal* in Boston, providing a more moderate perspective than the *Revolution*, and thus draining away possible support.

For a time it seemed that Dickinson would be sucked more completely into the *Revolution*'s vortex. On more than one occasion she had donated funds to the newspaper; beginning in December 1869 the *Revolution* ran a regular front-page notice listing Dickinson first among its prominent contributors.[58] When Anthony was pondering stepping down, she and Stanton considered inviting Dickinson to take over the reins. Stanton thought it an ideal solution. "If Anna Dickinson will be sole editor, I say, glory to God!" Others were less enthusiastic. Dickinson's mother, not one to mince words, urged her daughter to "keep independent of the *Revolution* and its stink. They would like to use thee, but don't let them." And her sister Susan, who had lost her enthusiasm for the famed feminists, concurred: "I hear the Bureau people in NY talk of offering thee a breakfast which I most earnestly hope thee will not accept nor permit. S.B.A. is nice enough in private, but in public thee can only hurt thyself by association with them & do them no good. . . . And E.C.S. is unendurable for <u>private</u> qualities beside. Do keep free of all entanglements with them. This is my entreaty, not someone else's (Reid's, for instance, though I told him I was going to make it & he'd like to endorse it). So does Ma, and Dr Mackenzie, & plenty of other friends of thine." These letters suggest that Dickinson at least toyed with accepting the editorship. In January the *Tribune* ran a story—almost certainly with Dickinson's approval—denying the rumor that she would be taking over the suffrage newspaper, and the *Revolution* promptly reran the article in its own pages.[59] In May Anthony transferred control of the paper to Laura Curtis Bullard, a woman with both radical and literary inclinations as well as substantial family funds. Bullard, working with the support of Theodore Tilton, would run the *Revolution* for a year and a half, gradually transforming the paper from its radical political roots into more of a "literary and society journal." Laura Bullard only knew Dickinson through mutual friends but almost immediately after becoming the editor she sought out the celebrated orator's advice and support. Before long the two were fast friends.[60]

Dickinson's extended *pas de deux* with the woman suffrage movement did not end with the movement's split into the competing NWSA and AWSA and her subsequent rejection of the *Revolution*'s editorship, but it certainly lost its centrality in her life. In mid-1870 Theodore Tilton engineered an abortive effort to stitch the divided movement back together, under the rubric of a new Union Woman Suffrage Society. Tilton would have loved to have had Dickinson's name in his corner, and in fact he offered her the presidency of the new society and, failing that, hoped to list her among the vice presidents, but Dickinson declined any association with Tilton's group. When her name was—inadvertently, he claimed —published as a member of the new committee, Tilton found himself apologizing repeatedly to both Dickinson and her sister.[61]

After this point Dickinson continued to speak about women's issues on platforms across the nation, and occasionally she attended suffrage conventions, but she avoided engagement with the associations themselves. Two letters in March 1871 illustrate Dickinson's occasional disdain for the official face of the women's movement. "Those disagreeable woman suffrage people did just what they have done every time I have been in Chicago for the last four years," she wrote home, "arranged a convention before & after my lecture—as tho it were a part of the programme & advertised me to be present." Dickinson regaled her mother with amusing anecdotes about avoiding the suffragists, who were "scurrying to & fro in pursuit of me" while she was doing her best to relax until her time to speak arrived.[62]

While she was honing her ideas in various lectures, Dickinson also toyed with several possible book projects during the early 1870s. In 1876 she published *A Paying Investment*, a short, serious-minded essay on an assortment of the nation's most pressing social and political ills. In many senses *A Paying Investment* represented the culmination of a chapter in Dickinson's public career. Having devoted much of the previous decade to research and lecturing on a wide range of the nation's pressing social ills, Dickinson used her "little book" to propose an integrated set of solutions. As she put the finishing touches on her manuscript, Dickinson contemplated various evocative titles ranging from "The Death of Citizenship" to "The Price of Liberty," before opting for the exhortative over the pessimistic.[63] The paying investment Dickinson had in mind was in human capital. Through an aggressive program of mandatory education and state-sponsored technical schools, the United States could develop a better-educated electorate and a more productive workforce, thus addressing a multitude of postwar challenges. As she had on many other occasions, Dickinson emphasized the importance of an engaged citizenry riding herd on politicians who were prone to corruption and self-interest. The problem was now that the war had been won, ordinary citizens were absorbed in the "grasping spirit of this generation" rather than the proper "recognition of the brotherhood of humanity" and "a full acceptance of the doctrine of individual responsibility," leaving the nuts and bolts of politics to unsavory political interests unchecked by an inattentive electorate. Worse, large pockets of voters remained illiterate and poorly versed in the requirements of citizenship. In the North, immigrants arrived in search of material wealth and were unschooled in their basic political responsibilities; in the Reconstructed South, African Americans had been robbed of opportunities for education, while poor whites remained loyal to a vanquished oligarchy that had "deprived them of land, of homes, of schools, of skill." In Dickinson's view, the state had as much of a responsibility to be proactive in combating illiteracy as they already were in battling smallpox or cholera.[64]

From politics, Dickinson turned to labor and class concerns. An outspoken critic of both monopoly capital and aggressive trade unions, she argued that the solutions to the nation's economic challenges would not come from debilitating strikes but a better trained, and thus more productive, workforce. Better for the government to invest in European-style training schools for the artisanal classes rather than in passing special legislation protecting trade unions. At the bottom of the social spectrum, Dickinson painted a grim portrait of filthy courts and alleys, and crowded almshouses populated by an underclass of uneducated paupers lacking the tools to overcome their circumstances. Building upon her extensive research on the nation's prison system, Dickinson devoted a chapter to a variety of reforms, including an expanded system of public defenders, speedier trials, and the separation of hardened criminals from those guilty of minor misdemeanors. Comparing the price of prisons and schools, Dickinson pointed out that "It costs more to neglect our duties than to accomplish them."[65]

Near the end of her book, Dickinson imagined her loyal readers wondering why she could "not find something better and finer and pleasanter" to write about. "While others have painted sunshine, and beauty, and prosperity, till your eyes are dazzled," she explained, "it is mine to stand within the gloom and the shadow, and, taking their voice, cry aloud, 'You ignore me, but I am here. Ah! for your own sake ignore me no longer!' " The dictates of both the "brotherhood of humanity" and "individual responsibility" demanded that those who enjoyed both means and a political voice use their powers to assist the needy, both for their own good and for the larger benefit of society. Those same readers might have been surprised that Dickinson, who they knew best as an advocate for women's issues, had woven her analysis through 14 chapters with no reference to the political and economic status of women. She waited until the conclusion to address that omission.

Dickinson began her final chapter by arguing that "whatsoever has been said in this little book to men, who have the conceded right to vote, is said to women, who ought to accomplish the duty of voting." Heretofore, she noted, many men had argued that since women did not fight in wars, they should not vote. She was willing to accept that "as long as politics meant wars and rumors of wars . . . there was no place for women's hands in this field." It was a measure of the progress of civilization that the nation had evolved to a point where politics was no longer merely the stuff of violent conflict. Instead, government had turned its focus on "questions sanitary, educational, social, [and] humanitarian," just the sorts of topics women addressed within their own homes. Thus, the nation's problems, and the particular challenges of emerging cities, required the political input of women. In response to those men and women who might respond that it was "unwomanly" for ladies to enter the public arena, Dickinson countered that it was really selfish for them to refuse to step forward where social ills called for their expertise. "Oh my sisters!" she exclaimed. "Where, then, are your woman's hearts, and your woman's consciences, that they are silent and still?" Rather than stay at home, she insisted, women should venture into the asylums, hospitals, jails, prisons, and reformatories, where their talents were desperately needed."[66]

As had become her pattern, in *A Paying Investment* Dickinson absorbed a wealth of information and ideas and produced an argument that was distinctly her own. She envisioned a postwar world of substantial governmental activism in the public interest, but also a deeply engaged citizenry in which every man and woman bore their own obligations to the collective good. The state should provide education to all voters, with particular attention to those immigrants, African Americans, and paupers who had fallen between the cracks. And, in return, those who failed to take advantage of that education had abdicated their right to vote. In making the case for woman suffrage Dickinson aligned herself with those who argued that women had a special set of skills and sensibilities that were particularly important as the problems of government had changed. She was not making the argument that women, merely by virtue of their status as citizens—or human beings —deserved an equal voice in politics. And rather than casting suffrage as a right that women should enjoy, Dickinson portrayed it as a responsibility that they should share. Placed within the larger context of the book, Dickinson's case for woman suffrage seems even more clearly an argument based on the public good rather than gender justice. Women should vote because they brought special skills to the public arena, and it would be selfish of them to deny society their insights. Interestingly, by phrasing the case in terms of civic obligation, rather than political rights, Dickinson seemed to be assuming—rather than asserting—gender equality.

As she was completing *A Paying Investment*, Anna Dickinson had high hopes for its commercial success. In fact, she wrote enthusiastically of a longer book about the status of women, which she had tentatively entitled "A Voice From the Wilderness" or perhaps simply "Men's Rights." But the book attracted little public interest and earned almost no royalties. In retrospect, it is hard to imagine why Dickinson would have expected anything else from such a high-minded, often technical, volume. Perhaps she overestimated her own popularity or, more precisely, she underestimated the extent to which her popularity was tied to her physical appearance and skillful performance.[67]

*Chapter 6*

# "WHAT NEW GRIEF HAS COME TO YOU?": THE PERSONAL AND THE POLITICAL

I N his 1885 novel *The Bostonians*, Henry James portrayed a triangle of distinctly American characters caught up in the women's movement of the 1870s. The story revolves around Verena Tarrant, the beautiful, captivating public speaker who rises to fame as an advocate for women's rights after the Civil War. Two other characters —Olive Chancellor and Basil Ransom—battle for Verena's heart and soul, providing James with fodder for dramatic tension and political satire. Olive is a strong-willed spinster, who has dedicated her life to a panoply of contemporary reforms and sees in Verena an ideal spokesperson for women as well as a magnetic object of her personal affections. Basil is a transplanted Southern gentleman, who appreciates Verena's charms but has little use for her politics. In the end, Ransom wins the day as Verena accepts his marriage proposal, abandoning both New England and the women's movement for a life with the charming Southerner.

The characters in *The Bostonians* were largely products of James's own imagination, and vehicles for his satirical commentary on a broad range of postwar issues, but it seems clear that he modeled the Verena-Olive-Basil triangle on the intertwined lives of Anna E. Dickinson, Susan B. Anthony, and Whitelaw Reid. Between May 1870 and May 1872 James lived in Cambridge, Massachusetts, where he had an excellent vantage point from which to observe the divisions within the women's movement, played out against the complex backdrop of the election of 1872 and a titillating sex scandal involving Henry Ward Beecher, Elizabeth Tilton, and Theodore

Tilton. For Dickinson, these were years when personal loyalties, private passions, and political commitments pulled her in various directions, with Anthony and Reid playing roles much like Olive Chancellor and Basil Ransom played in the life of Verena Tarrant. But if James's art imitated life, it did not quite duplicate it: Reid won Dickinson's political voice, but neither adversary captured her heart.[1]

In the half-dozen years following the Civil War, Dickinson's personal life followed the patterns she had established in her early twenties. Among dozens of admirers, a series of men and women grew particularly enamored with the captivating orator. Only months after Elias Irish succumbed to tuberculosis in 1866, Illinois congressman John Baker—two decades her senior—sent Dickinson several romantic notes before abandoning his quest when she failed to reciprocate his affections.[2] Two years later Iowa Congressman William B. Allison found himself under Dickinson's spell. The pair traveled together by train for portions of Dickinson's 1869 western tour, and she seemed to share the congressman's interest for a time. That September a jocular Dickinson told Susan that "I have had two regular, serious, bona fide offers this summer," including one from a congressman.[3] In May 1871 Dickinson visited Allison in Iowa as he was running for the Senate and she was amused to find herself billed as "their 'next Senator's lady.'" "All this tickles me hugely," she laughed, "seeing that I would as soon marry our John, as Billy."[4]

New York reporter Ralph Meeker was a particularly ardent—sometimes bizarre—Dickinson suitor in the postwar decade. The two became friends when Meeker was working for the *Tribune* and they continued to correspond about politics and woman suffrage as the young reporter bounced from position to position. Somewhere along the way Meeker became convinced that he and Dickinson were destined to marry, prompting him to make a strange visit to Philadelphia to meet Susan Dickinson—his future sister-in-law—in early 1871. Susan and Whitelaw Reid both sent Dickinson long, humorous accounts of this encounter, and nothing in Dickinson's correspondence suggests that she ever took his overtures seriously. But the two remained on good terms, and when Dickinson and her brother John traveled west in the fall of 1873 they visited Meeker at his family home in Greeley, Colorado.[5]

By the time Anna Dickinson reached her thirtieth birthday, in October 1872, she had grown used to persistent rumors about her love life and impending nuptials. During the war her friends enjoyed teasing her about various romances, both real and imagined, but such stories generally did not reach the press.[6] In the postwar decade gossip about the celebrated single woman became a staple in the newspapers. Near the end of 1865 a published rumor claimed that Dickinson was marrying an unnamed New York widower and newspaper editor. This worried New Hampshire's Benjamin Prescott, who asked "Is it so? You have too much work to do to get married."[7] Dickinson generally laughed off the marriage talk, occasionally forwarding the more outrageous letters to her sister. In early 1870 she wrote to a

Whitelaw Reid. Cabinet card of the editor and politician produced by Napoleon Sarony. Probably 1870s. Author's personal collection.

friend from an Ohio hotel that "I am growing such a wagabone that I doubt if I will ever camp down for long unless indeed I should marry (evil thought!) & in that case I fear me there would be an absconding, a suicide, or a murder,—none of which is wholesome."[8]

Among her many male companions, the only one who seemed a serious match for the quick-witted Dickinson was Reid, the Ohio reporter who had first crossed her path in 1864. Reid was only five years older than Dickinson, and in many senses on a comparable career trajectory when they first met. Immediately after the war, Reid toured the South, sending "dispatches" back to his Northern audience. For a time he tried his hand as a Southern planter, purchasing property in Louisiana, but when that venture failed he returned North where he accepted a position with Horace

Greeley's *New York Tribune*. By 1868, at the age of 31, he was managing editor of the nation's most powerful newspaper, and a major voice in the Republican Party. From his first visit to the Dickinsons' Locust Street home, Reid and Dickinson became fast friends. They wrote frequently and at length, in the language of close friends, political allies (although Reid was generally more moderate than Dickinson), and intellectual equals. Dickinson's male suitors commonly wrote in frothing tones, baring their souls while recalling precious moments spent alongside the enchanting orator. In contrast, Whitelaw Reid's letters were full of personal and political news, brotherly advice, and much good-natured bantering, broken with occasional bursts of real temper. After Dickinson agreed to endorse Lincoln's 1864 campaign, Reid called her "incurably wrong-headed." The following year some unknown row led him to send a blistering note, declaring that "some day I'll write the letter (or try) that your last deserved." But the two patched up their differences, and when Reid was in Louisiana he sent Dickinson long letters describing his Southern life.[9]

In December 1866 the wry journalist wrote that "this very day I read that [you] had been 'rejecting' . . . an elderly New York bachelor journalist. I felt thankful for that word New York. I once had the honor of figuring in a little western (far western) paper as having been 'accepted' by a young Quaker orator-ess. I was 29 years old the other day, which may surely be called elderly; was a bachelor & a journalist . . . so once more be the fates forever praised for the word New York. Being gazetted as 'accepted,' however tantalizing, was at least flattering. 'Rejected' was an ill-omened word." Reid certainly enjoyed kidding Dickinson about these stories. In early 1870 the press again reported that he and Dickinson were engaged. He gleefully told Susan he had received the clipping from any number of friends, including Vice President Schuyler Colfax who had congratulated him on his engagement to " 'that brilliant girl, Miss D.' " "I hope [Anna] bears it as stoically as I do," Reid joked.[10]

There was probably some truth beneath all the talk, or at least their mutual friends thought so. When fellow reporter Murat Halstead sent Reid a clipping about the couple, he added "if you want Anna don't let the damn fools scare you with their stuff in the papers." In early 1873 Charles Dudley Warner had not heard from Dickinson in several months, prompting him to ask, "Are you on the stage? Have you married Whitelaw?" The notion—or the notoriety—still appealed to Reid. Noah Brooks, one of Reid's young colleagues at the *Tribune*, told her that Reid was "rather tickled" with the most recent clippings, which he "carefully stored away."[11]

In fact, when Reid returned to New York, Dickinson routinely dropped by the *Tribune* offices to see him. And Reid became a regular visitor at the Dickinson home in Philadelphia. On several occasions the amiable bachelor spent part of the Christmas holidays with her family.[12] During the hectic years of the late 1860s and early 1870s they filled their letters with politics and scandals, but Dickinson and Reid also felt acute concern for each other, particularly because they shared a tendency to work themselves into exhaustion and illness. "Your reputation is made," Reid advised in late 1867, "devote yourself now to profiting by it" rather than wasting precious energy on other pursuits. When her letters grew despondent, a concerned Reid urged Dickinson to "learn moderation. Your store of vitality is not exhaustless."[13] The younger Dickinson sometimes mocked Reid's paternalistic tone by addressing her letters to "My Dear Mentor," but she voiced the same sentiments back to the oft-sickly Reid. "Be a good boy," she closed one note. "Be ambitious, be hard working, be as successful as you desire, only don't kill yourself in the effort. . . . there are one or two people who are by no means ready to part from you."[14]

Reid's position at the *Tribune* occasionally produced strains. After the paper mocked her calls for woman suffrage in May 1869, Dickinson held Reid responsible. Reid went to Susan Dickinson to plead his case, explaining that he was too proud to write directly to Anna. Several months later Dickinson finally extended a hand in friendship, because "I have more true friendship for you than false pride for myself." This letter seemed to thaw the tensions, for Susan reported that a jubilant Reid was pleased to accept an invitation for Christmas dinner.[15]

The following year the friendship evolved into more profound emotional intimacy. On December 13, 1870, after spending a quiet evening together, Dickinson began a letter with characteristic teasing about the *Tribune*'s coverage of her latest lecture, but her heart was not in the familiar quarrel because "you gave me something better, a few hours of rest . . . How good you are, how gentle, and how kind. You have seemingly always been afraid to give me anything save hardness, and yet, God knows, I am sore enough and worn enough to have a little fragment of coolness and softness bestowed on me." But then she seemed to shake herself out of her reverie, adding "Hah, what am I talking. I am what nature made me, and I live the life that nature ordains. I do not wish aught else: but I am glad that I know you somewhat better than I did, and that you have learned a little more of me." Reid responded that he was "more than glad of our talk—for many reasons, not the least being that I now know how you have been tortured & can therefore the better help you," and he promised to do his best to see her on Christmas. "We all want to see you, that you know," she replied, "and for myself—after that long talk with you I do not need to tell you how glad I shall be to see your face, and take your hand under my own roof."[16]

That winter the relationship grew more intense, until January 1871 when the couple had a painful conversation on the evening before Dickinson was slated to leave for a western tour. The details are unclear, but the following day Reid wrote to express his "mortification at having done the worst to make" her final night "as disagreeable as I would have had it bright." He assured her "that the end of the evening was as astounding to me as it must have been odious to you" and that her previous inclinations about their relationship had been correct. Still, Reid admitted that he was tempted to "dodge work" and follow her to the West. "But no," he sighed, "that is a dream." Reid was uncharacteristically emotional and affectionate in this long letter, referring to Dickinson as "darling" and hinting at his despair over their encounter. It seems likely that he proposed marriage, or at least suggested some unwelcome change in their relationship, leaving him concerned for "the friendship I have enjoyed so long." Later, the politician in him worried that perhaps he had said too much. Reid wrote in March and again in September urging Dickinson to destroy the letter or keep it hidden.[17] In his subsequent correspondence Reid never unveiled the same passion, but he continued for a time to behave like a suitor. On several occasions his letters included biting comments about other rumored Dickinson lovers, suggesting at least joking jealousy.[18] For her part, Dickinson was fond of Reid and for a time they shared a special bond, but there is no indication that she contemplated an ongoing romance with him, certainly not at the expense of her autonomy or career.

Dickinson's closest female friends enjoyed commenting on her actual and imagined romances, while they also loved examining how men responded to their charming young friend. Although some of her hosts worried that the rising star was in danger of becoming too full of her own fame, many seemed to see Dickinson as a sweet, essentially frail young woman. Shortly after the war, Milwaukee's Sallie Austin discussed Dickinson with a female friend and they concluded that Dickinson was "only a true tender loving little girl" who periodically drove "weak people"—like their husbands—"nearly crazy." Fortunately, Austin concluded, Dickinson was unlikely to be spoiled by these male attentions because only shallow women fell prey to such vanity, whereas women whose "character is pure and high . . . become more and more worthy of the sentiments they inspire."[19] Six years later New York newspaperwoman Laura Runkle had a similar chat with Samuel Bowles, the editor of the *Springfield Republican*, but their conclusions were different. Bowles found Dickinson not "above the pleasure of cajoling men from mere delight in power," and Runkle acknowledged some truth in these charges. "The result is that here are you, who do not seek nor want a husband <u>as</u> a husband, who do not mean to make any man your slave, who stand purely above the vulgar place of common flirtation, here are you, just by the virtue of the feminine instinct and impulse which are stronger than any princaple [sic] or plan, half-consciously and half-unconsciously spreading your 'strong [toils?] of grace' [over] man after man, simply <u>because</u> he is a man and you are a woman."[20] Such, perhaps, was the fundamental truth for Anna Dickinson. Although she had no need for, or interest in, a husband, she enjoyed the company of men and her very nature dictated that many of those men felt drawn to her presence.

While this series of men vied for Dickinson's attentions, she continued to develop close, often physically intimate, relationships with other women. During the Civil War, Dickinson and Bostonian Lou Brackett had been particularly close, although perhaps the young orator had felt some ambivalence at Brackett's passionate enthusiasm. After the war, Dickinson continued to correspond and exchange gifts with her old friend, but the two slowly drifted apart. As that relationship subsided, Dickinson developed warm relationships with several other women she met on the road. These relationships, however intense, did not always last long. Olive Logan wrote fondly of shared kisses and other intimacies, but the two public women never really established an enduring friendship. Sarah Bowman probably met Dickinson through Lou Brackett sometime shortly after the war. In August 1867 Bowman spent the evening with Dickinson at the Clifton House in Swampscott, Massachusetts, and wrote her a long note from Manhattan the following night. "My own wee darling," she began. "This time last evening you were sitting on my knee, nestled close to my heart and I was the happiest of mortals—tonight I am writing & dreaming of the pleasant memories which will remain with me always. Last night after leaving you I paused outside your door for it seemed I could not leave you, my heaven sent— . . . I see before me now, sitting all in a little heap in the bed, laughing at me with her great soft grey eyes—noble, tender, soul-lit eyes, and tempting me to kiss her sweet mouth, and to caress her until—well, poor little me, poor 'booful princess'—'How can I have thee, queen of my loving heart.'" Bowman—about whom little is known—acknowledged "[t]he wild rebellious wish that I could shelter you from yourself and the world. Can I never be a man!" she declared. She closed her long missive declaring that "my letters are like my kisses—lingering, lingering . . . Good-bye sweet pet." Bowman, who was married, sent Dickinson another half dozen notes over the next several years, occasionally recalling their time together at Clifton House, or speaking of Dickinson's beautiful eyes and their shared kisses.[21]

Dickinson's most complex and intriguing postwar relationship was with Susan B. Anthony. Anthony, more than 20 years Dickinson's senior, recognized a tremendous political asset in the popular orator and did her best to draw her into the movement's institutional world. But if the friendship between Anthony and Dickinson emerged out of their shared ideological commitments, it soon evolved into a more intense relationship. During the Civil War the two exchanged occasional notes about politics and reform strategies. One early letter illustrates the teenaged Dickinson's youthful exuberance. "The sunniest of sunny mornings to you," she wrote. "I want to see you very much indeed, to hold your hand in mine, to hear your voice, in a word, I want you—I can't have you?"[22] In those early years, Anthony adopted the maternalistic tone of a mentor and friend, guiding and cajoling Dickinson about politics while expressing motherly concern for her young friend's health. Their relationship evolved as Dickinson matured into her mid-twenties. In December 1866 Anthony promised to visit Dickinson in Philadelphia "and [I] hope to snuggle you darling closer than ever." A year later she wrote from a train in Ohio musing that "I do wish I could take you in these strong arms of mine this very minute."[23] By the time Anthony returned to the East she was writing much more freely about her desire for physical contact with Dickinson, whom she had taken to addressing with pet names like "Darling Dicky Dicky," "My Chick-a-Dee," and "My Dear Chicky Dick Darling." In early 1868 Anthony hoped that Dickinson would soon come to New York "and sleep with me in my fourth story bed room at Mrs. Stanton's ever so many nights . . . for I have many things to say which paper cant convey."[24] That March, Anthony urged Dickinson to come see her as soon as possible. "I have <u>plain quarters</u>—at 44 Bond St—<u>double bed</u>—and big enough & good enough to take you in—So come & see me—or let me know & I'll meet you at Depot—Hotel or any place you shall say—only let me see you—I do so long for the scolding & pinched ears & every thing I know awaits me. . . . What worlds of experiences since I last snuggled the wee child in my long arms—" Two weeks later Anthony promised Dickinson "one awful long squeeze" if only she would come to New York or agree to meet her in Philadelphia so that Dickinson could "spend a night with" her and have a long talk. By May, Anthony had grown more persistent. "I have—or aim to have—a nice hall bedroom—with bed large enough for you to have the half—provided you like so to do" she insisted, and a few weeks later she added: "Did I tell you that I had a big bed in a big room—all nice & cozy—at No. 116 East 23rd St now—and that the naughty teaze shouldn't be scolded a single if she will share it a few days?"[25]

We cannot know exactly what Anthony wished to discuss so urgently in the spring of 1868. It was during these months that Anthony was lobbying Dickinson —unsuccessfully—to attend the annual meetings of the American Equal Rights Association, and even accept a position as vice president of the Association. But Anthony had never been reticent about discussing such topics in writing, and in fact her letters during these months pushed Dickinson hard to attend the anniversary meetings. Moreover, in previous years Anthony's letters had not included such persistent references to warm embraces and sharing beds together, suggesting a change in their relationship. Whatever her intentions, Anthony was apparently disappointed. In May she sent Dickinson a short note. Speaking cryptically of herself and Dickinson she wrote sadly about how "this somebody didnt see that somebody after that and that somebody ran back to Phila and this somebody is left behind—alas for this poor somebody."[26] Following this meeting the two continued to correspond about politics and reform agendas, but Anthony's tone changed abruptly. Her letters remained affectionate, but they were no longer filled with references to physical embraces and possible nights together. Instead, Anthony returned to her earlier maternal role, calling Dickinson "darling child" and describing herself as her loving "Grandmother."[27] Over the next two years Anthony saw Dickinson periodically and they wrote occasionally, although far less often, as Dickinson consciously distanced herself from the various camps within the divided women's movement.[28]

Anthony's correspondence with Dickinson stopped completely in 1870, after nearly 70 letters over the previous six years. In December 1870 Anthony asked James Redpath for Dickinson's touring schedule, explaining that she hoped to meet her on the road, but there is no evidence that the two saw each other. The following year Anthony wrote to a mutual friend, saying "when Anna comes to see you, give my love to her [and] tell her I am the same 'Old blessed Susan.' She used to believe me. Not a line has she written in a whole year." In 1872 Anthony visited Dickinson in Philadelphia, but the meeting was short and unpleasant. Nearly a quarter century later, Dickinson—who had fallen upon hard times—wrote to Anthony about a fundraiser her old friend had assisted on her behalf. The sight of Dickinson's familiar handwriting led the aging Anthony into a moment of nostalgia. "I'm awfully glad to know you still live—and that I have a chance to tell you that my <u>motherly love</u>— my elderly sister's love—has never abated for my <u>first Anna</u>," she wrote. "I have had several lovely Anna girls—'nieces'—they call themselves now-a-day—since my <u>first Anna</u>," she continued, "but none of them ever has or ever can fill the niche in my heart that you did—my dear."[29]

The intense relationship between Susan B. Anthony and Anna Dickinson had various layers and meant different things to each of these powerful women. Anthony saw Dickinson as not only a political protégé but as the object of more intense personal, perhaps sexual, attraction. Even more so than Dickinson, Anthony spent most of her life on the road. She never married and was famously opposed to the constraints that the institution placed upon women, although—like Dickinson—she reportedly had various offers from male suitors. One need not speculate about the precise dimensions of their physical relationship to conclude that for a time Anna Dickinson was the subject of Anthony's passion and desire. And, when that aspect of their relationship cooled, Anthony eventually moved on to other "Annas," never to forget her moments with Dickinson. For Dickinson, who was a full generation younger, the relationship seemed different. She admired and wished to please Anthony, but at the same time family and friends—and her own political instincts—warned her about casting her lot too completely with the controversial women's rights advocate. Did she share Anthony's ardor? Perhaps for a time, but Anthony's letters in 1868 suggest a relationship that had become imbalanced and was bound to cool.[30]

Even as her relationship with Anthony was settling into a more distant, professional friendship, Dickinson found a true kindred spirit in Laura Curtis Bullard. Bullard first contacted Dickinson in 1870 when Anthony recruited the Brooklyn heiress to take over the *Revolution*. The two did not really see much of each other until 1872, but by February Bullard had already begun to fall under Dickinson's spell. "I want you to love me," she wrote. "I am sure I cant <u>help</u> loving you, or I am dangerously near it now, . . . Sweet Anna, I want to see you <u>often.</u>" A few weeks later Bullard was already proposing that they take "a little escapade together" at the first opportunity. "I am so glad you like me—for I like you amazingly well—I think I am very near <u>loving</u> you—so near it that I think of you very often & <u>long</u> to see you in a much impractical & <u>excessive</u> way."[31]

For the remainder of the year Dickinson and Bullard were together frequently, and wrote often. In March, Bullard closed a note with "My lovely sweet girl, good night—I kiss you & admire & love you & am yours." And, the following week: "Anna dear you dont know how you have found your way to my heart, nor how ardently you are cherished there . . . are you ready to be flaunted in the face & eyes of people . . . you will be, as <u>my</u> dear girl—. . . I kiss you a thousand times." Like Brackett, Bullard was married, and both of their husbands grew fond of Dickinson, prompting much joking about who would win Dickinson's heart. In early June Mr. Bullard was out of town, leaving Laura Bullard disappointed when Dickinson did not come to Brooklyn because "you should have had <u>your</u> place in my bed had you come." She closed with "Sweet Anna, I shall hope to see you soon & kiss your soft, tender lips." As if to underscore the point, a few months later Bullard wrote that "I dreamed of you last night & oh how I wanted you when I woke up." "I have lots & lots to say to you but will not say it now," she added. "As it might look foolish in black & white to put such a lot of sweet things, on paper, which I could whisper into your ear & nobody is the wiser."[32]

None of this affection and intimacy in any way called into question the continuing assumption that Dickinson would eventually marry a man. Bullard—again like Brackett—enjoyed teasing her friend about a variety of men. On July 14 Bullard wrote from her summer home at Long Branch, New Jersey, "So you are in love are you? Well tell us all about it & the lucky man & I will tell you whether I will give my consent or not." A few days later, in response to an emphatic denial from Dickinson, Bullard retracted her assertion, claiming that "My dear I <u>did not think</u> you were actually in love. I do so hate the idea of marriage, as it now exists, though I believe in true marriage, with all my heart." But while marriage might eventually be in Dickinson's future, Bullard persisted in claiming a special role in Dickinson's life. Bullard was rumored to be an advocate of free love, and in fact her name was often linked romantically with Theodore Tilton, but in August 1872 she assured Dickinson that "<u>Nobody</u> has made love to me—<u>nobody does</u>—I have a genius for friendships with men & women, but I am <u>not</u> one whom many men love. Sweet Anna <u>I love thee</u>—love thy Laura in return & come to her soon—I kiss you goodbye." When Dickinson visited Boston, Bullard urged her to return to New York, "where you shall share my <u>bed</u> as well as board. I love to have my <u>velvety peach</u> of a woman beside me, & feel the touch of her soft hand." And as Dickinson prepared to visit New York for a major speech, Bullard repeated the claim: "I am to be your <u>bed-fellow</u> on that occasion if you do not say nay."[33]

Although Laura Bullard seemed to offer, and assume, a sort of emotional exclusivity in their relationship, Dickinson simultaneously maintained relationships with several other women in the early 1870s, and in some cases these relationships also included physical attractions and intimacy. Most prominent among these was Fanny Edmunds who, perhaps not coincidentally, first became significant in

Dickinson's life a few months after Anthony drifted away. Dickinson occasionally visited Edmunds and her husband Charles in their East Boston home, and Fanny sometimes stayed with Dickinson in Philadelphia, but their relationship really developed on a series of trips between 1870 and 1874. Each year the pair spent several weeks vacationing together at Clifton House in Swampscott, Massachusetts, and in 1872 they also went hiking in the White Mountains. On several occasions Edmunds accompanied Dickinson while she was on tour. When they were not together Edmunds sent Dickinson tremendously long letters, addressed to "my darling little animile," declaring her affection and loyalty and sharing a range of political and personal gossip. When Dickinson first invited Edmunds to travel with her, her friend seemed almost ready to burst. "Is it possible that you love me any? It seems so strange, though God knows I love you dearly." Later, she asked "when do you want your lover, for you know I am that." Reflecting upon their relationship, she acknowledged that "I never loved anything [so] dearly as I have loved & do love & shall ever love you!" Edmunds also wrote fondly of sensuous caresses. If only she could look into "that sweet, sweet face & kiss it & watch it glow & change as you talk." The draw was particularly powerful when she sensed Dickinson was ill or unhappy. "Don't you want Fanny to go & rub your poor little back?" she asked. And, on another occasion, "would a little bit of petting & loving & comprehending hurt you any just now do you think?"

Like those who came before, Edmunds sometimes expressed uncertainty about Dickinson's desires. In planning one excursion to Swampscott, Edmunds offered to arrange a room for the two of them so that Dickinson would not have to room with a stranger, "even if you shouldn't want me." "Of course you are to have me, if you do want me," she added, "but are you sure you haven't thought better of it?" And, again like several other women, Edmunds sometimes implied that she wished that they were married partners. "Every day in my life I want you 'to have & to hold'" she closed one letter, and in a different note she chose very similar words, explaining that "You see how it is my dear—I want you 'to have & to hold.'"[34]

Dickinson also had occasional experiences with other women, like Sarah Bowman, who only appear briefly in her correspondence. In November 1871 a woman named "Nellie," who apparently knew Dickinson from her travels in the Midwest, heard the orator speak and found herself both moved and restless. "Do you know I came away from the Hall that night feeling so strange and almost sad," she wrote, "it was not natural to have you in the same city with me and each in different houses, different beds. I want to see you somewhere when I can stay with you all night in the old-fashioned way." Nellie closed the letter in frustration: "What is the use of trying to write to you as I want to talk I can't do it—Do you love me a little? Please say yes. Kiss me." In an undated letter, Nellie described similar longings following another encounter: "Your Good Bye kiss left my lips unsatisfied—it was so hasty—<u>both</u> kisses . . . all day my lips felt unfinished. . . . Kiss me—It is late & I must stop. Please kiss me. I love you—dont forget it."[35]

Taken as a group, the personal relationships that Dickinson developed in her twenties—between 1862 and 1872—suggest something of the social norms of her day as well as how Dickinson's highly distinctive life set her apart from those norms. Despite our contemporary assumptions about Victorian prudery and gender segregation, unmarried Northern women actually had substantial contact with single men, and marriages were commonly the result of extended courtship and shared affection rather than merely the product of family arrangement or economic need. On the other hand, courting women and men—particularly in the middle and upper classes—did have to navigate cultural rules governing when, where, and how they interacted, even though it was not difficult for them to find unchaperoned privacy. Anna Dickinson was of course a particularly active, highly independent woman, whose interactions with men commonly occurred hundreds of miles from the watchful eyes of her mother. Many of her male correspondents wrote fondly of private moments during outdoor excursions: picnics, hikes, horseback riding, and the like. Interestingly, although these men wrote glowingly of wondrous outings, warm conversations, and the particular power of Dickinson's beautiful gray eyes, they almost never mentioned kisses or the most innocent caresses, even though references to such physical contact were not unusual in contemporary love letters. In truth, most of these relationships probably never evolved from infatuations into full-blown courtships.[36]

While courting men and women moved within a nineteenth-century world that placed some restraints on their behavior, both sexes had every opportunity to develop far more deeply intimate bonds with members of their own sex. As historian Carroll Smith-Rosenberg has described it, young women matured into a "female world of love and ritual" almost entirely separate from male contact. Even if we should not imagine nineteenth-century women and men as thoroughly alien groups, those in the middle classes did live in often segregated gender worlds. All sorts of social, cultural, and political occasions directed men and women into separate groups, helping to forge close bonds within each gender while producing an intriguing, sometimes perplexing, cultural gap between women and men. One crucial aspect of this highly gendered world was that women (and men) commonly built particularly powerful, highly intimate, enduring relationships with peers of their own sex. Studies of extended correspondences—sometimes spanning decades—reveal close friendships formed in girlhood that flourished into adulthood, despite marriages, geographic separations, and the passage of time. Often these letters bespoke deep affection and physical longing, and they provide evidence that such female friends routinely shared beds and tender caresses.[37]

For the contemporary reader this is complex terrain. Nineteenth-century Americans routinely adopted flowery, sometimes effusive, language that sounds peculiar to the modern ear and can confuse our understanding of relationships. But there is ample evidence that some women within this separate female world expressed their mutual affection with varying degrees of physical intimacy. Prior to the end of the century, these women lived in a society without rigidly defined notions of sexual preference. That is, various degrees of homosocial intimacy, even explicit genital contact, did not necessarily suggest any particular label to either participant. Rather, the very absence of rigid definitions—or any culturally delineated sense of homosexuality as a distinct category—left nineteenth-century women with unusual freedom to experiment and experience without being forced into a complex act of self-definition, and without, at least in the immediate post–Civil War decades, necessarily confronting social stigmas. Many of these women went on to marry men, while often maintaining their loving relationships with their female friends. Others never married, or eventually abandoned unsatisfying marriages, and many of these women ended up living in households with their female partners.

Dickinson and her female friends clearly reflected this cultural world. It would be a mistake to discount these letters as merely the passionate Victorian rhetoric of essentially platonic friends. But it would be equally foolish to apply the label "lesbian" to all of these women, if the term is to imply something about self-definition as well as behavior. We cannot know, and from an historical perspective perhaps need not care, precisely what these women did in their nights together. Still, it seems clear that Dickinson had a series of female lovers in the 1860s and 1870s (with more to come). While Anthony—like Dickinson herself—never married, most of her other close female friends during these years had husbands, and in several cases it is clear that those marriages were quite happy and affectionate. And during her twenties nearly all of Dickinson's friends and acquaintances presumed that she would eventually marry a man, although some joined Anthony and Dickinson in questioning the institution as it was legally constructed.[38]

Anna Dickinson was quite typical of single women of her day in that she experienced various courtship rituals with several men, while enjoying a higher level of personal and physical intimacy with several women. Of course she was also distinctive in many senses. Her charisma and fundamental nature attracted a particularly wide array of male and female admirers. And the fact that she traveled so much, often returning to the same places, allowed for a complex tapestry of relationships that might have befuddled her more stationary peers. Yet she rarely managed to maintain the sort of enduring relationships that survived for decades. Although some men and women did remain in her life for quite some time, the women who wrote of more intimate relationships and who were most aggressive in declaring their love—Brackett, Logan, Anthony, Bullard, Edmunds, and a few others—all seemed to enjoy Dickinson's attentions for a relatively short period before she moved on to other companions, often leaving behind unfulfilled longings and regret.[39]

As a public figure, Dickinson grew accustomed to seeing her comings and goings reported in the nation's newspapers. She and her friends generally laughed off these stories, but this is not to say that Dickinson was indifferent to gossip or impervious to the potential dangers of her private affairs becoming public knowledge. Even as she moved away from the life of her girlhood, donning fancy clothes and an expensive lifestyle that belied her Quaker roots, Dickinson doted on her mother, sending her "Marmee" long letters from the road. Mary Dickinson responded with letters full of maternal love and unfettered worry. Mrs. Dickinson's greatest fear was that her youngest daughter would fall prey to unnamed dangers on the road. Again and again she warned of "the many snares and temptations of this wicked world," particularly because of Anna's "constant exposure to its <u>false</u> friendships and pleasures." Dickinson was probably not too concerned about those worldly perils, but she certainly worried about what her mother might read about her in the papers, and she also recognized that unflattering rumors could undermine her career.[40]

Meanwhile, Dickinson's fellow reformers had good reason to guard their own privacy and reputations. By challenging cultural norms about the proper roles of women and blacks in American society, the nation's reformers—and particularly Dickinson's sisters in the women's movement—faced the risk of heightened public scrutiny, and any stain on their private reputations stood to reflect ill on their larger causes. In the early 1870s the dangers of living with intensive public scrutiny struck close to home when salacious rumors spread about Dickinson's friends Theodore Tilton, Elizabeth Tilton, and the Rev. Henry Ward Beecher. The resulting scandal eventually became a national sensation, fueled by the notorious Victoria Woodhull, and for a time it seemed that the expanding rumors might cripple the broader movement and damage Dickinson's own career. The entire sordid Beecher-Tilton episode, and the broader controversies surrounding Victoria Woodhull, offered a powerful illustration of how private lives, public reputations, and political ideals periodically intertwined in the postwar decades.

Henry Ward Beecher, the brother of novelist Harriet Beecher Stowe and Dickinson's close friend Isabella Beecher Hooker, was one of the most celebrated ministers in the Northeast. A leading abolitionist, orator, and advocate for women's rights, he ministered to Brooklyn's Plymouth Church where Theodore and Elizabeth Tilton were members of the flock and part of the minister's inner circle. The handsome Tilton had an impressive reputation as a radical journalist, lobbying for the rights of women and blacks. Elizabeth Tilton had been poetry editor for the *Revolution*, and she was well known in their circle of reformers and journalists. From the pulpit Beecher spoke eloquently of the power of spiritual love. Privately, Beecher and Theodore Tilton developed an affectionate relationship that seemed to be the living embodiment of Beecher's broader teachings. Later in the decade, Beecher and Elizabeth Tilton became involved in their own loving, probably sexual, relationship. Elizabeth unburdened her soul to Theodore in July 1870, and Tilton confronted Beecher, hoping to force the minister out of his office while keeping the scandal quiet. But meanwhile, Elizabeth and Theodore Tilton selectively told their tale to a few chosen friends, and slowly the story spread.[41]

Dickinson had known both Beecher and the Tiltons for years; she had shared platforms with both men on numerous occasions, and she had corresponded with all three. Word of the scandal reached Dickinson shortly after Tilton confronted Beecher, and she sent Theodore several supportive letters.[42] In the meantime, Dickinson's own family troubles became a source of persistent worry, as Edwin and Susan bickered over household finances and turned to their sister to resolve their differences. In April 1871 she sent Whitelaw Reid an unusually melancholy letter about family and friends. "What new grief has come to you, that you write so despondently?" he asked. "I know how wearing is your life, but you speak as if there were something new & worse. One thing you must do. All these sudden interests in the misfortunes of your friends exhausts you utterly. You must learn moderation," he advised.[43]

The still somewhat private affairs of Henry Ward Beecher and the Tiltons became decidedly more public when Victoria Claflin Woodhull entered the scene. Celebrated, and in many quarters notorious, as spiritualists, free-love advocates, radical journalists, Wall Street stockbrokers, and defenders of women's rights, Woodhull and her sister Tennessee Claflin were two of the most fascinating, flamboyant figures in postwar America. The sisters had thrust themselves into the center of women's rights discourse in May 1870 when they published the first issue of *Woodhull & Claflin's Weekly*. Before long Woodhull and the *Weekly* were allied with the National Woman Suffrage Association, joining forces with Anthony and Stanton in opposition to their more moderate Boston-based colleagues.[44]

Woodhull's personal life and public pronouncements on free love drove away some supporters while providing ammunition for adversaries in the American Woman Suffrage Association, forcing Anthony and Stanton to reevaluate the cost of doing business with her. Both women objected to the hypocrisy that held Woodhull to a different standard than men in the movement. As Anthony told one friend in February 1871, "I have <u>heard gossip</u> of <u>undue familiarity</u> with persons of the <u>opposite sex</u>—relative to Beecher, Higginson, Butler, Carpenter, Pomeroy—and before I shall consent to an arraignment of <u>Woodhull</u> or any other <u>earnest woman worker</u> . . . I shall insist upon the <u>closest investigation</u> of <u>all</u> the <u>scandals</u> afloat about these men."[45] But neither Stanton nor Anthony saw a true kindred spirit in Woodhull, and Anthony in particular was troubled by the spiritualist's free-love beliefs, which she felt gave license to male promiscuity. Before long the leaders of the NWSA began distancing themselves from the controversial sisters, with only Isabella Beecher Hooker among the major figures remaining loyal to Woodhull.[46] Woodhull grew irate, accusing them of hypocrisy and threatening to reveal a secret world of promiscuous behavior among those who presumed to judge her. By the fall of 1871 Woodhull had heard the rumors about Beecher and the Tiltons and seemed prepared to share their secrets.[47] Perhaps to win her silence, Tilton befriended Woodhull and published an admiring biography of her in his newspaper, the *Golden Age*.[48]

Dickinson disapproved of the flamboyant spiritualist and free-love advocate, and watched her rise to prominence with chagrin.[49] When Woodhull and Claflin passed through Philadelphia with Isabella Beecher Hooker, Susan Dickinson reported that she would have been happy to entertain Mrs. Hooker, but under no circumstances would she have let the two sisters tell the world that they had been in the Dickinson home. In April 1871, as she toured in the Midwest, Dickinson referred to Woodhull as an "unprincipled woman," an assessment that annoyed Elizabeth Cady Stanton, who saw hypocrisy in Dickinson's rejection of Woodhull even while the orator supported the nation's more lowly "abandoned women."[50]

Before long Dickinson found herself drawn into the murky world of rumor and gossip. Betty Browne, who had previously worked with Susan B. Anthony, wrote of stories that Dickinson had spoken ill of Stanton while in the West, and that Stanton had made a few biting comments of her own in retaliation. In June 1871 Whitelaw Reid warned that the unpredictable Woodhull might spread her own lies about Dickinson. The following month Lillie Chace wrote obliquely of a distressing "fresh piece of scandal" she had just heard. A few weeks later, Dickinson told Theodore Tilton about "certain stories" circulating about her. "They antagonized me at first because no denial, & no absolute proof even can put to rest such lies when they are once put afloat," she acknowledged.[51]

Meanwhile, Dickinson grew worried about reports that Tilton had been behaving erratically and Elizabeth was in seclusion. In January 1872 she went to Brooklyn and found Theodore gone and Elizabeth anxious to talk. She stayed all night hearing Elizabeth's melancholy story, which included startling accusations that an erratic Theodore had invited Tennie Claflin to their home for "a free 'love feast.'" Dickinson recounted portions of this conversation to the Bracketts in Boston, who shared their own versions with several other friends. The tale found its way to James Redpath, who angrily confronted Theodore Tilton about the rumors. Tilton denied the whole story, and when he reported the conversation to his wife, Elizabeth promptly accused Dickinson of misconstruing "the spirit of my interview with you," which was intended to exonerate Theodore. A wounded Dickinson insisted that she had only told the story to illustrate the dangers in consorting with Victoria Woodhull and her sister, but clearly she had also been caught sharing a juicy piece of gossip about her friends.[52]

The whole affair was driving Dickinson to distraction. "I have seen such a lot of queer people, & listened to such an array of remarkable stories since I last saw you, that I hold on to the top of my head & am not quite sure, after all, whether all is right there" she told Susan Warner. But still she could not follow Reid's advice and divorce herself from the whole matter. Instead, she sent Theodore Tilton a long, frank letter. "Do you know how awfully & almost mortally, your fair fame & name have been wounded in the eyes of the whole country?" she demanded. Dickinson was less concerned with Tilton's conflict with Beecher than she was with his unseemly alliance with Victoria Woodhull. If Tilton wanted to continue serving the larger causes they both embraced, she insisted, he must cut his ties with Woodhull.[53]

Tilton appreciated Dickinson's strong words, and he soon broke with Woodhull. But in the spring Woodhull raised the stakes, threatening to publish—and perhaps even fabricate—rumors about leaders of the women's movement.[54] Perhaps spurred on by these blackmail threats, gossip in the movement swirled faster than ever. When stories circulated that both Mary Livermore and Phebe Hanaford—two major figures in the women's rights movement—had plans to leave their husbands, both Anthony and Dickinson blamed the other for spreading the tale (indicating that each must have been privy to the stories). In June, following a frank conversation with Hooker about various mutual friends, Stanton seemed to think better of her openness and cautioned Hooker that "whatever I have said to you touching social matters & some people is strictly confidential. . . . If A.D. ever in confidence tells you what she did me very well, but if not, do not make any statements as coming from Susan & me. Susan thinks I betrayed confidence in telling you but from my standpoint knowing that with you it was safe & that we both look upon these Platonic friendships as admissible, & discussed persons merely to illustrate principles."[55] Meanwhile, other stories circulated about Dickinson. Whitelaw Reid warned her about an unsavory story making the rounds about Dickinson and Senator Allison. Dickinson denied the tale and tweaked him for taking it seriously. Reid quickly brushed off the issue, but a week later he wrote that "I've been hearing a precious mess about you."[56] The following month Laura Runkle told Dickinson that she suspected Tilton had concocted stories about Dickinson so that he could then put them to rest "to make you his champion."[57]

Historian Ann Gordon speculates that in her letter to Hooker, Stanton was speaking of the rumors concerning Hanaford and Livermore, but perhaps she had also revealed confidences that Dickinson had shared about herself. Several months later John Hooker sent his wife a letter from Italy, responding to disturbing reports that Isabella had sent him from Connecticut. "What you write us is shocking & overwhelming beyond expression," John wrote. "The matter of Anna D was wholly new to me. I had heard a discreditable story about Phillips, but never a lisp of her being the other party. It is horrible—I can not conceive how she at her ripe age, & with her good sense, & her comprehension of the whole case, could submit herself to such a desecration. . . . I do not wonder that in her distress she should have divulged it to one or two confidential friends, but it is inconceivable that they should have told it to others. If they did they ought to be shot."[58] The Phillips in Hooker's letter is almost certainly Wendell Phillips. A generation older than Dickinson, Phillips had known the orator since the Civil War. For nearly a decade the two had been friends, finding common cause on the large issues but frequently clashing over political strategies and priorities. Their letters suggest an enduring friendship with occasional ups and downs, but nothing indicates that they were lovers or particularly intimate. It is certainly possible that there was some hidden romantic or even sexual encounter in their past that Hooker had somehow stumbled upon, but it seems equally likely that Phillips and Dickinson were victims of malicious gossip. Whether true or not, such a story would have been devastating to their reputations had Woodhull gotten wind of the rumor and put it in print.[59]

Fortunately for Dickinson and the women in the movement, Woodhull did not make good on her threats to publish an assortment of tales. She did, however, pull back the curtain on the Beecher-Tilton scandal. In September Woodhull delivered an angry address in Boston, lambasting the hypocrisy of those who had dared to criticize her morality, and accusing Beecher of having an affair with Elizabeth Tilton. She repeated and embellished on the charges in the October 1872 edition of *Woodhull and Claflin's Weekly*.[60] The entire story was now in the public domain, triggering three years of controversy and litigation, all covered in meticulous detail by the nation's newspapers. Woodhull ended up spending a month in jail for slander and obscenity, the victim of Anthony Comstock's moral purity campaign, and devoted many more months to legal wranglings. In the meantime, the controversial figure achieved a new level of fame when in 1872 she became the first woman to run for president. For Anna Dickinson, the rumbles of scandal eventually calmed down and she, too, turned her thoughts to the upcoming election.[61]

In 1868 the Republican Party turned to war hero Ulysses S. Grant as their standard bearer. Four years later President Ulysses S. Grant had given many in the party reason to feel alienated and ready to take some other path. High on the list of Grant's sins was his ham-handed effort to annex Santo Domingo, despite the vigorous protests of Republican Senators Charles Sumner and Carl Schurz. Grant's Republican enemies were also deeply disappointed with charges of corruption and cronyism in the White House and the president's indifferent record on Civil Service Reform. Meanwhile, news from the reconstructed South seemed unrelentingly bad and Grant's critics questioned whether he had the interest or ability to handle the problems. Upset by developments in their own party, and unable to wrest control from Grant and his people, a core of reformers bolted from the party and formed the Liberal Republican Party. They met in Cincinnati that May and, much to the surprise of many observers, nominated the *New York Tribune*'s idiosyncratic Horace Greeley. Caught up in the desire to unseat Grant, the Democrats also nominated Greeley at their national convention, thus creating some particularly strange political bedfellows. By nominating Greeley and allying with the Democrats, the upstart Liberal Republicans faced an interesting set of political challenges. Although the ex-Whig element in the party had placed tariff reductions on the platform, their standard bearer had an established record as a protectionist, leaving the Liberals with a two-pronged strategy stressing an end to corruption and reconciliation with the South. The latter proved a tough sell, as Republican cartoonist Thomas Nast persistently lampooned Greeley's call for clasping hands "across the bloody chasm" of war. Meanwhile, the bulk of the abolitionist leadership that claimed the Republican Party's moral center refused to abandon Reconstruction despite their distaste for Grant.[62]

As she observed these developments, Dickinson weighed a range of considerations. First, she disliked Grant with a venom born of public policy, personal distaste, and deep loyalty to the insulted Sumner. She also had ties with many of the insurgent Liberal Republican leadership, including Sumner, Schurz, Greeley, Reid, Tilton, and Samuel Bowles.[63] On the other hand, Charles Dudley Warner, Wendell Phillips, and many of her old abolitionist friends refused to abandon either the party or the freedmen. Dickinson was acutely aware that her good reputation was her meal ticket. Would there be a cost to backing the wrong candidate?

With the campaign season approaching, Dickinson toyed with a European tour, but she kept one eye on the political season to come, soliciting advice far and wide even while holding all parties at arm's length.[64] Finally, on April 2 Dickinson temporarily broke her political silence with a lecture in Pittsburgh. Still a month before the Liberal Republican's convention, Dickinson surprised her audience by attacking President Grant while praising the efforts of Republican dissidents Sumner, Schurz, and Greeley.[65] Bowles was "delighted that you have raised up your voice on this side," but Warner wrote, only half in jest, "You are now a democrat. I cannot write any more to a democrat now."[66] A few weeks later Dickinson repeated her attack on Grant at New York City's Cooper Institute, two days after a large rally for the president had been staged in the same hall. Anticipating themes that she would explore more fully on the eve of the election, Dickinson declared that "The war was only an act in a drama. What men did then they did not for the life or success of a party, but for the life and success of the nation." The question at hand was whether the next act should be left in the hands of the Republicans who gathered at Philadelphia, or with the new Liberal Republicans. So long as the Republicans clung to Grant, Dickinson was prepared to seek answers elsewhere.[67]

Although she attacked Grant, Dickinson was initially unprepared to throw her lot in with the insurgents. After their convention in May she seemed to have made up her mind. "Hurrah for Us!" she wrote to Reid, who was serving as Greeley's lieutenant, "next autumn I propose to do the best hooting I ever did in all my life in behalf of the good man and the good cause." But family and friends counseled against joining Greeley. Some felt she would be better off sitting out the election,

Horace Greeley *carte de visite*. Photographer unknown. Author's personal collection.

perhaps taking another stab at writing. The pressures grew progressively more intense. On June 6 Dickinson missed separate visits from both Reid and Bowles, two Liberal Republican leaders, and she received an unexpected and unwelcome call from Anthony, who was backing Grant. Meanwhile, the political rumors flew. That afternoon, Laura Bullard—who was strongly in the Greeley camp—heard that Dickinson had "given [her] . . . sanction to Grant & Wilson"; the following day Republican Senator Pomeroy wrote from Washington "I read that you hurrah for Greeley!" In fact, Dickinson had declined an invitation to speak for the Republicans and was still mulling over offers from the Liberal Republicans.[68]

The upcoming election was particularly challenging for woman suffrage advocates. Greeley had opposed immediate suffrage. Grant was hardly a strong suffragist, but he had offered his nominal support for the cause and his people had actively courted the movement's leaders, winning endorsements from Anthony and Stanton and most of the other leading suffragists. Then there was Victoria Woodhull, who spoke powerfully for women's rights, but had lost the support of most of the leadership. In July, Bullard admitted that Greeley was "no idol of" hers yet he was the right man for the moment. "I want you to speak, not only for Greeley because of patriotic motives, but because of the woman question," she argued. "[M]en will be sooner aroused to the injustice of denying us the franchise, by the sight of such a woman as you acting & swaying an election, than in any other way." That is, the cause of woman suffrage would be better served by Dickinson flexing her political muscle, rather than by supporting the nominally prosuffrage Grant.[69]

Bullard invited Dickinson to Long Branch, but Dickinson recognized this as a ploy to get her to meet with Greeley. Ironically, by declining Bullard's invitation Dickinson was in Philadelphia when Republican vice-presidential candidate Henry Wilson dropped in to make the Republican case. As she explained to her mother, "By avoiding one I fall into the claims of the other." A few days later Dickinson declined Theodore Tilton's invitation to meet Greeley in New York. If she went to see Greeley, "I would be in every paper in the country within twenty four hours." She was not ready for such public pronouncements. "If I want to go with the campaign," she concluded, "I will go with it, & get paid for it." With that in mind, she turned to Reid. "Do you want me to go into it," she asked him, "and if you do what will those vampires of the Com[mittee] pay me[?]"[70] Reid recognized that he was at once friend, advisor, and political partisan. "You have many friends, whose counsels you are accustomed to consider," he noted. "For myself, I am . . . hardly a dispassionate adviser." But then Reid tried to claim the ethical high ground, insisting that "I can't reconcile it with my notions of political honesty or patriotism to make one's entrance on great national questions . . . on whether one got paid enough to break silence." Greeley was the best man, and Dickinson should feel obligated to speak in his campaign. "You used to rate me for being unsentimental, practical, indifferent to the sentimental demands of this or that Great Cause," Reid continued. "Well, perhaps we've changed parts; & what I now write may seem a romantic idea of public duty that has no place in the calculations for a successful season."[71] But against this high-minded rhetoric, Dickinson had to weigh her mother's strong reservations. "Dear daughter, please [do] not have any more to do with politicks, political lectures and not much with politicians any more," Mary Dickinson implored.[72]

The lure of the campaign was finally too much to resist, and Dickinson tentatively agreed to speak for Greeley. But when the party initially refused to meet her price, Dickinson announced that she would sit out the campaign while writing a book.[73] A month later Bowles confided that he had heard from someone "high up in the Grant administration" that the Grant campaign was really behind the book offer merely to keep Dickinson off the stump. But if that had been the Republicans' devious plan, they had not properly reckoned on Dickinson's political drive. By the end of September, Dickinson and Reid were negotiating a Cooper Institute lecture in New York. Even if offered the best of terms, the veteran lyceum speaker recognized that appearing for Greeley would be a professional risk. "If I pay such price I do it because conscience compels and because I believe I can be made of really great service to Mr. Greeley and a great cause," she assured Reid.[74] On October 25, after many months of negotiating, Dickinson finally walked onto the platform of New York's Cooper Institute.

If Henry James were watching these political developments from afar, he might have concluded that Dickinson's support for Greeley represented the final victory of Whitelaw Reid in his competition with Susan B. Anthony for Dickinson's heart and soul. In the run-up to the October lecture that powerful triangle had both a private and a public aspect. When Anthony came to visit Dickinson in June, their private exchange was short and unpleasant. Dickinson told her sister that it was only through the maid's "carelessness" that Anthony—"the only one I especially wished to avoid"—even got past the threshold. Later she jokingly told Reid that Anthony "came to me a month ago, and was requested more emphatically than elegantly 'to leave.' "[75] Meanwhile, Grant's people proudly trumpeted the fact that they had the endorsement of most of the woman suffrage leaders. Only days before Dickinson spoke in New York, the Cooper Institute was the scene of an impressive gathering of the suffrage leadership—including Anthony, Stanton, Hooker (who had finally abandoned Woodhull for Grant), and Lillie Devereaux Blake—to endorse officially Grant's reelection bid. When Dickinson spoke in the same hall, Stanton and Blake reportedly came to witness Dickinson's political betrayal.[76] The timing of these two public events, and Dickinson's split with her suffrage sisters, was not lost on the press, nor was her history with Reid. One wag took special pleasure in the event and the subsequent praise from Reid's newspaper: "The fair Anna Dickinson has had her say in New York . . . Whitelaw Reid, whom she rejected some time ago for good and sufficient reasons, praises Anna in a gushing way in the *Tribune*, from which we infer that his angelic bosom is still torn by the tender passion."[77]

In April Dickinson had been more interested in burying Grant than praising Greeley; when she returned to the Cooper Institute in October she played the role of political partisan. In calling her lecture "Is the War Ended?" Dickinson adopted a clever rhetorical ploy. If the war was indeed over, one might reasonably ask why the United States maintained a war footing in the conquered American South, with an army of occupation enforcing Reconstruction. Moreover, if the war was truly over, Ulysses S. Grant could not merely run on his military record. Although Grant had been a fine general, Dickinson argued, as president he was "[a] man whose interest was first centered in a tap-yard; second in the blood he shed; and third in his cigar."[78] Grant's foibles had become popular targets for lampooning, but his political challengers still had some obstacles to overcome. While Dickinson was in the midst of an entertaining series of salvoes at the president, a voice cried out "'Who saved the country?'" The quick-witted Dickinson, perhaps recalling her jousts with wartime hecklers, took this popular memory head on. It was "the men who fought under Gen. Grant" who won the war, not the general himself, she declared. And in fact those men "had learned their lessons of loyalty through twenty-five years of the columns of the *New York Tribune*," the quick-thinking speaker retorted, implicitly crediting Horace Greeley credit for the victory.

But how could those radicals who had spoken up for the slave now seem to be abandoning the freedman? To address that thorny question, Dickinson turned to a metaphor that William Lloyd Garrison had employed in his inaugural issue of the *Liberator* in 1831. "He who runs to extinguish the flames of a house when the house is burning, does well," she acknowledged. But by that same token, "[h]e who checks the flow of water when the flame is extinguished, does also well, because the water, continuing, swamps the house, ruins the furniture, and brings decay and rot into the house." Now that the power of the North had extinguished slavery and subsequent amendments had expanded citizenship to include the freedpeople, Dickinson reasoned, the continued exercise of force could only harm the situation. "These blacks were slaves, then freemen, then citizens," she declared. "Before the law they stand on a level with the whitest white man here. That being the case there is not need and there should be no excuse for special legislation for any special class of people, since there is none such in the Republic." And following this logic further, "if they cannot defend themselves and exercise their right at the polls, then either we are in a state of war, and actual war power is brought to bear against them, and we ought to declare war and fight it out; or we are at peace, and being so, if millions of voters are unable to defend themselves . . . we might as well confess the experiment of the Republican Union is ended." If her audience wanted a return to war, so be it. If not, let the democratic process work its magic in the South. This tough-minded approach was consistent with Dickinson's longstanding belief that citizenship—and the electoral franchise—was not merely a birthright, but included heavy responsibilities. Her words also reflected the Liberal Republicans' overly optimistic, essentially naïve, perspective on the future of Southern racial politics.

It was bad enough that she seemed to be abandoning the Southern freedman, but in speaking for Greeley, Dickinson was apparently turning her back on woman suffrage. One response was simply that Grant's support of women smacked of cynical opportunism, backed by no real conviction. But she went on to quote Greeley's own words from 1860: "'When the women of the United States shall desire this, not merely as a privilege, but as a responsibility, then I am willing to give it.'" Dickinson, ever the maverick, added, "We have enough supine and lazy and careless voters already." Once again, she was equally concerned with rights and responsibilities, and she was willing to advocate for women while simultaneously belittling their insistence on immediate suffrage.

Much like her wartime campaigning, Dickinson's appearances for Greeley attracted substantial attention from the press. The *Providence Journal* admitted to "more than usual hesitation in dealing with a woman who has entered upon the domain of politics," but having overcome their scruples the editors characterized the lecture as "the most insipid and oft repeated slanders against General Grant, and an equally ludicrous and false glorification of Horace Greeley." The *Boston Journal* found "the sensational female declaimer," guilty of "demagogism." One Connecticut paper summarized the lecture and asked, in familiar patronizing terms, "Who wrote it?" In contrast, Bowles's *Springfield Republican* celebrated the speech as an "impressive plea for honest government and true national unity," adding that the "most eloquent of American women has performed the enoblest [sic] and most courageous actions of her life."[79] According to one Boston reporter, Dickinson's speech "recalled vividly the days of the war . . . when her woman's voice rang out through the country in defense of all that was just and noble." Still, times had changed. In the campaigns of 1863–64 Dickinson had been almost alone among women on the political stump. Eight years later, both parties competed for her endorsement, and when she threw her support behind Greeley, the Republican press proudly countered that they had the support of "nearly all the most gifted and famous women of the land."[80]

It was a performance that likely came at a cost. Liberal Republican Carl Schurz praised the "noble thing" she had done. Senator Ben Butler, who remained a loyal Republican, thought it "the <u>bravest</u> thing done through the campaign."[81] Perhaps Dickinson was driven by political ideology, perhaps by loyalty, perhaps merely by the lure of the stump. Whatever her true motivations—and they surely combined all three factors—Dickinson's appearance was in a losing cause, as Ulysses S. Grant beat Horace Greeley by a large margin.[82] For Greeley, the political defeat was dwarfed by his personal grief when his wife passed away on October 30. Within a month the distraught Greeley followed her to his grave, but not before Dickinson visited him one last time at the *Tribune* office. As Dickinson would later recall that final meeting, the famed editor expressed his heartfelt thanks for the sacrifices she had made for him, and he promised that the *Tribune* would always stand by her.[83]

Weeks after the election, Dickinson was back on tour again, speaking at her usual haunts in Pennsylvania, New York, and across New England before a planned trip west in the spring. As usual she rotated various lectures including her popular "Joan of Arc," but audiences were most interested in "What's To Hinder?" her new speech on women in the workforce. In many senses this new lecture was vintage Dickinson. Whereas other advocates of women's rights commonly stressed political and legal equality, for years Dickinson had nudged the conversation toward economic and class issues, urging her audiences to contemplate the plight of prostitutes, Mormon women, and poor working women. In "What's To Hinder?" Dickinson returned to familiar themes, noting that women had fewer career options than men and earned lower wages. And as she had argued a few years earlier in "Whited

Sepulchres," the gap between men and women commonly widened over time as men pursued professions of their choosing while too often women did not select careers but merely earned wages while waiting to find a husband. The solution, Dickinson concluded, lay largely with those "supine" women who were failing to grasp opportunities available to them. If they wanted equal opportunities and wages, they must grasp the professional training and experience that would yield better careers and wages. Too many, Dickinson charged, are simply lazy.[84]

"What's To Hinder?" was at its core a critique of an economic world fraught with gender imbalances, but Dickinson's critics honed in on her harsh words to women. How could this grand advocate for women's equality seem so dismissive of the true barriers that her sisters confronted, they wondered. In February the *Woman's Journal* took Dickinson to task in a particularly harsh editorial. "Being herself successful, does she count success easy for all?" the New England suffrage newspaper asked. Rather than blaming other women for their failure, "when God gives a woman great power, can she use it to better purpose than in elevating her own sex?" Lucretia Mott, who had known Dickinson since she was a teenager, heard the lecture in Philadelphia and was neither pleased nor impressed. "She seems to be rather losing her radical ground of late," Mott told a friend.[85] As Dickinson prepared to deliver the lecture in New York the *Tribune*—now under the editorship of Whitelaw Reid—ran an editorial critical of her themes. An irate Dickinson blamed Reid and lashed out in anger. As it turned out, Laura Runkle had penned the editorial "to help to fill your house," but despite Runkle's explanations, and Reid's protestations, the issue festered for months and the two never really recaptured the closeness they once shared.[86]

Mott was only partially correct in concluding that Dickinson had been "losing her radical ground." Between her endorsement of Greeley and "What's To Hinder?" Dickinson had certainly moved away from her radical roots and many of her former allies. But she would have argued that her call for individual responsibility and enhanced education in conjunction with equal treatment—the hallmark of her latest comments on both freedmen and working women—were perfectly in tune with the arguments she had been making for years about Chinese workers in San Francisco, Mormon women in Salt Lake City, and unionized laborers.[87] But as the public statements from the *Woman's Journal* and her private clash with Reid illustrated, the political and personal terrain had shifted, and with it her professional fortunes.

In early December, the Dickinsons suffered a family tragedy, as John's daughter, Florence, died unexpectedly. The death of her young niece—coming so soon after Greeley's death—took a particular toll on Dickinson, who was on the road and could not attend the funeral in New York. As if to underscore her sister's familial role, Susan wrote to Anna soon after Florence's funeral, itemizing the costs of the ceremony, much of which she hoped Anna would cover.[88] With these emotional and financial burdens weighing on her, Dickinson headed west in early March, passing through Ohio, Michigan, and Indiana on her way to Chicago. As she toured, letters from Dickinson's siblings conveyed their incessant bickering over the Philadelphia household. By April the rigors of the road and the pressures from home were taking their toll, forcing her to rest up in Chicago. The Chicago doctors concluded that she had "some form of epidemic catarrh, with typhoid symptoms," but certainly exhaustion helped drag her off the platform and into bed.[89] Later, when she reflected on those difficult weeks, Dickinson wrote that she "fell into a state of imbecility—or of general break-down, or something—which prevented me holding a pen, or doing work of any kind." Although her papers provide few concrete clues, judging from future events it seems likely that Dickinson was already consuming alcohol in large quantities, both socially and as a medical treatment. Even as she returned to work, bad weather, poor health, and mediocre audiences left her mentally drained. While she was in Chicago, Ralph Meeker journeyed from Colorado to hear her speak. Dickinson generally found him a bit of a nuisance, but the devoted Meeker did offer an enticing opportunity: why not visit him in Greeley, Colorado that summer?[90]

An exhausted Dickinson returned to Philadelphia in late May, and after a brief recuperation she headed with Fanny Edmunds to Swampscott. Although she had always enjoyed the beach resort, this time Dickinson found the weather cold, the people unpleasant, and her overall funk uncured. She asked her brother John, who was a minister in New York and still mourning the loss of his daughter, to join her for a western tour. In mid-August the two headed for Colorado.[91] Even though the rigors of the lyceum circuit often wore on Dickinson, she was an enthusiastic traveler, particularly when exploring new places and scenic sites. She once proudly proclaimed that she knew every railroad employee in the East. She was also an engaging raconteur, who loved spinning tales about life on the road. Whereas her notes home from the lecture circuit were often crisp and businesslike, when on vacation Dickinson entertained her mother with long, humorous letters. Only days after Dickinson and her brother set off by train, she sent her "Marmee" a 13-page missive from Denison, Ohio. She followed this with a lively 40-page account from Ralph Meeker's home near Denver, and in mid-September she sent an 85-page travel letter from Long's Peak, in the Rocky Mountains.[92] Many of her favorite tales featured complete strangers who interrupted her as she rode the rails. Some she found charming enough, but Dickinson preferred telling amusing stories of boorish passengers—usually men—who badgered her with silly questions and intrusive requests.[93]

It was a glorious, occasionally rugged, trip. Once they reached Colorado, railroad cars gave way to stagecoaches, horses, and the occasional burro. At each stage, Dickinson took joy in the experience and perhaps greater pride in rejecting commonly accepted gender rules and limitations. On stagecoaches, she preferred to sit in the open air beside the driver, rather than on the plush cushions on the inside, breathing the stuffy air. When one driver refused her request, explaining that company rules forbade such a practice because women might distract the driver, an irate Dickinson climbed down and walked in front of the stage until the driver relented.[94] An experienced horseback rider, Dickinson viewed the practice of requiring women to ride sidesaddle with similar disdain. Why, she wondered, should the supposedly weaker sex be forced into postures that were more awkward and much more dangerous than those adopted by men? Dickinson took pride in riding—astride—where no other white women had ventured, and she gleefully scandalized some of the locals by donning men's trousers for the task.[95]

Anna and John Dickinson devoted their three weeks to various excursions. For years Dickinson had been a dedicated hiker and mountain climber. In *A Ragged Register*, her memoir of her travels, Dickinson proudly claimed to have dined atop New Hampshire's Mount Washington on 28 occasions.[96] During their short stay in Colorado they ascended several of the 14,000-foot peaks towering over Denver, including Pike's Peak, Gray's Peak, Mount Lincoln, and Mount Elbert (the last ascent on the backs of borrowed United States government mules). Often in the company of Ralph Meeker, the Dickinsons climbed, or rode, in several small parties, led by some of the region's most celebrated hunters and guides. Dickinson was particularly proud of ascending Mount Elbert, the state's tallest peak, because—as she told her mother—few men and no women had ever made the ascent. Shortly before they were scheduled to leave, the intrepid threesome managed to join the survey team of Ferdinand V. Hayden for a climb up Long's Peak. In making this difficult ascent, Dickinson was credited as the first white woman to reach the top, besting mountain climber Isabella Bird by a month. During their climb, the Hayden team named two nearby peaks Mount Meeker and Mount Lady Washington. The former was in honor of Nathan Meeker, Ralph's father, and the latter was likely a nod to Dickinson and her affection for Mount Washington.[97] Between ascents, the Dickinsons wandered the region around Denver and Greeley, while Dickinson funded the trip by delivering a series of lectures. Using scenic Colorado Springs as a base, they explored the region's natural wonders. Always anxious to broaden her knowledge of the life of the working man, Dickinson studied the silver-ore miners "drilling and blasting" atop Mt. Lincoln. Later she toured the mines at Fairplay, venturing deep into the mine's tunnels.[98]

Dickinson loved the challenge of the Colorado peaks, and she clearly enjoyed the notoriety of being a trailblazer among women, but the true joy of the trip—and its essential healing qualities—came when she was high atop a mountain peak. "One goes to the top of a mountain for emotions, not descriptions," she later explained. Once she reached a summit she was content to spend hours gazing in all directions before clambering down, exhausted as night fell. After several climbs Dickinson convinced a guide to take them up Gray's Peak at night so she could view a spectacular sunrise from the mountain top, the high point of a glorious vacation.[99]

While in the mountains Dickinson "flourished like a Colorado sunflower." For a time she contemplated purchasing land in Colorado Springs, perhaps so that her ailing brother Edwin could take in the healthy mountain air. Of course, to escape her daily life was not to escape the drama that routinely surrounded her. During their time together, Ralph Meeker grew even more enchanted with Dickinson. When they visited Monument Park he sat rapturously at her feet basking in her presence; and as they rode down from Pike's Peak the enthusiastic reporter poured out words of unrequited love that later left him "sick at heart." "You can never know how deeply I was affected when you told us of your trials," Meeker later recalled. In discussing her own heartaches Dickinson must have felt a great catharsis, but the lovesick Meeker was hardly the emotional partner she might have selected for such a moment. Still, it was a very successful journey, and one that she would recall fondly into old age.[100]

When she reached the East, Dickinson returned to her previous "robustness" for a time. But the vacation from normal life did not relieve the pressures that still awaited her. Meanwhile, after two years of discussions Susan had finally resolved to sell the home on Locust Street in Philadelphia, and she and her mother had relocated to a boarding house on Arch Street. Dickinson agreed with the decision, but she worried about the effects of dislocation on her aging mother. These concerns piled up against the backdrop of national economic disaster, as the Panic of 1873 rocked the financial world. The lyceum circuit, already in decline, had a gloomy future.[101] For the upcoming 1873–74 lecture season Dickinson had already put her tour in the hands of O. G. Bernard and the National Lecture Bureau. It was another grueling schedule, and once again Dickinson's body threatened to break down before the end. She suffered from several ailments, including a debilitating case of hemorrhoids. While she was lecturing in Kansas that February Dickinson grew so ill—this time perhaps from a bout of malaria—that Susan worried that her sister's life was in danger. A few months later, after she had returned to the East, Dickinson suffered what may have been a nervous breakdown, leaving her—according to Susan—"in a hysterical condition that made dressing her seem impossible." She soon recovered, but it was more than a week before she could return to writing.[102]

As Dickinson faced new waves of personal and professional difficulties, she had several occasions to turn to Benjamin Butler for advice and assistance. One of the most powerful men of his day, Butler was a celebrated lawyer, wealthy financier, and influential politician. The two first met in 1863, when Dickinson was just shy of her twenty-first birthday, while the portly Bostonian—24 years older than Dickinson— was a major general in the Union Army. Dickinson came away impressed with the general's public persona, but she found him "a bore in private"; the General was pleased enough with Dickinson to write to her several times during the war.[103] Their paths crossed again two years later when Butler decided to try his hand as a lyceum speaker, and Dickinson helped him get an engagement.[104] Over the next several years

Ben Butler *carte de visite* produced by J. Gurney and Sons, New York City. Author's private collection.

they saw each other occasionally, and in one instance Dickinson turned to Butler to defend her against a libel suit. Although their contact remained limited and formal, Butler's periodic notes revealed that he would have happily seen much more of the vivacious Dickinson.[105] Following Dickinson's endorsement of Horace Greeley in 1872, a disappointed Butler still praised her honesty and sent her "a lovely bundle of flowers." The following year Butler had his opportunity to reenter Dickinson's life when she asked the powerful lawyer to intercede in a conflict with James Redpath, a task he tackled with zeal. Soon afterwards, Dickinson turned to Butler for help in securing her sickly brother Edwin a position. Butler happily complied, finding him a job as special agent in the Pension Bureau.[106]

Butler may have attached no strings to this assistance, but all concerned understood that he had hopes. Although Butler was married, for nearly a decade his bedridden wife had been suffering from a thyroid tumor that would soon cause her death.[107]
Privately, the Dickinsons had taken to joking about the general's agendas. When
Edwin met him to pick up the employment forms, Butler asked for Dickinson's
address. "So," Ed quipped, "I suppose thee'll have a love letter the day before or after
this reaches thee!" Indeed, Butler had already composed a long letter to Dickinson.
It was a peculiar note, and one that opened up a new chapter in their correspondence. He devoted most of the letter to his concerns about "our mutual friend L ___ "
who had only recently broken such an extended silence that he had feared "she had
taken some offense" at "a great favor" that he had asked and she had refused. Butler
also worried that "L___" was working too hard, thus suffering from "weariness, in
both body and spirit." Almost as an afterthought, he added that he looked forward
to his meeting with Edwin. The peculiar thing about this letter (beyond its
uncharacteristically personal tone) was that Butler and Dickinson had no mutual
friend "L___." In subsequent letters Butler spoke repeatedly of this troubled young
woman, who he began calling "Lizzie," but he was really speaking of Dickinson
herself, playing on her middle name, Elizabeth. In a half-dozen letters over the space
of a year and a half, Butler followed this odd convention, speaking to Dickinson
directly on business matters while directing his personal concerns and awkward flirta-
tions toward "Lizzie." Perhaps Butler worried that a third party might read his letters
and he wished to disguise his more personal affection for Dickinson. He even asked
Dickinson to stop including "<u>feminine</u> looking" sentiments in her business letters
because they were apt to make his clerks curious. Later he suggested that she mark
private letters "personal" to separate their public affairs from their private discourse.[108]

By 1874 it was clear that Butler hoped to play a larger role in Dickinson's life.
That spring he wrote frequently, seeking to make appointments to discuss her legal
dealings. And he was not above using Dickinson's brother to further these goals. In
June the still-ailing Edwin lost his position at the Pension Bureau, and Dickinson
turned once again to Butler for assistance. Ed worried that his chances were slim
unless the congressman received a pleasant "reception in Phila" when he went to
see Dickinson. The following month the persistent Butler suggested that perhaps
Edwin could be transferred to a position with a lighter workload in Boston, adding
that the overworked Dickinson might also wish to move to New England.[109]

Dickinson was indeed worn out and still ailing during the summer of 1874 as she
struggled to write and recuperate in preparation for the following year's labors.
Once again she concluded that she needed a vacation. A year after climbing the
peaks of Colorado, Dickinson turned to one of her other favorite relaxations: she
went to the beach with Lou Brackett. For several weeks Brackett and Dickinson
relaxed at an Atlantic City hotel, while Dickinson worked on several writing

projects. Unlike the western trip, which combined physical exertion with mental relaxation, during her Atlantic City stay Dickinson devoted her days to poring over newspapers between afternoons relaxing on the beach with Lou and sharing soothing visits to the hot sea baths.[110] Time and again she complained of fans and curiosity seekers interrupting her privacy. "The people seem to have learned no sense with the lapse of years," she grumbled. "While Lou was in the water & I alone, they gawked at me as diligently as of old." At dinner a woman made a great show of standing up to stare at her, explaining her rudeness by announcing that she owned a dozen photographs of Dickinson, and none did her justice. Dickinson and Brackett responded to all this unwanted attention by keeping to themselves as much as possible, prompting the local *Sunday Press* to criticize her for "shunning all the other guests."[111]

In her letters home from Atlantic City Dickinson revealed emphatic, sometimes quite disturbing, thoughts about African Americans. In her first letter she devoted several pages to a silly clash with an "impertinent" black maid over a leaking bathtub, followed by a more expansive commentary on how local hotels had been "substituting white help because they say their guests will not endure the manners of blacks." Later in the same letter she described a minor episode in which Brackett clashed with a black man in a local store, who turned to her and announced " 'I reckon I have a right to say what I please—I'm as free as you now.' " These racial themes were clearly eating at Dickinson as she wrote page after page about one incident after another. "It is certainly a marked thing that the colored people are growing so insufferably impudent that they are hurting themselves & making for themselves enemies out of even old friends," she complained.[112]

These private comments, less than a decade after emancipation, are striking coming from the pen of the woman who rose to prominence as an abolitionist and who later broke ranks with her woman suffrage colleagues over black manhood suffrage. One partial explanation is simply that even the most progressive white Americans in the nineteenth century were not free from racial and class prejudice, and Dickinson's comments reflect those sensibilities. In a broader sense, these private letters are consistent with Dickinson's most recent public statements on the race, gender, and class challenges confronting the nation in the early 1870s. In supporting Greeley in 1872 she celebrated black equality, but put the burden on black voters to defend their own political rights. In "What's To Hinder?" she had challenged women to grasp opportunities. And, when she turned to the ongoing battle between labor and capital, Dickinson took the side of workers, but in characteristic iconoclastic fashion she blamed the rank and file for casting their lot with unscrupulous union organizers. In short, Dickinson enjoyed delivering what she saw as harsh truths aimed at the politically disenfranchised, challenging them to work harder, behave better, and—in her view—show that they fully deserve political and economic equality. Viewed through that lens, Dickinson's letters to her mother were consistent with her political philosophy, which advocated equality while often criticizing the less fortunate for their complicity in their own plight.

While she was away in Atlantic City Dickinson avoided contact with Ben Butler, but her brother's job concerns persisted. By the end of August Ed had grown so anxious that Susan suggested Anna should "pacify" Butler with "a little note." Shortly thereafter Butler sent Ed a telegram about a new appointment.[113] It would be a year before Dickinson would once again turn to Butler for assistance. In the meantime, faced with declining speaking opportunities the resourceful Dickinson cast around for ways to supplement her income. Dickinson had fame, opinions, a quick wit, and unbridled confidence in her own abilities, but few obvious career alternatives. One option was to join the hundreds of postwar women who had begun making their livings as authors. *What Answer?* had earned some attention, but not much money. She had already arranged with publisher James R. Osgood to publish *A Paying Investment*, but even the optimistic Dickinson could not have anticipated major profits from a polemical tract on universal education. Meanwhile, she had already laid the groundwork for *A Ragged Register*, which promised to have more commercial appeal, but Dickinson found the writing process trying and she never imagined that she could live off her "scribbling" alone.[114]

While Butler persisted with his own secret agendas, Dickinson's circle continued to presume that some male lover would eventually come into her life. Not long after she returned from Atlantic City, Laura Bullard urged that "You must fall in love if you want to feel interested—an easy prescription you will say, but where is the man who will make one fall in love with him!"[115] In 1874 Chicagoan Leander Chamberlain fell deeply in love with Dickinson, only to face the same rejection as his predecessors. In what had become a familiar pattern, Dickinson's female friends enjoyed kidding her about the latest contestant for her heart, but nothing in their letters suggested that Dickinson was swayed by Chamberlain's efforts, although both Milwaukee's Sallie Austin and Laura Bullard put in a good word for the "Chicago adorer." "I hate to have you throw such a love & such a man away from you," Bullard wrote. "Is it <u>hopeless</u> for you to be happy under his strong protection & in his strong love?"[116] Before he disappeared from her life, Chamberlain sent Dickinson various love letters, including one heartbroken, eight-page note penned in the middle of a sleepless night. "Last Monday night I put your arms around my neck," he recalled. "[I]t was the weary reaching out of the heart for just one moment of that time, which seemed then so far off, when you yourself put them there in token of your trust in me and of tender pity for my great . . . love." But if there had been moments of physical tenderness in the past, after a night of "a thousand introspections" the melancholy Chamberlain "came to realize how mad and sad it would be for me to have been allowed to win your love. What had I to offer such a one as you!" But as Dickinson explained to her sister, "Leander is a good soul.—'Tis a pity he is not worth a million, & that I am not in love with him."[117]

As Dickinson continued to navigate her personal relationships, the continuing saga surrounding the Beecher-Tilton affair reached new depths. In 1874 Tilton's public accusations led Beecher to name a committee of church members to investigate the charges. When the Plymouth Church committee published a report exonerating their pastor, Tilton took Beecher to court, charging that the minister had committed adultery with his wife. Dickinson wanted no part of the public spectacle, but she devoured the published reports and privately grew disgusted with both men's behavior.[118] Throughout it all Dickinson worried that somebody might "try to drag [her] into the horrible whirlpool" and subpoena her to testify about the conversation she had had with Elizabeth Tilton. Meanwhile, Butler told her that he had been reading confidential materials associated with the case and found that "[t]here are many persons in the literary world of the female persuasion that are badly smirched by the documents submitted to me. Whether your friends or not I know not. Why will people write foolish letters?" he asked. Perhaps anticipating those concerns, Dickinson had just written to James Redpath asking him to destroy some of her letters.[119]

The trial began in January 1875. Although reporters had pestered her to speak about the case, in March Dickinson instead chose to reprise her popular lecture on prostitution at New York City's Steinway Hall. While others contemplated measures to register prostitutes, Dickinson focused on the economic inequalities that drove women into prostitution, and the double standard that attacked fallen women while looking the other way at the immoral men who bought their services. It was a lecture she had given many times before, but on this occasion Dickinson spoke with Theodore Tilton sitting at her side.[120] Her point was clear. While not weighing in on the details of the case, Dickinson appeared to suggest that women—like Tilton's wife, Elizabeth—are too often the victim of predatory men, like Beecher, who deserve to be punished. And, moreover, women who were in the public eye were particularly subject to the taint of sexual scandal in the postwar world.

As she looked back over the last several years, Dickinson had good reason to feel a pang of sadness at the demise of the Liberal Republicans and, perhaps even more so, at her strained relationships with Whitelaw Reid and Susan B. Anthony. For many years Dickinson had relied on those two powerful personalities for friendship and counsel, enjoying many of her most emotionally satisfying and intellectually stimulating moments in the company of one or the other. But both Anthony and Reid had wanted more from Dickinson than she was prepared to give, and it seemed almost inevitable that they each would drift from her life. Still, if her thoughts about the recent past were bittersweet, Dickinson also knew that she—and her sisters in the women's movement—had been fortunate to escape the whirlwind of rumor and innuendo that had surrounded the rise of Victoria Woodhull and the Beecher-Tilton debacle with their reputations intact. Dickinson's immediate challenge would be to find new ways to capitalize on that good name.

*Chapter 7*

---

# FROM THE PLATFORM
# TO THE STAGE:
# CLINGING TO FAME

A FTER the Panic of 1873 the lyceum circuit fell into decline. Dickinson still enjoyed tremendous popularity and could fill the occasional hall, but she would need new strategies to capitalize on that fame. Even as she climbed summits in Colorado and basked on beaches in New Jersey, Dickinson was contemplating her options. Since her youth, she had dreamed of going on the stage, but as long as lecturing provided an outlet for her passions it would have been folly to change careers. There were other barriers as well. Dickinson had been raised in a politically radical, but culturally conservative household. She grew up in a world full of journals, novels, and political debate, rather than one of theater going and light entertainment. The thought of Dickinson going on the stage troubled her mother and siblings, who worried for her genteel reputation.[1] They were not alone. During the war, many of Dickinson's closest friends argued that her talents were too important to waste on the stage. Alice Hooker, one of Isabella Beecher Hooker's daughters, confided that Dickinson had been the subject of serious talk in their Hartford household. Isabella worried that Dickinson would abandon her "noble useful life" to "gratify" her more worldly love of the theater. Alice agreed with her mother that "none of your best friends want you to act," but she promised to break family ranks and support Anna if she went on the stage.[2]

Even as she kept her distance from the theater, Dickinson grew friendly with several actors and actresses. For a short time flamboyant French actor Charles

Fechter took an interest in the compelling orator, and for several years Dickinson befriended Boston actress Melinda Jones, who encouraged her acting aspirations.[3] After the 1872 campaign the theater talk grew more serious. Susan Warner worried that acting would "seem a descent from your grand position," opening Dickinson up to "the caprices of a merciless public." But other friends encouraged the notion and offered to help her make contacts with theater owners and managers.[4] After she returned from Atlantic City in 1874 Dickinson edged closer to the theater. Jones argued that "you must go on the stage—and at once." Betty Browne reported a dinner conversation in which all around the table agreed that Dickinson would be a grand success on the stage. But Sallie Austin still felt that failure as an actress would undermine her "special reputation as queen of the platform." Whereas in the past Dickinson had pondered this option before quickly retreating to familiar ground, this time it seemed that the issue was only a matter of timing. How and when should she launch her acting career?[5]

In the short run, Dickinson selected the most conservative path. She postponed her theatrical debut for another year, declined to gamble on a European trip, and accepted Bernard's offer to manage a southern tour. Beginning in late March 1875 they toured the southern states for a month, starting in Richmond, and then moving south through Virginia, North Carolina, South Carolina, and Georgia, before heading north to Tennessee. Much like her 1869 cross-country trip to California and her Colorado excursion four years later, Dickinson's southern tour combined business and pleasure. While she hoped to attract audiences in these untapped markets, Dickinson was equally interested in exploring the old Confederacy to observe how Reconstruction was progressing. And, like those earlier working vacations, Dickinson sent her mother lengthy travel letters, recording the humorous and the poignant.[6]

Immediately after Appomattox, Dickinson had made a brief visit to the battlefields around Richmond and Petersburg. Now she was anxious to see how the South had evolved after ten years of peace. As soon as she headed into the Reconstructed states, Dickinson observed that "[e]verybody . . . white & black is poorer than poorly & regards a Northern person as a godsend to pick clean to the bones." In the weeks to come she found that poverty broken by pockets of prosperity—in Petersburg the tobacco plants were "in full blast" and Wilmington's port showed signs of activity—but time and again Dickinson observed once-majestic buildings in disrepair, citizens wearing threadbare clothing, and signs of economic despair.[7] She also found white Southerners still bitter about the Civil War, blaming Yankee invaders for economic destruction rather than taking responsibility for a war that they had provoked.

Dickinson, the wartime patriot, viewed the South's present through the lens of the past. Many of her longest and most poignant passages described visits to battlefields and soldiers' cemeteries. Outside Petersburg she explored the site of the Crater, where Union troops had tunneled under enemy lines to blow a huge hole in Confederate defenses, triggering a horrible bloodbath when the subsequent onslaught failed. A decade earlier, at nearly the same spot, her brother John had pulled a bayonet out of the ground only to discover a severed hand still grasping it. This time she toured with "a colored driver" who had been in the burial detail on that fateful day and who described a battlefield so full of corpses that " 'we couldn't stop widout treating on dem.' "[8] Dickinson would walk the ground at other battlefields, including Lookout Mountain and Chickamagua, but she was most profoundly moved by her visits to the prisoner-of-war burial grounds at Salisbury, North Carolina, and Andersonville, Georgia. As her plans to visit the site of the Salisbury camp (near Charlotte) became known, local whites did their best to discourage the inquisitive Northerner from visiting what they claimed was a small, insignificant site. But Dickinson insisted on seeing for herself, and was shocked to discover that 12,125 Union soldiers were buried at Salisbury, nearly all in 18 long, unmarked trenches. When she made a pilgrimage to the infamous Andersonville Prison, Dickinson sent a long, moving description home, concluding that "It was a terrible day, & yet a day I would not count out of my calendar for any reason." The thought of Union prisoners starving to death while the locals remained largely indifferent ate at Dickinson even more than the image of soldiers falling valiantly on the battlefield.[9]

During her southern travels the sharp-tongued Dickinson occasionally clashed with prying or hostile strangers. When she crossed swords with unreconstructed rebels, Dickinson gave as good as she got. In Georgia she happened to mention that she had seen "Valentine's statue of Lee" in Richmond. A Southern lady, the wife of a Confederate general, objected to Dickinson's informal tone, reminding her that " 'You mean Gen[eral] Lee.' " Rather than deflecting a potentially awkward moment with a quick pleasantry, Dickinson rose to the bait. " 'No, madame,' " she retorted, " 'I mean Lee.—Robert E. Lee—Lieut. Col. Lee. I know of no legitmate legal authority to make him more than that.' "[10] In other settings the Southern white elites, including ex-Confederate leaders, embraced the visiting Northerner or at least politely purchased tickets to attend her lectures, leading Dickinson to suspect that they were anxious that she come away with a good opinion of them and their region. But as she concluded in her final letter, "There is not one word nor effort spoken, nor made toward a 'reconciliation.' "[11]

While Dickinson was certainly drawn to how the memory of the Civil War permeated Southern life, she was even more concerned with the effects of Reconstruction. How was the South making the transition from a slave society to an interracial world of black and white workers and citizens? In Richmond she found that "the colored people manage to get along better than poor white Confederates," perhaps because "there is a wonderful unity among them for help & brotherhood." When they passed through rural South Carolina she observed a "region of colored folks who are working their own small places" as sharecroppers.

Whereas "<u>any</u> sign of work & property in their case is a thing to be glad of," she acknowledged that their "horrid looking little cabins, poor scratched land, starved looking mules or cows . . . were anything but savory sights."

On several stops Dickinson visited black schools. She found Raleigh's Shaw University, "a sort of academy for colored young men & women," to be sparsely equipped but "well-lighted & ventilated" and perfectly functional. Shaw's teachers were New Englanders of just the "disagreeable" sort who were bound to give the North a bad name, but she acknowledged that "a less cold, obtuse, self reliant & determined set of people" would likely "be driven away in short order." In South Carolina she noted that only black students were attending the new public schools, raising the possibility of a future with "at least reasonably well informed colored people & . . . absolutely ignorant whites." She praised Virginians—free of "carpetbag rule"—for establishing excellent "colored schools" with superb Southern teachers from the old master class rather than Northern women who, she claimed, could not be expected to truly understand their pupils. Echoing themes she had raised during the 1872 campaign and would reiterate in *A Paying Investment*, Dickinson confidently predicted that these Virginia schools would yield a generation of educated voters.[12]

If schools represented the future, Dickinson looked at prisons and penitentiaries as a window into contemporary race relations. Near Raleigh she saw a chain gang of black prisoners that looked distressingly like the slave gangs of a previous generation. She concluded that there were "more ignorant, lazy, & worthless whites than blacks," but she suspected that blacks were disproportionately incarcerated. In Charleston, South Carolina, things looked a bit more promising. At least the police force was evenly divided between blacks and whites. In Nashville Dickinson was discouraged to find that whereas white prisoners lived in decent cells and were taught a trade, "the negro cells" in the same penitentiary "were horrible holes" where inmates learned no skills.[13] Whenever possible Dickinson attended black church services. In her letters home she commented freely, and sometimes caustically, about the quality of singing, sermons, and the like. She was most pleased when worshippers honored their own traditions, singing spirituals that harkened back to slavery, and she was least impressed when she sensed that freedpeople were trying to imitate white religious behavior or when she heard black clergymen who had evidently spent much time in the North. On the other hand, Dickinson approved of the fact that young black women disdained the familiar turbans as "a badge of servitude" in favor of greater finery for Sunday services. At bottom, Dickinson was most encouraged when she sensed a "dignity & air of command" in the African Americans she met. In Georgia "the manners of the darkies are very like those of slavery . . . but in South Carolina they act like men."[14]

All of these postwar institutions evolved in a complex political context. Dickinson's letters imagined a positive future created by dignified blacks defining their own autonomous lives and reasonable whites, acting out of informed self-interest, developing economic and educational systems that would work best for all. She was skeptical about how much Northerners, even with the best intentions, could do to lead the South into that future. When she investigated the histories of Salisbury and Andersonville Prisons, Dickinson took pains to uncover and celebrate the efforts of a handful of kindly Southern white women who tried to smuggle food to the Union prisoners. While in Richmond she stayed with the famed Elizabeth Van Lew, who had spied for the Union during the war and had remained in her native Virginia as an example of good works and racial justice.[15] In contrast, Dickinson noted that transplanted Northern "carpetbaggers" remained social pariahs. In Columbia, South Carolina, Dickinson visited with Governor Daniel Chamberlain, the brother of her Chicago friend Leander Chamberlain. She found the Chamberlains to be entirely "refined, well disposed, elegant people, with no taint of obnoxious 'carpet baggery' about them." Still, after six or seven years in the state they had made no progress in breaking down the social barriers. Although she faulted local whites for their incivility, Dickinson concluded that the South's solutions would have to come from within.[16]

In Richmond she attended the state legislature and heard a series of "secession speeches" praising Robert E. Lee and Jefferson Davis, all while "six or seven colored members" sat by themselves in one corner. But, Dickinson wryly noted, they "had their revenge whenever a bill was pending" and the white legislators lobbied for their votes. Only a month earlier Congress had passed the Civil Rights Bill of 1875, banning segregation in public accommodations and conveyances. When Dickinson spoke in Wilmington the city opened the "great dingy opera house" for the first time since the bill's passage. As Dickinson later learned, most local blacks had "made a sort of compact among themselves" to preserve the peace by observing informal segregation, purchasing only the cheaper gallery tickets while leaving the more expensive reserved seats to the whites. One brave black man nearly provoked a riot by asserting his new legal right to sit in one of the best seats, surrounded by white ticket holders. Dickinson wrote admiringly of the defiant black customer, but she felt greater sympathy for those blacks who feared for their safety because of his audacity. A few weeks later Dickinson barely missed another violent episode in Charlotte. Only days before she arrived, a very light-skinned black South Carolina state legislator had stopped at the same hotel with his wife and child. The well-dressed black man managed to enter the dining room (alone) without attracting attention, but as soon as the white customers recognized his race a mob formed, forcing the legislator to flee. Meanwhile, the hotelier—cognizant that he risked a $500 fine—closed the building and did his best to keep the mob at bay. This, the sardonic Dickinson reported, was "a specimen of 'Civil Rights'" in action.[17]

Dickinson completed her southern tour with mixed feelings. On the one hand, she made no money. Even where the local press treated her well, too few Southerners could afford the price of a ticket, thus the tour failed to cover expenses. On the other hand, she came away with valuable insights and fodder for future writings. The following month she would write home from Chicago, seeking statistical data to support her bleak assessment of the state of Southern affairs. In particular, she sought "good reliable authority for an onslaught on the carpetbag governments," which she blamed "in part at least for the bad state of feeling." In her view, progress would only accompany internal evolutions within Southern society, both white and black, rather than political solutions imposed from the outside. She felt that Southern whites were particularly stymied by their hatred of the Northern government and their seeming inability to adjust to their new economic circumstances, Whatever her political sentiments, Dickinson was pleased to report that the warm weather had agreed with her and she had only been "very tired" once or twice during the trip. Despite the fine climate, as they left Nashville and headed north toward St. Louis, Dickinson and Bernard were "glad to get out of Dixie."[18]

From St. Louis Dickinson headed on to Chicago, one of her favorite cities. She spent several months holed up in Chicago's Palmer House, writing, thinking, relaxing, and raising cash by selling some local real estate she had purchased years before. As she explained to Susan, "If it were not for the puzzle of my own life, & the distraction about making money I would do very well." She expected to head for California for a new round of lectures, but those plans fell through and a frustrated Dickinson languished in Chicago, finishing A Paying Investment while drafting several plays.[19]

During her months in Chicago Dickinson befriended Frances Willard, who had emerged as a leading temperance advocate. The two spent long hours together, discussing women's rights and arguing about temperance. In later life Willard would date her own commitment to suffrage to those intense moments with Dickinson, and Willard's biographer argues that Dickinson became a valuable "role model" introducing Willard to "the world of the performer" who could influence audiences with her rhetoric. In early June Dickinson demonstrated that power when she "straggled into" a temperance convention and created a stir by speaking up for a woman suffrage proposal when, she claimed, the "shrieking sisters" present failed to rise to the occasion. Willard was impressed with the display, but Dickinson found the whole episode rather amusing and she shared the story with her sister in that spirit. Here she was, no teetotaler herself and completely unaffiliated with the temperance movement, drawn into a floor debate about suffrage largely because she felt the temperance women were concentrating their energies on men while ignoring the needs of working women.[20]

Before long the enthusiastic Willard began getting on Dickinson's nerves. In August, after one too many discussions, Dickinson sent Willard a long, frank letter. "If you care so much for Temperance meetings & religion let me learn that fact from somebody else," she implored. Although she valued Willard's friendship, she had her "own opinions about religion & life very different from" hers, and no good could come from Willard's incessant proselytizing.[21] In the years to come Dickinson and Willard remained in contact, although their conflicting political passions inhibited their friendship. Many years later, after they had had a falling out, a bitter Dickinson would recall the 1875 episode as the first sign of Willard's manipulative hypocrisy, evidenced by Willard's published assertions that the orator had appeared at the convention on her invitation, thus claiming Dickinson as a convert to a cause she never embraced.[22]

Although she gave a few paying lectures while in Chicago, Dickinson recognized that that professional chapter was essentially over. "It is no use Dickey," she wrote to her sister, "I have tried faithfully to stick to the platform, but the platform won't stick to me." She saw no solution other than defying her mother's wishes and finally turning to the stage as a playwright and actress. With that in mind, Dickinson wrote her mother a letter of explanation, which she sent to Susan for safe keeping. A lover of history, she contemplated Katherine of Aragon, Anne Boleyn, Lady Jane Grey, or perhaps the fictional Jane Eyre, as her first subject. Like her celebrated lecture on Joan of Arc, Dickinson hoped to create strong female characters, free of the critical assessments commonly placed upon them by judgmental and uncomprehending men.[23]

Finally things fell into place as Dickinson negotiated a preliminary agreement with Augustin Daly, a leading theatrical producer. Moreover, her old friend Betty Browne—who had recently married a much older man and become Betty Chatfield —offered Dickinson a room in their Elizabeth, New Jersey home, providing the perpetual vagabond with lodging in the East.[24] Meanwhile, she had broken nearly a year of silence with Ben Butler in search of some assistance with the land deal. Butler beamed at the attention, and did not seem to mind that Dickinson clearly had ulterior motives. In responding, Butler suggested that perhaps "Lizzie's" silence "was because of a misconstruction of my motives, wishes, and actions." He hoped that this new contact meant that Lizzie's "frame of mind" had changed, and that she would be willing to see him in person. Later, in the midst of another awkwardly flirtatious letter, the devious Butler pointed out that Edwin's job might again be in jeopardy but that he would intercede if need be.[25]

When she turned to the stage in 1876 Anna Dickinson opened herself up to particular national scrutiny. Her fame provided opportunities that would have been unavailable had she not already established her ability to attract paying audiences, but that fame and those opportunities also robbed her of the luxury of being a true novice. Some friends, fans, and critics would be especially supportive because of their affection for her public persona; others would jump at the opportunity to bring her down a notch.[26]

Dickinson selected Anne Boleyn as her first subject.[27] During the winter of 1876 she stayed with Laura Bullard in her New York apartment, drafting the script. Inspired by what she felt were unfair historical treatments of Henry VIII's ill-fated spouse, Dickinson hoped that her new play—*A Crown of Thorns, or Anne Boleyn*—would resurrect her subject as a noble woman of grand tragic dignity and purity, in contrast to the weak, immoral figure imagined by male historians.[28] As she prepared for the play's May 8 premier at Boston's newly rebuilt Globe Theater, the playwright and star reveled in her new career. "Mr. Waller, Mr. Cheney's stage manager is an old love," she gushed. At first "one or two of the actors . . . thinking they had a novice to deal with" presumed to assert their authority, but she "proceeded to sail in, take possession, & conduct my own rehearsal . . . as though I had been accustomed to it for twenty years."[29] While Dickinson and the cast prepared their performances, the Boston theater community—and in fact critics throughout the Northeast— were abuzz, anticipating the stage debut of the Queen of the Lyceum. Meanwhile, letters of support and impressive floral displays poured in.[30]

Opening night was, in the words of O. G. Bernard, "a magnificent triumph." The Globe Theater's packed house of nearly 3,000 included visitors from Philadelphia and New York, as well as an array of New England's most distinguished cultural and reform leaders, including Henry Wadsworth Longfellow, Ralph Waldo Emerson, Julia Ward Howe, Thomas Wentworth Higginson, and William Dean Howells. Most attended hoping for the best, but some probably joined Mark Twain—no great fan of Dickinson's—in anticipating "the crucifixion." Despite such cynicism, Dickinson was ebullient at night's end. "I have made a success," she declared, "& will do ten times better in the not far off future." The local critics were unanimous in praising the opening. Most found flaws in her technical skills, including her poor stage presence, her unconvincing accent, and her stilted gestures, but they graciously acknowledged that the power of her passion made the performance on balance a success. The optimistic Bernard agreed that the future looked bright, reporting to Susan that "she improved wonderfully last night on the first night's performance, & even that was even better than her most sanguine friends expected." Dickinson basked in the praise while reporting general satisfaction with the hastily composed script, which she concluded was "just about up to the mark" and was already attracting substantial offers, convincing her that "it has money in it."[31]

Whereas the New England press treated Dickinson fairly well, the more powerful New York critics who had traveled to Boston for the opening were less kind. The *Herald* praised the script but announced that Dickinson's "step from the rostrum to the stage [was] a mistake." The *Times* called it an "eminently dull play" and concluded that Dickinson was little more than a clever amateur. And the *Tribune's* notoriously caustic William Winter mocked both the play and the performance, adding that "we see no reason to encourage the idea that Miss Dickinson is an actress because she dresses herself in four gorgeous robes and goes into an ecstasy of elocution."[32] The savvy Dickinson had planned to postpone her New York debut until she had perfected her craft, but she could not control their "infernal"

Playbill for Anna Dickinson's play *Crown of Thorns*, about the life of Anne Boleyn. May 16, 1876. Author's personal collection.

reports from the provinces. In fact, as she told a Boston paper, "it was a foregone conclusion with the New York scalpers that I was to fail, and they were determined to make me seem to do so."[33] The Boston critics took umbrage at the implication that their own standards were too low. This sparked some interesting reportorial theater, as the Boston papers fired a few shots at their stuffy Gotham colleagues. Some even suggested that the most hostile New York critics had composed their reviews prior to watching the play.[34] Several newspapers called Winter's criticisms "ungentlemanly," echoing the rhetoric that wartime Republicans had used more than a decade earlier to defend her against partisan Democrats. But unlike the wartime debates, this time several of Dickinson's strongest defenses came from the pens of women who had only recently entered the field of journalism.[35]

Meanwhile, Dickinson also discovered that the Globe's charming Arthur Cheney had been guilty of "an abominable piece of sharp practice." As the play's author and star, Dickinson stood to share in the profits rather than earning a set salary. Dickinson and Bernard had understood that the first $500 of receipts from each night's performance would cover the actors' salaries and the play's other production expenses, but they learned that the actual agreement also reserved an additional $350 per night for the business management of the theater. In short, Dickinson would not start receiving profits until ticket sales exceeded $850 each night, a figure they rarely reached. Thus, she performed A Crown of Thorns in Boston for a fortnight without making any money, while learning a hard lesson about the theater business. In late May Dickinson took the play on the road, embarking on a ten-city tour of New England with members of the Globe Theater Company. The New England critics, like those in Boston, were gentle but mixed in their responses. As one put it, "Miss Anna E. Dickinson has attempted too much. In striving at one stride to place herself in the fore rank of play-writers and actors she has allowed her ambition . . . to warp her judgment."[36]

In October, Dickinson and the cast of A Crown of Thorns embarked on a rigorous six-week tour of the West, with stops in Cincinnati, Louisville, St. Louis, Cleveland, and a host of smaller towns and cities. Before they hit the road the optimistic Dickinson reassured an old friend that "I am not half the 'failure' they set me forth—& I have all the engagements I want for next season." From Ohio she reported that they had barely made expenses, but she felt confident that they would soon turn the corner. In fact, the entire tour turned out to be a draining grind, yielding valuable experience but little profit. To control costs, Bernard had arranged to work with local actors at each stop, thus producing perpetual new rehearsals and adjustments. Still, Dickinson was pleased that the local press had generally been supportive.[37]

Finally, in late November Dickinson returned to her home turf when she made her Philadelphia debut at the Arch Street theater. The Philadelphia crowds were large and the critics, like those in New England, generally complimentary. The

*Inquirer* dubbed the occasion "the most notable dramatic event" of the season and the *Evening Star*'s critic was pleased to report that both the play and Dickinson's acting had improved over the six months since the Globe Theater debut, although he acknowledged that she was far from a great actress.[38] The play ran at Arch Street for several weeks and, in the meantime, Dickinson put the finishing touches on another historical play, adapted from *Jane Eyre*, and began work on a contemporary comic melodrama, which she called *Laura, or True to Herself*.[39] In December, perhaps worried about continuing demand for *A Crown of Thorns*, Dickinson presented a hastily thrown together version of *True to Herself* to Arch Street audiences for a three-day run. It seemed an unwise decision. Even friendly critics found the play poorly written and the production hastily assembled.[40]

Following the New Year Dickinson took *A Crown of Thorns* on the road through upstate New York. Nearly a year after her Boston debut, and after months of performances across the North and Midwest, Dickinson finally opened her play in New York on April 4, 1877, at the Eagle Theater. It was far from the success she had envisioned. Once again the early audiences were large and generally enthusiastic, and the consensus among those who had attended the previous spring was that both actress and script had made impressive strides. Still, the New York critics remained unimpressed and uncharitable. "The truth is," the *World* declared, "Anna Dickinson is not an actor—never can be an actor." Better for her to return to the lyceum. The *Herald* panned the play and added that "of Miss Dickinson we have very little to say that is complimentary and therefore wish to say as little as possible." The *Tribune*'s Winter, perhaps conscious of the outcry his earlier review had sparked, wrote with uncharacteristic care. He found little in the play or the acting to praise, but stressed that Dickinson's great oratorical talents simply translated poorly to the stage.[41] As in Boston, Dickinson enjoyed particular support from female critics, including the *Daily Graphic*'s Jenny Cunningham Croly.[42]

Dickinson had reached a watershed moment, or so it seemed. Some critics saw her move to the theater as little more than a minor dalliance by an arrogant, overprivileged celebrity. Others claimed that her new career path reflected her abandonment of intellectually bankrupt women's rights issues.[43] Most saw it as an interesting adventure for an accomplished orator, but not much more than a brief experiment. Few seemed to understand how committed Dickinson was to her new career, or how much her livelihood depended on her success. After a year of hard work, she had finally presented herself to the New York theatrical world, and the critics had spoken. What would her next step be? The evidence before her was decidedly mixed. The New York critics were the nation's most powerful, and the most prominent of their number had almost taken glee in bringing her down a peg. Still, other professional eyes had watched her performances and found much to praise even while noting shortcomings. Moreover, many provincial critics had publicly accused the New York writers of unfair bias. Privately, letters of support from old friends and complete strangers arrived from across the country. Journalists and members of the theater community wrote assuring her that she had been unfairly treated.[44] As one supporter put it, "if you were not Anna Dickinson you would not have been so attacked." One of the only lukewarm responses came from Winter's employer, Whitelaw Reid; a mutual friend reported that the powerful editor was distinctly "noncommittal" about her performance and merely commented that " 'she is a very strong woman.' "[45]

Surely Dickinson had reason to feel aggrieved. Prior to her New York debut she had assembled a large stack of stories evaluating, and generally praising, her efforts. Now she had a fresh batch of clippings, with a generally harsher tone. For this most public of public women, those clippings defined her professional identity, and if the balance tipped the wrong way all was lost. In the past, Dickinson had had ample opportunities to speak directly to her public, using the platform to turn her sharp tongue on hostile editors and periodically publishing letters in selected newspapers, explaining her decisions, clarifying her positions, and lambasting her critics. Prior to opening *A Crown of Thorns* in New York, Dickinson had given several interviews in which she spoke openly about her acting career and the New York critics. But in response to this new round of criticisms Dickinson returned to her roots: she announced that following her April 9 performance she would speak directly to the public.

It was a remarkable moment. After the curtain went down on the final scene, Dickinson walked to the center of the stage, grasping a handful of newspaper clippings as her new prop. For the next hour she struck back at those who had written harshly about her, directing particular scorn at the *Tribune*'s Winter. Once again, Anna Dickinson was playing the role of transgressor, violating commonly recognized barriers. This time the ironies were thick. The actress who critics claimed performed too much like an orator muddied the lines between platform and stage even further, by lecturing to a theatrical audience while still in costume as Anne Boleyn. As she had in the past, Dickinson built her case with appeals to both evidence and emotion. She read from the most hostile reviews, juxtaposed against supportive commentary from both print and private correspondence. But in the process Dickinson added an unfamiliar chord to her familiar use of pathos by playing the role of the small, wounded female victim, thus casting *herself* in the role that she had in the past assigned to a host of other victims of injustice, from slaves, to prostitutes, to anonymous working women.[46]

As in the past, Dickinson did not really present herself in gendered terms throughout this conflict despite behaving in ways that violated normal gender prescriptions. Even in her teary-eyed attack on her critics, in which she offered herself as a relatively weak victim of powerful males, Dickinson did not stress her role as a helpless woman so much as a solitary individual dueling against a more numerous and powerful foe. (She did, however, speak of her New York critics as "these little men" to the delight of the *Chicago Tribune.*) In fact, rather than suggesting that she was being dismissed because she was a woman, Dickinson leaked a letter from powerful actor Dion Boucicault confirming her assessment that individuals in the acting profession were commonly at the mercy of unscrupulous and often corrupt critics.[47]

Dickinson's attack on her critics energized her personally and earned praise from friendly quarters, but the local press generally found her second performance of the evening unusual, amusing, and largely irrelevant. One called it "touching" but also "impertinent." Some noted sardonically that she was more biting than her worst adversaries. Those reporters who watched from a distance were more sympathetic. Journalist Murat Halstead remarked that "the fact is, the lady feels that the world should pet her a little; and she is more than half right about that."[48] George Warner was in the audience and dropped by her hotel afterwards to offer his support, adding that "I would rather you had made no sign, but it is well for others . . . that you did. The mere opinion of a single individual becomes in the columns of a newspaper a terrible power." Susan reminded her that even the great actress Clara Morris had risen to fame despite poor reviews, and in reference to "the Tribune's brutality" she added—suggesting a theme that would recur over the next several decades—"I hope Reid will get his just repayment some day for the way he has treated thee."[49]

For a short time Dickinson's direct public appeal seemed to bear fruit, as attendance at the Eagle Theater rose for the next several performances. But *A Crown of Thorns* closed abruptly on April 16 as Dickinson's squabbles with theater owner Josh Hart reached a boiling point. It had been an unhappy relationship from the outset, reflecting both Hart's managerial shortcomings and Dickinson's expectations that she should control her own play. The show had actually opened two days late because of mix-ups in the stage set, producing friction between actress and owner that persisted over the next week. These problems were magnified by the absence of Bernard, who Dickinson had dismissed following the western tour, forcing her to be author, star, and agent. For Dickinson, the final straw came when Hart replaced Edward Arnott in the role as Henry without consulting his star. An irate Dickinson walked into rehearsal the following day, collected the scripts and walked out the door. In the ensuing war of words both actress and owner accused the other of bad faith. Neither's heart seemed in the struggle, and both were happy to move on. In a dozen New York performances *A Crown of Thorns* had grossed less than $3,000.[50]

As this highly public drama came to a close, some observers persisted in casting the conflict as one between "unmanly" villains and Anna Dickinson who was, after all, "only a woman." A chivalrous Houston editor declared that "the little woman" deserved a "fair showing" purely "because she is a defenseless woman."[51] Several female observers offered more nuanced analysis. When Dickinson parted company with the Eagle, Mrs. J. M. Ellis praised the decision, noting that the theater had a seedy reputation that had precluded her and her female New York friends from attending Dickinson's performances.[52] The *Daily Graphic* accused the critics of being a cabal of "young men" of little maturity or judgment. Following Dickinson's counterattack from the stage, the *Graphic* ran a full-page cartoon depicting a schoolmarmish Dickinson towering over a group of childish boys wearing dunce caps, labeled "Herald," "Times," "World," and "Tribune." The caption read: "Anna Dickinson chastises the boys."[53]

It was poet and journalist Elizabeth Allen who truly tried to shake Dickinson by the shoulders and explain the larger truth behind her dispute. The problem was not Dickinson's acting, she wrote, but that "the jury is packed." "It isn't possible that you don't know why you have been singled out as the mark for all this cowardly insult, ridicule, and vituperation," she insisted. "Do you overlook it, or do you only choose to ignore it? . . . It is simply because you of all women who have come before the public as an artist, are the only one who has ever said a word or done a deed for the enlargement of women. You believe—and have preached that you believe—in the equality of men and women. You believe that a woman has a right to her own children and her own earnings and a voice in the laws that should govern but not oppress her. This is your offence." Allen pointed out that those public women who had declined to speak up for women, such as Gail Hamilton, Charlotte Cushman, or Kate Field, were destined to receive fair treatment from the male critics, while women like Dickinson would never get a fair shake. The best strategy, she argued, was to press on without wasting time battling on such terrain.[54]

As she approached her thirty-fifth birthday in 1877, Dickinson once again took stock. Although she had failed to win over the leading New York critics, Dickinson convinced herself that their reviews reflected unfair biases rather than a clear assessment of her potential. It seemed that she had enough support in the rest of the nation to press on with her new career. Certainly no better options appeared to be on the horizon. Unfortunately, more family tragedy was. With her mother and Susan living in modest rented quarters in West Pittston, Pennsylvania, that winter Dickinson once again accepted an offer to stay with Betty Chatfield and her husband in New Jersey, where she set to work on a new historic drama. Susan Dickinson had begun working as a journalist, thus reducing the financial burden on her younger sister and providing Anna with the rare opportunity to praise her sister's professional success. But that winter brother Edwin fell deathly ill with a lung ailment and had to move in with Susan and his mother. Suddenly Susan Dickinson found herself in the role of dual caretaker. "I cannot meet the requirements for nursing, & have any strength (& precious little time) left for writing!" she complained. For several months Susan soldiered on, with the aid of hired nurses, while Dickinson sent supportive letters from New Jersey. On April 20, 1877, the sisters lost a second brother, just under a decade after Samuel had died of tuberculosis.[55]

Edwin's death hit Anna particularly hard.[56] They had long maintained a lively correspondence, with Edwin often providing wry insight into the goings-on in the Dickinson household. And for years Dickinson had done her best to assist her older brother, lending him money, helping secure him jobs, and generally looking after his well-being. In her months of deepest despair Dickinson found herself once more in contact with Benjamin Butler, who had repeatedly used his influence to secure Edwin positions and thus Anna's affections. In the previous several years Butler had occasionally written to Dickinson about both professional and personal matters. Two years earlier—only months after Sarah Butler finally succumbed to her tumor— Dickinson had turned to the grieving Butler for a substantial loan to get *A Crown of Thorns* off the ground, but since then they had not corresponded.[57] A week before Edwin died, Butler sent Dickinson a brief note, telling her that it was important that he see her as soon as possible. When the distraught Dickinson failed to respond, he wrote a few months later inviting her to join him in Atlantic City for a private interlude. Dickinson initially agreed to this offer, so the exuberant widower hurried from Washington to the shore with great expectations. When his prey failed to arrive, the disappointed Butler poured out his sorrow in characteristically awkward style: "When one has planned schemed brought out any enterprise from which he promises himself advantage either of pleasure profits or still more happiness and fails therein because of accidents or circumstances wholly beyond his control the failure is very bitter, and is not alleviated because the hindering elements are not subject to his will or endeavor. . . . Robert Bruce's spider it is true tried thirteen times before he succumbed, but then he saw the defect lay in his own want of endeavor, and for no other reason. He was not disheartened by the fear or thought that perhaps another was fully employed in unweaving his web." Dickinson convinced Butler that her mother had fallen ill, keeping her from joining him in Atlantic City. But that was merely an elaborate ruse she devised to steer clear of Butler's web while still staying in his good graces. Still, it would be several years before Dickinson would once again turn to her patron for assistance.[58]

As she struggled with Edwin's death and Butler's advances, Dickinson was building a network of friends and contacts within the theatrical world and preparing her next move. Popular actress Rose Eytinge approached Dickinson about playing the role of Anne Boleyn in a new production of *A Crown of Thorns*, but the proud Dickinson would not part with the rights to her prized play.[59] In the meantime, Dickinson had grown close to actress Ann Wakeman, one of Eytinge's friends. For a time the two shared beds and other intimacies when they could find time together.[60] A few months later Dickinson offered her script based on *Jane Eyre*— which she called *Love and Duty*—to A. M. Palmer, who managed New York's Union Square Theater. Palmer assured her that he was anxious to produce a Dickinson play when she wrote a good one, but in his view *Love and Duty* did not fit that bill. Perhaps revealing more bluster than confidence, Dickinson replied that she was "reluctantly compelled to dissent" from this critical assessment.[61] During her winter with the Chatfields Dickinson had put the finishing touches on a new historical drama: *Aurelian, or Rome's Restorer*. Set in third-century Rome, *Aurelian*—like *A Crown of Thorns*, and *What Answer?*—had a strong woman and a tragic love story at its center. The gallant emperor Aurelian falls in love with Palmyra's independent-minded queen Zenobia, who initially resists his overtures before finally yielding to love, just in time to die protecting Aurelian from an assassin's hand.[62] When she wrote *Aurelian*, Dickinson was under the impression that famed actor John McCullough had already committed himself to the project, promising to support the play and star alongside Dickinson. But to her dismay McCullough found the script unacceptable.[63]

In 1879 Dickinson returned to the lecture circuit, but with a new wrinkle. In "The Platform and the Stage" Dickinson addressed those skeptics who claimed that her move to the theater constituted an abandonment of serious public discourse. Instead, she insisted, the contemporary stage was really a more powerful and influential forum than either the platform or the press. The new lecture was well received, particularly among colleagues in the theater. As had long been her pattern, Dickinson rotated this lecture with a revival of the ever-popular "Joan of Arc," as well as a few small readings from *Aurelian*.[64] She would continually return to the platform for brief stints over the next several years, but now Dickinson saw these interludes as temporary stopgaps between theatrical projects. Meanwhile, *A Ragged Register*—Dickinson's book based on her life on the road—finally appeared in print. The reviews were courteous and a few correspondents sent kind notes, but the book was a small, odd volume combining travel commentary, humorous anecdotes, and her own brand of social commentary, and it won no audience. In the next decade *A Ragged Register* would barely sell 100 volumes, earning her little more than $10, and providing the author with more evidence that writing could never be more than a sideline.[65]

With her plans in the East frustrated, Dickinson contemplated another junket to California. The idea was to tour the state, combining new theatrical performances with a few dependable lectures. Once again, Dickinson chose a man to serve as her agent. And, once again, she would come to second-guess those services. Dickinson had relied on her friend Leander Richardson, an editor with the *New York Dramatic News*, to act as the intermediary in her failed talks with John McCullough, and now she turned to him to negotiate an agreement with a New York dramatic agency for the California tour. Richardson returned with a contract guaranteeing a week of dramatic performances with the profits shared after the first $400 in receipts, and 20 speeches for a fee of $6,000. Dickinson found the length of the contract too short and the terms unacceptable, and rejected the deal. The problem arose when Richardson claimed that he had negotiated in good faith and had already signed the contract as her agent, an opinion that the gentlemen of Simmonds and Brown Dramatic Agents shared. Dickinson dug in her heels. She was not going to traipse across the country for less than a guaranteed three weeks of performances, and despite pressures from several quarters she was not going to honor a contract she had not signed and insisted that she had not approved.[66]

The aborted California negotiations revealed Dickinson in all her contradictions. She acted as an autonomous, strong-willed business woman, but she seemed frustrated by the burdens of these responsibilities. In August she sent Frank Lawlor, of Simmonds and Brown, a long letter explaining her position on the unacceptable contract, but also revealing her larger desires and frustrations. "All that ability, endurance & courage can do I have done," she explained. But she alone was powerless to break "down the barrier that a half dozen potent but conscienceless scribblers in New York" had put in her path. "What I need is a manager—Not an agent—not a fellow who will 'guarantee so much success for so many thousand dollars.' Not an engagement with a theater that will plan for the shortest possible length of time, or the closest margin of terms in the fear that I will be a 'failure', but a man or men . . . who will say this woman has a great name, she has . . . will, determination to succeed, she can write an admirable play for she has written one, & she can act, she knows too much to so utterly mistake what she can do & cant do as to make such a plunge as she has done without calculating her powers." In short, Dickinson wanted to put her career in the hands of a man who would gamble on her talents and her future, so that she could stop being mired in short-term arrangements that protected owners while leaving her with limited opportunities.[67] Dickinson was perfectly willing to yield her professional autonomy to a man. She just had not found any man who could do the job as well as she could do it herself.[68]

It was just as well that Dickinson's autumn excursion to California fell through. That spring she suffered from a kidney ailment followed by a bad bout of sciatica, and as the summer began she complained of an ailment that she described as malaria in her face. Once again, as they had so many times over the previous two decades, Dickinson's family members worried about her health while they continued to turn to her for financial assistance. Although Susan had been doing her best to build a journalism career, family finances had grown precarious and she and her mother contemplated another move from their rented rooms in West Pittson. In August Anna told Susan to "not fret about expenses." Although she was "as poor as Job's cat" Dickinson promised to "see them well & comfortably through the summer." It was a challenging time for both sisters. Their aging mother could be difficult under the best of circumstances, and in recent months her health seemed to be failing and she had made it clear that she wished to return to Philadelphia, where lodgings would be more expensive and Susan's career options limited. As Susan grew despondent, Anna did her best to raise her sister's spirits, but a few weeks later she still only had $50 to spare. Near the close of 1879 Susan and Mary Dickinson relocated to modest quarters in Honesdale, Pennsylvania while, meanwhile, Anna scratched together a living giving occasional lectures and readings but could only send small sums to her sister and mother.[69]

As she assessed her career, Dickinson still had reason to feel optimistic. In the decade and a half since the Civil War she had ridden the wave of postwar celebrity, enjoying the newly created trappings of fame that had emerged since the first wartime photographers had competed to sell her image. Dickinson's transition from the platform to the stage coincided with an explosion in collectible photographs of leading actors and actresses, and a transition in popularity from the small *cartes de visite* to larger "cabinet cards." Both Napoleon Sarony and Jose Maria Mora—two of the leading postwar theatrical photographers—produced images depicting Dickinson in costume and in various gowns.[70] For the photographers and album makers, the new postwar celebrities—lecturers, actors, politicians, war heroes—became a source of income. For the consuming public, the images produced a bond between the fan and the famous. For Dickinson and her peers these mass-produced photographs became a mechanism for underscoring and enhancing fame. Meanwhile, other entrepreneurs discovered new ways to capitalize on her celebrity and image. One company produced an elegant picture of Dickinson in a thick "milk glass"; another sold a walking cane with Dickinson's image carved into the head.[71] Dickinson's image also proved a popular advertising tool. At least two firms produced small advertising cards featuring Dickinson's image and a blank space for local companies to insert their own message.[72]

Much like other aspects of Dickinson's public life, this commodified celebrity had reflected her own decision making, the sweep of larger forces, and the serendipity of timing. In the same way that her political passions and oratorical talents had struck just the right chord in wartime audiences, Dickinson's established national reputation and appealing features had made her a popular subject for photographic studios throughout the 1860s and 1870s. Dickinson, along with her sister, had cooperated in this construction of a marketable image, arranging sittings with photographers, selecting favorite pictures, and patiently autographing stacks of cards and photographs for enthusiastic strangers.[73] But at the same time there is no indication that she ever trained her considerable entrepreneurial talents on honing her marketed identity. Rather, she had seemed content to be swept along in the explosion of *cartes de visite*, cabinet cards, advertising cards, and the like. As the 1870s came to a close, Dickinson still enjoyed a marketable name, but it was unclear how best to profit from that celebrity.

Her fortunes seemed to turn in mid-October, when theatrical star Fanny Davenport invited her to tea. Davenport was impressed with Dickinson's writing talents and had approached her about a new historical play for the upcoming season. For several months the two had been in contact through an intermediary, theater manager C. R. Gardiner, but they had failed to settle on an arrangement, so Davenport suggested that they meet face to face. This began a fascinating relationship between two of the most powerful public women in postwar America: the Queen of the Lyceum and the nation's leading diva.[74] It was not always a smooth relationship.

Advertising Card. Many small businesses used Anna Dickinson's image to advertise their products. This particular card was for a Maine establishment selling "Flour, Teas, Coffee, Spices, &c." This and similar images were used by other small establishments across the Northeast. Undated, but probably from the late 1870s or early 1880s. Author's personal collection.

Both women came away from this early exchange with the understanding that Dickinson would produce a play for Davenport, but the precise agreement remained unclear. The following month Bernard ran across Davenport in a Cincinnati hotel. A social call quickly became an earnest negotiation, with Bernard trying to convince Davenport that a contemporary play would work better than the historical drama

Davenport had in mind. By the following January the two large egos had already started to rub each other the wrong way. Dickinson had promised a play, but declined to say exactly what sort of play, so Davenport asked for a short synopsis in advance of a formal agreement. The author found this insulting, declaring that she was willing to write a play but not a synopsis. Davenport swallowed her own pride long enough to reassure Dickinson that she meant no harm and was anxious to star in an Anna Dickinson play.[75]

That spring Dickinson once again toured the Midwest, delivering lectures and dramatic readings from *Aurelian*, while making little progress on Davenport's play. In Toledo journalist Petroleum Nasby gushed over *Aurelian*, prompting a bitter Dickinson to blame the New York press, and actor John McCullough, for her professional frustrations. But still Dickinson maintained an optimistic front to her family, admitting that she was making little money but "laying a good solid foundation . . . for next season." In a long, revealing letter from Michigan she returned to familiar themes. "I have a cruel weight to carry in the shameful lies the New York papers told about me & my work" she declared. "Luckily Aurelian is the sort of thing that it is mighty hard even for prejudice to attack."[76]

Two days later—and more than a half year after they first met—Dickinson wrote to Davenport from Chicago, following up on negotiations between Bernard and Davenport. "Certainly I will be pleased to write you a play," she confirmed with no hint of irony, "tho' you are mistaken in saying I 'promised' it absolutely." She would only produce a script for $1,500 and an additional $350 a week in royalties. Davenport thought the terms a bit steep but reluctantly agreed to them, while reminding Dickinson that she had yet to see a word of the play. Perhaps, she suggested in particularly delicate language, Dickinson could send along scenes as they were completed so that the company could begin preparations. Dickinson was confident that she would hold up her end of the bargain, but she confided in Susan that Fanny "is a great dunce" who would need extensive coaching before she could play any part Dickinson wrote.[77]

In the past Dickinson had always been able to write on a deadline, preparing fresh new lectures for each season, but she struggled with this task. She made little progress during her weeks on the road, and after she returned to New Jersey Dickinson's continued silence began to worry Davenport, who sent a series of increasingly urgent letters and telegrams, pushing for a script even while she was assembling a cast and preparing the production of a play she had yet to see. On August 16, 1880, Dickinson replied with a long, testy letter. She was behind schedule because she had been suffering from "neuralgic gout," she explained. But even with her illness, she would have finished the script had Davenport been willing to accept the modern comedy she had originally offered rather than the Russian historical drama she had been drafting. Moreover, she had come to the realization that the new play's main character should spend most scenes dressed in rags, hardly suitable for the great Fanny Davenport. With these multiple concerns in mind, Dickinson suggested two rather extraordinary adjustments to their agreement. First, would Davenport consider substituting a comedy—*A Test of Honor*—that Dickinson had already written for the promised historical play, at least until Dickinson finished the Russian drama? And second, Dickinson suggested that she could play a supporting role in both productions.[78]

Davenport was predictably angry. "I feel as though I have received a blow in the face and from the last person in the world I expected it," she wrote. The star made it clear that she had no intention of sharing the stage with another female lead. Moreover, she found both the Russian drama and *A Test of Honor* unacceptable options. What had become of the American drama Dickinson had pitched in their earlier meetings? Under the circumstances, Davenport suggested that the

Fanny Davenport. Cabinet card of the famed actress produced by Napoleon Sarony. Probably 1870s. Author's personal collection.

two should cancel their arrangement and part as friends. Dickinson—desperate for a financial success—backpedaled quickly. She had never wanted to compete with Davenport on the stage, but only be a member of the supporting company, and she was happy to yield on that point. Meanwhile, she assured Davenport that she had been at work on an American drama "day and night" and had only offered the comic farce as a stopgap. This seemed to calm the waters for a time, and the following month Dickinson delivered a new drama, entitled *An American Girl*.[79]

Like many of Dickinson's other literary efforts, *An American Girl* featured a strong, attractive female lead, a passionate love story, and a series of misunderstandings that would keep the lovers apart for much of the play. But unlike her historic dramas, this time Dickinson wrote very close to home. Kate Vivian was a beautiful, charming young woman who turned to the stage when her family faced financial ruin. In so doing she overcame the social barriers that barred women of her status from the theater. Kate quickly became a great success, despite the malevolent efforts of the evil Julian Heirdon, who was intent on ruining her reputation and her career. In the end she won the love of Alleyn Cromarty, a struggling journalist who turned out to be a secret millionaire. Apart from the wondrous love affair, the plot sounded much like how Dickinson saw her own recent life, with Heirdon a lightly disguised version of editor Whitelaw Reid. And by situating her new play in a modern setting and choosing an actress for a heroine, Dickinson gave herself ample opportunity to comment on contemporary social mores and the roles of women, and particularly the theater as a worthy profession.[80] The script pleased Davenport, who saw ample opportunity for her beauty and talents, but the veteran actress felt that it needed work. In the weeks before the play opened Davenport rewrote substantial passages, much to Dickinson's annoyance. Rather than coaching the diva on the intricacies of her play, an irate Dickinson refused to attend the rehearsals and did not even appear for the opening.[81]

*An American Girl* opened in New York on September 20, 1880. In the first two weeks the play grossed over $13,000, testimony to the combined celebrity of Davenport and Dickinson. The playwright immediately began collecting her much-anticipated $350 a week in royalty checks. Even then the women bickered, as Dickinson insisted on bank drafts rather than the personal checks that Davenport preferred to send.[82] Although Dickinson's play and Davenport's performance received generally favorable—although not effusive—notices, and both sides seemed enthusiastic enough about the product, Davenport soon concluded that it could not support Dickinson's hefty royalties.[83] In December she sent Dickinson a brisk, businesslike memo from on tour in New Orleans informing the author that she must either "throw [the play] overboard" or reduce the royalties to $200 a week. Dickinson responded with a one-sentence note, instructing Davenport to "refer to the terms of our contract." She followed this two weeks later with a telegram threatening to "attach [Davenport's] property in New York" if her royalties were not paid in full.

Not one to be intimidated, Davenport replied by wire that "per contract" she had judged the play "a pecuniary failure" and would therefore close the show. *An American Girl* closed on December 30, 1880, after 100 performances.[84]

Dickinson was furious and bent on vengeance; she immediately took steps to sue Davenport for over a thousand dollars in unpaid royalties and for the lost proceeds for the rest of the season. Davenport, every bit the fiery entrepreneur that Dickinson was, countered that she had already overpaid Dickinson since she had essentially rewritten large portions of *An American Girl*. Old friend George Warner—who had heard versions of the conflict from his theater friends—urged Dickinson to consider Davenport's side of the affair, but she would have none of it.[85] Instead, she turned to Philadelphia lawyer James Heverin, who she had learned was known for "handl[ing] dishonest people without gloves." Later, after months of inactivity, she demanded that Heverin take those gloves off, or she would seek other counsel. In December, Heverin tried to have a writ served on Davenport as she performed "Lady Macbeth" in Philadelphia, but the actress managed to escape unmolested. The following week the lawyer finally filed the paperwork, suing Davenport for $1,050 in unpaid royalties.[86]

Dickinson never received further compensation from Fanny Davenport. The case did not come to trial, but the terms of the contract certainly appeared to support the actress's claims. For Dickinson, the entire episode seemed to symbolize her growing professional disillusionment while anticipating the personal decline to come. Years on the lyceum circuit had taught Dickinson to trust her own entrepreneurial instincts, but in her dealings with Fanny Davenport she had miscalculated. The actress might well have continued to perform *An American Girl* throughout the season had the playwright agreed to the reduced royalties. Instead, Dickinson had rejected the perceived insult and now faced an uncertain future.

At the close of 1880 Dickinson's name and talents could still open doors to meetings with actors, actresses, and theater managers. Although she was very new to the craft, several of her plays—including *A Crown of Thorns, Aurelian,* and now *An American Girl*—had earned a modicum of critical praise and each had generated modest income. But by this point the disappointments and perceived slights had begun to pile up. Certainly the greatest villains in Dickinson's own personal drama were still the New York theater critics. But she was also convinced that various theater managers and agents had treated her unfairly, and she fumed at actors John McCullough and now Fanny Davenport for rejecting the products of her labors.[87]

Given her early successes in life, and the praise that friends and strangers continued to heap upon her, it was almost impossible for Dickinson to assess her own abilities in this new professional arena. In 1882—two years after *An American Girl* closed—journalist Phebe Hanaford offered a dispassionate assessment of Dickinson's career in *Daughters of America or, Women of the Century*. In this large volume celebrating the nation's public women, Hanaford ranked Dickinson second only to Mary Livermore among "women lecturers" and devoted several pages to the Philadelphian's life. Hanaford closed her portrait with a telling assessment of Dickinson's new profession: "Many regret the change from the rostrum to the boards, while some think she will add new laurels to those already won. The matter is yet undecided; but she will always be best known as a lecturer, whose oratory was marvelous, and whom the whole country delighted to honor."[88]

Whatever her true prospects, only months after Davenport closed *An American Girl*, Dickinson signed a contract with Boston theater manager John Stetson. With this new "Memorandum of Agreement" Dickinson took a risky professional step: she contracted to play the male role of "Claude Melnotte" in the popular play, *The Lady of Lyons*. The experiment would begin the following month, in April 1881, with a short run at Philadelphia's Chestnut Street Opera House, followed by four shows at Stetson's Globe Theater. Dickinson and Stetson also discussed the possibility that she might soon tackle the role of Hamlet. This time Dickinson insisted on receiving a share of the entire gross, increasing from one-quarter to one-third if the receipts exceeded $800.[89]

Dozens of women had played "breeches parts" on the American and British stage, most notably the great American actress Charlotte Cushman. In some cases, the appeal of these cross-dressing actresses reflected the novelty of women appearing in male clothing, often including close-fitting tights and tunic that revealed the female form in unfamiliar and titillating ways. But some nineteenth-century actresses, including the talented Cushman, turned to male roles largely because those were often the meatiest parts. Whatever their impulse, when female actresses donned male breeches their performances implicitly challenged cultural norms about gender identity and sexuality. In the relatively safe space of the "legitimate" stage, this handful of actresses could walk, talk, and emote as men, temporarily violating seemingly hardened categories. Cushman's cross-dressing performances also resonated with her personal life. On occasion she adopted aspects of male fashion while in public, and further away from the public's gaze she entered into a series of relationships with women.[90]

By the time Dickinson agreed to play Claude Melnotte the landscape had changed. The heyday of the breeches roles had ended by the 1870s, as audiences had grown resistant to cross-dressing women and suggestions of transgendered behavior, while the larger culture had gradually defined—and marginalized—homosexuality, and thus all hints of lesbianism were pushed further underground. But despite these shifting norms, this new departure made perfect sense for the still-popular Dickinson. Since her early days on the lyceum circuit Dickinson had been associated with her popular portrayal of Joan of Arc, the gallant French peasant girl who grew to fame dressed in man's armor. On the stage as Anne Boleyn, Dickinson had been least convincing in the tender love scenes and much more successful when the script called for rhetorical power. And when she gave public readings of *Aurelian,* audiences were impressed with her portrayal of the strong male characters. Dickinson probably approved of the political connotations of portraying male characters, but it is most likely that she embraced the notion because it promised strong parts while the novelty might attract curious audiences. Moreover, as several contemporary critics noted, by playing male roles Dickinson was consciously following in the footsteps of the great Charlotte Cushman.[91]

Shortly after signing with Stetson, Dickinson began to have second thoughts about the tight timetable. She discovered that she was slated to perform with a stage company that would arrive in Philadelphia in time for only a single dress rehearsal, and she learned that Stetson had been giving her inferior billing while emphasizing the performances of Italian star Tomasso Salvini, who would be performing on the same stage on alternate nights. Moreover, the actress who had been cast as her leading lady was taller than the diminutive Dickinson. Recognizing that it would be her reputation on the line, the temperamental star adamantly refused to perform in Philadelphia under such circumstances and warned Stetson that he was in danger of losing her Boston performances as well. The manager of Philadelphia's Chestnut Street Opera House refused to release Stetson from the contract. This put Stetson in the awkward role of intermediary, sending telegrams from Boston imploring Dickinson to do her best rather than break her contract. Finally, the day before Dickinson was slated to open in Philadelphia, a desperate Stetson telegrammed a revised schedule of rehearsals, adding that "You are losing the best chance of your life." But a stubborn Dickinson preferred to break a contract rather than risk humiliation in a poorly prepared play.[92]

Dickinson's battles with Stetson soon became public property. Stetson released damaging telegrams to the *Press,* and the theater world became engrossed with Dickinson's movements as Stetson threatened to sue for damages.[93] Boston journalist Lilian Whiting watched with growing concern. The previous July Whiting had written a very flattering portrait of Dickinson's new theatrical career, and in March the *Boston Traveller* reporter had approached Dickinson for an interview to give her perspective on her battles with the New York press. Now Whiting wrote to Dickinson as a casual acquaintance, fellow professional woman, and journalist insider. She had discussed the whole affair with Stetson and concluded that he had behaved fairly and thus it would be a public relations disaster if Dickinson were to break the contract. Worse, she added, "a public woman of all other women cannot afford to be capricious."[94] Dickinson did not take this counsel well. She sent Whiting a long, blistering letter dismissing the reporter's claims of friendship and noting that Whiting had blithely accepted Stetson's version of events without hearing her side of the story. A distraught Whiting trumped Dickinson with an even longer missive, in which she insisted that she had always had Dickinson's interests in mind.[95]

Once again Dickinson took her case directly to the public. On April 18 she addressed a long public letter to the *New York Herald*, in which she proclaimed that she would take the high ground in her battle with Stetson, refusing to air the details in the press. Prior experience had taught her that in any controversy her antagonist seemed to earn journalistic praise while she received only condemnation. This time she sought popular sympathy. She was too famous to get a fair hearing in the theater from either critics or managers, she complained, and too poor to fund her own productions on her own terms. Stetson responded in the *Tribune* with carefully worded condescension, declaring that he was "sorry for her, as well as angry at her." The following week an irate Dickinson had had enough; she released a public letter to the Philadelphia papers attacking Stetson for negotiating in bad faith and then distorting his actions in the press. The local papers confirmed the essentials of Dickinson's version, including that Stetson had indeed changed the leading lady without consulting Dickinson.[96]

The mainstream press found Dickinson's letter to the *Herald* "a very pathetic one."[97] As Whiting had feared, even if her message rang true, its power was largely lost in the hostile medium. Still, while many in the press mocked her, Dickinson also received words of encouragement. Lucy Stone, who Dickinson had not heard from in many years, sent a supportive note promising her that "you may be sure of large sympathy from your own sex." And true to her word, Stone—who edited the *Woman's Journal*—published a supportive editorial calling on "her countrywomen to aid her defence" in the spirit of "fair play." An anonymous female correspondent to the *Boston Commonwealth* agreed, arguing that women must rally to Dickinson's cause, specifically because "she was Anna Dickinson, the women's rights lecturer, the woman who wanted to vote," and thus she was bound to get poor treatment from male critics "who prefer the yielding, clinging and unquestioning women to the strong, sagacious, clear-eyed and resolute."[98]

The following month Dickinson remained on the offensive, giving a long interview to the *New York Dramatic News*. In the immediate future she expected to go on tour playing both Claude Melnotte and Hamlet. When the interviewer questioned why she—such a tiny woman—would make such choices, Dickinson patiently explained that a careful reading of *The Lady of Lyons* would reveal that Melnotte should be played as a young man, almost a boy, for much of the play. Moreover, she argued, Shakespeare intended Hamlet to be a "creature of poetry, of imagination, and of intellectual force" rather than the "big, loud butcher" too often presented on the stage. Dickinson closed the interview by appealing to her past to explain her future: "When I started as a public speaker everybody said it was ridiculous for a young girl like me to deal with the weighty matters of the nation. But when they came to hear me I soon made them forget whether I was man or woman. Now they say I cannot play men's characters. If I have the chance I will show them, just as I did in public speaking—including John Stetson of Boston."[99]

Dickinson would not have to wait long for her next opportunity to show her doubters. On July 1, 1881, she signed a contract with Charles A. Mendum for the next season. This time the star commanded a contract guaranteeing her 50 percent of the profits through the first $1,500 in revenues (after allowing $1,200 a week in expenses), rising in increments to 80 percent if the tour should exceed $4,500 a week. The plan was to rotate *Hamlet* and *The Lady of Lyons*, while perhaps experimenting with *Macbeth*. If all went according to expectations, Mendum would arrange a London opening that April. In announcing the tour, Dickinson stressed that she would offer her own distinctive readings of these male characters, and in response to earlier criticisms she insisted that with her "hair combed down over the brow" she would appear "neither effeminate nor boyish." Mendum released a statement, stressing that the crucial issue was not that a woman would be playing these male roles, but that Anna Dickinson would be doing so. The agent added that the advertising would be "modest and quiet" because " 'Miss Dickinson strongly objects to being 'circused.' "[100]

In January 1882 Dickinson, accompanied by Betty Chatfield and a personal maid, set out for two months on the road with Mendum and their touring company, playing the male leads in *Hamlet* and *Lady of Lyons*. They began in Rochester, before heading west with stops in Ohio, Nebraska, Missouri, Illinois, and Indiana. She threw herself into the part of Shakespeare's Dane, tailoring the role to fit her strengths and sensibilities, donning a distinctive purple tunic as opposed to the traditional black, and even studying fencing to ensure convincing swordplay. The trip was hard, the returns modest. In one week in February she performed seven shows and received only $226.33 after expenses. Two weeks later Dickinson's hotel bills exceeded her share of the net returns. On March 20 Dickinson debuted her *Hamlet* at Haverly's Fifth Avenue Theater in New York. In financial terms it was a complete disaster. The show closed after only nine performances, at which point Dickinson switched to *A Crown of Thorns* for several shows before leaving the city in humiliation. The low point of the tour came in New York when a nervous Dickinson, after having played Hamlet dozens of times, forgot the words to the "To be or not to be" soliloquy, forcing her to turn to the prompter for her lines. Between March 23 and March 29 the company performed eight shows and only sold $212.70 in tickets. After adjustments for expenses, Dickinson had to *pay* Mendum $800 for the week's labors. In Philadelphia sales were only slightly higher, as the company continued to run in the red. In April the troupe headed north through New York and Connecticut before bringing the disastrous tour to a close.[101]

The 1882 tour left Dickinson with absolutely no reason for optimism. In the provinces, audiences had been modest and reviews lukewarm; in the eastern cities the critics had been unforgiving and the ticket receipts an embarrassment. But although the tour was a financial disaster, the cross-dressing actress did succeed in sparking some serious discussion about Shakespeare's play, and even about the

Anna Dickinson as Hamlet. This cabinet card (roughly 4.25" × 6.5") produced by New York's theater photographer Mora, depicts Anna Dickinson in costume as Hamlet. Early 1880s. Author's personal collection.

nature of gender identity. The *Home Journal* ran a lengthy analysis of Hamlet's supposedly "feminine elements," noting that "in a certain refinement of imagination and of the nervous system . . . he has much of what is usually termed the feminine habit and condition" but his general hesitancy in the face of crisis, the *Journal* contended, was hardly the stuff of feminine nature. Others noted that Dickinson's stature and appearance led her to present a boyish Hamlet, which raised further questions about character and plot. A Scranton paper declared that "Anna Dickinson is a woman of ideas," and—like it or not—her portrayal of the character's feminine traits matched her own distinctive vision of the Bard's design. Even the newspapers that were unrelentingly negative generally criticized Dickinson's acting skills and conception of the character, rather than emphasizing the fact that she had strayed onto male terrain. The harshest New York critics seemed no more appalled by Dickinson's Hamlet than her Anne Boleyn.[102]

Dickinson resolved to give acting one more serious try. Within months she was making inquiries about a competent new manager for the upcoming season. After much discussion she signed with Boston's J. W. Wentworth and Percy Hunting for a fall tour, playing several roles.[103] For six weeks she played towns and small cities in West Virginia, Ohio, Michigan, and Illinois, wisely steering clear of eastern cities. From her first days on the road, Dickinson complained that the new schedule was too grueling and the managers lacked sufficient experience. By early October she was contemplating abandoning Wentworth—the "dull old fogy"—and Hunting for new management. Still, she seemed pleased with her performances and reported home that the audiences were animated, even while the receipts were limited and the touring company amateurish.[104] Clearly part of Dickinson's frustrations stemmed from her being a 40-year-old professional, who had spent the better part of the previous 20 years on the road, while her latest managers knew the theater but lacked her experience in touring. But it was also a familiar gendered story. As she explained to her mother: "I believe the man never lived who did not think he could do a thing he knows <u>nothing</u> about a deal better than any woman could suggest or could help him." This was the rub. It was bad enough that they had done a poor job of scheduling the tour, but infuriating that they refused to listen to her voice of experience. When the tour reached Detroit, Wentworth abandoned the company. Stranded and financially strapped, Dickinson became the object of charity. A small group of Detroit women, supported by actor John McCullough and sculptor Laura Kellogg, arranged for a benefit performance to help the company get back on its feet. But after two more weeks of touring, the company folded and a defeated Dickinson took refuge in Chicago.[105]

# Part III

# DECLINE AND FALL

# Chapter 8

# DECLINE AND FALL

As 1883 ended, Dickinson again found a haven in Chicago's Palmer House Hotel, short on funds, physically and emotionally drained, and with no clear direction. For five months she remained in the city that had become one of her favorite sanctuaries, while gradually depleting her limited savings by staying at one of Chicago's more luxurious hotels. As was so often the case, Dickinson devoted her energies to various schemes for earning a living. She remained convinced that there was money in playing Hamlet, if only she could find the right manager. In the meantime, she toyed with lecturing. The problem, she discovered, was that "the very best prices now are worse than the very worst used to be." As the weeks passed, she grew more desperate. "I will do what I said I never would do" she declared, " 'make bricks without straw' for the sake of money. But nobody wants to buy them." In the meantime, she sent depressing letters home complaining of neuralgia in her shoulder and general despair. "I believe I would run a gambling saloon for the sake of getting ahold of some money," she admitted.[1] Dickinson still harbored hopes that back payments from Fanny Davenport would eventually come her way, and she engaged a new lawyer who was to "jump onto" the actress whenever she came into town. But Davenport managed to escape her legal clutches with "nothing save a bad scare."[2] Faced with an array of legal concerns and in increasingly desperate financial straits, Dickinson's thoughts turned once again to Ben Butler.

Since Butler's failure to lure his quarry to Atlantic City back in 1878 the Dickinsons had followed Butler's sometimes hapless political career with amusement, sharing unflattering jokes when his name appeared in the newspapers.[3] Following a defeat in the Massachusetts gubernatorial election in 1879, Butler had written Dickinson a short note, leading her to conclude that "I presume the campaign being ended he has to look after his other defeat." "My dear, I don't <u>know</u> 'what to do,'" Susan replied "except <u>ignore</u> him as long and completely as possible." But even in their jesting Dickinson noted the huge sums that Butler had spent on campaigning, and imagined "[w]hat a lot of good & happiness <u>we</u> could get out of it."[4] Dickinson had initially responded to Butler's notes with limited pleasantries, but in 1881 she wrote to him as she prepared to do battle with Fanny Davenport. The general had responded with his typical enthusiasm, and even offered to help serve Davenport with papers when she passed through Boston.[5] From Chicago Dickinson sent Butler a creative proposition. Perhaps he could loan her a thousand dollars and then use his legal expertise to get the money out of Fanny Davenport? But Butler failed to respond, so Dickinson turned to Susan for advice, wondering "whether there is any good in any approach to the old rooster." Her problem was that she could not be sure how he really felt about her without journeying to Boston to see him face to face. Was he really as "'beaten' & 'old'" as the papers claimed, or would a "talk with the woman he has professed to adore" bring him out of his funk?[6]

Meanwhile, lecture agent Henry Slayton assembled a slate of speaking engagements for early 1884. But a series of ailments grounded her at the Palmer House for several more months. Finally, in April 1884 Dickinson hit the road for a brief midwestern tour before joining her sister and mother in Pennsylvania that spring. During her travels she managed to scrape together small amounts of money to send home, but the experience merely magnified her frustrations. "I am sick to death of being poor," she told her sister. "I think sometimes if I had any faculty of managing I would do better,—but the quality seems to have been left out of my composition."[7]

When Dickinson returned East in 1884 a chapter of her public life was nearly closed. It would be years before she would return to the road, and she would never recapture her earlier fame. With her sister and her aging mother living in modest rented rooms in West Pittston, Dickinson no longer had a home base. For several years she had stayed with Betty Chatfield, but although she remained close to Betty, Dickinson eventually tired of Mr. Chatfield's drinking (and it seems likely that he lost patience with his perpetual house guest) and she sought other arrangements. When she returned home from Chicago she stayed for several months with Susan and her mother, but by 1885 she was back to hotel living, renting rooms in New York's Victoria Hotel on Fifth Avenue. Although she was almost certainly living beyond her means and draining limited savings, Dickinson maintained the trappings of her earlier professional life.[8]

In March Susan wrote suggesting new strategies for approaching Butler. Why not, she suggested, visit Boston in order to "prospect around" about Butler's movements and then orchestrate some chance meeting on the streets? Once in contact, Anna could remind him "'gently but firmly' of what thee had done for him" over the years. This conversation, Susan suggested, would pave the way for a large request. Dickinson should ask Butler to sponsor a proposed summer in England, both for her health and her career. If their friendship and Dickinson's need were not sufficient, then the memory of his past ardor (and, by implication, the reminder that she too remembered) might do the trick.[9] Dickinson apparently followed her sister's plan, and she and Butler had a frank conversation that spring. The wealthy Bostonian promised to provide substantial financial assistance, particularly if she were to attempt a foreign tour. But by January 1886 he had grown weary, even testy, with Dickinson's persistent demands. "I fear you keep no account," the exasperated financier wrote. "You desired $1,000. I gave you two hundred sent you $500 and three hundred more." In fact, he noted, in the course of seven months he had sent her $2,500 even though the European trip had never materialized. There was no reason why she should be spending money so quickly, he insisted, and nothing in their relationship that would indicate that he should supply it.[10]

Dickinson and her sister were pursuing a delicate strategy. On the one hand, Dickinson had often turned to Butler in the spirit of friendship and charitable kindness, interwoven with talk of business arrangements that a man of Butler's sensibilities could support. But there was always another story just beneath the surface: In the past—even prior to his wife's death—Butler had acknowledged a deeper affection for the much younger Dickinson, and one that he would rather not see made public. When Butler chastised her for overspending, Dickinson responded with an angry note of her own, including comments that Butler deemed "so offensive as to make silence impossible." He scribbled back a quick, furious note enclosing $100 to meet the "wants of not a friend but of a sick woman." Apparently in her desperation Dickinson had crossed a line, accusing Butler of improprieties that he would not acknowledge.[11]

During her months in Chicago and then New York, Dickinson's circle of friends and correspondents shrunk as she gradually settled into a life of quiet obscurity. Few of the old names still wrote. Even more so than a decade before, Dickinson surrounded herself with a handful of female friends. Many of these confidants were also public women of various stripes, who seemed best prepared to understand what she had accomplished, and the obstacles she had faced. In Chicago, she spent much of her leisure time with popular British orator Emily Faithfull. When Dickinson first met Faithfull more than a decade earlier she had been unimpressed, but in Chicago the two warmed to each other, visiting frequently and exchanging amused caustic comments and rumors about other public women.[12] While at the Palmer House Dickinson had also enjoyed visits from temperance advocate Frances

Willard, although it took some time for the two to negotiate their longstanding differences about alcohol and reform.[13]

Some of these women intermingled affection with pity. Mary Livermore, one of Willard's close friends and an old Dickinson acquaintance from the war years, wrote to encourage the fading orator. "It is to many of us evident that you are not to be allowed to succeed" on the stage, Livermore commiserated. She assured the depressed Dickinson that "[y]ou are mistaken in supposing that women are hostile to you—all your old friends have mourned over your ill-luck on the stage, and rejoice at any prosperity that can come again to you." In closing, Livermore added: "I wish you could know how dear you still are to all your old friends—to <u>women</u>."[14] Dickinson was not ready to accept Livermore's kindness. She passed the letter onto her sister, with a sardonic comment: "Here . . . is a queer letter from Mary Livermore. I think one might safely say to it 'thank you for nothing.' . . . As to lectures & bureaus, I presume I will not have to go to her to learn how to make the one, or understand which is the best. . . . she doesn't amount to a row of pins one way or the other."[15] Sculptor Laura Kellogg also objected to the critics who had derailed Dickinson's theatrical career and were not "worthy of unloosing your shoes." Kellogg insisted "that every woman who I have heard speak of you is in love with you and swears eternal allegiance to your standard." Later, recalling their time together in Detroit, Kellogg wrote: "How I wish I could take you in my arms once more but I hope it will never be to kiss away tears as it was before."[16] These words of solidarity and support rang hollow to Dickinson, who was not yet ready to contemplate her celebrity as a thing of the past. In Chicago she also encountered the latest in a long string of young female orators who declared that Dickinson had been "the inspiration of her life." "It is a queer irony of fate," a discouraged Dickinson told her sister, "that makes me & has made me the 'inspiration' of so many successful movements & lives—yet dooms me to nothing but disaster & heart break in my own!"[17]

In her prime, Dickinson counted many of the nation's leading newspapermen among her close friends, but as she drifted from public notice most of those friendships seemed to wane. Dickinson's relationship with journalist Lilian Whiting was symptomatic of her changing public identity. Whiting began work on Murat Halstead's *Cincinnati Commercial* in 1879; the following year she moved East to take a position with Boston's *Evening Traveller*.[18] Whiting had not been on the job long before she contacted Dickinson with unsolicited advice on how to deal with the critics and the press. Periodically thereafter Whiting would send Dickinson effusive letters, full of flattery and suggestions for how Dickinson could further her career. For her part, Dickinson tolerated the younger woman, and on occasion they would visit with each other in Boston or New York, but to her family she described Whiting as an "unmitigated goose."[19]

Nonetheless, Whiting seemed to grasp something of Dickinson's essence. In 1884, as she contemplated a biographical sketch of Dickinson, Whiting told Susan that

"I think I can see—as I never did before—how those reformers have jarred upon your sister in ways that she could not make any one understand." As she assessed Dickinson's early career, Whiting astutely concluded that "because of her war record they wanted to absorb & appropriate her while she only flashed into unison with them at one point." The reformers could never really grasp "her imaginative powers—her color—intensity—poetry of nature." "Imagine Mrs. Stanton, or Miss Anthony, or Mrs. Stowe or even Mrs. Howe comprehending Anna Dickinson —of course they couldn't."[20] Susan shared Whiting's letter with Anna, who was unmoved by these sentiments: "I don't need defense against any insignificant fool who thinks my work in the past amounted to nothing. It is of no moment in the long run so far as <u>fame</u> is concerned, & of less than no moment so far as present work & the outcome of money are concerned,—but it is of vital import to me & mine what judgment the papers help the public make on the work on which any future for me seems to depend. She gushes over my stage doings, & my play writing & the rest of it in personal letters, & leaves the whole matter alone or utterly begs the question when she speaks to the public."[21] Whiting, like Livermore, seemed to be celebrating Dickinson as a great woman of the past, while Dickinson was more concerned about her future.

While at the Victoria in New York City, Dickinson spent nearly every day with a woman named Carol Rich, and often the pair were accompanied by a third woman they called L.L. The two first met in 1877, when—as Rich later recalled— she "fell in love . . . 'at first sight.'" Like various other women in Dickinson's past, Rich was a devoted and intimate friend, and perhaps a lover. When Dickinson traveled out of the city, Rich sent affectionate notes signed your "little beaux," or (when left alone) her "widdy woman," or simply "your 'little girl,'" and her notes often spoke fondly of kisses and embraces.[22] Dickinson's life in New York with "Caro" and "LL" was full of pleasures but also frustrations. She spent her days pursuing various professional and legal schemes, only to be "disappointed" at every turn.[23] Meanwhile, as had been the case for many years, Dickinson suffered from a variety of physical infirmities and what Carol Rich described as "anxieties within."[24]

By this point Dickinson's medical and emotional problems were probably affected by some level of alcohol abuse. Dickinson's correspondence only hints at her alcohol consumption over the years, so it is impossible to judge when it might have begun affecting her behavior and health. When she was in her twenties, Dickinson had arranged for Susan to send her cases of wine at various stops along the road. On one visit to Kansas she mentioned ordering a glass of brandy and rosewater, and in the context of discussions of Frances Willard and temperance she periodically defended the propriety of drink in moderation.[25] Dickinson, like many of her contemporaries, also drank alcoholic beverages on the advice of her doctors. Prior to seeing a Dr. Thomas in 1870, Dickinson had been drinking whiskey to assist her digestion. The doctor warned her off this remedy, suggesting instead that she drink "a good malt liquor" or "scotch ale" after consuming meat. And, recognizing that a woman of her stature might have difficulties getting ale on the road, he wrote a prescription for the cordial curaçao, which he suggested that she drink diluted. Nearly a decade later a different doctor gave Dickinson medications for a kidney ailment and instructed her to drink a glass of wine each morning, while he also advised her to halt the regular consumption of brandy, which had apparently become her habit.[26] Although the evidence is thin, it does seem that Dickinson occasionally drank socially in addition to her regular use of alcohol for medicinal purposes. For Christmas 1885 Carol Rich sent her friend a bottle of brandy. A few days later she suggested a fine cider and whiskey drink that her grocer had concocted.[27]

In June 1887 Dickinson began feeling pains in her side that became so severe she took refuge with her mother and sister in the small resort town of Honesdale, Pennsylvania, high in the Poconos.[28] For a time, it seemed that Dickinson was on death's door. Her doctor performed emergency surgery on the ailing orator; an announcement went out across the village silencing the Sunday church bells, so that she could rest quietly. The following week local churchgoers were pleased to learn that Dickinson was on the mend, and doctors declared the danger past. The precise nature of Dickinson's illness is not clear, but numerous accounts agreed that she had nearly died. One newspaper attributed her symptoms to "overwork and worry," another said that she suffered from "nervous prostration" brought on by "overwork and worry," seemingly confirming Rich's earlier concern for "anxieties within." Friends and strangers sent letters of support, demonstrating how in this exceedingly private moment, Dickinson's health was once again a matter of public discussion.[29]

It would take many months before she would recuperate fully, but in the meantime Dickinson faced serious medical bills and no source of income. As her sister lay in bed, Susan Dickinson wrote to various men from Dickinson's past, including Butler, old beau William Allison, and editor Samuel Bowles, in search of help. When Dickinson was well enough to put pen to paper, she too turned to Butler, seeking help with her medical bills as well as funding to cover a therapeutic European trip for her and her ailing mother. At first Butler seemed prepared to step in with substantial assistance, but he soon backed away from his more ambitious offers, explaining that recent financial setbacks limited his flexibility.[30] Dickinson was distraught, angry, and moved to hyperbole. Honesdale had become like a "prison house" to her, and her medical debt a "poison." "I want to get away from this place," she insisted, "& I can't get away till you take me away." And, in closing a long and poignant letter, she added her hope that "while you find more or less fault with me, that you carry me always in your heart." Dickinson's letter may have touched Butler, but it did not change his finances; he responded with a check for $500 and an offer to talk to her surgeon about the debt. When Dickinson persisted, an exasperated Butler—who was ailing himself—finally replied that he regretted "the events which have so affected you with evil but do not see they were within my power to prevent."[31]

At this point the gap between Butler and Dickinson was substantial, but not insurmountable. Butler continued to send Dickinson money, even while he balked at the much larger sums she had requested, and it was entirely possible that he would have continued supporting her as far as his finances would allow. But then, as had so often been the case, a newspaper story complicated Dickinson's life. In June 1888 the *New York Daily Graphic* ran a small piece on her recent misfortunes, including a detailed description of the "open secret" that as a younger woman she had refused proposals of marriage from both Butler and "the editor-in-chief of a prominent paper" (certainly referring to Whitelaw Reid). In a sense this was a rather commonplace occurrence for Dickinson, whose name had been linked with various suitors for years. But while the press had often been free with Dickinson's name, they usually spoke of the public men in her life only obliquely, without naming names. The stately Butler was not pleased that his name had been so openly linked with the orator and failed actress. He wrote to Dickinson, explaining that the story had embarrassed his daughter, and asking her to issue a public statement denying the rumor. If the story had bothered Butler, his request infuriated Dickinson. Why should she disavow a story that was in fact true? She had indeed refused Butler's proposals in the past. Moreover, Butler's request seemed to imply that to have his name linked to Dickinson's reflected poorly on him, his daughter, and his deceased wife. Outrage indeed. Dickinson and Butler met in person shortly thereafter, but the meeting did not go well. She refused to write the letter disavowing their past; he, in turn, refused to honor his earlier promises.[32] Dickinson and her sister were not quite ready to give up on their meal ticket, but for the time being turned to other strategies.

It had been 16 years since Anna Dickinson had spoken on the political stump. Since then her public pronouncements and private thoughts had drifted from partisan concerns. When she returned from her tour of the South, she spoke on the state of Reconstruction, but for the next decade she steered clear of partisan topics. Few of her old Republican friends remained in her world. That is not to say that Dickinson had lost all interest in politics. Every four years, she felt the pull of the presidential campaign, not so much out of a passion for a candidate but out of a love of the battle itself. But she watched as an outsider. Partially this was because she was a woman without a party. "The Republican Party read me out eight years ago," she wrote in 1880.[33]

In 1888 all this changed.[34] Only months after her angry meeting with Benjamin Butler, and barely a year after she lay near death in Honesdale, the crafty Dickinson granted an interview with *The (NY) Press* in which she spoke eloquently and expansively about party politics, calling on the Republican Party to take up "the negro question" with renewed vigor. A few days later the *Press* ran a series of letters celebrating Dickinson's return to politics, and within a few weeks the Republican papers had picked up the story. By July she was negotiating with the Republican National Committee to assist in Benjamin Harrison's bid to unseat the incumbent President Grover Cleveland.[35] In powerful testimony to Dickinson's enduring celebrity, party boss James S. Clarkson—the vice president of the Republican National Committee—offered Dickinson 20 speeches at a fee of $100 for each appearance. This written offer became the starting point for face-to-face negotiations, and Clarkson upped Dickinson's guarantees to 30 nights at $125 for a total of $3,725 plus expenses. Dickinson would later insist that Clarkson and his fellow Republicans Matthew S. Quay, the party chairman, and William W. Dudley promised to pay a bonus of $1,275—raising the total to $5,000—in the event of a Harrison victory.[36]

In September Dickinson spoke for Harrison in western New York, before heading west to Indiana and Michigan, as part of a particularly hard-fought and partisan campaign. Dickinson's own letters and subsequent recollections indicate that she dropped back into the political saddle as if she had never left, drawing enthusiastic crowds and firing rhetorical shots at new adversaries as if it were 1864 again. Drawing on her own patriotic past, she drew ties between the modern Democratic Party and the rebels of the Old South, and mining familiar veins in her postwar rhetoric she called the Republican Party the true friend of labor. She wandered from the party script in saying relatively little in support of the party's tariff plans, opting instead to focus on workers and African Americans, while criticizing the excesses of the temperance movement. And she adopted a particularly adversarial tone in attacking Cleveland with the same biting rhetoric she once used to lambaste McClellan and eviscerate Copperheads. Still, Dickinson felt confident that her manner and message had been perfectly tailored to her midwestern audiences. Her Indianapolis lecture seemed particularly like old times. While she entertained a large audience, the Democrats gathered for their own event nearby, firing a cannon and doing their best to disrupt the Republican orator. But just as she had deftly put down wartime hecklers, the quick-witted Dickinson turned the disturbance to her advantage, remarking that "all the noise of hell cannot suppress the truth."[37]

Dickinson's early reports were exuberant, and local Republican newspapers seemed to agree. In fact General and Mrs. Harrison invited Dickinson to dine with them at their home when she passed through Indianapolis.[38] But while Dickinson basked in her Midwest successes, the Democrats began firing back with more than ceremonial cannons. The *Indianapolis Sentinel* called her local speech "a coarse, vulgar, brutal, insane harangue, fill of vituperation and scurrility, and reeking with passion, malice and hatred." "The charitable view is, we think, that Anna Dickinson is insane," declared another editorial. One Republican paper reported that an offended Logansport Democrat had formally requested that Dickinson "take a little vinegar out of her address." In South Bend, Indiana the Democratic *Daily Times* turned to old wartime gender tactics in describing the female orator as short haired, dressed "like a boy," and displaying "a somewhat muscular appearance."[39]

Dickinson was distressed to discover that some eastern papers had begun picking up unflattering tales about her tour. If she was drawing crowds, they were composed disproportionately of women, some suggested. And insofar as she was reaching potential voters, they claimed that her combative style was out of synch with contemporary mores, thus alienating Republican supporters rather than bringing voters into the fold.[40] In the meantime, Dickinson soon discovered that the state political committees were more amateurish than her worst lyceum agents. Before long she was complaining of excessive travel and poor accommodations. And far more frustrating, after a handful of engagements in Indiana, she learned that her itinerary beyond a few Michigan appearances had not been set. The original plan had been to stay in the West, but in early October the party called her back East. Clarkson did his best to orchestrate matters from New York. He flattered Dickinson on her successes and assured her that the gaps and alterations in her schedule reflected poor state organization and no disrespect to her. At first Dickinson accepted these explanations, but she wondered how Clarkson intended to replace all the missed dates he had promised. Her worries grew more pronounced when she returned to New York and days passed without an assignment. Dickinson, never slow to sense a conspiracy, accused the National Committee of "trying to enforce [her] silence" and threatened to take her story to the Democratic press if her agreement was not honored.[41]

When the New York committee finally began arranging dates, a battle-weary Dickinson insisted on "large places, short distances, day travel & no Saturday nights." She wanted a New York City audience, while the state Republicans only offered engagements in places like Poughkeepsie and Auburn.[42] While state and national party officials took turns apologizing to their temperamental star, local Republicans weighed her performances. One Steuben County newspaper publisher reported that Dickinson's Bath, New York lecture was "simply terrific" as a piece of oratory, but politically "she did us harm" with her zealous "vituperation upon the Democratic party." "You want to sit down on her hard," he advised. "Tell her that she must not call Cleveland a hangman, and that she must not wave the bloody shirt quite so vigorously." But three days later the same man had concluded that upon reflection the controversial speech "did us more good than harm" by energizing local Republicans. As they had in the Midwest, Dickinson's fiery lectures charged up the Republican base while alienating local Democrats.[43] By using the combative rhetorical techniques she had perfected a generation earlier, Dickinson enjoyed some success but she was essentially out of step with contemporary political mores.[44]

A week before election day the New York state committee informed Dickinson that they had no further need of her services, forcing her to turn to neighboring New Jersey for a few final engagements.[45]

The 1888 campaign worked out well for Harrison and the Republicans, as they successfully defeated Grover Cleveland despite losing the popular election by a slim margin. That electoral college success owed much to close victories in the crucial battleground states of Indiana and New York.[46] Dickinson's own experience was more mixed. She had enjoyed large crowds, in both the Midwest and back East, but her old methods had also raised hackles in a new political climate. Whether owing to inefficiency or political calculation, the Republicans only sent Dickinson onto the stump 17 times. Still, the Committee paid her for the promised 30 engagements at the agreed-upon fee, totaling $3,750. But Clarkson and his colleagues balked when Dickinson reminded him that he had—as she recalled it—promised to pay $5,000 if the party won. They denied that there had been such a commitment, and privately they were outraged that Dickinson, who had been paid so handsomely, had the audacity to complain at all. Dickinson was unmoved. After all, $125 a night was well below her normal fees, and she was desperate for money to cover her debts and her mother's medical expenses. Within weeks Dickinson had engaged the aggressive law firm of Howell and Hummel to begin proceedings against the Republican National Committee.[47]

The next two years were tough times for Anna Dickinson. Her suit against the Republicans dragged on, dominating her thoughts and sending her into an emotional decline. She began to see various injustices melded together into a complex morass. In addition to the relatively modest unpaid fees from 1888, which amounted to little more than a thousand dollars, she claimed that the Pennsylvania Republicans still owed her for services rendered during the Civil War. Meanwhile, she stewed over the grand sacrifices she had made to stand by Horace Greeley in 1872, and the insults heaped upon her by the *Tribune*, under the leadership of Whitelaw Reid. She became convinced that Reid had been complicit in Greeley's death, as part of his grand plan to rise to power. And harkening back to the harsh reviews her acting had received from the New York critics, Gotham's press turned her case against the G.O.P. into a subject of ridicule, mocking her excessive demands and reprinting angry letters she had sent to Clarkson and his colleagues.[48]

Only months after she returned from the campaign trail Dickinson suffered what Dr. Theodore Johnson would later call a "nervous breakdown," brought on by "'neurasthenia, in conjunction with liver trouble.'" According to Johnson's courtroom testimony, during the 18 months Dickinson was under his care she exhibited "a great deal of excited talk," broken by periods of emotional quiet and despair. He further recalled that she had been in the habit of drinking whiskey to excess and grew belligerent when he refused to prescribe alcohol for her various ailments, concluding that liquor would harm her damaged liver. Finally, Johnson reported that in 1889 Dickinson was struggling through a difficult menopause. While he was not prepared to state that Dickinson had been insane when he treated her, Dr. Johnson did later testify that she exhibited symptoms that were "liable" to lead to "lunacy."[49]

That spring, with her mother failing and her sister once again in the care of specialists, Susan Dickinson cast around desperately for funds. She again wrote to several men who had been Anna's friends and admirers, including the always reliable Benjamin Butler. Butler responded with a short note, dictated to his personal secretary. "Several months ago I had an interview with Miss Dickinson on this subject," he noted. But the conditions he had offered had been "wholly repudiated" and in fact he had been "insulted" by her response. Thus, he concluded, "I shall . . . not answer any communication from you." Anna was incensed when she heard of Butler's response. She wrote a long, angry response, taking care to file a copy for future reference. Playing on the romantic letters Butler had sent 14 years earlier, Dickinson told him that she had been consulting with her friend "Lizzie"—her own alter ego created in 1875 by a lovesick Butler—who described his latest letter to Susan. This, she explained, called to mind Butler's letter of the previous June, when he had asked her to deny his alleged marriage proposals. She went on to assail him for his outrageous demands. "Lizzie," she confided, had found his request "the letter of a scoundrel" and she was perfectly willing to share a cache of his old letters with Butler's daughter or anyone else who would care to see them. Lest he be confused about the implications, she went on to quote extensively from an October 1, 1875, letter from Butler—written while his wife was still alive—that spoke frankly of his affection for "Lizzie." And, to put the pieces together more precisely, Dickinson noted that he was not merely a scoundrel for his insulting letter but because he had reneged on "voluntary" promises made to her in the past. In short, an agitated Dickinson was reminding the powerful Butler that if he persisted in refusing her financial support she might humiliate him with his own love letters.[50]

On May 12, 1889, barely a month after Susan Dickinson had appealed to Butler, Mary Dickinson died in West Pittston at the age of 90. Faced with her mother's unpaid medical bills and an ailing sister, Susan tried progressively desperate measures. In March 1890 she sent ex-Republican President Rutherford B. Hayes a long appeal. Anna, she explained, had suffered from a "total nervous breakdown from years of overwork," exacerbated by her undercompensated labors for the party in the 1888 campaign. Hayes had heard Dickinson lecture many years before, but they had never met. Still, Susan hoped that her sister's patriotic work and their sad plight might move Hayes to lend her $300. But Hayes never responded, leaving the sisters to their own devices.[51]

Mary Dickinson had been ill for years, and had long since lost much of her mental acuity, but her death was still a blow to her daughters, whose relationship with each other had always been shaped by their shared devotion to their strong-willed mother.[52] Anna had only been two and Susan 12 when their father John had died, leaving Mary Dickinson behind with almost no savings and five children to raise. When Dickinson emerged as a highly paid public speaker, these family roles became curiously distorted. With their three older brothers scattered, and none demonstrating much earning capacity, Anna and Susan had settled into an unusual division of labor. Mrs. Dickinson's youngest child spent much of her early adulthood on the road, sending large sums home, while Susan ran the Philadelphia household and tended to much of Anna's correspondence and business matters. Susan, like her sister, never married. Although for many years she seemed to accept her own role, by the 1870s—as she entered her forties—the older sister had grown anxious for outlets for her own considerable intellectual gifts and progressively worried about finances. At first she had written the occasional newspaper article or book review, but as Anna's earnings dwindled in the early 1880s, Susan had supported herself and her mother with her journalism, supplemented by only occasional checks from Anna. When their mother declined, it once again fell to Susan Dickinson to abandon her budding career and become the principal caretaker. Now that their mother had died, the two middle-aged sisters—Anna was 46 and Susan ten years older—would have to renegotiate their relationship under different terms. With brothers Samuel and Edwin long since deceased, and John living in California, no family buffers remained between these two strong personalities.

Dickinson, still under Dr. Johnson's care, channeled her energy and sorrow into her grievances against the Republican Party. Only two weeks after Mary Dickinson died, Dickinson took her case directly to new President Benjamin Harrison, explaining the details of the broken agreement and declaring that she had only agreed to campaign for him at all because of her dying mother. Harrison's representatives responded cordially, but unsupportively, passing her letter on to the National Committee where it was bound to be ignored.[53] Finding this avenue blocked, Dickinson turned to her lawsuit. In August 1889 the press reported that she had been confined to her bed in Philadelphia, but she released a statement insisting that she would soon return to the platform and even the stage. But the following February she was still too ill to proceed with the upcoming trial and instructed her lawyers to seek a postponement. That summer Dickinson left Philadelphia and joined her sister in West Pittston. She had healed enough to seek a new trial date, but she was far from fully recovered.[54] She complained of headaches and mysterious pains in her extremities; various West Pittston citizens later testified that Dickinson had the peculiar habit of asking people to pull on her fingers or stamp on her toes, apparently to relieve these pains. She also suffered from a new flareup of the pains and swelling in her side and lower back that had plagued her for several years. This time a new doctor diagnosed the problem as "enlargement of the spleen" and prescribed medications which Dickinson found "innocuous" if not particularly salutatory. As she recuperated, Dickinson settled into a strange new living situation. Whereas she had grown accustomed to urban hotels, and the companionship of close female friends, Dickinson now found herself in the small town of West Pittston, living in a modest rented house with her older sister and a Welsh maid—Martha —who had a deep loyalty to Susan Dickinson and no affection for Anna. It was bound to be an awkward time.[55]

As Dickinson would later tell it, her life in West Pittston was quiet and lonely. Whereas Susan seemed to know everyone in town, Anna was an outsider with little interest in mundane chat and small-town gossip. Dickinson would also claim that her sister had a long history of obsessive, almost pathological concern about money, which became worse as the two settled into a life of limited means. Susan, supported by Martha and the testimony of various neighbors, would paint a very different portrait. They claimed that Anna's behavior became increasingly erratic, with sudden outbursts of temper and at least one occasion when she cut Susan with a pair of scissors. Casual acquaintances from the town reported conversations in which Dickinson spoke wildly of conspiracies involving Whitelaw Reid, Ben Butler, Jay Gould, and the Republican Party. Meanwhile, the local wine dealer recalled that she habitually ordered large quantities of liquor to be delivered to her home. And several people testified to her seemingly bizarre requests to ease pains in her extremities. In short, Dickinson portrayed herself as a somewhat aloof loner, whereas those who observed the celebrity in their midst seem to have concluded that she had become an eccentric crank.[56]

While her new neighbors were dissecting her behavior at home, Dickinson's attention turned to her case against the Republicans pending before the New York State Supreme Court. In January she wrote to her old friend and ex-suitor, Republican Senator William B. Allison, urging him to use his influence prior to the trial or she would release embarrassing documents to the press. In addition to correspondence pertaining to the campaign, she claimed to have personal letters from James Clarkson that he would not wish to see in public. To her dismay, Allison declined to answer and Clarkson—perhaps coincidentally—made plans to leave the country.[57] Days after she wrote to Allison, her attorney reported that the trial date could be within the month. Dickinson threw herself into preparations, going over correspondence and documents and jotting down notes for the trial. After further delays, events took an unexpected turn on February 10, when A. H. Hummel telegrammed that there had been a change in the docket and the trial would commence within the next two days. At first Dickinson prepared to rush to New York City, but then her suspicions began to take hold. How could the trial date have changed so quickly? Somehow she concluded that her Republican adversaries had forged the telegram in order to lure her to New York for nefarious purposes. Best to stay put until she could confirm the truth.

When Dickinson failed to appear in court on February 13, her lawyer had no choice but to accept another extended postponement. Three days later, on the sixteenth, an agitated Dickinson spent several hours at the local telegraph office composing a long telegram to A. H. Hummel. Although Hummel had explained that the changed date was owing to a shift in court dockets, she remained convinced that this was evidence of evil machinations, and she insisted that he do whatever he could to return to the original trial date.[58] Following this latest disappointment, Dickinson grew anxious and suspicious. For quite some time she had been in the habit of threatening various public men with embarrassing exposure, claiming that she had letters that the likes of Butler, Reid, and Clarkson would wish to keep hidden. These boxes of letters and clippings were the trump cards she held in case all else failed. She now came to suspect that Susan and Martha were somehow conspiring to steal or tamper with her boxes of letters. She thought that she had caught Martha sneaking around, barefoot to make no sound, in the room where her boxes were stored. As she went over her files, certain key letters seemed to be missing or out of place, and others appeared to have been tampered with. As her suspicions grew, Dickinson thought she detected strange crystals at the bottom of her coffee cup, leading her to conclude that her sister aimed to drug her. She decided that the wisest strategy would be to sequester herself in her own room, organizing her clippings and letters, until the court date arrived and she could abandon West Pittston for good. When Dickinson refused to come downstairs, even for meals, Susan and Martha took to bringing trays up to her room. Dickinson picked over these with care, checking for signs of tampering.

On February 23, exactly a week after Dickinson's anxious visit to the telegraph office, Susan and Martha tried to enter Dickinson's rooms to collect the used food trays. Some sort of violent altercation ensued, and the two women retreated in haste. At this point Susan Dickinson concluded that her sister needed further medical help. She approached John Courtright the borough's director of the poor, and the two prepared a plan for moving Anna to the state asylum for the insane at Danville. On February 25 Dr. John Heilman knocked on Dickinson's door. Dickinson knew Heilman from previous visits, but she had not been treated by him recently, nor had she called for him. She refused to open the door, and when he asked if she needed any assistance she insisted that she was perfectly fine. At that point, the door was forced inward and seven people stormed into the room. Dr. Heilman was accompanied by Courtright, in his capacity as overseer of the poor; Dr. Gideon Underwood, of the Luzerne County home for the poor; George B. Thompson, the Dickinsons' landlord; Henry Bryden and Allan Eggleston, two men from the community; and Mrs. Griffith, an elderly neighbor. Susan Dickinson was nowhere to be seen.

From this point onward, each of the actors in the day's drama behaved precisely as one would expect, given their roles as they understood them. Dickinson responded like a perfectly sane middle-aged woman who was suddenly faced with a gang of kidnappers. She challenged their authority; she refused to cooperate; when it became apparent that she was helpless against their numbers, she demanded the right to dress properly, secluded from the prying eyes of these hostile men. The invaders—both the professional men and the good-hearted neighbors—saw a wild-eyed woman living surrounded by the accumulated squalor of a week's seclusion. They ignored what she had to say, wrapped her in a cloak, and hustled her—bodily—out of the house and into a waiting carriage. Dickinson fought as best she could; and they restrained the tiny woman as gently as possible. They took her to the local train station, where she demanded the opportunity to send telegrams to her brother and her lawyers. But she had already made the transition from citizen to mad woman, and the teller and conductor both refused her desperate pleas. By prior arrangement, the train made an unscheduled stop at the State Hospital for the Insane at Danville. There Doctors Heilman and Underwood signed the appropriate papers to have Dickinson committed. Later, when they discovered that Heilman was technically unable to sign such a legal document, local physician Dr. James Oglesby stepped in to execute the proper certificate, although he had never treated the patient.[59]

From that day forward, Susan and Anna Dickinson never again spoke; they only saw each other face to face across a variety of courtrooms. Meanwhile, Dickinson's private humiliation quickly became a public event. The local press picked up the story within 24 hours. On February 27 the New York headlines read: "Anna Dickinson Insane."[60] Within days Dickinson had gone from the feisty, combative, sometimes brilliant, often arrogant, always interesting public figure she had been for nearly 30 years, to an object of speculation, pity, and charity. Within less than a month various friends and celebrities had taken steps to raise money for her support. It is hard to know which humiliation cut the deepest. For the next 30 years Dickinson would devote much of her limited public life to a series of increasing desperate attempts to sever the word "insane" from her name and legacy.

Dickinson remained at Danville for five weeks and a day. Dr. S. S. Schultz, the asylum's head physician, signed off on Dickinson's condition upon her arrival, describing his new patient as suffering from "mania, and with respect to bodily health and condition, impaired." Hardly a docile person in the best of circumstances, an agitated Dickinson gave her new caretakers ample reason to doubt her stability. She declined to speak when questioned and initially refused food and water; she resisted attempts to bathe her, demanding her accustomed privacy; and she spent her time scribbling furtive notes on scraps of paper, in hopes that she could smuggle them to potential liberators. Even while those who monitored the celebrated patient's behavior saw evidence that she was insane, Dickinson still managed to win friends and supporters among the nursing staff and her fellow patients. Eventually these bonds would serve her in good stead. But for the time being she felt abandoned and alone.

After several weeks of isolation from the outside world, Dickinson discovered a posted notice explaining that each patient had the right to mail one letter each month. She immediately combined two letters into a single packet and insisted that they be mailed. The first she addressed to the State Board of Charities in Philadelphia, demanding a formal medical examination. With that note she enclosed a long letter to her lawyers, Howe and Hummel. To Dickinson's great surprise, the Board of Charity's Dr. Henry M. Wetherhill—accompanied by a lawyer—came to see her in the asylum on March 18, shortly after receiving her letter. Their quick visit caught Dickinson unprepared and she was too suspicious to speak freely with the doctor, particularly in the presence of a lawyer. Perturbed that Dickinson had requested his attention and then refused to speak, Wetherhill came away convinced that the middle-aged woman was insane.[61]

While these small dramas unfolded behind the walls of Danville's State Asylum, a much more public drama was acted out in the nation's newspapers. Two days after Dickinson arrived in Danville, Susan Dickinson issued a statement through the Associated Press explaining that Anna was not insane, but merely suffering from insomnia and overwork. The statement circulated widely, but it was accompanied by reports of a crazed Dickinson wielding a butcher's knife, abusing drugs, and generally betraying symptoms beyond simple sleeplessness. One reporter journeyed to Danville, where Dr. Schultz characterized Dickinson as "sullen and resentful" and generally uncooperative. The public story was clear. Anna Dickinson, worn out by years of overwork and strain, had reached a breaking point, leaving her loving but impoverished sister with no choice but to place her in a public institution.[62] The fact that the Dickinson sisters had become destitute soon became a central piece of this tale. On March 8 journalist Laura C. Holloway Langford sent a public letter to the New York Times announcing a new fund to assist Dickinson, in recognition of both her immense "public services" and her noble "private character." Langford hoped that her appeal would generate $20,000. A few weeks later the media-savvy Susan gave an interview about her sister's deteriorated mental health. Susan claimed to have nothing to do with the fundraising efforts, but she approved of their goals and noted that if destitute wives of Civil War heroes were deserving of public munificence, the nation surely owed Anna Dickinson similar consideration. By early April, Dickinson's supporters had announced a broader fund, under the auspices of Philadelphia financier A. J. Drexel, "for the aid of destitute women who have rendered public service," starting with Anna Dickinson. The plan included separate fundraising efforts in a variety of urban centers. Susan B. Anthony herself volunteered to orchestrate the effort in the nation's capital. Anna Dickinson was officially the object of public charity.[63]

On April 2 a serendipitous turn of events changed the direction of Dickinson's story. Susan Dickinson had hoped that the charitable funds would enable her sister to move to a more appealing private institution. Dr. Frederick W. Seward's large, rambling home in Goshen, New York—which he called "Interpines"—seemed like just the solution. On the second Dr. Seward visited Dickinson and arranged to take her back with him to Goshen. Seward, an accomplished homeopathic physician and the nephew of famed Republican William Seward, spent the next several days in extended conversation with his new patient and soon came to a startling conclusion: in his view Dickinson was perfectly sane.[64] The transformation was remarkable. One moment Dickinson had been in despair. Her worst fear was that she would be shuttled off to a private asylum and never heard from again.[65] But in the sympathetic Frederick Seward she had an advocate who believed her story and who had the credentials and authority to support her case. Seward concluded that Dickinson needed an extended rest, but before she attended to her physical health Dickinson insisted on starting on the path toward rehabilitating her name. A week after the two left Danville, Dickinson and Seward journeyed together to New York City where she launched her counteroffensive.

While in New York, Dickinson met with her lawyers in the Astor Hotel, and she agreed to an extended interview with a reporter from the *New York Herald*. The *Herald*'s story spanned six columns on April 10, largely told in Dickinson's own words. Finally given the chance to tell her own story, Dickinson took the opportunity to contest many of the small details that had found their way into the press and to offer her own version of several episodes that had been used to illustrate her insanity. Developing an argument that she would return to over the next several years, Dickinson revealed that "for many years my sister Susan has been a monomaniac on the subject of money." Faced with Anna's reduced earnings and the specter of an impoverished future, Susan had grown erratic and hostile. Meanwhile, Dickinson claimed, her sister had constructed some murky schemes involving the sensitive letters to Dickinson from various public men. Although she did not claim to know all the details behind the plan, Dickinson wove a compelling tale explaining how her incarceration was not a result of her own insanity but the product of sinister forces intent upon silencing her and stealing her correspondence. The *Herald* included a short statement from Dr. Seward, declaring that "Miss Dickinson is perfectly sane . . . that I can assure you. I have studied her case attentively and believe there is nothing the matter with her." The press quickly picked up this startling story, paying particular attention to Seward's testimony and the titillating hints of powerful men whose reputations might be compromised by Dickinson's claims.[66]

For decades Susan Dickinson had used her contacts in the press to promote and protect her sister's public reputation. Now she used those considerable talents to defend her own name. She issued a long statement expanding her side of the story, and she arranged for her lawyer to send Dr. Seward a telegram—also published— threatening him with libel. Susan also denied that she had any control over the funds raised for her sister. To support that point, Frances Willard, who had played a major role in creating the original fund, issued a statement from Chicago offering her complete confidence in Susan Dickinson. The following week the press reported that Susan Dickinson lay "dangerously ill" in a Pittston hotel, struck down by the "constant worry and strain" about her younger sister.[67]

Following her brief trip to New York City, Dickinson returned to Interpines where she settled in and prepared her next step. With lines of communication now open, friends and strangers wrote or visited Goshen, offering words of concern and support. Old friend Ellen Everett asked for permission to assemble a discreet new fund to help cover Dickinson's expenses, as "proof of friendship and esteem." The ever-faithful Lilian Whiting promised her support. Perhaps, she suggested, Dickinson's trials were part of a divine plan to shed light on the criminal abuses within insane asylums. This notion struck a chord with Dickinson. With the *New York Gazette*'s Charles MacGeacy serving as her agent, Dickinson prepared to return to the platform.[68]

On April 25, Dickinson walked onto the stage at New York's Broadway Theater to lecture on "Personal Liberty." Perhaps she intended to speak on the larger social and political issues surrounding insanity and state asylums, but she instead turned the lecture into a highly personal, rambling attack on a wide range of enemies and injustices. Her core narrative concerned the 1888 campaign and the duplicity of the Republican operatives who had belittled her contributions and reneged on their promises. But this time Dickinson ventured onto more sensitive terrain, accusing a series of public men of various improprieties. Whitelaw Reid, Benjamin Butler, James S. Clarkson, and Postmaster General John Wanamaker all became targets of Dickinson's ire. The reporters who were present spoke gingerly of Dickinson's tirade. They noted that several ladies in the audience walked out rather than endure her scandalous talk, but the published reports declined to repeat what they deemed to be the most offensive details. One report did quote Dickinson's comments on Butler. " 'Yes, Mr. Butler has written me letters,' she explained, 'and they were addressed to Lizzie. He is the only man who has ever addressed me by my middle name. He knew what he was doing, but he will answer for it in a court of law.' " Judging from her later court testimony, Dickinson also probably claimed that Reid had turned on her after she had refused his offer of marriage.

The press took Dickinson's scandalous and nearly incoherent presentation as evidence that she had indeed lost her mind. But Dickinson and Seward did not back off. Seward claimed that the press had twisted their accounts to paint his patient in an unfavorable light. Moreover, he told reporters, it was perfectly true that "several prominent men had tried to make Dickinson wife or mistress" and "she had the documents to prove it." Dr. Seward must have felt privately conflicted about his patient's performance. He was confident that Dickinson's charges were largely true. In the case of her claims against Butler, the general's own letters confirmed what Dickinson had described. Yet if her goal had been to repair a damaged reputation, the Broadway lecture was an abject failure. Even if her charges had been accurate, the press ridiculed them as unbelievable and wildly inappropriate. Worse, her manner had provoked more pity than praise, leading Seward privately to conclude that the nervous Dickinson had consumed too much whiskey before taking the platform. Still, for better or for worse the doctor had hitched his wagon to this star.[69]

Dickinson next gave an interview, published with the headline "Anna Dickinson Justifies Her Talk," in which she reiterated that she possessed private letters by Republican J. S. Clarkson "which his wife would not like to see," "love letters from General Butler," and various other evidence of misdeeds by leading Republicans. And she added, ominously, that "these men knew that I had letters affecting them, and I was sorting these letters when my door was burst open and I was carried away." "I am not ashamed of my speech," she declared, "I am ashamed of the men who compelled me to make it." The reporter found Dickinson deeply embittered, but not ranting or seemingly insane.[70] The following week Dickinson sallied forth again, this time speaking at New York's Hermann's Theater. Dressed in red velvet and white silk, and sporting several diamond rings to counter the charge that she was a pauper, Dickinson asked "Are you ready for your own incarceration in an asylum?" As she had hundreds of times in the past, Dickinson tried to involve her audience in a tragic, poignant tale, before using that anecdote to illuminate larger social evils. But much like her unsuccessful attack on New York's theater critics 14 years before, Dickinson found it impossible to play the simultaneous roles of victim and advocate. It was a tearful performance, full of pathos and free of the earlier explicit attacks on public men, but it failed to attract much public attention or praise.[71]

Following this second New York City appearance, Dickinson returned to Goshen and Interpines, where she settled into a quiet life as something between patient and houseguest. During the day she was free to roam the streets of the sleepy village. In the evening the residents and staff dined together as an extended family. Before long "Miss D"—as they came to call her—and Sallie Ackley, Interpines' housekeeper, had become inseparable, enjoying long drives and intimate chats. Mrs. Ackley and her husband George, who did odd jobs around the grounds, were long-term Goshen residents who had invested their own funds in Interpines when Seward opened the institution in 1890. In the evenings the Ackleys would join Dickinson and Seward's young son for long hours of card playing and good company.[72] Although Dickinson was resting up, this was hardly the sort of draconian "rest cure" that Silas Weir Mitchell would prescribe for Charlotte Perkins Gilman later in the decade.[73] Free to come and go as she pleased, Dickinson—with Seward's encouragement— gradually returned to delivering lectures and readings in the Goshen vicinity. Reports of her successful recovery soon filtered out to the national press. "The people of Goshen say that if she is insane they hope it will prove contagious," chuckled the New York Herald.[74] In August the Goshen Independent Republican sent a reporter to visit Interpines, where he found Dickinson to be perfectly happy, lucid, and charming. The reporter also interviewed Dr. Seward, who reiterated his conviction that the orator had been sane all along.[75]

Although he had yet to share his full thoughts with the media, at some point Seward concluded that while Dickinson was not insane, she had been suffering from "alcoholic mania" in February 1891. Perhaps this had not been apparent when he picked Dickinson up from Danvers, but after a few months in Goshen Seward observed that Dickinson and Sallie Ackley were in the habit of drinking together late into the evening. Roles that had been intentionally blurred in the hospitable Interpines now became hopelessly muddled. It is impossible to know whether Dickinson's alcohol consumption had in fact crossed some line from social drinking to true alcohol abuse, but clearly for Dr. Seward it was intolerable for one of his employees to be drinking with a patient whom he believed had suffered from alcohol abuse. In early 1892 the issue came to a head, and the Ackleys severed their ties with Seward and moved out of Interpines. Dickinson sided with the Ackleys and abandoned her comfortable refuge when they left.[76]

# Chapter 9

# A REPUTATION
# DEFENDED

E VEN before Dickinson left Interpines, she had already begun her campaign to repair her reputation and resurrect her public career. For the next five or six years Dickinson devoted her energies to a series of legal battles. She hoped that these trials would both restore her good name and win her financial reward. Each battle had its own complex strategies, delays, and frustrations, and over the years she worked with a variety of lawyers. In the end she would win more judgments than she lost, but the biggest victories remained out of her reach.

First on Dickinson's agenda was her pending lawsuit against the Republican National Committee. In February 1891 this case had been the catalyst that seemed to push her into increasingly erratic and destructive behavior. During her initial visit to New York, Dickinson met with lawyers from Howe and Hummel to reconfirm her commitment to the suit. It was no easy task getting the case back on the court's docket. Finally, in May 1892, Dickinson's case against James Clarkson, Matt Quay, W. W. Dudley, and several other Republican defendants came before the New York Supreme Court. Dickinson appeared for her day in court decked out in black silk and a red straw hat, ready to do battle with her powerful adversaries. The trial made excellent theater, with the glamorous Dickinson crushing the popular perception that she had become a crazed madwoman, while A. H. Hummel basked in the glow of yet another high-profile case. The financial stakes were actually small. Dickinson sought a mere $1,250 in unpaid funds. That figure was certainly significant to the impoverished Dickinson, but she was equally interested in vindication. On the first day of testimony Dickinson fared quite well, twisting the Republican National Committee's attorney in knots while managing to not only tell her version of the 1888 events but to get in an extended discussion of her wartime services to the party. Although Dickinson scored quite a few points with the press, and presumably with the jury, these gains proved for naught. Judge Truax threw the entire case out, citing a little-known 1842 New York law disallowing contracts compensating any person for aiding in the election of a state or federal candidate. The decision was a disappointment, and the lost $1,250 sorely missed, but Dickinson could leave the courtroom with the knowledge that she had outperformed the opposing counsel and finally earned high marks in the press.[1]

Long before her case against the Republican National Committee came to trial, Dickinson had taken steps to punish a bigger prey: those responsible for putting her in the asylum. Here again Dickinson had multiple goals. Furious at how she had been treated, Dickinson wanted to bring her accusers to justice. She also recognized that her professional identity required that she erase the stain on her reputation. It turned out to be a complicated, often frustrating, legal journey, which saw Dickinson passed from lawyer to lawyer before she finally settled on a legal team combining the efforts of prominent New York attorney Judge A. H. Dailey and Wilkes-Barre lawyer William L. McLean.[2]

As her lawyers gradually steered Dickinson's cases through the judicial system, she also struggled to reestablish her career. In her first months in Goshen, as she was testing her legs on the local lecture circuit, she contemplated various writing projects. One concerned correspondent urged her to turn her back "on the things that annoy" and those men who had "wronged and abused" her, and instead write a series of magazine articles on education, insanity, and similar topics, with an eye toward an eventual book. Several people approached her about writing her life story or some other similarly marketable volume; others suggested journalistic projects that could capitalize on her fame.[3] In June 1892 she received $100 for a long, retrospective piece to the *New York Herald* on "Lecturing Then and Now."[4] In the meantime, she did her best to rekindle her speaking career. With the election of 1892 approaching she even offered her services to both major parties to speak on tariff reform, an offer they not surprisingly declined given her recently completed trial.[5]

Meanwhile, Dickinson turned one more time to Benjamin Butler. It had been three years since she had heard from the General, and that final exchange had been an unpleasant one. But Dickinson had endured much in the previous three years, and these were desperate times. Still, the proud woman did not approach Butler on bended knee. "I want to see or hear from you at once," she insisted. "If I do not, you will see every letter you have written to me in print within the month. This is neither blackmail, nor the letter of a mad woman—You know what was,

Anna Dickinson in later life. This photograph, which appeared in a volume on famous Americans, was probably taken in the early 1890s, when Dickinson was in her early fifties. Author's personal collection.

I am—You know what you have written about many matters. Among others you may remember a letter written while your wife was dying, it will make good food for the public's palate . . . I have endured all I am going to suffer. Enough is enough. Do you understand? I need it immediately—it will be better for both, if you come here—if not send a check. It is no moment to me if you put this in print tomorrow . . . But it will be of moment to you if I do not hear from you at once. Do you want to stand friend or foe?" The old general was not about to cave into such threats, perhaps because Dickinson had already floated these scandalous charges before a New York audience, and he appeared insulated by her new status as an insane person. When close friend Ellen Miles and her partner Phebe Hanaford followed up with their own appeal for assistance in Dickinson's name, Butler responded with a businesslike note informing them that it was "inexpedient that as matters stand that there should be any further correspondence concerning" Dickinson, "or that I should give her further aid."[6] With that, Butler closed the books on his relationship with Anna Dickinson.

On February 4, 1893, Dickinson's lawyers finally filed three separate suits against eight individuals in the United States Circuit Court in Scranton, Pennsylvania. She sought $50,000 in damages from the six men who took her from her home, an additional $50,000 from Dr. Gideon Underwood (who was named in two suits), and $25,000 more from Danville surgeon Dr. James Oglesby. Not long after filing the papers, McLean told Dickinson that he had run into the Pittston lawyers for the defendants, who warned portentously that if the case were to go forward "many things would have to be told that would be disagreeable to you." McLean replied that his client "knew all their plans and schemes" and was unafraid. Two weeks later Dailey's New York firm started proceedings against four leading New York morning papers for libel based on their reports of Dickinson's incarceration and their subsequent unflattering accounts of her public lectures in May 1891.[7]

During her entire career in public life, Dickinson had sought professional advice from a wide variety of skilled experts—authors, publishers, agents, politicians—but she had also trained her own skills and energies on these concerns, often second-guessing the services she received. As a litigant she revealed the same traits. From the time she left Danville, Dickinson had thrown herself into preparations for her various legal battles. She filled notebooks with detailed thoughts on her upcoming cases, critiquing witnesses, pointing out flaws in her opponents' stories, scratching lengthy marginal comments alongside libelous newspaper articles, and generally playing the role of an active and engaged client. As her court dates approached, Dickinson wrote to doctors, ex-Interpines and Danville inmates and employees, various public officials, and anyone who might conceivably help her cases.[8] She was also sometimes a frustrating client. Her frequent queries, and periodic lapses in contact, strained the patience of several lawyers, but in their occasional letters to each other Dickinson's lawyers consistently revealed a true affection for their difficult and penniless client.[9]

It appeared that Dickinson would have her day in court a year after she filed suit, but in March 1894 the United States Circuit Court continued her case when Drs. Underwood and Oglesby both fell ill.[10] Not until the following March would Dickinson again take the stand. In the weeks before the court date McLean met with Mrs. Jessie Winterstein, who had been one of Dickinson's attendants in Danville. Winterstein promised to be a superb witness, telling the lawyer that she had found Dickinson to be perfectly rational and "poorly treated." Later McLean deposed Dr. Oglesby, who described Dickinson as having been shabbily dressed and agitated, with a "wild" look in her eyes when he first met her. But Oglesby acknowledged that he made only the most cursory examination and that he had very little experience with mental illness. Meanwhile, McLean reported that while the official documents described Dickinson as suffering from "paranoia," at least one person said that "the problem was <u>alcoholic</u>."[11]

The case opened in the United States Circuit Court in Scranton on March 25, 1895, with Dickinson's testimony beginning on the second day. Like her performance in the trial against the Republicans, and distinctly unlike her two volatile New York lectures four years earlier, Dickinson performed marvelously. She was, according to one local reporter, "the most brilliant witness ever heard in this city." It was high drama and received extensive newspaper coverage. Dickinson, who had not laid eyes on Susan in more than four years, initially refused to acknowledge any blood relationship with her only sister. In extended testimony, Dickinson sketched her celebrated life story and her recent miseries, testifying for a spellbinding four hours before coming to the events that had brought them there. She denied some of the more outrageous claims about her behavior in 1891, and offered seemingly cogent explanations for other quirky episodes. Under cross-examination she sparred effectively with the defendants' highly paid counsel. In response to claims of alcohol abuse, she acknowledged drinking alcohol for medicinal purposes and taking therapeutic alcohol baths that she speculated might explain claims that she had smelled of drink. One of the many dramatic subplots that cropped up in Dickinson's extended cross-examination concerned her charge that Susan B. Anthony owed her $5,000 for an unpaid debt. When tracked down in Rochester, Anthony explained to reporters that Dickinson was probably confused about a note that Dickinson—along with several other leading women—had cosigned to help support the *Revolution*. Anthony assured reporters that there was no outstanding debt, and she declined to offer any opinion on Dickinson's mental health.

Following Dickinson's testimony, her lawyers called a series of witnesses, including Sallie Ackley, Jessie Winterstein, and ex-maid Louisa MacDonald, to establish that Dickinson had been perfectly sane prior to entering Danville, and that she had been horribly treated during her five weeks of incarceration. The defense countered with a long list of witnesses who testified to Dickinson's peculiar behavior in West Pittston, but their case clearly rested on the performance of her older sister. When her turn finally came, Susan Dickinson told a slightly different version of their early days and Dickinson's failed theatrical career, claiming a greater role in her sister's early career and insisting that since the early 1870s Anna had frequently depended on her for financial assistance. When her testimony turned to February 1891, Susan told a poignant tale of an unstable sister who had finally lost her reason following their mother's death. She also claimed that her sister had been using chloroform in order to sleep for nearly a year and that by the end Dickinson was consuming between a half gallon and a gallon of liquor each week. The conflicting testimony from the two sisters offered pathetic views of a private world in collapse.[12]

Susan Dickinson. Portrait from Frances E. Willard and Mary A. Livermore, eds., *A Woman of the Century* (1893; New York: Gordon Press, 1975). Date and photographer unknown.

The trial lasted through the first week in April. In purely legal terms, Dickinson did not have much of a case. The defendants who carried her off to Danville almost certainly proceeded on the honest understanding that they were acting for the best, accepting the word of Susan Dickinson. The doctors who signed the commitment papers may have acted hastily, but probably not illegally, and the most culpable physician had already died. Susan Dickinson had not been named in any of the suits, but the trial really came down to which sister the jury would believe. And in the end the 12 jurors could not agree. On April 10—following a day of debate—Judge Marcus Wilson Acheson convened the court and declared a hung jury, explaining that further deliberations were impossible because the wife of a juror had just died. By the end of the day the press had learned that Dickinson had won over eight of the jurors, providing her with a modicum of vindication if no monetary compensation.[13] Two days later she received a long letter from M. J. McMahon, a grocer who had served on the jury. McMahon, speaking for the other seven supportive jurors, offered words of "kindly feeling and sympathy" and complete disgust with "those 4 miserable rats" who had blocked the forces of justice. He claimed that one of "those contemptible scoundrels" had been a "particular friend of Dr. Underwood," while another had been seen talking with an opposing counsel "in violation of his oath." All eight, he promised, were ready to serve her in any way they could.[14]

Perhaps spurred on by these words, and aware that her libel suit probably depended on a victory in the damage case, Dickinson vowed to press on. Unfortunately, ill health and unsupportive partners forced Judge Dailey to step down from her legal team. Dickinson turned to William McLean for direction. McLean agreed to pursue a retrial, but in the meantime he urged Dickinson to return to the platform. "Certainly the trial of last spring has broken through some of the wall built between me & my public," she acknowledged, "but nothing but the entire truth will destroy it." Moreover, having devoted many years to a host of progressive causes, Dickinson now worried that she was too conservative for current "'fads'" and "somewhat at a loss to determine a theme," particularly since she had burned her partisan political bridges. Instead Dickinson spent much of that winter on preparations for the next round of trials. In February Dailey arranged for Julius M. Ferguson, Esq., a New York City lawyer, to take over Dickinson's case, only weeks before the scheduled March 23 trial date.[15] But shortly before that date Susan Dickinson fell on some ice and broke her wrist, forcing the judge to postpone the retrial. A few days later an exhausted McLean abandoned Dickinson's legal team, having earned nothing from his labors.[16]

Almost precisely a year later, in March 1897, United States Circuit Court Judge Acheson finally called the case to order, with Julius Ferguson representing the plaintiff. Dickinson, along with Winterstein and Ackley, testified much as she had in the first trial, but now the orator was two years further removed from the asylum and that much more persuasive as a thoroughly sane victim. This time Judge Acheson left little room for jury discretion. In his charge to the jury, the Circuit Court judge offered a summary of the evidence and the issues tilted heavily in favor of the defendants. All the jury had to do was conclude that Dickinson had been mentally deranged on the day in question, and the judge made it clear that he felt that had certainly been the case. Nonetheless, the men of this new jury again offered Dickinson a modicum of vindication. They voted unanimously that Thompson, Eggleston, Heilman, Underwood, and Bryden were all guilty of "unwarranted incarceration" in the case, but they granted Dickinson a mere 6¼ cents as a symbolic judgment.[17] The decision was a financial disappointment, but Dickinson chose to see it as a victory. She wrote to all the jurors, praising one for "the clear judgment . . . that turned a monstrous scheme of defeat to a magnificent triumph." The jury, she concluded, had opted to give her no damages for fear that the unconscionably biased Judge Acheson would throw out any other verdict. And, in eloquent testimony to Dickinson's enduring charisma, not only did Dickinson hear from most of the latest jurors, but several of the men from two years earlier also wrote to congratulate her.[18]

Fresh from the Scranton case, Dickinson and Ferguson shifted their attentions to the libel suits against the New York press. Once again, Dickinson filled notebooks with observations. Whereas she had cast Susan as the central villain in the damage suits, Whitelaw Reid played that role in the new cases. She transcribed long passages from books and articles dealing with Reid's career, and jotted down cryptic comments about the journalist's malevolent doings.[19] Whereas the earlier trials concentrated on the events of February 1891, Dickinson's libel cases emphasized their accounts of her behavior after she escaped Danville and spoke in New York. In late February 1898 the State Supreme Court in New York City began hearing Dickinson's case against the *World*. Much of the trial was taken up with the court stenographer reading aloud the testimony from the earlier trials, after which Dickinson took the stand for a day. The defense attorney declined to cross-examine Dickinson, dismissively acknowledging that she seemed to believe her own story. This proved a poor strategy, as the jury awarded Dickinson $1,250 in damages.[20]

In her suit against the *New York Press*, the trial for which the records are most complete, the libel charges concerned three newspaper articles, published on April 11, April 27, and May 4, 1891. The jury heard several weeks of testimony, read transcripts from the Pennsylvania trials, and inspected stories published by the *Press* and other city newspapers. But once again the case came down to Dickinson's own testimony. In Scranton, Dickinson had twice spun her life story for the jury, culminating with the Republicans' duplicity in 1888 and Susan's disloyalty three years later. In this latest testimony Dickinson took as her script the lecture she had delivered at the Broadway Theater. Whereas in April 1891 she was agitated from her recent stay in the asylum and probably suffering the ill effects of drink, from the witness stand the eloquent orator was in complete command of her narrative and her audience.

She began her story not during the war, or even during her halcyon days on the lyceum circuit, but in November 1872 when Whitelaw Reid beckoned her into the *Tribune* offices to meet with Horace Greeley. In what would be their final meeting, the editor expressed his profound gratitude to Dickinson for her sacrifices during his failed presidential campaign and promised his paper's uncompromising support in her future endeavors. Soon Greeley would be dead, in what Dickinson implied were mysterious circumstances, and Reid—her old friend and one-time suitor—rose to power. As she spun her tale it was as if two decades of travails dated to that moment, and Greeley's broken promise. She moved seamlessly from 1872 to 1888, and the injustices she endured at the hands of the Republicans. Among

Clarkson's broken promises was an agreement that the National Committee would protect her from Whitelaw Reid and "the ill-will of the *Tribune.*" She recounted how the *Tribune,* through the powerful hand of theater critic William Winter, had undermined her acting career, and how she had tried to fight back against those injustices to no avail. As her lawyer led her through her notorious lecture, Dickinson praised various public men, excoriated others, and insisted that, while her comments had been biting, she had "never said conspiracy" or betrayed paranoia.

Finally the testimony turned to her charges of immoral conduct by various public men. Dickinson acknowledged speaking of Clarkson's letters, but denied accounts that she had claimed his letters—if seen by his wife—"would make a domestic tempest." On her relationship with Reid, Dickinson spoke much more freely. Her wild accusations against Reid from the Broadway Theater stage had been at the heart of the published accounts that she had been a ranting madwoman, and thus her defense turned on convincing the jury that she had spoken the truth. Her story began back during the war, when Reid was "a poor scribe" who made a name for himself by praising her speech in the House of Representatives. In subsequent years, Reid— through "a fine scheme of advertising"—managed to have his name romantically linked in the press with the heralded young orator, thus riding her fame to greater notoriety. In fact, Dickinson revealed, Reid suffered from disease he had inherited "from the tainted blood of his father and the epileptic blood of his mother," forcing him to take poisonous medications "to make a man of himself." Teary eyed, she had told the New York audience humiliating stories—recounted to her by several public men—of how a jocular Whitelaw Reid would regale his buddies with bawdy claims that whenever Anna Dickinson was in town his size 17 shoes could be found outside of her hotel room. These tales were, she declared, not merely abominable lies, but beyond the physical capabilities of the epileptic Reid. The newspapers had claimed that many scandalized audience members walked out at these revelations, but Dickinson recalled instead that they stood to applaud her courage. Dickinson went on to offer a brief account of her Hermann's Theater appearance the following week, emphasizing that in this second lecture she criticized the journalists in attendance for distorting her previous performance and urged them to treat her fairly this time. Rather than heeding her words the gentlemen of the press belittled her talk as the continued ravings of a madwoman. The time had finally come, she told the jury, for justice to be done.

Justice Beckstaver instructed the jury to base its findings on Dickinson's mental stability as she was in early 1891, not her condition as they observed her seven years later, but no expert testimony or yellowed newspaper clippings could convince them that the clear-eyed, quick-witted woman who sat soberly before them was the same deranged madwoman of these old accounts. The jury found against the *Press* and awarded Dickinson $2,750 on May 10, 1898. Of the other two libel cases, surprisingly little is known. Dickinson apparently lost one case and the last suit seems never to have come to trial.[21] Whereas her earlier trials had been the subject of extensive newspaper coverage, these final public acts received only limited attention from the press; the New York newspapers adhered to a strict policy of not publishing news concerning libel suits against any of their number.[22]

What should one take from the stormy chapters in Anna Dickinson's life, beginning in 1891 and culminating with the libel suits seven years later? The courts certainly heard diverging versions of the events of February 1891, often pitting one sister against the other, but many portions of that narrative are fairly clear. During the winter of 1890–91 Dickinson had been physically worn down, emotionally drained, and in serious financial distress. Her behavior had grown erratic, and she was almost certainly experiencing the physical and emotional effects of alcohol abuse. As Frances Willard would attest, it is hard to cast Susan Dickinson in the villain's role in the drama, as much as her embittered sister swore it was so. Still, Susan was far from a passive observer or disinterested party. Over the years she had periodically revealed jealousy at Anna's celebrity, concern for her sister's contentious and occasionally profligate ways, and persistent worry about their financial future. When she took the witness stand the long-suffering Susan cut a sympathetic figure, but sometimes at the expense of the truth. She exaggerated her role in Dickinson's early career, testifying incorrectly that she had traveled with her younger sister on the road during the early days, and claiming—again untruthfully—that Anna had been entirely dependent on her earnings as a journalist since the early 1880s. When she discussed Dickinson's relationships with public men, she adopted a cautious strategy peppered with half truths. She acknowledged that Reid had been upset with her sister at some point, but said that she had never claimed there was a conspiracy. In fact, she had pointedly accused Reid of mistreating her sister in his newspaper. Susan told the court that Ben Butler had provided modest financial assistance as thanks for Dickinson's support of his wartime actions in New Orleans. She may have chosen that path out of a concern for her family's reputation, but the fact remains that she had actively schemed with her sister about how best to parlay Butler's affections into financial gains, and when called to testify she dishonestly contradicted Anna's allegations.[23]

These inconsistencies aside, Susan's testimony—supported by various loyal townspeople—still suggests that in February Dickinson's behavior had grown peculiar, but she was probably not a danger to herself or others. They told of only one minor violent episode, in which Dickinson either accidentally or intentionally cut her sister's finger with a pair of sewing shears. But it is also true that Dickinson sequestered herself in her room for several days, refusing food. Dickinson herself acknowledged that she suspected that her sister was trying to poison her, hardly the behavior of a perfectly sound mind.

Why had Susan Dickinson acted so aggressively in orchestrating Anna's commitment? Was she worried about what Dickinson might do or say at her pending suit against the Republican National Committee? Dickinson suspected that her sister had some ulterior motives, either to stop her from testifying against the party or to silence her before she revealed embarrassing stories about various public men. Her claims that her sister and maid were conspiring to steal her letters smacks of paranoid delusions, but Dickinson really did have letters from major figures like Butler and Reid that would have been awkward had they appeared in public. Nothing in the written record can confirm such suspicions.[24] Even Dickinson did not claim to know precisely what Susan had in mind. In her notes to her lawyer, Dickinson guessed that Susan's editor friend John Barrett, who was a part owner in the *Scranton Republican*, might have had a hand in the plot. "If there is anything in what was reported of the letters he probably thought to make some barter with W. Reid," she speculated. She believed that Barrett had certain letters in his safe, and that Susan "proposed to make money in some way out of them. It was <u>money</u> from first to last, & <u>destruction</u> for me."[25]

It is also possible that Dickinson's suspicions were imaginative delusions containing a kernel of truth. Perhaps Susan Dickinson had sought to remove or tamper with her sister's letters at the behest of these men. Even if Susan had no interest in silencing her sister, she may have acted out of financial practicality, as well as sisterly love. Anna had mounting medical bills and no expectations of future earnings. Worse, it was impossible to predict what Anna might do—or spend—when she went to New York. By arranging to have her sister committed, Susan ensured that Anna would be cared for at the public expense while blocking any future losses. Moreover, once Dickinson became a ward of the state, Susan had an ideal opportunity to raise funds, capitalizing on her sister's past glories and her present humiliations. Thus, by forcibly moving her sister from West Pittston to Danville, Susan Dickinson had acted to preserve her sister's financial well-being, and her own.[26]

The evidence from other witnesses is similarly mixed. The folks in West Pittston had no particular reason, beyond perhaps their loyalty to Susan Dickinson, to claim that Dickinson had behaved peculiarly. But some of those peculiarities were probably explained by her headaches and medical symptoms, and others reflected the fact that the good people of West Pittston had no experience with a woman like Anna Dickinson, and she had little interest in them. Meanwhile, those women who got to know her well stood by Dickinson throughout these trials and insisted that she was sane and unfairly treated. While several doctors who had had little personal contact with their patient testified that Dickinson was insane, Frederick Seward, who spent the most time with her, concluded that Dickinson was perfectly sane. In the 1898 libel case against the *Press*, Seward—who was no longer on good terms with Dickinson—testified that his ex-patient had suffered from "alcoholic mania," but even then he stopped short of describing her as insane.[27]

The trials themselves offer another window into Dickinson's mental health. She was sometimes a difficult client, but she was a superb advocate for her own legal interests. In her two damage suits Dickinson convinced 20 of 24 jurors that she had been wrongfully kidnapped. Then she went on to win two of three libel suits, persuading new juries that the journalists who had called her insane had behaved improperly. If Dickinson had lost control of her faculties in February 1891, she seems to have regained them by the time Dr. Seward took her off to Goshen.

Dickinson managed to present a highly competent, eloquent public face when circumstances required it. Yet those closest to her periodically saw quite a different private person. Not long after she left Interpines, Dickinson had a falling out with Sallie Ackley. In March Ackley wrote twice, expressing despair that Dickinson "no longer want[ed] [her] for a friend." For roughly a year Dickinson refused all contact with her devoted companion. She lived in New York's Fifth Avenue Hotel for a time before moving on to a less expensive boarding house on West 12th Street, under the concerned care of three women: Ellen Miles and her partner Phebe Hanaford, and their friend Phebe C. Hull.[28] All three—and particularly Miles—were devoted to Dickinson and committed to her welfare, but as was so often the case with Dickinson's friends, tensions and suspicions eventually fractured the relationships. For a year and a half Dickinson stayed with—or near—Miles and Hanaford. But that autumn yet another angry clash precipitated a new move.[29] In October she turned to actress Marion Booth Douglas to help her find a new flat, where she lived for several months. And in the spring of 1894 Dickinson apparently moved into Douglas's home for a time, breaking off all contact with Miles, Hanaford, and Hull. Later that year Dickinson stayed with friends in Mount Vernon, New York.[30] While Dickinson was moving from place to place, the Ackleys left Goshen for Middletown, New York and then they relocated to New York City, where they opened a bakery. Even while Dickinson was refusing contact with Sallie Ackley, Dickinson's close friends recognized Ackley as a valuable asset. Miles and Hull both wrote to reassure Ackley that her friend still needed her, and eventually the two mended fences. In early 1895, roughly three years after she left Interpines, Dickinson moved into the Ackleys' residence on East 50th Street.[31]

From the time she left Goshen until she was reunited with Sallie Ackley, Dickinson relied on the support of a network of devoted female friends. These women privately adopted a maternalistic attitude toward Dickinson, sometimes speaking of her almost as a child or invalid who required their intercessions and guidance to navigate her day to day life. In February 1893, Miles confided in Ackley that "the dear child needs some one to stand by her in her great time of need. And some one who loves her well enough to bear with her little peculiarities." Phebe Hull, Miles worried, "was foolishly fond of Anna" in a way that "Anna cannot reciprocate" and was bound to produce heartache. Meanwhile, Frances Willard—well aware that Dickinson had long since turned on her—wrote to Miles and Hanaford from England, inquiring after "the most eloquent woman that our country has produced" and about "your & her ideas for her future."[32]

Time and again this good will wore thin. When Dickinson broke with Miles and Hanaford, the latter told a mutual acquaintance that after a year and a half together Dickinson became so "abrupt in speech and unjust and unkind in manner . . . that I was half inclined to believe her insane, as so many have declared her to be. We have always said she was not, and we have strenuously declared that she used no liquors or drugs," Hanaford admitted. "But her behavior has been so ungrateful and unaccountable, that I am at a loss for a reason or an excuse." Miles seemed to agree, writing to Ackley that while her "love for and interest in Anna will never cease. . . . I cannot longer have her impose upon my friends. My mind is fully made up as to her mental condition. God pity her." A wounded Miles told Dickinson that "most gladly would I serve you, were it in my power. But my dear you built the barrier yourself, and you alone can crumble it in pieces." Precisely as Miles had feared, Hull proved less philosophical when disappointment struck. By December 1894, the two had clashed, and Hull sent Dickinson a crisp note promising that "some day I shall call you to account for the many stories told about me."[33]

By that point there had been all sorts of tales circulating among Dickinson's friends. Miles found it particularly galling when Dickinson turned on her in favor of women who she had previously spurned. Not long before, Miles reminded Dickinson, she had said "many unkind things" of friends Lizzie Sargent Dickinson and Marion Booth Douglas, and now she was accepting the hospitality of these past pariahs. A wounded Miles revealed that "it was so often said to me 'Anna Dickinson will turn her back on you as she does on every one else who is helpful to her,'" but she had never really believed that her time would come. "Why Anna, I have lied for you, but never of you," she insisted.[34]

While these battles raged close to home, Dickinson corresponded with a handful of other women. Most prominent among these was S. May Isom, a Professor of Elocution at the University of Mississippi. Isom and her partner Frances Tucker, an artist, met Dickinson in 1892 when they were visiting Hanaford and Miles in New York City. Isom became a devoted correspondent, writing long letters from Oxford, Mississippi, expressing her affection for Dickinson while sharing detailed stories about her often-unsettled personal relationship with Tucker. Two years later Tucker, upon hearing of Dickinson's conflicts with Hanaford and Miles, wrote commiserating about how Dickinson had "suffered by two women so greatly your inferiors who ought to have felt honored by your friendship." Before long Isom and Tucker had their own falling out, and Tucker moved to Chicago, but both stayed in touch with Dickinson. In 1896 Isom visited New York and sought out Dickinson, only to be rebuffed. "Do you know you have almost broken my heart?" she wrote. Following a now-familiar pattern a distraught Isom declared that "I cannot in any way explain your very peculiar treatment since my arrival in this city." She had been "the truest & most loyal friend that you will ever know," and Dickinson had repaid her with "cruel, heartless & altogether inexplicable treatment."[35]

It was indeed a complex world of friendships and jealousies, with all sorts of voices vying for Dickinson's attentions and affection. Whereas several decades earlier, many of Dickinson's closest friends were married couples, as she entered her fifties she lived almost exclusively in the company of other women. And while friends and family members had always worried about Dickinson's physical and emotional well-being, the comments by Miles, Hanaford, Hull, and Isom suggest that they saw their friend as suffering from diminished capacity rather than illness or exhaustion. In 1893, after she interviewed Dickinson for a magazine profile, journalist Ann Jenness Miller exchanged concerned notes with Ellen Miles about Dickinson's health and future. "The woman has done a grand work in the world," Miller added, "and has been a very good woman. If she has foibles, that is no more than the rest of us have, and she is entitled to some as an overflow of her virtues."[36]

While those in the closest proximity to Dickinson were sometimes the disillusioned victims of these foibles, Dickinson's aggressive campaign to reconstruct her public identity took other victims as well. Not long after she escaped Danville, Dickinson had gotten wind of the various fundraising efforts launched in her name. Furious at this discovery, she demanded to know who was behind these humiliating efforts. She began her investigations with Ellen Everett, who had collected a small sum from friends shortly after Dickinson moved to Interpines. Everett had some knowledge of the fund managed by A. J. Drexel, but insisted that she knew few of the details. She tried to assure Dickinson that "Miss Willard has your interest at heart" and that in her view everyone involved in the fund "wanted to help you" and they all "were very sincere in the matter."[37]

In 1895 Everett finally sent Dickinson a printed circular, dated April 2, 1891, soliciting contributions to the Drexel fund. Dickinson wrote directly to Drexel and his associates at Drexel and Company, requesting any relevant records. The Philadelphia bank acknowledged that there was indeed such a fund, with $47 still on deposit, but Dickinson suspected that other funds may have been transferred to Susan.[38] The circular letter included the names of a short list of prominent acquaintances, among them Susan B. Anthony, Frances Willard, and several leading Philadelphians. To Dickinson, this document was the smoking gun, identifying those who had publicly labeled her a "pauper lunatic." Ignoring Everett's explanations, Dickinson wrote to the named sponsors, demanding to know each person's role in "this ostensibly friendly letter," which was "in reality a criminal libel."[39] Many responded like Hon. Henry M. Blair, who told her that as best he could recall he had signed the document at the request of "Miss Willard or one of her agents . . . thinking that I was doing an act of kindness to a noble & brilliant woman."[40] The *Philadelphia Press*'s Talcott Williams claimed that he could not "recollect ever signing or authorizing the use" of his name, but Dickinson insisted that she would accept nothing short of a sworn affidavit disavowing the document.[41] Dickinson was most furious with Willard, who had once been a friend and who had, in Dickinson's hour of greatest need, cast her lot with Susan Dickinson.[42] In letter after letter, Dickinson hectored the people named on the circular, answering their seemingly gracious responses with demands for further information and legally binding retractions. Only Anthony seemed to dodge this harassment. In response to Dickinson's initial inquiry, the aging Anthony responded with true joy at seeing her old love's "pen tracks once more" after nearly a quarter century. "It don't matter if its contents do seem a bit scolding," she wrote playfully, "I'm awfully glad to know you still live." Anthony devoted the rest of her letter to reminiscing about their past together, completely ignoring any talk of a circular letter.[43]

The most poignant moments in this campaign came when Dickinson turned to Robert Purvis. For decades the Purvises had been among Philadelphia's most prominent African American families, and their patriarch one of the North's great abolitionists. Dickinson and Harriet Purvis had been childhood friends, and in 1868 she used the Purvis family as the model for the interracial family in *What Answer?* But somehow three decades had erased those memories for Dickinson, and all she could see was that Robert Purvis had attached his name to the insulting circular. She wrote to Purvis as she had the others, with a letter that combined equal parts legalistic bluster and belligerence. Harriet Purvis replied for her elderly father, telling Dickinson that Purvis was too ill to write himself, but that he had no memory of lending his name to the circular. Harriet told Anna that she and her father spoke of her often and fondly, and added that "father is <u>very</u> poorly." Dickinson did not take this hint. She wrote back to Robert Purvis, insisting that even if he was ill he could sign a dictated letter disavowing the circular. When the elderly man failed to respond, Dickinson sent testy letters to Harriet Purvis and her brother Dr. Charles Purvis, speaking of their father's "criminal libel." An annoyed Dr. Purvis finally took up the task. "I am surprised at the tone & spirit of your note," he wrote. "My father has always been a staunch friend of yours. He is old now & has lost most of his mental vigor, he is entitled to kind & gentle expressions from those who are many years younger." Shockingly, Charles's appeal to Dickinson's better nature failed to find its target. Instead, her rhetoric grew more hostile. If Purvis was indeed "a staunch friend" he would produce a legally valid affidavit, and if he failed to do so she was prepared to take him to court. Although she did not follow through on her threats, Dickinson had burned one more bridge to her happy past.[44]

Once she had made the complete transition from public figure to private citizen, Dickinson stopped leaving much of a mark on the public record. She lived with George and Sallie Ackley in New York City from 1895 until 1910, when the trio moved back to Goshen, where the Ackleys opened a confectionary shop. Even as a bystander, Dickinson maintained her passion for public life. She took several newspapers and continued her lifelong habit of clipping and saving articles on public affairs. Some of these were retrospective pieces mentioning her own past exploits, but more and more she behaved as an observer rather than a chronicler of her own life.[45]

Although she had moved to the margins of political discourse, Dickinson did her best to keep her name before the public. One option was to write her auto-biography. Throughout the 1890s Dickinson entertained occasional proposals from literary agents and publishers who felt sure that her life story would win an enthusiastic readership.[46] The problem was that the tale she wished to tell was not about a young Civil War patriot who faced down angry miners in Pennsylvania, influenced elections across the Northeast, spoke before leading politicians in Washington, and had a personal interview with Abraham Lincoln. The book she had in mind would settle old scores against people like Reid, Clarkson, Butler, and Willard. In 1897 a literary agent told her that the proposed book "has its difficulties" and no "prudent publisher would promise to publish" it. Better, he argued, to "give the world the master production of your life" rather than concentrating on these battles.[47]

With the libel trials behind her, Dickinson turned to an aggressive letter-writing campaign, aimed at punishing the government for the horrors she had endured. Her first target was Pennsylvania Governor Daniel H. Hastings, whom she called upon to "rectify the monstrous wrong" and "to expose & . . . punish the hideous crime you know has been done against me." Hastings proved politely unreceptive, passing her letters on to the state attorney general.[48] In 1901 Dickinson took her case to the United States Senate. She worked her way down a list of sitting senators, send-ing each man a long letter enumerating her trials at the hands of the government. Not only had the state regulations made it appallingly easy to toss her into the asylum, but biased judges had denied her a fair trial in the federal courts.[49] Most senators ignored this plea for justice, and those who acknowledged it did not take its author seriously. For the next seven or eight years Dickinson followed up this original mailing with dozens more letters, growing increasingly irate with the realization that she was being ignored.[50] Dickinson eventually tried yet another strategy: she turned to New York's Governor Charles Evans Hughes. Although the events of February 1891 had occurred in Pennsylvania, and were tried in federal court, she argued that as a long-term citizen of New York she had a right to the governor's intercession, through which "a giant wrong will be righted." When Governor Hughes simply passed Dickinson's letters to a secretary for a cursory response, Dickinson tried writing to Mrs. Hughes, but to no avail.[51]

It is impossible to read Dickinson's letters in the early 1900s without feeling a sense of pathos. Four decades earlier, congressmen and senators were happy to receive her letters and pleased to offer her advice or solicit her political support. And she and her sister had enjoyed exchanging caustic remarks about the peculiar strangers who sent her incoherent letters seeking her aid or counsel. Now the worm had turned, and it was Dickinson who was pestering public figures with long, rambling letters. Even if her core arguments were sound, a senator would have had every reason to conclude that the author had lost touch with reality.

Desperate for funds, Dickinson pursued every avenue at her disposal, attempting to capitalize on all accumulated resources. She approached Josiah Quincy, Henry Deming, and William Lloyd Garrison, Jr., all prominent sons of men Dickinson had known in her youth. Garrison—who recalled how during the Civil War the young orator had charmed his family—turned out to be the embodiment of gentlemanly deference, graciously answering Dickinson's queries and lending his support to several schemes, even while doing his best to extricate himself from further obligations.[52] With both her efforts at political vindication and her schemes for earning money stymied, Dickinson turned back to her proposed memoir. Ignoring all advice, she drafted a book proposal, bitterly recounting the election of 1888, Reid's misdeeds, the various failures of the press and the courts, and her disheartening campaign to find justice.[53] Hoping to find some "old time Republican" to embrace the project, Dickinson wrote to famed populist William Jennings Bryan and Toledo's reform Mayor Brand Whitlock for advice. Mary Bryan, Bryan's wife and publishing partner, responded from Nebraska with a few possible publishers, but warned that they knew of "no publisher who would be likely to publish a book because of sentiment." Whitlock steered her toward Charles Merrill, of Bobbs-Merrill, but Merrill rejected the proposal as unmarketable.[54]

Dickinson pressed on, filling notebooks with a draft of her memoir. It was a meandering manuscript, moving back and forth across time as she followed narrative threads wherever they took her. As promised, Dickinson wrote almost exclusively of those who had mistreated her, rather than of her own past successes. She devoted the bulk of her invective to Reid, Willard, and the New York press, but she also sought retribution against William Winter, actor John McCullough, Senator William Allison, and Clarkson and his Republican cronies.[55] In May 1908 she wrote to Allison, warning him that "the book of which we talked is about finished" and a publisher had been lined up. There was still time for the Republican National Committee to square its debts before the book appeared. But in fact there was no publisher, and this was little more than another attempt to shake further compensation out of the GOP.[56]

In one final effort to get her story out in her own words, Dickinson turned to Aggie Day Robinson, an old friend with connections in the publishing world. Robinson's daughter, Edith Day Robinson, was a journalist with the *New York Times* and immediately expressed interest in Dickinson and her project, The two met with Dickinson and Sallie Ackley, but once again Dickinson's suspicions scuttled the plans. Edith Robinson's editor, W. C. Reicke, had suggested publishing an interview with Dickinson, which would be an ideal way of announcing her work in progress. But Dickinson recalled that two decades earlier Reicke had worked for the hated *Tribune*, so she refused to cooperate. Robinson later told Ackley how disturbed and insulted she had been at the encounter. "I felt like crying 'What have I done?'" she wrote.[57]

As these efforts foundered, Dickinson concentrated for a time on shaping and correcting how others remembered her. In early 1910 she agreed to an interview with journalist Ida Tarbell, who was writing a brief profile on her for *American Magazine*. She followed up that meeting with several letters and clippings clarifying minor details of her early life.[58] A month after Dickinson met with Tarbell, the Associated American Press distributed an article on "Women Who Knew Lincoln," including a short discussion of her wartime career. A few days later Aggie Day Robinson sent the editor a list of corrections, probably on Dickinson's instructions.[59] But this campaign to keep her name before the public seemed bound to fail as the years rolled by. One can only imagine how Dickinson felt in August 1910, when she discovered a short letter to the editor in a local paper inquiring about her whereabouts. The editor replied that "Miss Dickinson died about ten years ago." She clipped the page, circled the story several times, and set it aside to be saved in a scrapbook.[60]

# Chapter 10

# CONCLUSION:

# MEMORIES AND LEGACIES

A NNA Dickinson was nearly 70 years old when she returned to Goshen with George and Sallie Ackley in 1910. It would be tempting to conclude that the once-famous orator settled into the life of a recluse, but more accurate to say that she lived the life of an elderly woman out of the public eye. This final chapter was not a short one. Despite the many illnesses that had plagued her earlier life, Dickinson lived for more than 20 years in Goshen before dying on October 22, 1932, less than a week before her ninetieth birthday.[1] After devoting so much of her life to supporting her family, Dickinson lived out her final years without relatives. John Dickinson—her only surviving brother—died in 1899. Susan followed in 1915. Susan sent her sister a telegram about John's death; Anna learned about Susan's passing through a newspaper story. In Dickinson's eyes, she had lost both siblings in 1891.[2] The much greater loss came in 1927, when Sallie Ackley died. At her passing, a heartbroken Dickinson stood at the top of the stairs and delivered a eulogy to her departed friend, as friends and neighbors gathered to hear the great orator deliver one final, poignant speech.[3] Mrs. Ackley left behind a curiously mismatched pair: her 74-year-old husband, George Ackley, and the 85-year-old Anna Dickinson. Uncertain how he was going to run his Goshen household, Ackley invited his two half sisters to move in with him and Dickinson. This arrangement quickly collapsed when an angry Dickinson resisted the unwanted interlopers. The two sisters soon fled, not to return until Dickinson had followed their brother's wife to the grave.[4]

Less than a decade after Dickinson's death, a young historian—James Harvey Young—journeyed to Goshen in search of clues about her life.[5] In 1941 he interviewed several people, including George Ackley, his half-sister Bertha, and Dr. Frederick W. Seward, Jr., who directed Interpines 51 years after his father opened the private asylum. Seward spoke fondly of evenings playing euchre and whist with Dickinson and the Ackleys, and he recalled the rift with his father that followed accusations of late-night drinking. In his typed notes, Young recorded that "Dr. Seward gives it as his opinion that Miss D. was abnormal. Mrs. Ackley was a vigorous individual, more 'masculine' than her husband, and Dr. Seward feels it to be highly probable that there was a strong attraction between her and Miss D." There are any number of layers to peel away here, as we imagine the two men— one quite young, the other in his seventies—chatting in 1941 about two women Seward had observed 50 years before. But setting aside their notions of sexual pathology and delicacy, it is clear that Seward believed the two women had been lovers.[6]

When Young met with George and Bertha Ackley he learned that "the Ackleys treated Miss D. as if she had been visiting royalty." She had the best room in the house; her own personal maid; clothes purchased in New York City; special foods and soaps; and breakfast in bed. For more than 30 years George Ackley shouldered these bills without complaint, and both described "Miss D" as thoroughly ungrateful. The unassuming Ackley, with a twinkle in his eye, kept saying "she was a devil." His younger sister spoke much more harshly, calling her a "witch" and worse. They agreed that Dickinson and Sallie Ackley had been constant companions. A bemused Bertha Ackley told Young "that Anna had some sort of an odd power over Mrs. A; whatever she wanted, Mrs. Ackley was willing to get." Here again, Young's interview refracted the life that Dickinson and Sallie Ackley actually led through several lenses. Both Ackleys portrayed Dickinson as almost otherworldly, reminiscent of the wartime editorials that had praised her as a heaven-sent Joan of Arc. The "odd power" that Bertha Ackley claimed Dickinson had over her sister-in-law suggests a Svengali-like figure, rather than simply a loving relationship between two devoted friends, or lovers.[7]

Sallie Ackley left an ambiguous written record. During the short period in the 1890s when she and Dickinson were separated, Ackley wrote Dickinson many short notes, including a few she signed "Cupid." These letters revealed great devotion and pain that Dickinson had spurned her. "I will not force you to see me," she wrote, "but God knows that I love you." When set alongside the correspondence from Dickinson's many worldly and erudite female friends, Ackley's notes seem like the words of a devoted, but much less articulate, admirer, and hardly an intellectual equal.[8] The occasional letters from Phebe Hull and Ellen Miles to Ackley suggest that they initially saw the one-time Interpines housekeeper as little more than a sweet woman who had been good to their friend. On the other hand, several of these women eventually concluded that Sallie Ackley was a woman to be reckoned with.[9] Even if the Goshen household revolved around Dickinson's needs and demands, it was Sallie Ackley who really controlled her husband and dictated the arrangements.

When Sallie Ackley died she left Dickinson $7,000.[10] For the next five years George continued to pay the household bills, with the understanding that Dickinson would leave him what remained upon her death. George and Bertha Ackley were convinced that Dickinson drank heavily during this period, thanks to the assistance of her maid.[11] Dealing the kindly confectioner one final humiliation, Dickinson died intestate and her modest $6,000 was earmarked for a distant cousin in New Jersey. George Ackley arranged for Dickinson to be buried in Goshen's Slate Hill Cemetery, at Sallie Ackley's feet. A small granite headstone marked the spot.[12] When Ackley died, he left instructions to be buried beside his wife of many decades, with both their names etched into an impressive headstone. Anna Dickinson lay only a few feet away.

By the time she moved to Goshen, Anna Dickinson had long since drifted from the public memory. For a woman who had devoted so much of her life to guarding her reputation, measuring her stature against the yardstick of newspaper clippings, this obscurity must have been galling. Still, the failure of memory is hardly a measure of Dickinson's true importance. Dickinson was most obviously significant as a partisan orator and Civil War patriot. In her early twenties audiences had filled halls to hear her brand of Radical Republicanism blended with fervent patriotism. Abolitionists embraced her as one of their most eloquent advocates; contemporaries credited her with swaying several crucial state elections; party leaders invited her to address them in the House of Representatives. For years after the war Dickinson was among the nation's most popular—and handsomely paid—public speakers, devoting her talents to defending the rights of women, workers, and African Americans. Frederick Douglass recalled that she helped craft the language that became the Fifteenth Amendment. In her novel *What Answer?* and later in *A Paying Investment*, Dickinson used other means to engage audiences. Even as a playwright and actress, Dickinson challenged cultural assumptions about the proper roles of women. In each guise Dickinson sought to cajole, educate, and reform, as well as entertain. Even when audiences came to witness a show, Dickinson invariably served up a political message.[13]

Through all the lectures and performances, Dickinson rarely consciously presented herself as a woman entering the public arena. Still, her audiences were acutely aware that Dickinson was unique among women as a partisan political orator and her early exploits left a powerful legacy. By 1872 other women had joined her on the political stump, but Dickinson remained a distinctive attraction among public women, worthy of aggressive recruiting from both the Republicans and the Liberal Republicans. Moreover, Dickinson's public performances—and her great fame—had a major impact on an entire cohort of young women who saw her as a model for success, indicating professional paths and possibilities they might not otherwise have considered. Several prominent nineteenth-century women, most notably Isabella Beecher Hooker, Frances Willard, and Olivia Langdon Clemens, dated their expanded political consciousness and entry into the women's movement to late night conversations with the young Anna Dickinson.[14]

That fame represented another strand in Dickinson's historical significance. The Civil War era saw important transitions in how celebrity became defined and commodified and Dickinson found herself at the center of these developments. As one of the war's most famous figures, Dickinson became one of the nation's first widely photographed celebrities. Strangers displayed her photograph in family albums; advertisers used her image to hawk their wares. Here again, Dickinson's significance lies both in the magnitude of her fame and in her early rise to celebrity. While those women who devoted their wartime energies to nursing or voluntary societies eventually earned postwar tributes for their heroism and sacrifices, Dickinson's Civil War activities placed her in a public world of men, and thus her *cartes de visite* circulated among those of generals and politicians, sending further messages to young women and men that ran counter to popular gender assumptions.

When Dickinson abandoned the lyceum circuit she turned to career paths where other women had already led the way, trying her hand as an author, playwright, and actress. Even when she decided to play male roles, Dickinson raised a few eyebrows, but she was hardly moving onto unfamiliar terrain. Nonetheless, Dickinson put her own unique stamp on these new professional endeavors. Never content to turn her career over to others, Dickinson become a talented and aggressive businesswoman at a very young age. She fired managers, challenged theater owners, attacked critics, interrogated publishers, and sued a leading actress.

Dickinson's behavior in later life no doubt damaged her legacy, tarnishing the public image she had fought so hard to cultivate and protect. Some of the traits that eventually undermined her had been present throughout her career. Dickinson had always had a strong personality and an explosive temper. Her first public speech as a teenager had been delivered in anger, when she stood to give a foolish father of several daughters a piece of her mind, and throughout the Civil War she was often most effective when hecklers stoked her fiery rhetoric. At the height of her success, Dickinson periodically drove friends and admirers away with bewildering bouts of rage. As Mark Twain had once observed, her harsh sarcasm was both "her best card" and likely to be her ruin.[15]

Even as she rose to stardom with seeming ease and unbridled confidence, those closest to her worried about Dickinson's emotional and physical fragility, and on at least one occasion she probably suffered an emotional breakdown. But if her earlier years contained seeds of her future destructive behavior, for quite some time Dickinson managed to maintain a highly successful public career despite a draining travel schedule and persistent family pressures. Even when she took on the New York theater critics in the mid-1870s, her anger seemed justified—or at least defensible—and her decisions carefully considered. But when she broke with Fanny Davenport, Dickinson let her anger and her ego compromise her professional future, and her irate charges against the Republican National Committee seemed wildly out of proportion to the party leaders' actual behavior, suggesting that her grasp of her professional situation had begun to slip.

By 1891 the balance had shifted. Perhaps Susan Dickinson acted prematurely or even deviously in having her sister committed, but there is no denying that Dickinson's behavior had grown erratic in the months after their mother's death. Had the sisters been from a wealthy family, or had Anna married a rich man, the entire narrative might have been very different, and certainly less public. After her release from Danville and her subsequent speeches in New York City, Dickinson settled into a quieter existence, fighting her public battles in the courtroom. But while she presented herself as the picture of sanity on the witness stand, Dickinson's personal correspondence in the 1890s suggests that she never fully recaptured her previous mental sharpness. Certainly the Dickinson of old would never have treated the aging and dignified Robert Purvis as she did. Meanwhile, close friends came to view Dickinson differently, questioning not only her health and behavior, but also the state of her mind.

It is impossible to know precisely what caused Dickinson's decline. Near the end of her very long life, Mary Dickinson suffered from some form of dementia, but there is no evidence that any of her other children exhibited any signs of mental illness. By the time Anna was in her late forties alcohol abuse was almost certainly a factor in her physical and emotional difficulties, and she was likely drinking to excess long before that point. Perhaps liquor was the root cause of her problems, but it seems equally likely that she turned to alcohol in response to frustration, despair, and emotional deterioration, thus accelerating a decline that was already underway.

Dickinson's public actions only began to appear erratic after she started facing professional disappointments. Having achieved great success at an early age, she grew accustomed to both the trappings of fame and the political influence that accompanied it. When she returned from her 1875 southern tour, Dickinson clung to celebrity for a time by turning to the stage, but she no longer enjoyed a public role nor a reliable income. Like many other public figures who achieved great fame at an early age, Dickinson was in a sense a victim of her own success. Not only had she come to expect continuing triumphs and a substantial income, but her audiences and critics measured Dickinson's later efforts against the mark set by her earlier accomplishments. Her eventual frustrations and despair may not have been preordained, but they were certainly not a surprising coda to a career that began with such startling success.

Of course this narrative of professional achievements followed by crashing disappointments occurred within a rigidly circumscribed world of gender rules and expectations. During the Civil War Anna Dickinson walked on the very edge of culturally acceptable female behavior. Her unique role as an attractive young woman on the political stump helped draw enthusiastic audiences, but it was her oratorical skill and political acumen that won her continuing success and influence. After the war Dickinson tried her hand at many of the public roles available to a woman of her talents. In a sense Dickinson's public career mapped out the multiple ways a woman could enter the public arena in the mid-nineteenth century. But the flip side was that Dickinson faced barriers because of her gender. By her early forties she had taken to writing despairing letters home, expressing frustration that she had run out of professional alternatives. "I would run a gambling saloon for the sake of getting ahold of some money," she wrote from Chicago.[16] Had she been a man with the same ambitions and talents she would have enjoyed a much wider range of options.

Those professional disappointments are easy to document, even if we can only speculate about how they might have affected Dickinson's emotional health. Her personal frustrations are less clear, but they were perhaps equally debilitating. For nearly 30 years, from the time she first left for Boston until the day her sister had her removed from her West Pittston bedroom, Anna Dickinson lived a peculiarly peripatetic existence. She spent long periods on the road, and between tours her home base was often a hotel or a friend's home. Even when the family still had a house in Philadelphia, Dickinson rarely spent much time there, often opting to vacation in the mountains or at the shore. Although she was often alone and always adamantly individualistic, Dickinson valued close companionship. She routinely traveled with a friend, and when she lived in hotels in Chicago or New York, Dickinson generally had a female companion with her. Throughout her twenties and thirties Dickinson enjoyed the company of male suitors, and at least on occasion she seems to have reciprocated their affections if not their passions. Friends and family assumed that she would marry, and although Dickinson expressed doubts about compromising her career for a marriage, and she period-ically lectured on the institution's flaws, there is no evidence that during those early years she dismissed the notion entirely. Meanwhile, she had several physic-ally intimate relationships with women, but most only lasted a few years. Perhaps these experiences left Dickinson unhappy or depressed, longing for a more per-manent relationship, but nothing in her surviving correspondence hints at such an emptiness.

Dickinson finally found such a lasting relationship with Sallie Ackley. The two were together for over 30 years, albeit in a household with George Ackley, and by all accounts they were happily inseparable. Before she moved in with the Ackleys Dickinson had lived for several years in the company of women, and most of those women were in open relationships with other women. Despite these relationships there is no way of knowing what Dickinson thought about her own sexuality, or whether those thoughts changed over time.[17] Perhaps in her earlier days she was conflicted about her own inclinations and actions, or perhaps the common assumption that she would—or should—marry a man produced its own set of internal tensions. But there is no direct evidence that Dickinson suffered any emotional difficulties because her reality deviated from social expectations.[18] Perhaps more emotionally damaging, Dickinson's conservative mother would likely have disapproved of her daughter's relationships with women, particularly if any had developed into an open partnership. While Mary Dickinson still survived, Anna had many circumspect relationships with other women, often many miles from her mother's home. But it is probably no coincidence that Dickinson's relationship with Ackley began shortly after her mother's death.[19]

As is commonly the case with revolutionary figures who survive to old age, the world that Anna Dickinson watched from Goshen evolved well beyond the society that had launched her into fame, and that she had critiqued for so many years. In some senses that world had already passed Dickinson by well before her collapse in 1891. The changing antebellum political culture that had accommodated her radical abolitionism and embraced her scorching partisan rhetoric had given way to the politics of professional wire pullers. In the 1888 campaign she had won some appreciative audiences with her anachronistic, bellicose style, but the whole experience merely underscored how much had changed in a quarter century. Moreover, during the Civil War Dickinson's fame was at least partially owing to her unique position as a female political orator; by 1872 she was still a voice to be reckoned with, but hardly the novelty she had once been.[20]

As an orator and playwright, Dickinson had taken pride in cutting her own path, selecting topics according to her political and ideological impulses, even while her contemporaries entertained audiences with lighter fare. But by her early forties Dickinson was forced to admit that she felt out of synch with contemporary mores and unsure how to reach new audiences.[21] On the stage, Dickinson's plays revolved around complex romantic plots but her writing style ran toward heavily oratorical dialogue and intellectualized gender themes. By the 1880s the American theater had begun to change, as had the role of women on the stage. As one historian has explained it, the new era in the theater celebrated "female spectacles": including the "overwrought emotionalism" of actresses like Sarah Bernhardt, the humor of a new breed of "girl comedians," and—eventually—the "tastefully displayed" sexuality of the Ziegfeld girls. In her youth, Dickinson's appearances on the platform had been a spectacle in their own right, and no doubt some of her patrons had been drawn to her physical beauty, but by the 1880s her beauty had waned and her performances were out of step with these new theatrical trends.[22]

But if Dickinson's public career and identity were always defined by the memory of her Civil War exploits, rooting her celebrity in the past even while events around her rushed forward, she was also an important voice shaping nineteenth-century discourse and anticipating future developments. Time and again in her speeches and plays Dickinson created strong, independent female characters, from Joan of Arc to Anne Boleyn to Kate Vivian, whose personal strengths shared much in common with the autonomous "New Woman" of the turn of the century. Dickinson also told poignant tales of women, including Hester Vaughn and Abby McFarland, who fell victim to gender injustice (even her female heroines commonly suffered at the hands of men), and through these narratives she assailed the legal and cultural double standards that persisted into the decades to come.

From her vantage point in New York City and then in Goshen the aging Dickinson watched political developments with care, clipping newspaper stories particularly when they pertained to old friends or adversaries. As she relived her political and personal battles from the past, nearly everyone she fought with or alongside passed away. Ben Butler, Fanny Davenport, and Frances Willard, all subjects of her continuing ire, each died in the 1890s. Whitelaw Reid, the greatest villain in

Dickinson plaque. In 2001 the New York branch of the Sons of Union Veterans of the Civil War installed two copies of this plaque in Goshen, New York, one at her gravesite and the other at the site of her home.

Dickinson's personal narrative, lived until 1912. Meanwhile, the women who led the nineteenth-century fight for suffrage gradually passed from the scene. Elizabeth Cady Stanton died in 1902 and Susan B. Anthony followed four years later. Dickinson's chief female rivals on the lyceum circuit, Olive Logan and Kate Field, died in 1908 and 1909.[23] With the new century a new generation of suffrage leaders who Dickinson did not know stepped forward to take up the fight. Anna Dickinson would be 78 years old before women finally won the franchise in 1920. She would never exercise her right to vote.

In 2001 the Sons of the Union Veterans of the Civil War, Camp 124, Department of New York, erected a plaque at Dickinson's gravesite in Goshen, New York, and a second one at the home where she once lived. Those plaques are an extraordinary piece of historic memory: "In January 1864, President Lincoln invited Anna to address Congress, the Cabinet, and the Supreme Court, to rally support for the Union Cause and the fight against slavery" they begin. "Anna devoted the rest of her life to justice, liberty, and basic human rights for all people: male or female, black or white, rich or poor; and contributed to the 15th Amendment, prohibiting the disenfranchisement of every person based on race, sex, color, or previous servitude. Anna Dickinson lived at this site, in the Village of Goshen, for the last forty-one years of her life."[24] At the most basic level, these commemorative plaques absolutely captured Dickinson's essence. She likely would have been pleased to be remembered as an advocate for basic human rights, regardless of gender, race, or class. Still the sometimes persnickety Dickinson might have chafed at the errors that have now become a part of the public memory. She actually only lived in Goshen for 22 years, not the full 41 years from the first day she moved into Interpines until the day of her death. Although Abraham Lincoln attended her 1864 lecture, he was hardly responsible for inviting her to the capital, and in fact she treated the president quite harshly on that memorable day. And, in a piece of irony that one hopes would have made the orator chuckle, the Fifteenth Amendment that Dickinson had supported guaranteed the vote to black men while ignoring the interests of women. In supporting that amendment, and approving the line drawn between black men and all women, Dickinson had followed her heart and her own political philosophy, while alienating her sisters in the suffrage movement. They would never forget.

# BIBLIOGRAPHIC ESSAY

## Manuscript Sources

Throughout her career Anna Dickinson took pains to collect and preserve her personal papers. Shortly after Dickinson's death the Library of Congress (LC) in Washington, D.C. acquired a large trunk of these materials. The LC later added several additional scrapbooks and the research notes assembled by biographer Giraud Chester. Today the Anna E. Dickinson Papers (AEDP) comprise roughly 10,000 items, nearly all of which have been microfilmed.[1] In addition to thousands of letters received by Dickinson, the correspondence files include the letters she sent to both her mother and sister, drafts of dozens of letters she sent to various correspondents, and a handful of letters received by Sallie Ackley.

Dickinson's scrapbooks are an invaluable source. In preparing this book I have turned to her scrapbooks and clippings for evidence of what she did and how others responded to her actions. This invites an obvious question: did Dickinson filter out unflattering articles, producing scrapbooks that distorted the historic record? During the Civil War Dickinson saved roughly 200 clippings describing her lectures and other exploits. As a test for possible biases, I consulted 11 wartime newspapers from New York, Hartford, and Chicago (and their vicinities).[2] This research yielded 63 stories on Dickinson's wartime lectures, 23 of which (36 percent) also appeared in the scrapbooks. A comparison of the scrapbook stories with the material from this independent research suggests that although Dickinson missed stories, she was probably not filtering out unwelcome clippings. After the war Dickinson seemed to grow even more concerned with assembling a full record in her scrapbooks. Her letters home from the road routinely included packets of clippings and instructions about gathering more. During the 1872 presidential campaign Dickinson only spoke a handful of times, once in April and then several times in October and November. Yet her scrapbook includes nearly 70 clippings on those appearances. Given this vast and apparently unbiased body of clippings, I elected to rely on Dickinson's scrapbooks for news stories about her activities, supplemented by selective research in individual newspapers and contemporary journals and material from three newspapers available online: the *New York Times*, the *Brooklyn Eagle*, and the *Washington Post*.

In addition to the correspondence (personal and family) and the scrapbooks, the AEDP also house a wealth of Dickinson's notes and writings; printed copies of several scripts; notebooks full of reading notes, aphorisms, and snippets from writing projects; a very rough draft of a proposed autobiography; and folders of unfiled clippings. Most of Dickinson's legal papers are filed in separate containers. In the notes to this volume I have included container numbers when citing letters that are not found in the alphabetical correspondence files, or clippings that are not in the chronologically labeled scrapbooks.

More than a half century ago, two authors—Giraud Chester and James Harvey Young—wrote biographies of Anna Dickinson. Both left behind valuable materials for future scholars. Chester donated his research notes to the LC, where they appear in container 29 of the AEDP. These notes include partial transcripts of letters from Dickinson to Whitelaw Reid that Chester identified as from private papers made available to him by the Reid family. These letters do not appear among the Whitelaw Reid papers in the LC. I have been unable to locate these letters, and thus I have relied on Chester's detailed notes. James Harvey Young authored a dissertation on Dickinson's war years, several articles on specific topics, and an unpublished biography. Young's papers—which are housed in the Special Collections Department, Robert W. Woodruff Library, Emory University (JHYP)—include two boxes of research notes and the draft of his Dickinson biography. I thank Dr. Young for permission to consult his notes and manuscript. In the case of Dickinson's letters to Theodore Tilton, which are catalogued in the New York Public Library, I relied on Young's notes because the originals have been lost. In 1941 Young corresponded with Dr. Frederick W. Seward, Jr., and he interviewed Dr. Seward, George Ackley, and Bertha Ackley about Dickinson. Seward's letter and the transcripts of these conversations offer invaluable information on Dickinson's final years. The JHYP also include complete copies of Dickinson's correspondence with Charles Dudley Warner and Susan Warner. The originals are housed in the Watkinson Library, Trinity College, Hartford, Connecticut.[3]

While the AEDP proved to be the major source for Dickinson's papers, quite a few isolated letters are housed in other archives, and I also turned to these other librarians for material on Dickinson's contemporaries. The Huntington Library, San Marino, California, holds a superb collection of books, published journals, newspapers, and manuscripts pertaining to nineteenth-century America. The manuscript collections include a dozen scattered letters from Dickinson as well as quite a few useful letters and diaries that spoke of her. The Huntington also holds an extensive run of the *Revolution*, the Isabella Beecher Hooker Project (on microfiche), and most of the important popular journals of the day. The Harriet Beecher Stowe Center Library in Hartford houses valuable correspondence from many of Dickinson's Nook Farm friends, including Isabella Beecher Hooker and her husband John Hooker, Susan and Charles Dudley Warner, and various of their children and other relatives. The holdings of the Connecticut Historical Society, Hartford, include a long list of Connecticut newspapers as well as several useful diaries.

The Arthur and Elizabeth Schlesinger Library, Radcliffe College, Harvard University, Cambridge, Massachusetts, has an immense collection of materials related to U. S. women's history, including about a dozen letters from Dickinson to various correspondents. The Sophia Smith Collection, Smith College, Northampton, Massachusetts also contains an excellent collection of materials on American women's history. Although the collection includes almost no Dickinson correspondence, quite a few letters in the Garrison Papers speak of Dickinson and contextualize her activities. The Manuscripts and Archives Division of the New York Public Library includes 14 Dickinson letters in the Anthony Collection. Other letters from Dickinson are noted in the catalogue but were missing in 2000. The holdings of the Friends Historical Library, Swarthmore College, Swarthmore, Pennsylvania, include 14 Dickinson letters. The Nantucket Historical Association Research Library has two letters from Frances Willard to Phebe Hanaford (1892 and 1893) discussing Dickinson. In 1890 Susan Dickinson wrote to Rutherford B. Hayes about her sister. This valuable letter is in the Rutherford B. Hayes Presidential Center, Fremont, Ohio.

Several of the most valuable collections of personal papers are available on microfilm or in published volumes. Whitelaw Reid's papers are in the LC (Reid Family Papers) and available on microfilm. This large collection includes some useful correspondence from both Anna and Susan Dickinson, several letters mentioning Dickinson, and a few important copies of letters sent to Dickinson in Reid's personal letter books. Unfortunately, the Reid papers do not scratch the surface of the Dickinson-Reid relationship. Many letters from Reid to Dickinson in the AEDP do not appear in his letter books, and there are almost no letters from Dickinson among his incoming correspondence despite the fact that they were regular correspondents for nearly a decade. As noted above, Giraud Chester received access to additional Dickinson letters from Reid's descendents, and it seems likely that Reid's papers have been culled for personal correspondence related to Dickinson. Dickinson also enjoyed an extensive correspondence with Susan B. Anthony. The letters that survive are included in "The Papers of Elizabeth Cady Stanton and Susan B. Anthony," an ambitious microfilm project edited by Patricia G. Holland and Ann D. Gordon. Unfortunately, Anthony destroyed most of her letters including nearly all those that she received from Dickinson.[4] The notes to this volume include citations to several published collections of letters.

## Scholarship on Anna Dickinson

For many decades the biography of record on Dickinson has been Giraud Chester, *Embattled Maiden: The Life of Anna Dickinson* (New York: G. F. Putnam's Sons, 1951). This is a lively narrative with no citations and limited analysis, and Chester—who was a journalist and not an historian—freely acknowledged that he invented some dialogue. Still, it appears to be based on substantial readings in the AEDP, supplemented by about 50 letters from the Reid family papers and a few other items. Chester also interviewed Miss Bertha Ackley, who knew Dickinson in her old age. In addition to his unpublished Dickinson biography, James Harvey Young wrote a dissertation entitled "Anna Elizabeth Dickinson and the Civil War" (Ph.D. dissertation, University of Illinois, 1941) and three articles: "Anna Dickinson and the Civil War: For and Against Lincoln," *Mississippi Valley Historical Review* 31 (June, 1944), 59–80; "A Woman Abolitionist Views the South in 1875," *Georgia Historical Quarterly* 32 (December, 1948), 241–51; and "Anna Dickinson as Anne Boleyn," *Emory University Quarterly* 5 (October, 1949): 163–69. Judith Anderson's master's thesis, "Anna E. Dickinson, 1842–1932" (M.A. Thesis, Lehigh University, 1934), written only a few years after AED died, includes evidence from interviews with some of Dickinson's childhood acquaintants.

Joseph Duffy, "Anna Elizabeth Dickinson and the Election of 1863," *Connecticut History* 25 (1984), 22–38, is a useful description of one of Dickinson's first political campaigns. Professor of Rhetoric Karlyn Kohrs Campbell examine Dickinson's most famous lecture in "*La Pucelle D'Orleans* Becomes An American Girl: Anna Dickinson's "Jeanne D'Arc," in Michael C. Leff and Fred J. Kaufield, eds., *Texts in Context: Critical Dialogues on Significant Episodes in American Political Rhetoric* (Davis, CA: Hormagoras Press, 1989), 91–111. For an earlier discussion of Dickinson's rhetoric see Philip George Prindle, "An Analysis of the Rhetoric in Selected Representative Speeches of Anna Elizabeth Dickinson," (Ph.D. diss., Stanford University, 1971). For an analysis of Dickinson as a playwright and actress see Stacey A. Stewart, "Nothing Ladylike About It: The Theatrical Career of Anna Elizabeth Dickinson," (Ph.D. diss., Department of Theater, University of Maryland, 2004).

Several recent works have begun incorporating Dickinson into broader studies of nineteenth-century women. See Wendy Hamand Venet, *Neither Ballots nor Bullets: Women Abolitionists and the Civil War* (Charlottesville: University of Virginia, 1991); Lyde Cullen Sizer, *The Political Work of Northern Women Writers and the Civil War, 1850–1872* (Chapel Hill: University of North Carolina Press, 2000); and Melanie Susan Gustafson, *Women and the Republican Party, 1854–1924* (Urbana: University of Illinois Press, 2001). In her recent history of Northern women during the Civil War, *Daughters of the Union: Northern Women Fight the Civil War* (Cambridge, MA: Harvard University Press, 2005), Nina Silber devotes several pages to Dickinson's life.

As I have been preparing this biographical study I have published several essays on various aspects of Dickinson's career. Although many of the ideas in these essays appear in this volume, the essays generally explore the themes in greater depth. See Gallman, "An Inspiration to Work: Anna Elizabeth Dickinson, Public Orator," in Joan E. Cashin, ed., *The War Was You and Me: Civilians in the American Civil War* (Princeton: Princeton University Press, 2002), 159–82; Gallman, *"Touched with Fire"?: Two Philadelphia Novelists Remember the Civil War* (Frank Klement Lecture Series No. 10) (Milwaukee, 2002); Gallman, "Introduction," in Anna E. Dickinson, *What Answer?* (1868; Amherst: Humanity Books, 2003); Gallman, "Anna Dickinson, America's Joan of Arc: Public Discourse and Gendered Rhetoric During the Civil War," in Wendy Gamber, Michael Grossberg and Hendrik Hartog, eds., *American Public Life and the Historical Imagination* (Notre Dame, IN: University of Notre Dame Press, 2003), 91–112; and Gallman, "Is the War Ended? Anna Dickinson and the Election of 1872," in Alice Fahs and Joan Waugh, eds., *The Memory of the Civil War in American Culture* (Chapel Hill: University of North Carolina Press, 2004), 157–79.

## Secondary Literature

This study attempts to place Anna Dickinson's remarkable life within the context of a nineteenth-century world in flux. I have turned to a wide array of specialists for guidance in this task, many of whom are acknowledged in the notes to this volume. The next few paragraphs are intended to point the reader toward some of the scholarship that has been most central to my thinking, although this short list barely scratches the surface of my intellectual debts.

The classic studies of antebellum, middle-class, Northern women include Nancy Cott, *The Bonds of Womanhood: 'Women's Sphere' in New England, 1780–1835* (New Haven: Yale University Press, 1977); Barbara Welter, "The Cult of True Womanhood: 1820–1860," *American Quarterly* (Summer 1966): 151–74; and Mary Ryan, *The Cradle of the Middle Class: The Family in Oneida County, New York, 1790–1865* (New York: Columbia University Press, 1981). For later works on women in the public arena see, Lori Ginzberg, *Women and the Work of Benevolence: Morality, Politics and Class in the 19th-Century United States* (New Haven: Yale University Press, 1990); Glenna Matthews, *The Rise of Public Woman: Woman's Power and Woman's Place in the United States, 1630–1970* (New York: Oxford University Press, 1992); and Michael D. Pierson, *Free Hearts & Free Homes: Gender and American Antislavery Politics* (Chapel Hill: University of North Carolina Press, 2003). On women and writing see, Mary Kelley, *Private Woman, Public Stage: Literary Domesticity in Nineteenth-Century America* (1984; rev. ed., Chapel Hill: University of North Carolina Press, 2002); and Sizer, *The Political Work of Northern Women Writers.*

On the Northern home front during the Civil War I have relied on my own previous work, including Gallman, *Mastering Wartime: A Social History of Philadelphia During the Civil War* (New York: Cambridge University Press, 1990); and Gallman, *The North Fights the Civil War: The Home Front* (Chicago: Ivan R. Dee, 1994). For more recent studies on Northern women (in addition to those noted above), see Jeanie Attie, *Patriotic Toil: Northern Women and the American Civil War* (Ithaca, NY: Cornell University Press, 1998); and Judy Giesberg, *Civil War Sisterhood: The U.S. Sanitary Commission and Women's Politics in Transition* (Boston: Northeastern University Press, 2000). Many studies of Confederate women provide a crucial context to these Northern experiences. See especially, George Rable, *Civil Wars: Women and the Crisis of Southern Nationalism* (Urbana: University of Illinois Press, 1989); Drew Gilpin Faust, *Mothers of Invention: Women of the Slaveholding South in the American Civil War* (Chapel Hill: University of North Carolina Press, 1996); and LeeAnn Whites, *The Civil War as a Crisis in Gender: Augusta, Georgia, 1860–1890* (Athens, GA: University of Georgia Press, 1995). On both the North and the South, see the essays in Catherine Clinton and Nina Silber, eds., *Divided Houses: Gender and the Civil War* (New York: Oxford University Press, 1993); and Cashin, ed., *The War Was You and Me.*

On the history of woman suffrage, Elizabeth Cady Stanton, Susan B. Anthony, and Matilda Jocelyn Gage, *History of Woman Suffrage*, three vols. (1881; reprinted New York: Source Book Press, 1970) is still an invaluable source. Ellen Carol DuBois's *Feminism and Suffrage: The Emergence of an Independent Women's Movement in America, 1848–1869* (Ithaca, NY: Cornell University Press, 1978) is the best short history of the women's movement in the mid-nineteenth century. Jean H. Baker's *Sisters: The Lives of America's Suffragists* (New York: Hill and Wang, 2005) appeared in print as this volume neared completion. I thank Dr. Baker for sharing a draft of her chapter on Susan B. Anthony. James M. McPherson's *The Struggle for Equality: Abolitionists and the Negro in the Civil War and Reconstruction* (1964; reprinted Princeton, 1995) remains a crucial study of the politics of abolitionism. See also, Venet, *Neither Ballots nor Bullets*. On the sometimes complex relationship between race and the women's movement, see Louise Michele Newman, *White Women's Rights: The Racial Origins of Feminism in the United States* (New York: Oxford University Press, 1999). Among the many biographies of Dickinson's peers, some of the most useful are, Ruth Bordin, *Frances Willard: A Biography* (Chapel Hill: University of North Carolina Press, 1986); Kathleen Barry, *Susan B. Anthony: A Biography of a Singular Feminist* (New York: New York University Press, 1988); David Blight, *Frederick Douglass's Civil War: Keeping Faith in Jubilee* (Baton Rouge: LSU Press, 1989); and Venet, *A Strong-Minded Woman: The Life of Mary Livermore* (Amherst: University of Massachusetts Press, 2005).

For the political culture of the nineteenth century see, Mary P. Ryan, *Civic Wars: Democracy and Public Life in the American City during the Nineteenth Century* (Berkeley: University of California Press, 1997); Glenn C. Altschuler and Stuart M. Blumin, *Rude Republic: Americans and Politics in the Nineteenth Century* (Princeton: Princeton University Press, 2000); and Mark W. Summers, *Party Games: Getting, Keeping, and Using Power in Gilded Age Politics* (Chapel Hill: University of North Carolina Press, 2004).

Some of the most exciting recent scholarship concerns the role of women in partisan politics. See Ronald J. Zboray and Mary Saracino Zboray, "Whig Women, Politics, and Culture in the Campaign of 1840: Three Perspectives from Massachusetts," *Journal of the Early Republic* 17 (Summer, 1997): 277–315; Elizabeth Varon, *We Mean To Be Counted: White Women and Politics in Antebellum Virginia* (Chapel Hill: University of North Carolina Press, 1998); Janet L. Coryell, "Superseding Gender: The Role of the Woman Politico in Antebellum Partisan Politics," in Alison M. Parker and Stephanie Cole, eds., *Women and the Unstable State in Nineteenth-Century America* (College Station: Texas A & M University Press, 2000), 84–112; Faye Dudden, "New York Strategy: The New York Woman's Movement and the Civil War," in Jean Baker, ed., *Votes for Women: The Struggle for Suffrage Revisited* (New York: Oxford University Press, 2002); and Gustafson, *Women and the Republican Party*.

See the notes for numerous sources on the history of the lyceum circuit. On female oratory see, Karlyn Kohrs Campbell, *Man Cannot Speak for Her, volume I: A Critical Study of Early Feminist Rhetoric* (Westport, CT: Greenwood Press, 1989); Campbell, ed., *Women Public Speakers in the United States, 1800–1925: A Biocritical Sourcebook* (Westport, CT: Greenwood Press, 1993); and Nan Johnson, *Gender and Rhetorical Space in American Life, 1866–1910* (Carbondale, IL: Southern Illinois University Press, 2002). On women and the theater see, Faye E. Dudden, *Women in the American Theatre* (New Haven: Yale University Press, 1994); Elizabeth Reitz Mullenix, *Wearing the Breeches: Gender on the Antebellum Stage* (New York: St. Martin's Press, 2000); and Susan A. Glenn, *Female Spectacle: The Theatrical Roots of Modern Feminism* (Cambridge, MA: Harvard University Press, 2000). The best study of women and alcohol is Catherine Gilbert Murdock, *Domesticating Drink: Women, Men, and Alcohol in America, 1870–1940* (Baltimore: Johns Hopkins University Press, 1998).

The scholarship on romantic and sexual relationships, both heterosexual and homosexual, is vast. On courtship, see Ellen K. Rothman, *Hands and Hearts: A History of Courtship in America* (New York: Basic Books, 1984); and Karen Lystra, *Searching the Heart: Women, Men, and Romantic Love in Nineteenth-Century America* (New York: Oxford University Press, 1989). On relationships between women see, Carroll Smith-Rosenberg, "The Female World of Love and Ritual: Relations Between Women in Nineteenth-Century America," *Signs*, 1 (Autumn 1975), 1–29; Lillian Faderman, *Surpassing the Love of Men: Romantic Friendship and Love Between Women from the Renaissance to the Present* (1981; expanded, New York: William Morrow and Company, 1998); Faderman, *To Believe in Women: What Lesbians Have Done For America—A History* (Boston: Houghton Mifflin, 1999); and Martha Vicinus, *Intimate Friends: Women Who Loved Women, 1778–1928* (Chicago: University of Chicago Press, 2004).

Many scholars have been drawn to the Beecher-Tilton scandal and the flamboyant career of Victoria Woodhull. Barbara Goldsmith's *Other Powers: The Age of Suffrage, Spiritualism, and the Scandalous Victoria Woodhull* (New York: A. A. Knopf, 1998) is a useful volume, although I disagree with some the details. See also Richard Wightman Fox, *Trials of Intimacy: Love and Loss in the Beecher-Tilton Scandal* (Chicago: University of Chicago Press, 1999); and Amanda Frisken, "Sex in Politics: Victoria Woodhull as an American Public Woman, 1870–1876," *Journal of Women's History* 12 (2000), 89–111.

# NOTES

## Abbreviations

HL = The Huntington Library, San Marino, CA.

LC = Library of Congress, Washington, D.C.

SDC = Stowe-Day Collection, Stowe Center Library, Hartford, CT.

SSC = Sophia Smith Collection, Smith College Archives, Northampton, MA.

AEDP = Anna E. Dickinson Papers, LC.

WRP = Whitelaw Reid Papers, LC.

WR-GC = Whitelaw Reid correspondence transcribed by Giraud Chester, notes in AEDP.

JHYP = James Harvey Young Papers, Special Collections, Robert W. Woodruff Library, Emory University, Atlanta, GA.

WP = Warner Papers, Watkinson Library, Hartford, CT; copies of these letters are on file in the JHYP.

JHY, "AED" = James Harvey Young, "Anna Elizabeth Dickinson," unpublished manuscript, JHYP.

*Selected Papers* = Ann D. Gordon, ed., *The Selected Papers of Elizabeth Cady Stanton and Susan B. Anthony,* vol. 1, 1840–1866 (New Brunswick: Rutgers University Press, 1997); vol. 2, 1866–1873 (New Brunswick: Rutgers University Press, 2000).

*ECS-SBA Papers* = Patricia G. Holland and Ann D. Gordon, eds., *The Papers of Elizabeth Cady Stanton and Susan B. Anthony* (Wilmington, DE: Scholarly Resources Ind., 1989, microfilm).

*IBH Project* = Isabella Beecher Hooker Project, microfiche, HL.

AED = Anna Elizabeth Dickinson

ED = Edwin Dickinson

MD = Mary Dickinson

SD = Samuel Dickinson

SED = Susan E. Dickinson

SBA = Susan B. Anthony

BB = Benjamin Butler

LCB = Laura Curtis Bullard

FDP = Fanny Davenport (Price)

IBH = Isabella Beecher Hooker

WR = Whitelaw Reid

ECS = Elizabeth Cady Stanton

TT = Theodore Tilton

CDW = Charles Dudley Warner

VCW = Victoria C. Woodhull

## Notes to Introduction

1  *Cincinnati Gazette*, January 18 [?], 1864, AED scrapbook.
2  The letter of invitation is in the AEDP. The invitation and AED's response, are reprinted in Elizabeth Cady Stanton, Susan B. Anthony, and Matilda Jocelyn Gage, *History of Woman Suffrage*, 3 vols. (1881; reprinted New York: Source Book Press, 1970), 47.
3  *Independent*, January 7, 1864, AED scrapbook.
4  For a recent historiographic overview see Catherine Clinton and Christine Lunardini, eds., *The Columbia Guide to American Women in the Nineteenth Century* (New York: Columbia University Press, 1999). See the bibliographic essay for a discussion of scholarship on AED.

## Notes to Chapter 1

1  *Evening Gazette*, May 23, 1889, AED scrapbook; *New York Herald*, June 19, 1892, AED scrapbook.
2  The only published biography of AED is Giraud Chester, *Embattled Maiden: The Life of Anna Dickinson* (New York: G. F. Putnam's Sons, 1951). James Harvey Young, who also wrote a dissertation on AED's wartime career, authored a biography ("Anna Elizabeth Dickinson") that has never been published. The best contemporary account of AED's early life is Elizabeth Cady Stanton, "Anna Elizabeth Dickinson," in James Parton et al., *Eminent Women of the Age* (Hartford: S. M. Betts & Company, 1869), 479–512. For AED's biographical sketch of her parents see *New York Herald*, June 19, 1892, AED scrapbook. In 1880 the *Boston Times* published a two-part biography of AED that also includes some useful information on her early life. *Boston Times*, October 10, 1880 and November 10 [?], 1880, AED scrapbook.
3  Stanton, "Anna Elizabeth Dickinson," 482; Judith Anderson, "Anna E. Dickinson, 1842–1932" (M.A. thesis, Lehigh University, 1934), 13–14; Nancy Cott, *The Bonds of Womanhood:'Women's Sphere' in New England, 1780–1835* (New Haven: Yale University Press, 1977).
4  Philip George Prindle, "An Analysis of the Rhetoric in Selected Representative Speeches of Anna Elizabeth Dickinson," (Ph.D. diss., Stanford University, 1971), 412. Quote from AED, "Whited Sepulchres," as reported in *Missouri Democrat*, March 5, 1870.
5  The ages of AED's siblings can be calculated from various references in the AEDP. JHYP.
6  *Liberator*, February 22, 1856.
7  Cott, *The Bonds of Womanhood*; Mary Ryan, *The Cradle of the Middle Class: The Family in Oneida County, New York, 1790–1865* (New York: Columbia University Press, 1981); Lori Ginzberg, *Women and the Work of Benevolence: Morality, Politics and Class in the 19th-Century United States* (New Haven: Yale University Press, 1990).
8  In this volume I will use the term "gender" to describe socially constructed roles based on perceived sexual difference. For a classic discussion see, Joan Wallach Scott, "Gender as a Useful Category of Historical Analysis," *American Historical Review* 91 (December 1986): 1053–75.
9  Barbara Welter, "The Cult of True Womanhood: 1820–1860," *American Quarterly* (Summer 1966): 151–74.
10  Cott, *Bonds of Womanhood*.
11  Ellen Carol DuBois, *Feminism and Suffrage: The Emergence of an Independent Women's Movement in America, 1848–1869* (Ithaca, NY: Cornell University Press, 1978); Lori D. Ginzberg, *Women in Antebellum Reform* (New York, 2000).
12  Moreover, by midcentury both factory work and domestic service had lost much of their respectability among native-born Americans. For brief surveys of antebellum labor patterns see Lynn Y. Weiner, *From Working Girl to Working Mother: The Female Labor Force in the United States, 1820–1980* (Chapel Hill: University of North Carolina Press, 1985), 13–18; Glenna Matthews, *The Rise of Public Woman: Woman's Power and Woman's Place in the United States, 1630–1970* (New York: Oxford University Press, 1992), 95–99.
13  SED to AED, January 27, 1861, December 6, 1862. Both SED's and AED's careers are summarized in Frances E. Willard and Mary A. Livermore, eds., *A Woman of the Century* (1893; republished New York: Gordon Press, 1993), 1: 241–2.

14   AED to Ida Tarbell, February 1, 1910.

15   MD's later letters to AED often expressed a concern for her daughter's moral and spiritual health while on the road and engaging in public activities.

16   DuBois, *Feminism and Suffrage*, 24 and *passim*; Ginzberg, *Women in Antebellum Reform*; Michael D. Pierson, *Free Hearts & Free Homes: Gender and American Antislavery Politics* (Chapel Hill: University of North Carolina Press, 2003).

17   On women and antebellum rhetoric see Karlyn Kohrs Campbell, ed., *Women Public Speakers in the United States, 1800–1925: A Biocritical Sourcebook* (Westport, CT: Greenwood Press, 1993); Campbell, *Man Cannot Speak for Her, Volume I: A Critical Study of Early Feminist Rhetoric* (Westport, CT: Greenwood Press, 1989), 1–87; Lillian O'Connor, *Pioneer Women Orators: Rhetoric in the Ante-Bellum Reform Movement* (New York: Columbia University Press, 1954); Nan Johnson, *Gender and Rhetorical Space in American Life, 1866–1910* (Carbondale, IL: Southern Illinois University Press, 2002); Anne Mattina, " 'I am as a bell that cannot ring': Antebellum women oratory," *Women and Language* 16 (Fall 1993); Matthews, *The Rise of Public Woman*, 110–17. On Sojourner Truth, see Nell Irvin Painter, *Sojourner Truth: A Life, A Symbol* (New York: W. W. Norton Press, 1996). See also Gregory Clark and S. Michael Halloran, eds., *Oratorical Culture in Nineteenth-Century America: Transformations in the Theory and Practice of Rhetoric* (Carbondale, IL: Southern Illinois University Press, 1993), 1: 28.

18   In addition to other sources cited in this chapter see Mary Kelley, *Private Woman, Public Stage: Literary Domesticity in Nineteenth-Century America* (1984; rev. ed., Chapel Hill: University of North Carolina Press, 2002), espec. vii–xxiii.

19   This paragraph summarizes an emerging literature on politically engaged women in the antebellum years. See Ronald J. Zboray and Mary Saracino Zboray, "Whig Women, Politics, and Culture in the Campaign of 1840: Three Perspectives from Massachusetts," *Journal of the Early Republic* 17 (Summer, 1997): 277–315; Janet L. Coryell, "Superseding Gender: The Role of the Woman Politico in Antebellum Partisan Politics," in Allison M. Parker and Stephanie Cole, eds., *Women and the Unstable State in Nineteenth-Century America* (College Station: Texas A & M University Press, 2000), 84–112; Elizabeth Varon, "Tippecanoe and the Ladies, Too: White Women and Party Politics in Antebellum Virginia," *Journal of American History* 82 (September, 1995): 494–521; Varon, *We Mean To Be Counted: White Women and Politics in Antebellum Virginia* (Chapel Hill: University of North Carolina Press, 1998); Melanie Susan Gustafson, *Women and the Republican Party, 1854–1924* (Urbana: University of Illinois Press, 2001), 7–24; Pierson, *Free Hearts & Free Homes*.

20   Michael F. Holt, *The Political Crisis of the 1850s* (New York: Wiley, 1978).

21   Gustafson, *Women and the Republican Party*, 18–24; Pierson, *Free Hearts & Free Homes*, 3, 46–69, 81–96, 139–50; Sylvia D. Hoffert, *Jane Grey Swisshelm: An Unconventional Life, 1815–1884* (Chapel Hill: University of North Carolina Press, 2004), 111–24. Pierson argues that as women became increasingly engaged in politics, the terms of political discourse became more gendered and the two parties exhibited distinct gender cultures.

22   Glenn C. Altschuler and Stuart M. Blumin, *Rude Republic: Americans and Politics in the Nineteenth Century* (Princeton: Princeton University Press, 2000), 47–86; Mary P. Ryan, *Civic Wars: Democracy and Public Life in the American City during the Nineteenth Century* (Berkeley: University of California Press, 1997), 158–9 and *passim*.

23   *New York Herald*, June 19, 1892. ECS's biographical sketch suggests that this encounter actually occurred at AED's second visit to Clarkson Hall the following Sunday. Stanton, "Anna Elizabeth Dickinson," 485–6.

24   SED checked the newspapers to see "whether thy remark has been reported there with addenda and ornaments." SED to AED, January 11, 1860.

25   Unidentified newspaper clipping, AED scrapbook; James Miller McKim to AED, note on announcement of annual meetings of the Pennsylvania Anti-Slavery Society, AEDP; Mary Mott Bowman to AED, November 30, 1860; JHY, "Anna Elizabeth Dickinson and the Civil War," (Ph.D. diss., University of Illinois, 1941), 10–14. On divisions within the abolitionist movement over slavery and the Constitution see Pierson, *Free Hearts & Homes*, 47–57.

26   Philadelphia *Evening Bulletin*, n.d.; *West Jersey Pioneer*, n.d. (quoting *Philadelphia Press*), AED scrapbook; Lucretia Coffin Mott to Lydia Mott, January 22, 1861, in Beverly Wilson Palmer, ed., *Selected*

*Letters of Lucretia Coffin Mott* (Urbana: University of Illinois Press, 2002), 305–6; JHY, "Anna Elizabeth Dickinson and the Civil War," 22–23. On February 4, 1861, shortly before delivering this lecture, AED signed two petitions addressed to the state legislature. The first called for legislation protecting fugitive slaves, the second sought to protect the economic and legal rights of married women. These two public documents illustrate AED's principle political passions. RG-7, House File, Box 16, 85th Session, 1861, folder 6, State Archives of Pennsylvania, Harrisburg, PA. My thanks to David G. Smith for transcripts of both petitions.

27  J. Matthew Gallman, *Mastering Wartime: A Social History of Philadelphia During the Civil War* (New York: Cambridge University Press, 1990).

28  See Lillie Atkinson to AED, June 17, 1861.

## Notes to Chapter 2

1  Lillie [Atkinson] to AED, June 17, 1861 (this letter is misfiled with the Lillie Chace letters); William Lloyd Garrison to Helen E. Garrison, October 29, 1861, Walter M. Merril, ed., *The Letters of William Lloyd Garrison* V: 42 (Cambridge: Harvard University Press, 1971); AED to Ida Tarbell (draft?), February 1, 1910.

2  Elizabeth Cady Stanton, Susan B. Anthony, and Matilda Jocelyn Gage, *History of Woman Suffrage*, 3 vols. (1881; reprinted New York: Source Book Press, 1970), 2: 42. In her March 16, 1862, letter to Garrison, AED explained that she had lost her job "in consequence of my abolition sentiments & the yet graver offense, being a woman of expressing them in public." AED to William L. Garrison, draft, March 16, 1862. It is unclear when AED delivered this lecture. The West Chester meetings of the Pennsylvania Anti-Slavery Society occurred a few days after the Battle of Ball's Bluff, but Garrison's October 29 letter makes no mention of these charges, so perhaps she added these remarks at a subsequent appearance.

3  AED to William L. Garrison, draft, March 16, 1862; AED scrapbook; William L. Garrison to AED, March 22, 1862. Garrison's four 1862 letters to AED are also reprinted in vol. V of *The Letters of William Lloyd Garrison*.

4  Garrison to AED, March 27, 30, 1862, April 3, 1862; AED to SED, April 15, 1862, SED to AED, April 21, 1862; *National Anti-Slavery Standard*, April 26, 1862; various clippings in AED scrapbook.

5  AED to SED, April 28, 1862. The Mrs. Dall AED refers to was author Caroline Dall.

6  Fanny Garrison to AED, June 23, July 27, September 14, 1862; Frank Garrison to AED, September 12, 1862.

7  Samuel May, Jr., to Mrs. Elizabeth Buffum Chace, April 27, 1862, in Lillie Buffum Chace Wyman and Arthur Crawford Wyman, eds., *Elizabeth Buffum Chace* (Boston: W. B. Clarke Company, 1914), I: 286; Stanton, et al., *History of Woman Suffrage*, 2: 42.

8  *National Anti-Slavery Standard*, May 3, 17, 1862; *New York Herald*, May 7, 1862; AED scrapbook. In late May AED returned to Boston for the annual convention of the New England Anti-Slavery Society.

9  AED to Elizabeth Buffum Chace, June 16, 1862, in Wyman and Wyman, eds., *Elizabeth Buffum Chace*, 1: 240.

10  Stanton, et al., *History of Woman Suffrage*, 42–43; SED to AED, October 18, 1862; MD to AED, November 18, 1862.

11  *National Anti-Slavery Standard*, November 22, 1862; Charles Slack to AED, May 14, September 27, 1862; AED scrapbook.

12  William S. McFeely, *Frederick Douglass* (New York: W. W. Norton & Company, 1991), 215.

13  SED to AED, December 6, 1862, January 17, February 9, 1863.

14  Linus A. Gould to AED, October 30, November 10, 1862, January 22, 1863.

15  Joseph Ricketson to AED, numerous letters, 1862. See also Samuel May, Jr., to AED, January 13, 1863.

16  Benjamin F. Prescott to AED, numerous letters, 1863; *Granite State Free Press*, March 14, 1863, AED scrapbook; Stanton, *History of Woman Suffrage*, 43–44.

17  Lucretia Coffin Mott to Mary Hussey Earle, February 20, 1863, in Beverly Wilson Palmer, ed., *Selected Letters of Lucretia Coffin Mott* (Urbana: University of Illinois Press, 2002), 332–3.

18  Mrs. J. Olmsted to Benjamin Prescott, March 23, 1863. This letter is filed with Prescott's letters to AED. Prescott to AED, April 2, March, 23, 24, 1863. Prescott mentioned the fee on the twenty-third; the quotation is from the twenty-fourth.

19  Samuel May to AED, March 30, 1863.

20  Benjamin Prescott to AED, March 25, 1863; *Hartford Courant*, March 25, 28, 1863, numerous Hartford papers.

21  *Middletown Constitution*, undated clipping, AED scrapbook. The term "Copperhead" was used to describe anti-war Northern Democrats.

22  Unidentified clipping, AED scrapbook. The article pointed out that the only local factory that had not raised wages was run by Democrats.

23  *Hartford Courant*, April 4, 1863; *Hartford Post*, April 6, 1863; unidentified clippings, AED scrapbook.

24  This section represents a distilled version of J. Matthew Gallman, "Anna Dickinson, America's Joan of Arc: Public Discourse and Gendered Rhetoric During the Civil War," in Wendy Gamber, Michael Grossberg, and Hendrik Hartog, eds., *American Public Life and the Historical Imagination* (Notre Dame, IN: University of Notre Dame Press, 2003), 91–112.

25  Unknown newspaper, n.d. [October 1860?], AED scrapbook. Of course contemporary accounts of male orators also reported on their appearance and physical bearing, although without the same scrutiny.

26  *United States Gazette* [?] [handwritten notation], n.d. [roughly March 26, 1862]; *Philadelphia Press*, March 26, 1862, AED scrapbook; *New York Herald*, n.d., quoted in *National Anti-Slavery Standard*, April 25, 1863. As she became more successful, AED took to wearing custom-made dresses and flashy jewelry, a change that was not lost on the press.

27  *Providence Press*, [April 1862], reprinted in unknown newspaper, n.d.; unknown newspaper, December 15, 1862; *Independent*, [April 1863], reprinted in unknown newspaper, n.d. All AED scrapbook.

28  *Republican*, April 23, 1863; unknown Philadelphia newspaper, [May 1863]; "Correspondent to the *Philadelphia Press*," reprinted in several unknown papers, October 29, 1864; *National Eagle*, March 10, 1863. All AED scrapbook.

29  *Hartford Daily Post*, March 24, 1863; *Hartford Courant*, March 25, 1863.

30  *Republican*, April 23, 1863, AED scrapbook. See also *Chicago Tribune*, November 11, 1863.

31  Unknown newspaper, [late 1862], AED scrapbook. For similar sentiments see *Luzerne Union*, n.d., AED scrapbook.

32  *Hartford Courant*, March 25, 26, 1863; *Hartford Times*, March 24, 30, 1863.

33  Unidentified Hartford newspaper clipping, AED scrapbook; Lyman Beecher Stowe, *Saints, Sinners and Beechers* (New York: Blue Ribbon Press, 1934), 346; Joseph S. Van Why, *Nook Farm* (Hartford: Stowe-Day Foundation, 1975). See IBH's praise of AED in IBH to Edwin Stanton, April 1863, SDC.

34  *Liberator*, May 8, 1863; J. G. Batterson to AED April 9, 1863; Batterson to [?], April 18, 1863; Prescott to AED, March 23, 1863; SED to AED, February 9, 24, March 5, 30, 1863; JHY, "AED," III: 18; Joseph Duffy, "Anna Elizabeth Dickinson and the Election of 1863," *Connecticut History* 25 (1984), 22–38.

35  Unidentified clippings, AED scrapbook, March and April 1863; AED to "Dear Friend," April 10, 1863, HM 10528, HL.

36  *New York Herald*, April 22, 1863; *Republican*, April [?], 1863, AED scrapbook.

37  ECS to Martha C. Wright, April 22, 1863, ECS Papers, LC. Transcript in JHYP; Elizabeth Cady Stanton, "Anna Elizabeth Dickinson," in James Parton, et al., eds., *Eminent Women of the Age* (Hartford: S. M. Betts & Company, 1869), 500.

38  Stanton, "Anna Elizabeth Dickinson," 500.

39  Twenty-two New York men to AED, April 22, 1863; 20 Philadelphia men to AED, April 24, 1863. Both filed in AEDP under "Group Letters." AED spoke in New York on May 2 and in Philadelphia on the fourth.

40  Jno. Young to Judge Kelley, May 5, 1863; Judge Kelley to AED, May 9, 1863; William Lloyd Garrison to Oliver Johnson, May 5, 1863. Reprinted in *Letters of William Lloyd Garrison*, V: 149; misc. clippings, AED scrapbooks.

41  SED to AED, April 13, 1863.

42  Wyman and Wyman, eds., *Elizabeth Buffum Chace*, 1: 252.

43  AED to James C. Beecher, June 2, 1863, Schlesinger Library, Cambridge, Massachusetts.

44  AED to CDW, June 2, 1863, WP.

45  Undated clipping from [*National Guard?*], AED scrapbook. This lengthy story, signed "Agate" (Whitelaw Reid's pen name) and identified as "Special Correspondence of the *Cincinnati Gazette*," is dated June 22, 1863. A slightly abbreviated version of the same story appears in James G. Smart, ed., *A Radical View: The 'Agate' Dispatches of Whitelaw Reid, 1861–1865*, vol. 2 (Memphis: Memphis State University Press, 1976), 121–4. Two months later the *Ladies' Repository* reprinted Reid's entire story in its "Wayside Gleanings" section. *Ladies' Repository* vol. 23 (August 1863): 507–8.

46  *Addresses of the Hon. W. D. Kelley, Miss Anna E. Dickinson, and Mr. Frederick Douglass, at a mass meeting . . . Philadelphia, July 6, 1863, for the promotion of colored enlistments*, (Philadelphia, 1863) pamphlet, LC; AED to Milo Adams Townsend, July 7, 1863, in Peggy Jean Townsend and Charles Walker Townsend III, eds., *Milo Adams Townsend and Social Movements of the Nineteenth Century* (1994) online documents; Thomas Wentworth Higginson to AED, October 27, 1863.

47  Undated clipping, AED scrapbook. AED would make the exploits of the U.S. Colored Troops a central part of her novel, *What Answer?* (1868; reprinted Amherst: Humanity Books, 2002).

48  Lou Brackett to AED, August 18, 1863; SED to AED, several letters, fall 1863; William Hay to AED, October 16, 1863; Fanny Garrison to AED, October 4, 1863; Prescott to AED, September 28, November 15, 1863; Stanton, "Anna Elizabeth Dickinson," 504. One unidentified clipping lists 12 Pennsylvania speaking engagements between September 29 and October 12, 1863. In this crucial election Pennsylvania's Republican Governor Andrew Curtin defeated challenger George Woodward.

49  [Webler?] to AED, October 1, 1863, filed in container #14; *Philadelphia Press*, October 9, 1863, AED scrapbook. It is difficult to separate fact from legend in the Shamokin story. In 1868 ECS asked AED's permission to include the episode in a biographic sketch, arguing that it was already in wide circulation. AED's reply does not survive, but the story did not appear in Stanton's "Anna Elizabeth Dickinson." Stanton to AED, May 21, [1868]. In the early 1900s AED drafted an autobiography in which she treated the story as fact. AED, "Unidentified Manuscript," container #20, AEDP.

50  See William Quentin Maxwell, *Lincoln's Fifth Wheel: The Political History of the United States Sanitary Commission* (New York: Longmans, Green, 1956); George Fredrickson, *The Inner Civil War: Northern Intellectuals and the Crisis of Union* (New York: Harper and Row, 1965); J. Matthew Gallman, *The North Fights the Civil War: The Home Front* (Chicago: Ivan R. Dee, 1994); Gallman, "Voluntarism in Wartime: Philadelphia's Great Central Fair," in Maris A. Vinovskis, ed., *Toward a Social History of the American Civil War: Exploratory Essays* (New York: Cambridge University Press, 1990), 93–116.

51  Mary Livermore to AED, August 17, September 12, 22, October 1, 11, 1863; SED to AED, October 1, 1863. Livermore's first letter to AED was sent in care of Lucretia Mott.

52  *Chicago Tribune*, November 5, 7, 9, 11, 1863; *History of the Northwestern Soldiers' Fair* (Chicago: Dunlop, Sewell, and Spalding, Printers, 1864), 39–44; Wendy Hamand Venet, "The Emergence of a Suffragist: Mary Livermore, Civil War Activism, and the Moral Power of Women," *Civil War History* 48 (June 2002): 153–60; Venet, *A Strong-Minded Woman: The Life of Mary Livermore* (Amherst: University of Massachusetts Press, 2005), 113–15.

53  *Chicago Tribune*, November 12, 1863; unidentified clippings; *Peoria Morning Mail*, November 14, 1863; *Quincy Daily Whig*, November 14, 1863; *Portland Press*, November [?], 1863, all AED scrapbook.

54  Numerous clippings, AED scrapbook; SED to AED, several letters, 1863; JHY, "AED," III: 32.

55  [Rochester?] *Courier and Union*, November 18, 1863, AED scrapbook.

56  SED to AED, December 23, 1863.

57  MD to AED, February, 11, 1864.

58  On AED's research and requests for information from friends and acquaintances see Caroline Dall to AED, August 16, 1862; Samuel May, Jr., to AED, March 30, 1863; Samuel Pomeroy to AED, July 2, 1863; TT to AED, July 10, 1863.

59  Samuel Pomeroy to AED, May 27, July 2, November 2, 1863. Printed flyer, dated February 1864, filed among the letters from Pomeroy to AED. This flyer, which was reportedly sent to only a few hundred leading Republicans, has a handwritten notation labeling it "private." David Donald, *Lincoln* (New York: Simon and Schuster, 1995), 482.

60 Invitation in AEDP; SED to AED, December 23, 1863; William D. Kelley to AED, December 8, 14, 1863, January 9, 1864. The invitation and AED's response, are reprinted in Stanton et al., *History of Woman Suffrage*, 2: 47.

61 SD to AED, December 14, 1863.

62 Diary of Annie G. Dudley, January 16, 1863, HL.

63 For summaries of the lecture see *National Anti-Slavery Standard*, January 23, 1864; *Cincinnati Gazette*, n.d.; *Independent*, January 18, 1864; *Missouri Democrat*, January 25, 1864, all in AED scrapbook.

64 *National Anti-Slavery Standard*, January 23, 1864. This story cites a report from the *New York Post*.

65 William D. Kelley to Abraham Lincoln, January 16, 1864, Robert Todd Lincoln Collection, Abraham Lincoln Papers, LC; JHY, "AED," IV-8. Young cites the *Springfield Weekly Republican*, January 23, 1864.

66 WR to AED, January 17, 1864; Samuel Pomeroy to AED, [January 17, 1864?]; CDW to AED, January 19, 1864. AED apparently was annoyed with Pomeroy for keeping his distance immediately after the lecture. Pomeroy to AED, February 15, 1864.

67 The AEDP include invitations from Cincinnati, Philadelphia, Harrisburg, and Columbus, Ohio, each signed by long lists of dignitaries.

68 WR to AED, January 23, 1864; SED to AED, February 6, 9, 20, 27, 1864; AED scrapbook.

69 Unknown newspaper quoting both the *World*, AED scrapbook; *Geneva (NY) Gazette*, [March 1864?], reprinted in *National Anti-Slavery Gazette*, April 2, 1864.

70 *Rochester Evening Express*, March 15, 1864, AED scrapbook.

71 William Lloyd Garrison, Jr., to Ellen Wright, April 28, 1864, SSC; Martha Coffin Wright to Ellen W. Garrison, January 22, 1865, SSC.

72 Misc. clippings, AED scrapbook.

73 WR to AED, February 3, 1864; Benjamin Prescott to AED, March 13, 1864.

74 Lillie B. Chace to AED, March 12, 1864; Benjamin Prescott to AED, March 30, 1864; WR to AED, April 3, 1864. Reid's letter refers to a March 12 letter from AED.

75 William D. Kelley to AED, July 24, 1864; William Lloyd Garrison, Jr., to Ellen Wright, April 28, 1864, SSC; JHY, "AED," IV: 17–21. For another critique of AED's attacks on the president see [Fairchild Anders?] to AED, March 15, 1864.

76 For abolitionists and the election of 1864 see James M. McPherson, *The Struggle for Equality* (1964; reprinted Princeton, 1995), 260–86.

77 Phillips was at the core of the Frémont movement, but he did not attend the Cleveland convention. McPherson, *The Struggle for Equality*, 269.

78 WR to AED, April 3, 1864. One Republican canceled a lecture engagement because of AED's attacks on Lincoln. G. Ames to AED, May 13, 1864.

79 TT to AED, June 30, 1864; SBA to AED, July 1, 1864.

80 AED to [ECS], July 12, 1864, HL. AED shared similar sentiments about Lincoln in a letter to Elizabeth Buffum Chace. Elizabeth Buffum Chace to Lucy F. Lovell, July 2, 1864, in Wyman and Wyman, eds., *Elizabeth Buffum Chace*, 1: 263.

81 TT to AED, July 13, 1864; William D. Kelley to AED, July 24, 1864; William D. Kelley to Abraham Lincoln, August 1, 1864, Robert Todd Lincoln Collection, LC.

82 Lillie B. Chace to AED, August 21, 1864. Chace describes a conversation with Douglass.

83 AED to [?] Reaves, August 29, 1864, Chicago Historical Society. Transcribed in the JHYP.

84 McPherson, *The Struggle for Equality*, 281.

85 David Donald, Jean Baker, Michael Holt, *The Civil War and Reconstruction* (New York: W. W. Norton Press, 2001), 523.

86 McPherson, *Struggle for Equality*, 282.

87 *New York Independent*, September 8, 1864. A handful of other leading women had already placed their political opinions in print. Elizabeth Cady Stanton had publicly endorsed the Frémont movement, and on May 1 Bostonian Caroline Dall published a response in the *Liberator* declaring that women should be interested in national concerns but not expect to "dictate" politics. Faye Dudden, "New York Strategy: The New York Woman's Movement and the Civil War," in Jean Baker, ed., *Votes for Women: The Struggle for Suffrage Revisited* (New York: Oxford University Press, 2002), 67–68.

88  TT to AED, September 5, 1864; BB to AED, September 8, 1864; Edwin Hawkins to AED, September 9, 1864; WR to AED, September 11, 1864. For more praise of AED's letter in the *Independent* see T. B. Pugh to AED, September 15, 1864; Emma Wood to AED, September 18, 1864; Oliver Johnson to AED, September 22, 1864.

89  Lillie B. Chace to AED, September 19, 1864; TT to AED, October 4, 1864 (TT's letter quotes from AED's letter to him); *Philadelphia Press*, November 3, 1864; several unidentified clippings AED scrapbook.

90  Donald, Baker, and Holt, *Civil War and Reconstruction*, 425–6.

91  CDW to AED, November 10, 1864.

92  *Pittsburg Evening Gazette*, December 15, 1864, AED scrapbook.

93  AED delivered the same lecture in Maine, Brooklyn, and finally at New York's Cooper Institute. (Augusta, Maine) *Gospel Banner*, February 18, 1865; *Transcript*, February 18, 1865; *New York Tribune*, February 15, 1865, all AED scrapbook.

94  *New York Times*, February 22, 1865; *New York World*, March 10, 1865; *Providence Journal*, March 15, 1865; *Lawrence Sentinel*, April 1, 1865, AED scrapbook; Oliver Johnson to AED, February 24, 1865; CDW to AED, February 25, 1865.

95  Oliver Johnson to AED, April 20, 1865; unidentified to AED, April 20, 1865; Lillie B. Chace to AED, April 23, 1865.

96  *New York World*, May 11, 1865, AED scrapbook.

## Notes to Chapter 3

1  Glenn C. Altschuler and Stuart M. Blumin, *Rude Republic: Americans and Their Politics in the Nineteenth Century* (Princeton: Princeton University Press, 2000), 152–83; Mary Ryan, *Civic Wars: Democracy and Public Life in the American City during the Nineteenth Century* (Berkeley: University of California Press, 1997).

2  MD to AED, February 11, 1864.

3  Fanny Garrison to AED, June 23, September 14, October 12, 1862; Lilly G. [Warner] to AED, February 1, 1864 (this is a portion of a note filed in the letters from IBH); Lilly G. Warner to AED, July 17, 1865, January 16, 1868.

4  Caroll Smith-Rosenberg, "The Female World of Love and Ritual: Relations Between Women in Nineteenth-century America," *Signs*, 1 (Autumn 1975), 1–29.

5  Joseph Allyn to AED, May 15, 31, July 21, 1863. On March 30 Allyn wrote to Secretary of the Navy Gideon Welles, praising "the little Quakeress" he had just heard speak. Giraud Chester, *Embattled Maiden* (New York: G. F. Putnam's Sons, 1951), 56. Allyn was born in Hartford in 1833. On his background see John Nicolson, ed., *The Arizona of Joseph Pratt Allyn: Letters from a Pioneer Judge* (Tucson: University of Arizona Press, 1974), 3–42.

6  SED to AED, August 13, 1863. Two years later a letter from Benjamin Prescott seemed to confirm that AED had declined Allyn's marriage proposal. Prescott to AED, December 29, 1865.

7  Nicolson, ed., *The Arizona of Joseph Pratt Allyn*, 6–8, 37. Allyn's letter was published in the *Hartford Evening Press*, December 24, 1863. Allyn remained in the West until 1867 when ill health forced him to resign and return home. He died shortly thereafter of tuberculosis.

8  Elias Irish to AED, December 20, 1864, March 16, August 20, 1865.

9  Elias Irish to AED, January 21, 1866.

10  SED to AED, November 6, 15, 1866, December 31, 1867; Frank Irish to AED, December 1, 1866. AED remained in touch with Irish's siblings, and when Frank Irish died a few years later he left Anna a book that had once belonged to Elias. Ellen Irish to AED, September 29, 1869.

11  MD to AED, May 26, 1866.

12  Charlotte M. Crowell to AED, November 20, 1866.

13  "Louise" [Brackett] to AED, March 9, 1863, filed among "miscellaneous" letters.

14  Louise Brackett to AED, June 15, July 11, 24, 1863. Later letters from Brackett mentioning this judge would seem to indicate that he was from New Hampshire and remained in the East after Allyn was

long gone. It is possible that SED's letter of August 13 actually refers to the judge Louise Brackett was mentioning. In any case, both men were clearly taken with AED, and she seemed uninterested in either.

15  Louise Brackett to AED, June 15, July 24, 1863.

16  Louise Brackett to AED, May 29, 1863, March 4, 1864.

17  James Beecher to AED, January 8, 1864. This letter is filed among "fragments." The first 4 (of 12) pages are missing. See also AED to James Beecher, June 2, 1863, Schlesinger Library, Cambridge, MA.

18  James Beecher to AED, October 2, 1864.

19  "Louise" [Brackett] to AED, April 1, 1863; Louise Brackett to AED, May 29, June 15, 1863.

20  Louise Brackett to AED, July 11, 24, August 18, November 2, 1863, March 4, 1864.

21  We shall consider AED's relationships with Brackett and several other women in chapter 6.

22  Joseph Ricketson to AED, June 24, 1862; Frank Garrison to AED, September 12, 1862; Louise Brackett to AED, April 1, 1863. See also SED to AED, December 22, 1862, Ruth [Duzdeely?] to AED, March 29, 1862 [?].

23  Lillie Chace to AED, February 18, 1863, March 12, 1864, December 30, 1865; TT to AED, June 5, 1865; Oliver Johnson to AED, July 6, 1865.

24  On the development of *cartes de visite* see William C. Darrah, *Cartes de Visite in Nineteenth Century Photography* (Gettysburg: W. C. Darrah, 1981); Oliver Mathews, *The Album of Carte-de-Visite and Cabinet Portrait Photographs 1854–1914* (London, 1974). For a case study of one celebrity's use of *cartes de visite* to shape her identity see Nell Irvin Painter, *Sojourner Truth: A Life, A Symbol* (New York: W. W. Norton, 1996), 185–99.

25  Frank Garrison to AED, September 12, 1862; Edward Anthony to AED, April 27, May 19, 1863; SED to AED, August 13, 20, 1863. In 1864 the Edward and H. T. Anthony included a stereoview of AED in their "portrait gallery" of famous Americans. *Stereoworld* 25 (September, October, 1998), 19–21. Five years after the war, a Union veteran sent AED a copy of the engraving he said he had carried in his knapsack throughout the war. John H. Duhme to AED, July 21, 1868.

26  Author's collection.

27  Emma Fisher to AED, October 15, 1865. For another request for a lock of hair see Louise Lockett to AED, April [?].

28  Thomas Seville to AED, June 12, 1863; W. M. Boucher [?] to AED, April 6, 1864. For other marriage proposals see E. M. Bruce to AED, October 20, 1864; R. P. Minier [?] to AED, November 27, 1865.

29  Lillie [Atkinson] to AED, March 12, 1861, June 1, 1863. Most of the Lillie Atkinson letters are misfiled with the Lillie Chace letters in the AEDP.

30  Fanny Garrison to AED, June 23, 1863, September 14, October 12, 1862.

31  Lillie Chace to AED, February 18, March 30, April 17, 1863; December 17, 1866.

32  Frances E. Willard, *Glimpses of Fifty Years: The Autobiography of an American Woman* (Chicago: H. J. Smith & Co., 1889), 570.

33  Lillie Chace to AED, March 12, 1864; Emma F. Foster to AED, April 15, 1865; Harriette A. Keyser to AED, February 20, 1866; Charlotte Garrique to AED, November 1, 1865; Annie McCarthy to AED, February 12, 1865; Marie P. Kendall to AED, December 16, 1865; L. A. Plympton to AED, November 30, 1862.

34  AED's most popular postwar lecture was a tribute to Joan of Arc. At some point during the war AED jotted down a list of references to her as "Joan of Arc" on a scrap of paper, AEDP.

35  Frank Moore, *Women of the War: Their Heroism and Self Sacrifice* (Hartford: S. S. Scranton & Company, 1867); Linus Pearpont Brockett and Mary C. Vaughan, *Woman's Work in the Civil War: A Record of Heroism, Patriotism and Patience* (Philadelphia: Zeigler, McCurdy, & Company, 1867).

36  See Nina Silber, *Daughters of the Union: Northern Women Fight the Civil War* (Cambridge: Harvard University Press, 2005), 41–86.

37  Faye Dudden, "New York Strategy: The New York Woman's Movement and the Civil War," in Jean Baker, ed., *Votes for Women: The Struggle for Suffrage Revisited* (New York: Oxford University Press, 2002). Quotation from 71. See also Wendy Hamand Venet, *Neither Ballots nor Bullets: Women Abolitionists and the Civil War* (Charlottesville: University of Virginia, 1991), 94–122 and *passim*.

38  Venet, *Neither Ballots nor Bullets*, 129–30; AED scrapbook.

## Notes to Chapter 4

1 Phrenological chart, dated June 21, 1866, container #24. Charles Sumner, one of AED's idols, embraced phrenology, the popular science based on the study of the skull and brain. David Donald, *Charles Sumner and the Coming of the Civil War* (New York: A. A. Knopf, 1960), 104. Walt Whitman was also fascinated with the possibilities of phrenology. David S. Reynolds, *Walt Whitman's America* (New York: A. A. Knopf, 1995), 246–8 and *passim*.

2 AED had made a few unpaid appearances in aid of freed slaves or to encourage African American enlistment.

3 SD to "Family," January 3, 1866; MD to AED, March 4, 1866; SD to AED, March 6, December 4, 1866; ED to AED, November 15, 1866; SED to AED, December 1, 1866.

4 Robert Julius Greef, *Public Lectures in New York, 1851–1878* (Chicago: University of Chicago Press, 1945). For contemporary analysis see "The Popular Lecture," *Atlantic Monthly* 15 (March 1865), 362–71; Thomas Wentworth Higginson, "A Plea for Culture," *Atlantic Monthly* 19 (January 1867), 29–35; Higginson, "The American Lecture-System" *Every Saturday* (April 11, 1868), 489–94; "The Lyceum Lecture," *The Nation* (April 8, 1869), 271–2. See also Carl Bode, *The American Lyceum: Town Meeting of the Mind* (New York: Oxford University Press, 1956).

5 Greef, *Public Lectures in New York*; Charles F. Horner, *The Life of James Redpath and the Development of the Modern Lyceum* (New York: Barse & Hopkins, 1926); Major J. B. Pond, *Eccentricities of Genius: Memories of Famous Men and Women of the Platform and Stage* (New York: G. W. Dillingham, 1900).

6 "The Popular Lecture," *Atlantic Monthly* 15 (March 1865), 362–71; Pond, *Eccentricities of Genius*, 540–1.

7 Container #19, folder #2, AEDP; JHY, "AED," chapter X.

8 Dickinson family correspondence; John B. Gough to AED, June 29, July 18, 1865; John B. Gough, *Autobiography and Personal Recollections* (Springfield, MA: Bill, Nichols, & Co., 1869), 550; SED to AED, February 13, 1866; JHY, "AED," X: 10–1.

9 T. B. Pugh to AED, March 14, 1868 and numerous letters. AED also assisted Pugh by steering several colleagues—including Phillips and Butler—toward her old friend.

10 Pond, *Eccentricities of Genius*, 152–3; Horner, *The Life of James Redpath*, 144–5; Albert Bigelow Paine, ed., *Mark Twain's Autobiography* (New York: Harper & Brothers, 1924); JHY "AED," X: 18–19. These figures appear in AED's papers. In June 1870 the *Brooklyn Eagle* reported that AED was charging $250 per lecture for the upcoming season, *Brooklyn Eagle*, June 24, 1870.

11 James Redpath to AED, December 16, 1869, May 30, August 8, 1870, February 11, 1872; AED to CDW, June 3, 1870, WP; Horner, *Life of James Redpath*, 144–5; Harrison, *Culture Under Canvas*.

12 JHY, "AED," X: 19; Horner, *The Life of James Redpath*, 156–79.

13 AED to MD, February 3, 1871, February 2, 1873; AED to SED, October 12, 15, November 14, 1873; ED to AED, May 21, 1872.

14 Betty Browne to AED, August 29, 1871.

15 O. G. Bernard to AED, August 19, 1873, May 19, June 6, August 19, 1874; AED to SED, November 18, December 2, 1873; SED to AED, December 12, 1873, March 28, 1874.

16 The text of AED's "Joan of Arc" lecture is in AEDP, container #15. For a full transcript and analysis see Karlyn Kohrs Campbell, "La Pucelle D'Orleans Becomes An American Girl: Anna Dickinson's 'Jeanne D'Arc'," in Michael C. Leff and Fred J. Kaufield, eds., *Texts in Context: Critical Dialogues on Significant Episodes in American Political Rhetoric* (Davis, CA: Hormagoras Press, 1989), 91–111, 279–309. Quotes from pp. 285, 290.

17 AED scrapbooks; Philip George Prindle, "An Analysis of the Rhetoric Selected Representative Speeches of Anna Elizabeth Dickinson," (Ph.D. diss., Stanford University, 1971).

18 *Revolution*, August 5, 1869; *A Ragged Register*, 25–32; Prindle, "Speeches of Anna Elizabeth Dickinson," 18.

19 *Revolution*, October 21, 1869; *Brooklyn Eagle*, November 20, 1869; Philip George Prindle, "Speeches of Anna Elizabeth Dickinson," 387–413 (full transcript, copied from *Daily Missouri Democrat*, March 5, 1870), quotes from pp. 401, 405, 400, 408.

20 Barbara Goldsmith, *Other Powers: The Age of Suffrage, Spiritualism, and the Scandalous Victoria Woodhull* (New York: Alfred A. Knopf, 1998), 203–6, 216; *Brooklyn Eagle*, January 13, 1871; Prindle, "Speeches of Anna Elizabeth Dickinson," 204–7.

21 See CDW to AED, June 12, 1871; ED to AED, August 20, 1871; Samuel Bowles to AED, September 23, 1871; Horace White to AED, July 14, 1872; AED to CDW, June 6, 1871, WP.

22 Prindle, "Speeches of Anna Elizabeth Dickinson," 214–8; Oliver Johnson to AED, November 17, 1871; Ira Steward to AED, October 11, 1871.

23 AEDP include several notebooks with notes, drafts, and polished lectures.

24 *San Francisco Alta California*, April 5, 1867, online at www.twainquotes.com; Paul Fatout, *Mark Twain on the Lecture Circuit* (Bloomington: Indiana University Press, 1960), 68. On AED's tense relationship with Twain see Laura E. Skandera-Trombley, *Mark Twain in the Company of Women* (Philadelphia: University of Pennsylvania Press, 1994), 141–50.

25 In addition to the sources noted above, see Harry P. Harrison as told to Karl Detzer, *Culture Under Canvas: The Story of Tent Chautauqua* (New York: Hastings House, 1958), 217–28.

26 "Woman in the Lyceum," *Nation* (May 18, 1869), 371–2. Six months later Parker Pillsbury assessed "Woman in the Lyceum" for the *Revolution*, paying particular attention to the offerings by Kate Field and Olive Logan, but also taking note of the most recent lecture by AED, *Revolution*, November 25, 1869.

27 Lizzie M. Powell to AED, November 13, 1866.

28 Tynesea W. Harris to AED, November 2, 1868. See also Ida Blanche Keedy to AED, May 19, 1870; Adelle Hazlett to AED, August 28, 1871; Emma [?] Harriman to AED, April 16, 1873; Leila E Patridger [?] to AED, August 18, 1874. In her memoirs, celebrated suffragist and orator Anna Howard Shaw recalled in her youth hearing AED give her "Joan of Arc" speech. She found the lecture inspirational, but AED proved dismissive in person. Anna Howard Shaw, *The Story of a Pioneer* (New York: Harper & Brothers, 1915), 66. Various contemporary novelists created characters who turned to AED for inspiration. See Harriet Beecher Stowe, *The Chimney Corner* (Boston: Ticknor and Fields, 1868), 36–37; Marcus Mills Pomeroy, *Nonsense, or, Hits and Criticisms on the Follies of the Day* (New York: G. W. Carleton, 1868), 181; Joseph Hertford, *Personals, or Perils of the Period* (New York: privately printed, 1870), 316; Martha J. Lamb, *Spicy* (New York: Appleton, 1873), 104.

29 *Brooklyn Eagle*, April 14, 1870. Contemporary novelists and satirists also used AED's name to mock female orators and women in public. See Sarah A. Dorsey, *Lucia Dare* (New York: M. Doolady, 1867), 9; George W. Peck, *Adventures of One Terence McGrant* (New York: J. H. Lambert, 1871), 69. In her novel, *The Widower*, Julie P. Smith's young character Pauline has two cats, a docile female named "General Grant" and a feisty male named "Anna Dickinson." (New York, G. W. Carleton, 1871), 205.

30 On the camaraderie on the lyceum circuit see also Paine, ed., *Mark Twain's Autobiography*; Elizabeth Cady Stanton, *Eighty Years and More: Reminiscences 1815–1897* (New York: European Pub. Co., 1898), chapter XVII.

31 SED to AED, November 20, 1868; Olive Logan to AED, May 31, 1869. Logan was actually three years older than AED, but she clearly looked up to her as a role model in their early interactions.

32 See William M. Martin to AED, June 2, 1869; T. H. Jackson to AED, July 21, 1870; Olive Logan to AED, n.d.; E. M. Davis to AED, October 19, 1871.

33 *Revolution*, June 3, 1869. AED promptly sent a copy of Logan's article to a friend in Michigan. Edward Evans to AED, June 7, 1869.

34 Olive Logan to AED, June 21, October 8, 1869. See also Logan to AED, April 10, June 12, 1870.

35 Olive Logan to AED, May 31, June 21, 1869.

36 SED to AED, November 2, 1870. Samuel Bowles expressed similar sentiments in an April 8, 1871, letter to AED.

37 Olive Logan to AED, December 12, 1871. This is the final letter from Logan in the AEDP.

38 See Carolyn J. Moss, ed., *Kate Field: Selected Letters* (Carbondale, IL: Southern Illinois University Press, 1996). Both Logan and Field appeared in Pugh's Star Course in 1872. Pugh to AED, February 27, 1872. Like Logan, Field was actually a few years older than the more experienced AED. The sardonic Mark Twain recalled that both Field and Logan "should have been house-emptiers" despite their early successes. Paine, ed., *Mark Twain's Autobiography*.

39 Kate Field to AED, July 14, August 19, 23, 1870; WR to Kate Field, February 24, 1870 (letter book), WRP; Kate Field to WR, November 6, 1870, in Moss, ed., *Kate Field*, 62; Kate Field to AED, December 24, 1874.

40 SED to AED, February 10, 1870; Melinda Jones to AED, July 13, 1872; Lou Brackett to AED, November 27, 1874. See also Edward Evans to AED, February 4, 1870; Lou Brackett to AED, April 27, 1871; Melinda Jones to AED, August 21, September 4, 1874. Laura Bullard was friends with both women and often mentioned Field in letters to AED. LCB to AED, November 27, December 20, 1873; August 17, October 29, 1874. In the early 1870s Reid was occasionally linked romantically with both AED and Field. This may have added another layer to their professional rivalry. See WR to Murat Halstead, February 4, 1870, WRP.

41 AED to SED, August 21, 1879.

42 AED to SED, February 27, 1880. See chapter 7.

43 *Revolution*, June 3, November 25, 1869.

44 Fanny Edmunds to AED, March 2, 1871; AED to CDW, March 16, April 13, 1871, WP; CDW to AED, March 28, 1871; Samuel Bowles to AED, April 18, 1871. In preparation for this proposed trip, AED secured a letter of introduction from author John Greenleaf Whittier to British M. P. John Bright, Whittier assured the famed English orator that AED was "the most eloquent female speaker in the US." John Greenleaf Whittier to John Bright, April 8, 1871.

45 LCB to AED, October 5, 10, 13, 30, December 29, 1872; AED to MD, February 2, 1873.

46 Sallie F. Austin to AED, November 11, [1872], March 9, [1873]; E. P. Bullard to AED, February 23, March 1, April 8, 1873.

47 AED to MD, February 7, 1871. Robert Julius Greef linked Edgarton with Logan and Field as a trio of "thoroughly feminine and attractive young ladies" who began lecturing after the war. *Public Lectures in New York*, 23.

48 AED to CDW, March 16, 1871, WP; WR to AED, March 22, 1871, WRP.

49 SED to AED, February 28, 1871; Noah Brooks to AED, April 7, 1873.

50 ECS to Milo A. Townsend, April 5, 1871, Garrison Papers, SSC. ECS's comments came in response to negative comments by AED and Field about VCW. See Martha Coffin Wright to Ellen Garrison, April 12, 1871. See chapter 7.

51 ECS to Harriot Eaton Stanton, January 8, 1879, in Theodore Stanton and Harriot Stanton Blanch, eds., *Elizabeth Cady Stanton: As Revealed in Her Letters, Diary and Reminiscences* (New York: Harper & Brothers, 1922), II: 156–7; container #19, folder #5, AEDP.

## Notes to Chapter 5

1 Lillie Chace to AED, May 22, 1865; E. H. Irish to AED, May 25, 1865; John W. Blassingame and John R. McKivigan, eds., *The Frederick Douglass Papers* (New Haven: Yale University Press, 1991), 4: 80; James M. McPherson, *The Struggle for Equality* (Princeton: Princeton University Press, 1964), 304.

2 Ellen Carol DuBois, *Feminism and Suffrage* (Ithaca, NY: Cornell University Press, 1978, 1999), 53–55.

3 McPherson, *Struggle for Equality*, 245–6, 341–56.

4 Lillie Chace to AED, April 23, 1865; Benjamin Prescott to AED, July 17, 1865; misc. clippings, AED scrapbook; JHY, "AED," V: 22–25; McPherson, *Struggle for Equality*, 308–40.

5 CDW to AED, April 22, 1866, CDW Papers; William D. Kelley to SED, May 4, 1866. A few weeks later SD reported that a congressman had cornered him to complain about mistreatment at the hands of his celebrated sister. See MD to family, May 17, 1866 (SD's note is at the end of this letter).

6 T. E. Longshore to AED, August 1, 1866; Pugh to AED, August 8, 17, 1866.

7 William D. Kelley to AED, August 7, 23, 1866; Colonel Francis Jordan to AED, August 16, 24, 1866; SED to AED, August 18, 1866.

8 AED to IBH, August 29, 1866, IBH Papers; IBH Diary, April 12, 1867, *IBH Project*.

9 McPherson, *Struggle for Equality*, 358–60.

10 McPherson, *Struggle for Equality*, 360–3; Eric Foner, *Reconstruction: America's Unfinished Revolution* (New York: Harper & Row, 1988), 270; William S. McFeely, *Frederick Douglass* (New York: W. W. Norton & Co., 1991), 251–2; David Blight, *Frederick Douglass's Civil War: Keeping Faith in Jubilee* (Baton Rouge: LSU Press, 1989), 193–4. The entire proceedings were printed in the *Washington Reporter*, 33–40 (September 17 through November 5, 1866). For AED's speech see the *Reporter*, 37 (October 15, 1866): 12–15.

11 Frederick Douglass to AED, September 10, 1866. On several occasions in the decades to come Douglass credited AED and TT with turning the tide at this crucial moment, paving the way for black male suffrage. See Philip S. Foner, *The Life and Writings of Frederick Douglass* (New York: International Publishers, 1955), 4: 28–30, 46, 352–3. See also Douglass's address delivered in Albany, NY, April 22, 1870, in Blassingame and McKivigan, eds., *Frederick Douglass Papers*, 4: 268.

12 Henry Barr to AED, September 12, 1866; George Marcy to AED, September 12, 1866. See also Frances Lewis to AED, October 5, 1866; CDW to AED, October 22, 1866; WR to AED, November 11, 1866. The day after she spoke the members of the convention also passed a special resolution thanking AED for her "able and eloquent address." *Reporter*, 39 (October 29, 1866): 15.

13 JHY, "AED," V: 48.

14 Henry Wilson to AED, September 7, 8, 1866; AED to Henry Wilson (draft), September 19, 1866.

15 L. Edwin Dudley to AED, May 7, June 15, 26, 1867; TT to AED, May 16, 1867; Frederick Douglass to AED, May 21, 1867.

16 DuBois, *Feminism and Suffrage*, 63–65; Ida Husted Harper, *The Life and Work of Susan B. Anthony*, (Indianapolis: Bowen-Merril Company, 1899), 1: 256–62.

17 Oliver Johnson to AED, May 14, 1866; Harper, *The Life and Work of Susan B. Anthony*, 1: 258.

18 DuBois, *Feminism and Suffrage*, 71–72.

19 Oliver Johnson to AED, May 19, 1867.

20 SBA to AED, April 3, 1863 (this letter is also reproduced in the *ECS-SBA Papers*). SBA shared her hopes that AED would attend the meetings with other members of the women's movement. SBA to Amy Kirby Post, April 13, 1863, *Selected Papers*, 1: 481.

21 SBA to AED, August 6, October 23, 1866; SBA to SED, November 7, 1866; SED to AED, November 15, 1866.

22 Numerous letters in AEDP speak of her December illness, which was serious enough that SED traveled to Chicago to tend to her sister. SD to AED, December 14, 1866.

23 DuBois, *Feminism and Suffrage*, 66–104; Harper, *The Life and Work of Susan B. Anthony*, volume 1, chapter XVII; SBA to AED, February 18, March 24, 1867; Lucy Stone to ECS, April 10, 1867, *Selected Papers*, 2: 48. See also Samuel N. Wood to AED, several 1867 letters; Wood to SBA, April 21, 1867, *Selected Papers*, 2: 54. Wood was the Corresponding Secretary of the State Impartial Suffrage Association in Kansas.

24 SBA to AED, June 11, July 2, 12, 1867; SED to AED, July 9, 1867; AED to SBA, July [before 31] 1867, in Harper, ed., *The Life and Work of Susan B. Anthony*, 1: 280; DuBois, *Feminism and Suffrage*, 87–88. See also, SBA to AED, May 17, 1867, June 14, 19, 1867.

25 DuBois, *Feminism and Suffrage*, 89–91; SBA to AED, August 15, September 23, 1867 (The September 23, 1867 letter is reprinted in *Selected Papers*, 2: 92–93); SED to AED, August 2, 16, 1867. Samuel Pomeroy also wrote to AED pushing a Kansas trip. See Pomeroy to AED, October 16, 1867 and SED to AED, October 23, 1867.

26 Lucy Stone to AED, December 10, 1867; SED to AED, February 23, 1868; DuBois, *Feminism and Suffrage*, 93–101.

27 SBA to AED, November 28, 1867 (reprinted in *Selected Letters*, 2: 114–5). AED's relationship with SBA will be considered in the next chapter.

28 DuBois, *Feminism and Suffrage*, 193, quoting Elizabeth Cady Stanton, Susan B. Anthony, and Matilda Jocelyn Gage, *History of Woman Suffrage*, 3 vols. (1881), 2: 266–7.

29 Harper, *The Life of Susan B. Anthony*, 1: 202–3. Harper republished the entire story. The original appeared in the *Cincinnati Commercial*, April 5, 1868 (clipping in AED scrapbooks).

30 Lucy Stone to AED, March 5, 1868; SBA to AED, March 31, May 4, May [?], 1868; Harper, *The Life of Susan B. Anthony*, 1: 303–4; *Revolution*, May 7, 1868; Lillie Chace to AED, May 29, 1868. As she

had done two years earlier, AED pleased, and perhaps appeased, SBA a bit by sending the AERA a large contribution of $100 in 1868. SBA to AED, May 22, 1868.

31  *Revolution,* April 9, 23, May 7, 1868.

32  Book contract for *What Answer?* with Ticknor & Fields, Boston, August 27, 1868, container #22, AEDP.

33  AED's correspondence include only occasional references to the idea of writing a novel, and no discussion of plot lines or writing strategies. TT to AED, August 1, 1864; WR to AED, June 18, 1866. A few letters indicate that AED was writing and copyediting in the summer and fall of 1868. Lillie Chace to AED, July 9, 1868; Emma Wood to AED, July 16, 1868; Charles Wood to AED, August 8, 1868; AED to MD, September 1, 1868; SED to AED, September 7, 1868.

34  Harriet Beecher Stowe to AED, n.d. See also Harriet Beecher Stowe to James T. Field, [July 1868?], J. T. Field Collection, HL; *Hartford Courant,* n.d., AED scrapbook.

35  See Gallman, "Introduction," in Anna E. Dickinson, *What Answer?* (1868; Amherst: Humanity Books, 2003). See also, Gallman, *"Touched with Fire"?: Two Philadelphia Novelists Remember the Civil War* (Frank Klement Lecture Series No. 10) (Milwaukee, 2002); Lyde Cullen Sizer, *The Political Work of Northern Women Writers and the Civil War, 1850–1872* (Chapel Hill: University of North Carolina Press, 2000), 232–44.

36  AED modeled Francesca and her family on the family of Robert Purvis, one of Philadelphia's most prominent black abolitionists. AED and her family were friendly with the Purvises, and AED and Hattie Purvis were particularly close.

37  Oliver Johnson to AED, September 30, 1868; TT to AED, October 9, 1868; SED to AED, March 16, 1873 (quoting a conversation with Purvis, who had spoken with Sumner). AED received comparable letters praising the novel from BB, WR, IBH, CDW, Wendell Phillips, and D. R. Locke and numerous other friends and strangers.

38  Lillie B. Chace to AED, October 27, 1868; WR to AED, October 12, 1868; Martha Coffin Wright to Ellen Garrison, November 5, 1868, SSC. Prior to reading the novel, CDW told IBH that "I guess it is a short work about a colored woman who was the wrong color for this wicked world." CDW to IBH, November 2, 1868, IBH Project.

39  *Revolution,* November 12, 1868; AED scrapbook; copies of *What Answer?* in the author's possession. There was also talk of translating the novel into both French and German. SED to AED, March 9, 1869; J. G. Hertwig to AED, December 20, 1869.

40  *Springfield Republican,* September 23, 1868; *Philadelphia Press,* September 26, 1868; *New York World,* September 30, 1868. These are among the over 30 reviews in the AED scrapbooks.

41  *Nation,* October 29, November 12, 1868; IBH to AED, November 23, [1868]; IBH to Robert Allen, November 28, 1868, IBH Project. See also Robert Purvis to AED, November 2, 1868; Lillie Chace to AED, January 10, 1869. Chace noted that Wendell Phillips found the *Nation's* review much too harsh; Martha Coffin Wright (cited above) called the *Nation* characteristically "savage."

42  AED to Burt G. Wilder to AED, January 19, 1910. In 1869 AED sought advice from Harriett Beecher Stowe about her unsatisfactory royalty payments. Harriett Beecher Stowe to AED, May 22, 1869; Walter Brackett to AED, May 18, [1869].

43  *Revolution,* October 22, 1868. For a discussion of the racial dimensions of the women's rights movement, and particularly the attitudes of Stanton, see Louise Michele Newman, *White Women's Rights: The Racial Origins of Feminism in the United States* (New York: Oxford University Press, 1999), 3–21, 57–65.

44  *Revolution,* November 5, 1868.

45  James Parton et al., *Eminent Women of the Age: Being Narratives of The Lives and Deeds of the Most Prominent Women of the Present Generation* (Hartford, CT.: S. M. Betts & Company, 1869). For an extended discussion of Stanton's essay see Gallman, "An Inspiration to Work: Anna Elizabeth Dickinson, Public Orator," in Joan E. Cashin, ed., *The War Was You and Me: Civilians in the American Civil War* (Princeton: Princeton University Press, 2002), 159–82. For a critical analysis of this volume's rhetorical assumptions see Nan Johnson, *Gender and Rhetorical Space in American Life, 1866–1910* (Carbondale, IL: Southern Illinois University Press, 2002), 115–8, 137–9. Perine's engraving was based on a popular CDV of Dickinson.

46 SBA to [SED?], February 3, 1868; [SED?] to SBA, February 4, 1868; George E. Perine to SBA, May 23, 1868 (letter forwarded to AED and filed under "Misc. P"); SBA to AED, May 25, June 3, 1868; S. W. Betts to AED, July 16, 1868; ECS to Martha Coffin Wright, March 2, 1868, ECS Papers, SSC. Perine's engraving was based on a popular CDV of AED.

47 *Revolution*, January 29, June 4, September 17, October 8, 15, 22, 29, November 5, December 31, 1868, January 7, 1869; SBA to AED, July 8, 1868.

48 SBA to AED, October 15, 27, 29, 1868; *Revolution*, November 5, 1868.

49 *Revolution*, September 17, November 12, 19, December 10, 1868, January 21, 1869; DuBois, *Feminism and Suffrage*, 145–7; Lutz, *Susan B. Anthony*, 156–7; Harper, *Life and Work*, 1: 309; Angela G. Ray, "Representing the working class in early U. S. feminist media: the case of Hester Vaughn," *Women's Studies in Communication* 26 (Spring 2003). Most of the contemporary sources spelled the name "Vaughan," but Ray notes that it was actually "Vaughn."

50 *Revolution*, February 25, March 18, 1869; Stanton, Anthony, and Gage, *History of Woman Suffrage*, 2: 564–570; Harper, *Life and Work*, 1: 316.

51 *Revolution*, March 18, 25, April 1, 8, 15, 22, 29, May 13, 20, 27, 1869 (the letter from AED was published on April 22). Although the newspaper published numerous letters supporting the annual meetings, none arrived from AED.

52 SBA to AED, January 15, 1869; MD to AED, May 10, 1869; DuBois, *Feminism and Suffrage*, 162.

53 *Revolution*, December 31, 1868, February 18, April 8, 22, May 20, 27, 1869; *Harper's Bazaar* (June 12, 1869), 38. The newspaper spelled the name "Cozzens."

54 DuBois, *Feminism and Suffrage*, 162–99.

55 *Revolution*, June 3, 1869; SBA to AED, June 1, 1869. This edition republished the *Tribune's* article.

56 See, for instance, N. Kinney to AED, May 30, 1869; Olive Logan to AED, May 31, 1869; Edward Evans to AED, June 7, 1869; Ralph Meeker to AED, June 2, 1869.

57 WR to AED, June 2, 1869, June 1870; WR to ECS, June 2, 1869, HM 10542, HL; SED to AED, September 27, 1869.

58 At some point AED cosigned a $3,000 note to help keep the *Revolution* afloat. *Elmira Telegram*, April 14, 1895, container #23.

59 Harper, *Susan B. Anthony*, 1: 354–61 (Stanton quote on page 361); *Revolution*, December 9, 1869 and *passim*; SBA to AED, January 21, 1870; MD to AED, November 6, 1869; SED to AED, December 6, 1869; *Revolution*, January 20, 1870 (reprint of story from the *New York Tribune*).

60 Harper, *Susan B. Anthony*, 1: 361–3; LCB to AED, May 24, 1870; TT to AED, undated [May 1870?]; Denise M. Kohn, "Laura Jane Curtis Bullard (1831–1912)," *Legacy* 21 (2004): 74–82.

61 Stanton, Anthony, and Gage, *History of Woman Suffrage*, 2: 770–1; SBA to AED, March 22, 1870; TT to AED, [June 1870?], November 13, 14, 1870; SED to AED, November 11, 19, 1870; WR to SED, April 24, 1870, WRP.

62 AED to Mother, March 19, 1871. This long letter recounts several weeks of activities.

63 CDW to AED, December 9, 1870, WP; AED to CDW, April 13, May 18, 1871; AED to SED, August 26, 1872, July 8, 10, 1875; AED to MD, July 7, 1875.

64 Anna E. Dickinson, *A Paying Investment* (Boston: James R. Osgood and Co., 1876), 9, 28, 30.

65 Dickinson, *A Paying Investment*, 96.

66 Dickinson, *A Paying Investment*, 108–17.

67 AED to SED, July 7, 10, 1875. AED's correspondence included very few responses to *A Paying Investment*. One exception was a short note from BB on March 27, 1876.

## Notes to Chapter 6

1 Henry James, *The Bostonians* (1885; reprinted New York: Penguin Books, 1984); Sara deSaussure Davis, "Feminist Sources in *The Bostonians*," in *American Literature* (December, 1979), reprinted in Louis F. Budd and Edwin H. Cady, eds., *On Henry James: The Best from "American Literature"* (Durham: Duke University Press, 1990), 209–26. See also Charles R. Anderson, "Introduction," James, *The Bostonians*, 7–30. I have found no reference to James or the novel in the AEDP.

2  John Baker to AED, March 9, July 4, 7, 11, 1867; SED to AED, April 6, 1867.

3  William B. Allison to AED, July 15, September 5, 1869, and several undated notes; visiting card from Allison filed among letters from William Kelley; undated visiting card from "W.B.A." in Unidentified Letters folder; AED to SED, September 29, 1869. While in California AED acquired another suitor who apparently also proposed marriage. John H. Lewis to AED, September 11, 1869.

4  AED to MD, May 26, 1871. AED and Allison remained friends, and romantically linked in the press, for several years. Allison to AED, various letters; Fanny Edmunds to AED, June 28, no year; Susan Warner to AED, June 2, 1873.

5  Ralph Meeker to AED, June 2, 1869, September 26, [1870?], December 23, 1870, October 6, 19, 1873; SED to AED, March 28, 1871; WR to AED, March 27, 1871.

6  Louise Brackett to AED, June 15, 1864; James Beecher to AED, January 8, 1864; TT to AED, October 4, 1864; Abbe Harris to AED, August 4, 1865. CDW teased that she should consider advertising for a suitable husband. CDW to AED, December 22, 1866.

7  Benjamin F. Prescott to AED, December 29, 1865. For other comments see Lillie B. Chace to AED, December 30, 1865; SED to AED, February 13, 1866; R. N. Austin to AED, September 22, [1867?] (Filed with letters from Sallie Austin); John Hutchinson to AED, March 10, 1868.

8  AED to Susan Warner, January 19, 1870. WP.

9  C. Vann Woodward, "Introduction," *Whitelaw Reid, After the War: A Tour of the Southern States, 1865–1866* (1866; New York: Harper & Row, 1965), ix–xxi; WR to AED, June 6, 26, 1864, October 31, 1865.

10  WR to AED, November 11, 1866, March 18, 1870; WR to SED, January 21, 1870. Further reports about AED and WR cropped up over the next several years. See S. F. Austin to AED, November 11, [1872]; ED to AED, February 19, 1873; SED to AED, February 21, 1873.

11  Murat Halstead to WR, December 15, 1870, WRP; CDW to AED, March 12, 1873; Noah Brooks to AED, March 11, 1873. Brooks was also pleased to note that his name had been linked to AED's on occasion. WR sent Halstead a joking letter about his rumored courtships with both AED and Kate Field. WR to Murat Halstead, February 4, 1870, Reid Letterbook, WRP.

12  See WR to AED, December 20, 1867, December 20, 1870; SED to AED, December 6, 1869.

13  WR to AED, August 18, [1867?], June 17, 1870, April 8, 1871.

14  AED to WR, August 2, 1872, WR-GC.

15  SED to AED, September 27, 1869; AED to WR, November 15, 1869, WR-GC; SED to AED, December 6, 1869. See also WR to ECS, June 2, 1869, HL.

16  AED to WR, December 13, 22, 1870, WR-GC; WR to AED, December 20, 1870.

17  WR to AED, February 1, March 22, September 14, 1871, WRP. None of these letters appear in the AEDP. In her libel suit against the *Tribune* AED testified about WR's marriage proposal. See chapter 9.

18  WR to AED, March 27, 1871. For other examples of this sort of apparent jealousy see March 18, 1870 (on BB), March 27, 1871 (on Meeker), July 30, 1872 (on Allison). See also WR to SED, March 16, 1871, WRP.

19  Sallie F. Austin to AED, March 23, 1866.

20  L. G. Runkle to AED, August 27, 1872.

21  "Ida" to AED, August 28, 1867 in container #14. The context of this letter suggests that "Ida" was almost certainly Mrs. Sarah Bowman. A later letter from "Ida" in the same folder has the penciled notation "Mrs. Bowman" on the back. See SED to AED, August 28, 1867; Sarah H. Bowman to AED, six letters, no years, filed under "Misc. B" letters.

22  AED to SBA, n.d. Typescript in Ida Harper, *The Life and Work of Susan B. Anthony*, 3 vols. (1898–1908; reprint, New York: Arno Press, 1969), 1: 220–1. In *ECS-SBA Papers* the editors date this letter as 1862.

23  SBA to AED, December 6, 1866, November 28, 1867.

24  SBA to AED, n.d. The context suggests that this letter was written in early 1868.

25  SBA to AED, March 18, May 4, 25, 1868.

26  SBA to AED, May 18, 1868.

27  SBA sent at least eight more letters in 1868, and another eight over the next two years. The quotations are from July 8, October 29, 1868.

28  See SBA to IBH, [September/October?] 1869, *IBH Project*; SBA to AED, March 22, 1870.

29  SBA to James Redpath, December 23, 1870, *Selected Papers*, 2: 388–9; Betty Browne to AED, October 10, 1871?; SBA to AED, November 5, 1895. The 1872 encounter will be discussed later in this chapter.

30  For discussions of AED's relationship with SBA see Jean H. Baker, *Sisters: The Lives of America's Suffragists* (New York: Hill and Wang, 1995), 74–78; Lillian Faderman, *To Believe in Women: What Lesbians Have Done For America—A History* (Boston: Houghton Mifflin, 1999), 25–7. Unfortunately, whereas many of SBA's letters to AED remain among the AEDP, SBA burned many of her letters, including nearly all those from AED. See Patricia Holland and Ann D. Gordon, eds., *The Papers of Elizabeth Cady Stanton and Susan B. Anthony: Guide and Index to the Microfilm Edition* (Wilmington, DE: Scholarly Resources, Inc., 1992), 3–5. Frances Willard biographer Ruth Bordin has pointed out that SBA's letters to AED were much more "passionate" than her letters to Willard, who SBA also liked and admired. Bordin also notes that Willard's letters to AED were also more passionate than her normal correspondence with female friends. Ruth Bordin, *Frances Willard: A Biography* (Chapel Hill: University of North Carolina Press, 1986), 46.

31  LCB to AED, May 24, 1870, February 22, March 6, 1872.

32  LCB to AED, March 18, 25, April 2, June 6, 1872, August 23, [1872?] (filed with undated letters). The AEDP include 28 letters from LCB dated between March 1872 and the end of the year. Numerous letters in the AEDP indicate that LCB was often with her on her travels.

33  LCB to AED, July 14, 18, August 26, 1872, undated (early 1870s), November 24, [1872]. On the rumors about LCB, and about LCB and TT, see Richard Wightman Fox, *Trials of Intimacy: Love and Loss in the Beecher-Tilton Scandal* (Chicago: University of Chicago Press, 1999), 387n37.

34  Fanny Edmunds to AED, July 5, 10, [1871?], April 12, [?], May 2, [?], June 23, [?], March 2, [?], undated, July 19, [1871?], May 29, [?], undated. None of Edmunds's letters include the year. The dates and locations of her travels with AED are based on AED's family correspondence.

35  Nellie to AED, November 8, 1871, n.d. These letters are filed with the Ellen (Nellie) Miles letters although it is not clear that either came from Nellie Miles. Beginning in about 1870, Miles was the partner of activist minister Phebe Hanaford. Hanaford wrote to AED in 1868 and twice in 1873, and Miles and Hanaford would play a major role in AED's life in the 1890s, but there is no clear evidence that Miles was in contact with her in 1871. "Nellie's" letters refer to Cincinnati, which suggests that she could be Nellie Hutchinson, the reporter for the *Cincinnati Commercial* who profiled AED's visit to the *Revolution* offices in 1868.

36  See Karen Lystra, *Searching the Heart: Women, Men, and Romantic Love in Nineteenth-Century America* (New York: Oxford University Press, 1989); Ellen K. Rothman, *Hands and Hearts: A History of Courtship in America* (New York: Basic Books, 1984).

37  Carroll Smith-Rosenberg, "The Female World of Love and Ritual: Relations Between Women in Nineteenth-century America," *Signs*, 1 (Autumn 1975), 1–29.

38  Whereas Brackett, Bullard, and Edmunds all had husbands, many of AED's closest friends later in life lived with female partners.

39  My thoughts on how to understand and interpret AED's sexuality have been influenced by John D'Emilio and Estelle B. Freedman, *Intimate Matters: A History of Sexuality in America* (New York: Harper & Row, 1988); Lillian Faderman, *Surpassing the Love of Men: Romantic Friendship and Love between Women from the Renaissance to the Present* (1981; expanded New York: Quill Books, 1998); Faderman, *To Believe in Women*; Baker, "In the Company of Women"; Martha Vicinus, *Intimate Friends: Women Who Loved Women, 1778–1928* (Chicago: University of Chicago Press, 2004); Nancy Sahli, "Smashing: Women's Relationships Before the Fall," *Chrysalis* 8 (Summer 1979), 17–27; Leila J. Rupp, " 'Imagine My Surprise': Women's Relationships in Historical Perspective," *Frontiers* 5 (Fall 1980), 61–70; Estelle B. Freedman, " 'The Burning of Letters Continues': Elusive Identities and the Historical Construction of Sexuality," *Journal of Women's History* 9 (Winter 1998): 181–200; Sally Newman, "Lesbian Historiography, or a Talk about the 'Sweaty Sheet Fantasies' of Certain Modern Tribades," *Eras* (online journal) 5 (November 2003) www.arts.monash.edu.au/eras/edition_5/newmanarticle.htm; Bordin, *Frances Willard*, 44–48.

40  MD to AED, March 22, 1868. See also MD to AED, August 16, 1872.

41 On the Beecher-Tilton scandal see Fox, *Trials of Intimacy*; Barbara Goldsmith, *Other Powers: The Age of Suffrage, Spiritualism, and the Scandalous Victoria Woodhull* (New York: A. A. Knopf, 1998); Altina Waller, *Reverend Beecher and Mrs. Tilton: Sex and Class in Victorian America* (Amherst, MA: University of Massachusetts Press, 1982).

42 TT to AED, February 23, April 1, 1871; AED to TT, March 18, 1871, Autograph Collection of Charles Francis Jenkins, Friends Historical Library, Swarthmore College, notes in JHYP; WR to AED, April 18, 1871.

43 ED to AED, March 8, April 12, May 8, 1871; SED to AED, April 10, 15, 19, 1871; Fanny Edmunds to AED, March 2, 8, April 8, [1871]; WR to AED, March 8, 1871. During these same weeks AED was also worried about the health of her friend, columnist David Locke, who wrote under the name Petroleum Nasby.

44 SBA to VCW, February 4, 1871, *Selected Papers*, 2: 415; Goldsmith, *Other Powers*, 212–23. On VCW see Amanda Frisken, "Sex in Politics: Victoria Woodhull as an American Public Woman, 1870–1876," *Journal of Women's History* 12 (2000), 89–111 and the various studies of the Beecher-Tilton scandal noted above.

45 SBA to Martha Coffin Wright, March 21, 1871, *Selected Papers*, 2: 425–6. See also ECS to Lucretia Coffin Mott, April 1, [1871], *Selected Papers*, 2: 427–8; SBA to Laura De Force Gordon, February 9, 1871, *Selected Papers*, 2: 418; ECS to Milo Townsend, April 5, 1871, SSC.

46 CDW to AED, October 24, 1871; Olympia Brown to IBH, December 9, 1871, IBH Project; Henry B. Blackwell to SBA, September 7, 1872, *Selected Papers*, 2: 519; John Hooker to IBH, September 21, 1872, SDC.

47 WR claimed that VCW had told him stories about Beecher maintaining a harem of women in Brooklyn. WR to CDW, October 13, 1871, IBH Project. See also WR to AED, August 18, 1871.

48 Waller, *Reverend Beecher and Mrs. Tilton*, 135–6.

49 See Betty Browne to AED, May 16, [1871], September 16, 1871; WR to AED, August 18, 1871; SED to AED, May 12, 1871; AED to Jeanne Carr, September 17, 1871, HL.

50 Martha Coffin Wright to Ellen Garrison, April 12, 1871, SSC; ECS to Milo A. Townsend, April 5, 1871, Garrison Papers, SSC.

51 SED to AED, March 21, 1871; Betty Browne to AED, May 16, [1871]; WR to AED, June 3, 1871, WRP; Lillie B. Chace to AED, July 1, 1871; AED to TT, July 24, 1871, New York Public Library, notes in JHYP. (In 2000 AED's letters to TT were missing from the NYPL.)

52 AED to MD, December 3, 1871, January 12, 1872; AED to SED, December 6, 1871; James Redpath to AED, February 11, 1872; Elizabeth Tilton to AED, January 26, 1872, filed with Family Correspondence; AED to Elizabeth Tilton, February 10, 1872.

53 AED to Susan Warner, February 14, 1872, WP; AED to Theodore [Tilton], [February ?] 20, 1872 (filed among Misc. Letters). See also Oliver Johnson to AED, March 8, 1872.

54 TT to AED, March 26, April 4, 1872; Moses Coit Tyler to AED, June 30, 1872; SBA Diary, May 6, 1872, *Selected Papers*, 2: 492. Waller, *Reverend Beecher and Mrs. Tilton*, 136.

55 ECS to IBH, June 14, 1872, *Selected Papers*, 2: 512, 2: 513n8. Gordon cites SBA diary, June 7, 1872. The following year Hanaford—who had left her husband and was living with Nellie Miles—wrote to AED, blaming SBA for speaking having spoken ill of AED, Livermore, and herself. Phebe Hanaford to AED, February 9, 1873.

56 AED to WR, July 23, 1872, WR-GC; WR to AED, July 30, August 6, 1872.

57 L. G. Runkle to AED, August 31, 1872. It is impossible to know what these various rumors involved and which ones were based on a grain of truth.

58 John Hooker to IBH, October 31, 1872, SDC.

59 In two letters Phillips spoke of brief private moments together, but most of his letters were quite formal and paternalistic. Wendell Phillips to AED, August 13, 1867, October 28, 1868. In April 1871 AED sent a private note to Phillips through Lou Brackett and grew agitated when the Bracketts forgot to confirm delivery, but no letters hint at a secret relationship. Louise Brackett to AED. April 23, 1871. Barbara Goldsmith cites Hooker's letter and accepts the rumor as fact. *Other Powers*, 174, 322–3.

60 Fox, *Trials of Intimacy*, 156–7.

61 On VCW's 1872 campaign see Goldsmith, *Other Powers*, 324–36, 363–73.

62 Earle Dudley Ross, *The Liberal Republican Movement* (New York, 1919; New York: AMS Press, 1971); Matthew T. Downey, "Horace Greeley and the Politicians: The Liberal Republican Convention in 1872," *Journal of American History*, 4 (March 1967), 727–50; James M. McPherson, "Grant or Greeley? The Abolitionist Dilemma in the Election of 1872," *American Historical Review*, 71 (October 1965). For a longer discussion of the election of 1872 see J. Matthew Gallman, "Is the War Ended? Anna Dickinson and the Election of 1872," in Alice Fahs and Joan Waugh, eds., *The Memory of the Civil War in American Culture* (Chapel Hill: University of North Carolina Press, 2004), 157–79.

63 See AED to MD, February 2, 1871. On Bowles see Richard A. Gerber, "Liberal Republicanism, Reconstruction, and Social Order: Samuel Bowles as a Test Case," *The New England Quarterly* (September, 1972): 393–407.

64 See Oliver Johnson to AED, March 8, 1872; John Dickinson to AED, March 7, 1872.

65 *Pittsburgh Daily Post*, April 3, 1872, AED scrapbook.

66 Samuel Bowles to AED, April 5, 1872; CDW to AED, May 11, 1872, WP.

67 *New York World*, April 20, 1872; *Springfield Republican*, April [20?], 1872; *St. Louis Dispatch*, April 20, 1872; *Boston Post*, n.d.; *New York Sun*, April 20, 1872; all AED scrapbook.

68 AED to WR, May 11, 1872, WR-GC. LCB to AED, May 31, June 6, July 14, August 9, 1872; Robert Collyer to AED, July 28, 1872; Betty Browne to AED, July 29, 1872; CDW to AED, May 9, 11, 1872; AED to SED, June 7, 1872; M. S. Pomeroy to AED, June 7, 1872; Henry Wilson to AED, June 11, 1872.

69 Melanie Susan Gustafson, *Women and the Republican Party, 1854–1924* (Urbana: University of Illinois Press, 2001), 50–51; LCB to AED, July 7, 1872.

70 AED to MD, July 10, 12, 15, 1872; AED to SED, July 10, 1872; SED to AED, July 11, 1872; TT telegram to AED, July 12, 1872; AED to WR, July 23, 1872, WR-GC.

71 WR to AED, July 30, 1872. On the same day Oliver Johnson, another Greeley supporter, sent AED a similarly long and high-minded letter. Oliver Johnson to AED, July 30, 1872, filed among unidentified letters.

72 MD to AED, August 16, 1872. MD might have been influenced by a visit from Wendell Phillips that afternoon.

73 WR to AED, August 22, 1872; Wm [?] Hayes Ward to AED, August 26, 1872; Oliver Johnson to AED, August 27, 1872; AED to SED, August 26, 30, September 2, 1872; AED to SED, [1872?], filed with undated family letters; AED to MD, August 27, 1872. For the newspaper notices see *Independent*, August 27, 1872; *Golden Age*, August 31, 1872; *New York Tribune*, August 30, 1872; *Evening Chronicle*, August 28, 1872, all in AED scrapbooks. AED told her mother and sister that she had a contract for a new book, promising a $10,000 guarantee.

74 Samuel Bowles to AED, September 27, 1872; AED to WR, October 3, 1872, WR-GC. For lost lecture opportunities see Sue Warner to AED, September 28, 1872; Moses Coit Tyler to AED, October 2, 1872.

75 AED to SED, June 7, 1872; AED to WR, August 7, 1872, WR-GC.

76 *Boston Pilot*, October 30, 1872; *New York World*, October 26, 1872, AED scrapbook.

77 *National Republican*, n.d., AED scrapbook.

78 Numerous newspapers published detailed accounts of AED's lecture. Most of this narrative comes from the *New York Sun*, October 25, 1872.

79 *Providence Journal*, October 29, 1872; *Boston Journal*, October 29, 1872; *Waterbury (CT) Evening American*, October 26, 1872; *Springfield Republican*, October [?], 1872. AED scrapbooks includes roughly 30 clippings on her Cooper Institute lecture.

80 *Boston Post*, October 30, 1872; *Boston Journal*, October 29, 1872. The election of 1872 is also significant because of SBA's arrest and trial for voting in the election. Kathleen Barry, *Susan B. Anthony: A Biography of a Singular Feminist* (New York: New York University Press, 1988), 249–74.

81 Carl Schurz to AED, November 3, 1872; AED to MD, November 14, 1872. AED quoted BB in her letter to her mother.

82 Grant won the popular vote 3,597,132 to 2,834,125. David Herbert Donald, Jean Harvey Baker, Michael F. Holt, *The Civil War and Reconstruction* (New York: W. W. Norton, 2001), 619.

83 AED to SED, November 8, 1872.

84 AED unveiled "What's To Hinder?" on November 8, 1872. AED to SED, November 8, 1872. This summary from *Buffalo Courier*, February 28, 1873, AED scrapbook.

85 *Woman's Journal*, February 22, 1873, AED scrapbook; Lucretia Coffin Mott to Martha C. Wright, March 18, 1873, Beverly Wilson Palmer, ed., *Selected Letters of Lucretia Coffin Mott* (Urbana: University of Illinois Press, 2002), 478; SED to AED, March 23, 1873.

86 *New York Tribune*, February 11, 1873; L. G. Runkle to AED, February 16, 1873; LCB to AED, March 1, June 21, 1873; Noah Brooks to AED, March 11, May 16, July 31, 1873; AED to WR, October 12, 1873, WR-GC; LCB to AED, November 27, 1873. Soon friends were reporting rumors that Reid was seeing another woman.

87 By this point AED was already shaping the ideas that would become *A Paying Investment*.

88 AED to MD, November 29, 1872; John Dickinson to AED, November 30, 1872; SED to AED, December 2, 1872. In January John Dickinson wrote to AED about an overdue bill, apparently related to the funeral. John Dickinson to AED, January 7, 1873.

89 ED to AED, February 19, March 11, 1873; Charlotte Crowell to AED, February 28, 1873; AED to SED, April 7, 1873. On AED's illness see also SED to AED, April 4, 1873; AED to Susan Warner, April 15, 1873, WP; Betty Browne to AED, April 22, 1873; Phebe Hanaford to AED, May 22, 1873.

90 AED to CDW, September 4, 1873, WP; AED to Jeanne Carr, April 10, 1873, HL; SED to AED, April 16, 1873; AED to SED, April 17, 1873. Given the timing of her Colorado trip, I have surmised that Meeker made the offer during this visit.

91 SED to AED, May 27, 1873; AED to SED, July 17, 1873; AED to MD, July 29, August 2, 1873; MD to AED, July 31, 1873; John Dickinson to AED, July 31, [1873?].

92 AED to MD, August 12, September 4, 11, 1873. Later, in 1879, she wove many of her favorite travel stories—often taken almost verbatim from those letters—into *A Ragged Register* (New York: Harper and Brothers, 1879; reprinted Longs Peak, Colorado: Temporal Mechanical Press, 2000).

93 Dickinson, *A Ragged Register*, 51–52, 181. An 1873 etiquette book used AED as an example illustrating the fact that "ladies very frequently travel without any escort" and without serious problems. Alex. M. Gow, *Good Morals and Gentle Manners: For Schools and Families* (Cincinnati: Wilson, Hinkle, & Company, 1873), 240.

94 Dickinson, *A Ragged Register*, 20–22. This anecdote was probably from her 1869 trip.

95 Dickinson, *A Ragged Register*, 37–38; Janet Robertson, *The Magnificent Mountain Women: Adventures in the Colorado Rockies* (Lincoln: University of Nebraska Press, 1990), 10; *Greeley Tribune*, October 22, 1873, transcript at the City of Greeley Museum, Greeley, CO.

96 Dickinson, *A Ragged Register*, 6.

97 AED to MD, September 4, 11, 1873; Robertson, *The Magnificent Mountain Women*, 8–11; Harold M. Dunning, *Over Hill and Vale: In the Shadows of Colorado's Longs Peak*, 3 vols. (Boulder, CO: Johnson Publishing Company, 1956–71), 3: 57; Dickinson, *A Ragged Register*, 157–76. Forty-one years later the Colorado Geographic Board honored her feat by naming a 11,381-foot peak Mount Dickinson.

98 *Greeley Tribune*, August, 3, September 17, 20, 24, 1873, transcripts in the City of Greeley Museum; Dickinson, *A Ragged Register*, 183–5; AED to MD, September 4, 1873.

99 Dickinson, *A Ragged Register*, 164, 171–5.

100 AED to CDW, September 4, 1873; AED to ED, September 4, 1873; *Greeley Tribune*, December 10, 1873, transcript in City of Greeley Museum; Betty Browne to AED, September 9, [1873]; SED to AED, September 28, 1873; Ralph Meeker to AED, January 26, 1874; AED to Clara M. Olson, May 29, 1910.

101 SED to AED, September 28, October 24, November 1, 1873; MD to AED, October 25, 1873; AED to SED, October 12, 30, 1873.

102 O. G. Bernard to AED, August 19, 1873; AED to SED, November 16, 1873; SED to AED, January 30, February 2, 4, 27, March 23, 1874; ED to AED, February 8, March 25, 1874; AED to Susan Warner, April 20, 1874, WP; SED to WR, June 10, 1874, WR-GC; WR to AED, July 10, 1874.

103 *Biographical Dictionary of the American Congress, 1774–1949* (GPO, 1950), 926; Lou Brackett to AED, June 15, July 11, 24, 1863; Lillie Chace to AED, September 14, 1863; SED to AED, February 9, October 1, 1863; BB to AED, September 8, 1864.

104 BB's relationship with Pugh grew strained when the general backed out of an engagement. BB to T. B. Pugh, January 2, April 20, 1867 (these letters filed in the AEDP with BB's letters); T. B. Pugh to AED, March 21, April 5, 17, 1867; SED to AED, March 22, April 19, 22, 1867.

105 BB to AED, January 10, 1869, February 6, September 20, 1870, September 5, 1871; *Brooklyn Eagle*, August 26, October 20, 1871.

106 AED to MD, November 14, 1872, November 14, 1873; AED to SED, October 12, 1873; SED to AED, October 15, December 16, 1873, February 2, 1874; BB to AED, December 7, 1873.

107 Robert S. Holzman, *Stormy Ben Butler* (New York: MacMillan, 1954), 209. Butler's wife died in 1876.

108 ED to AED, February 8, 1874; BB to AED, January 31, May 7, June 30, 1874.

109 ED to AED April 12, June 25, 1874; MD to AED, July 12, 1874; BB to AED, July 24, 1874. BB wrote about meeting with AED on May 1, 7, June 3, 18, 24, July 11, 1874.

110 The AEDP include 18 letters from AED to MD and three to SED written from Atlantic City between August 13 and September 5, 1874. This vacation turned out to be the last hurrah for AED and Brackett. The final letter from Louise Brackett was dated March 17, 1875.

111 AED to MD, August 14, 24, 1874. AED was paraphrasing the *Press.*

112 AED to MD, August 20, September 2, 4, 1874.

113 ED to AED, August 13, 19, September 4, 1874; SED to AED, August 28, 1874; AED to MD, September 2, 1874.

114 James R. Osgood to AED, April 14, August 6, 1873, June 26, 1874, January 3, 1876; Charles Shepard to AED, March 30, 1874. Osgood and Shepard both also mentioned the possibility of AED writing short essays for fees. Both *A Paying Investment* and *A Ragged Register* sold poorly and neither made much profit. "Receipts, 1883–1930," container 22.

115 LCB to AED, November 27, 1874.

116 Leander [Chamberlain?] to AED, August 8, 1874, filed in Leander Richardson folder; LCB to AED, May 26, 1874; Sallie Austin to AED, May 29, 30, June 27, August 7, September 20, [all 1874?]. Austin's letters commented simultaneously on two lovesick men. The other was probably Ralph Meeker.

117 Leander Chamberlain to AED, n.d., filed under "Misc. C" letters; AED to SED, June 1, 1875.

118 AED to CDW, July 17, 1874; AED to MD, July 19, August 5, 1874; AED to Susan Warner, August 14, 1874, WP; AED to SED, August 16, 22, 1874; AED to Oliver Johnson, August 22, [1874?] (draft.); Sallie Austin to AED, August 6, [1874?]. For evidence that AED was following these events see Ralph Meeker to AED, April 26, 1873; Henry Ward Beecher to AED, July 19, 1874; AED to Henry Ward Beecher, July 22, 1874; Oliver Johnson to AED, August 17, 1874; James Redpath to AED, August 25, 1874. The jury finally found Beecher innocent. Fox, *Trials of Intimacy*; Waller, *Reverend Beecher and Mrs. Tilton*; Goldsmith, *Other Powers.*

119 AED to Susan Warner, August 14, 1874; AED to MD, August 18, 1874; AED to ED, August 19, 1874; BB to AED, August 29, 1874; James Redpath to AED, August 25, 1874. Ellen Everett was pleased that AED's "name has not been dragged in" to the "miserable Brooklyn muddle." Ellen Everett to AED, August 29, 1874.

120 *Brooklyn Eagle*, March 6, 1875.


## Notes to Chapter 7

1 See SED to AED, December 6, 1862; SD to AED, June 30, 1865. Public attitudes toward women in the theater, both as actresses and audience members, were already in flux during the antebellum decades. By midcentury there was an established middle-class theater, where women could comfortably attend. By 1870 acting at all levels had grown to be a large occupation, employing 20 times as many women as newspapers. Ironically, this numerical expansion in the profession went hand in hand with a decline in women's power and autonomy within the theater. See Faye E. Dudden, *Women in the American Theatre* (New Haven: Yale University Press, 1994), 78–82, 118–22, 177–84 and *passim.*

2 Alice B. Hooker, to AED, May 3, [??]. For further evidence that AED was considering the theater see Benjamin Prescott to AED, January 28, 1863; Lillie Chace to AED, February 18, 1863; W. J. Burton to AED, July 2, 1864; A. G. Draper to AED, April 6, [1865?].

3  Charles Fechter to AED, January 16, August 23, September 21, 26, 1871 (these letters are misfiled with letters from Daniel Froham); Lou Brackett to AED, April 23, 1871. On one occasion AED feigned a headache to avoid Fechter's overtures. See LCB to AED, June 16, 1873; Melinda Jones to AED, April 6, June 11, July 13, November 22, 29, 1872, February 14, April 4, 1873.

4  Susan Warner to AED, March 8, 1873; LCB to AED, April 30, June 21, 1873; E. L. Davenport to AED, May 1, 1873; Jenny West to AED, May 24, 1873. See also S. F. Austin to AED, February 21, [1873]; CDW to AED, March 12, 1873.

5  LCB to AED, August 17, 1874; Melinda Jones to AED, August 21, September 4, October 23, 1874; Betty Browne to AED, November 8, [1874]; Sallie Austin to AED, November 11, [1874]. See also Louise Brackett to AED, November 23, 1874; O. G. Bernard to AED, September 16, 1874.

6  As she toured, AED sent four long letters home, totaling nearly 40,000 words. AED to MD, April 10, 25, 30, May 3, 1875. AED dated each letter when she started writing, not when they were mailed. For a short essay on this trip see JHY, "A Woman Abolitionist Views the South in 1875," *Georgia Historical Quarterly* 32 (1948), 241–51.

7  AED to MD, April 10, 1875.

8  AED to MD, April 10, 1875.

9  AED to MD, April 28, 30, 1875.

10 AED to MD, April 30, 1875. AED quoted directly from this conversation. As she explained to her mother, Robert E. Lee was a lieutenant colonel in the United States Army before resigning his commission to join the Confederacy.

11 AED to MD, May 3, 1875.

12 AED to MD, April 10, 28, 1875.

13 AED to MD, April 28, May 3, 1875.

14 AED to MD, April 28, 1875. AED attended at least four black church services during her trip.

15 AED to MD, April 10, 1875. A large portion of this letter, including most of AED's description of Van Lew, is misfiled with "Unidentified Letters" in the AEDP. On Van Lew, and AED's visit, see Elizabeth R. Varon, *Southern Lady, Yankee Spy: The True Story of Elizabeth Van Lew, A Union Agent in the Heart of the Confederacy* (New York: Oxford University Press, 2003), 227–8.

16 AED to MD, April 28, 1875. AED made the same observations about several other "carpetbaggers" she encountered on her journeys.

17 AED to MD, April 10, 28, 1875.

18 AED to MD, May 3, 1875; AED to Elizabeth Warner, June 1, 1875, SDC.

19 AED to SED, May 5, June 21, 1875. The AEDP do not indicate when AED purchased the Chicago property.

20 AED to MD, June 1, 1875; AED to SED, June 1, 4, 1875; *Chicago Tribune*, June 4, 1875, AED scrapbook; Ruth Bordin, *Frances Willard: A Biography* (Chapel Hill: University of North Carolina Press, 1986), 83–85, 101.

21 AED to [Frances Willard?], August 8, 1875 (a copy of the original); AED to SED, August 16, 1875. AED sent a draft of her letter to SED for advice on the relationship.

22 AED to MD, March 20, 24, 26, 1880, January 22, 25, 27, March 4, 1884, November 12, 1885; "Unidentified Manuscript," container #20, AEDP; Frances Willard, *Glimpses of Fifty Years: The Autobiography of an American Woman* (Chicago: H. J. Smith & Co., 1889), 570–2.

23 AED to SED, June 4, July 10, 20, August 5, 1875; LCB to AED, September 8, 21, 1875.

24 AED to SED, August 10, October 27, 1875; Sallie Austin to AED, October 3, October 21, [1875?].

25 BB to AED, August 24, October 1, 1875, March 27, 1876. This extraordinary letter was written only a few weeks before Sarah Butler died. Holzman, *Stormy Ben Butler*, 209.

26 For a recent analysis of AED's career as an actress and playwright, see Stacey A. Stewart, "Nothing Ladylike About It: The Theatrical Career of Anna Elizabeth Dickinson," (Ph.D. diss., Department of Theater, University of Maryland, 2004).

27 See JHY, "Anna Dickinson as Anne Boleyn," *Emory University Quarterly* 5 (October 1949): 163–9; Stewart, "Nothing Ladylike About It," 78–104.

28 The previous summer AED had read James Anthony Froude's unflattering portrayal of Anne Boleyn in his *History of England* and she told Susan that "I would like to wack him with a club." AED to SED, July 20, 1875; *New York World*, April 2, 1877, AED scrapbook.

29  Script of *A Crown of Thorns*, container #16. She copyrighted the play on March 25, 1876, container #18. AED to SED, May 4, 1876.

30  AED's scrapbooks include dozens of short squibs and longer editorials announcing her debut and speculating on her performance, container #28.

31  O. G. Bernard to SED, May 10, 1876, filed among Family Letters; Samuel Clemens (Mark Twain) to William Dean Howells, April 25, 1876, in Albert Bigelow Paine, ed., *Mark Twain's Letters* (New York: Harper & Brothers, 1917), 1: 277–8; AED to SED, May 16, 1876. On local responses see, for example, *Boston Herald*, May 9, 1876, *Boston Evening Transcript*, May 9, 1876, *Boston Daily Globe*, May 9, 1876. AED scrapbooks. Several of the local papers listed the famous people in the audience. Howells recalled that he and Twain agreed that the opening was a disaster. William Dean Howells, *My Mark Twain: Reminiscences and Criticisms*, ed. Marilyn Austin Baldwin (1910; Baton Rouge: LSU Press, 1967), 48–49.

32  *New York Herald*, May 9, 1876; *New York Times*, May 9, 1876; *New York Tribune*, May [?], 1876, all in AED scrapbook, container #28. Numerous contemporary clippings quote Winter's review. See also *Brooklyn Eagle*, May 9, 1876.

33  AED to SED, May 16, 1876; *Boston Times*, May 14, 1876, AED scrapbook. AED actually asked WR to send the *Tribune*'s theater critic to Boston for the debut. AED to WR, May 4, 1876, WRP; WR to AED, May 8, 1876, Reid Letterbook, WRP.

34  This account is based on dozens of clippings from AED's scrapbooks and the *Brooklyn Eagle*, April 2, 1877. The *Philadelphia Evening Bulletin*, n.d., the *Boston Times*, May 14, 1876, and the *Danbury News*, July 22, 1876, AED scrapbook, are particularly useful in tracking the rift between the New York and Boston critics.

35  *Boston Times*, May 21, 1876; *New York Daily Graphic*, May 18, 1876; several unidentified clippings, AED scrapbook. During the war there were few identified women who weighed in on AED's performances, but a decade later there were far more female journalists in the field. Of course AED had also moved out of the male-dominated world of partisan politics.

36  AED to SED, May 16, 1876; *Brooklyn Eagle* May 9, 1876; *Worcester Daily Sun*, June 7, 1876, AED scrapbook.

37  AED to [Hal Spollord?], August 26, 1876, New York Public Library; AED to SED, November 16, 1876; misc. clippings, AED scrapbook, container #28.

38  AED to SED, May 16, 1876; *Philadelphia Evening Star*, November 28, 1876, *Philadelphia Inquirer*, November 28, 1876, AED scrapbook.

39  AED copyrighted *Love and Duty* (based on *Jane Eyre*) on September 29, 1876 and "Laura, or True to Herself" on December 7, 1876, container #18, AEDP.

40  *Philadelphia Evening Bulletin*, December 10, 1876; [*Philadelphia?*] *Item*, December 10, 1876; *American and Gazette*, December 8, 1876; AED scrapbook.

41  *New York World*, April 5, 1877; *New York Tribune*, April 5, 1877, AED scrapbook; George C. D. Odell, *Annals of the New York Stage* (New York: Columbia University Press, 1938), X: 261–2.

42  *New York Daily Graphic*, April 5, 1877, AED scrapbook. A few days earlier Croly's daughter confirmed to AED that her mother was going to do a piece on the play for the *Graphic*. May Croly to AED, April 1, 1877.

43  See *Brooklyn Eagle*, April 2, 1877.

44  See Thomas Habbershon to AED, April 5, 1877; E. M. Halford to AED, April 21, 1877; A. E. Lancaster to AED, April 12, 20, 1877; Edmund Clark to AED, April 17, 1877; Edward Willett to AED, April 23, 1877.

45  R. W. L. Mitchell to AED, April 17, 1877; W. A. [Crofful?] to AED, April 11, 1877.

46  AED filled an entire scrapbook with hundreds of accounts of this event and the immediate aftermath, published in New York and throughout the country, from as far away as Florida, Utah, Nebraska, and California. This summary relies on the *New York Herald*, April 10, 1877, *New York Evening Express*, April 10, 1877, AED scrapbook, container #24.

47  *New York Daily Graphic*, April 10, 1877; *Chicago Tribune*, April 13, 1877, both in AED scrapbook; AED to Dion Boucicault, April 17, 1877 (draft?). Only a few years earlier the New York theater world had been rocked by stories of critics accepting bribes from agents and actors, *Brooklyn Eagle*, April 15, 1877.

48 *New York Sun*, April 15, 1877, Unidentified clipping quoting Halstead, AED scrapbook, container #24. Numerous clippings from New York and across the nation, container #24. See also R. G. Fitch to AED, April 28, 1877. Fitch was a reporter for the *Boston Post*.

49 George Warner to AED, April 10, 1877; SED to AED, April 12, 1877. See also ED to AED, April 12, 1877.

50 AED sent an open letter to the *World* on her conflicts with Hart, dated April 17, 1877, that was republished by several papers. Hart countered with his own open letter, in which he claimed that he was suing AED for breach of contract. *New York Evening Post*, April 10, 1877; *New York World*, April 17, 1877; *New York Daily Tribune*, April 17, 1877; unidentified clippings; all in AED scrapbook, container #24; Edward Arnott to AED, April 10, 1877; R. B. W. to AED, April 18, 1877. On AED's break with Bernard see O. G. Bernard to AED, September 24, 1877.

51 See *Elmira Daily Gazette*, April 11, 1877; *Houston Daily Telegram*, April [?], 1877; AED scrapbook.

52 Mrs. J. M. Ellis to AED, April 18, 1877.

53 *Daily Graphic*, April 10, 14, 1877, AED scrapbook.

54 Elizabeth A. Allen to AED, April 19, 1877.

55 AED to SED, January 1, February 1, 1878; MD to AED, October 9, 1877; SED to AED, December 28, 1877, January 9, March 13, 1878; AED to ED, February 1, March 11, 1878. JHY, "Anna Dickinson," XVI: 38. JHY cites ED's date of death in the Dickinson family Bible.

56 See Robert Collyer to AED, April 3, 1878.

57 BB lent AED $1,500 on July 13, 1876. JHYP, box 5, folder 8.

58 BB to AED, April 14, July 13, 22 (quote), 26, 1878. On July 15 AED wrote to SED instructing her to send an urgent telegram saying "mother says to come at once" adding that she would explain later. AED to SED, July 15, 1878.

59 Rose Eytinge to AED, January 22, February 24, April 1, May 10, July 19, 1878; AED to Rose Eytinge, April 6, 1878. AED suggested that Eytinge could produce the play in London.

60 Ann Wakeman to AED, January 4, 1878.

61 A. M. Palmer to AED, April 20, 1879; AED to A. M. Palmer (draft), April 25, 1879. AED copyrighted *Love and Duty* on September 29, 1876, container #18.

62 AED copyrighted *Aurelian* in January, 1879, container #18. For an analysis of the play see Stewart, "Nothing Ladylike About It," 104–24.

63 John McCullough to AED, June 21, 25, July 30, 1878, February 13, [1879?]; AED to SED, January 12, 1879; Margaret Sullivan to AED, January 21, 1879; Leander Richardson to AED, January 29, 1879; *New York Dramatic News*, February 1, 1879, *New York Tribune*, March 17, 1879, AED scrapbooks. Richardson acted as AED's agent in negotiations with McCullough..

64 AED to SED, January 12, February 25, March 11, 1879; AED to MD, February 4, 1879; A. M. Palmer to AED, January 21, 1879; Sallie J. White to AED, February 7, 1879; *New York Tribune*, January 18, 1879, *New York World*, January 18, 1879, numerous other clippings, container #24.

65 Contract for *A Ragged Register*, July 5, 1879, container #22; royalty statements from Harper & Brothers, container #22; AED to SED, July 31, August 16, September 5, 1879. AED hoped that the book would bring much-needed funds. SED to AED, December 22, 1879, January 28, 1880.

66 Leander Richardson to AED, January 29, February 15, May 24, July 26, 1879; contract from Morris Simmonds Agency, May 22, 1879, filed with Richardson correspondence; AED to MD, February 4, September 17, 1879; AED to SED, February 14, March 11, 1879; AED to Leander Richardson, July 25, 1879; AED to Frank Lawlor, August 26, September 17, 1879; Frank Lawlor to AED, August 22, September 6, 1879; AED to Morris Simmonds, September 5, 1879 (filed with the Lawlor letters under "misc. L"); AED to W. B. Barton, August 26, 1879.

67 AED to Frank Lawlor, August 26, 1879 (copy in AED's handwriting). AED shared very similar sentiments with Leander Richardson in AED to Richardson, July 25, 1879.

68 One theater manager criticized AED for relying on "amateur managers" rather than working with a professional. C. R. Gardiner to AED, February 21, 1879.

69 SED to AED, April 8, November 5, 1879; AED to SED, May 4, June 3, August 7, September 18, October 1, 28, 31, 1879; MD to AED, May 10, September 20, 1879.

70 This summary of AED's photographs is based on the author's collection. On the photographing of nineteenth-century celebrities see Robert Taft, *Photography and the American Scene* (New York: Dover,

1938), 149–50 and *passim*; William C. Darrah, *Cartes de Visite in Nineteenth-Century Photography* (Gettysburg: W. C. Darrah, 1981); and Alan Trachtenberg, *Reading American Photographs* (New York: Hill and Wang, 1989). AED's correspondence includes dozens of letters requesting photographs, autographs, and other artifacts. Napoleon Sarony photographed AED in 1873 and probably on at least one other occasion. Betty Browne to AED, April 15, 1873.

71 The author has inspected both items at trade shows.

72 The author has several cards, including two separate images and designs, in his possession. The advertisers include a Maine Coffee and Spice dealer, a Connecticut school supplies merchant, and a Connecticut music teacher.

73 Numerous letters refer to photographs and photographers, indicating that AED was involved in selecting and distributing images of herself. See SED to AED, November 8, 1867, January 24, November 26, 1869, January 11, 1870; SBA to AED, June 3, 1868; James Redpath to AED, May 30, 1870; AED to MD, April 14, 1880.

74 FDP to AED, October 21, 1879; C. R. Gardiner to AED, May 25, July 17, 1879; AED to FDP, November 6, 1879. Price acted under the name Fanny Davenport, but used her married name in legal dealings. Her letters to AED are filed under Price.

75 O. G. Bernard to AED, November 19, 20, 1879; AED to FDP, January 16, 1880; FDP to AED, January 29, [1880], January [?], 1880.

76 AED to SED, April 19, 22, 1880. AED made similar comments about the Democratic and Republican press on several occasions during this tour.

77 AED to FDP, May 9, 1880 (draft); AED to SED, May 16, 23, 1880; FDP to AED, May 13, 1880; contract between AED and FDP, July 27, 1880, container #22.

78 FDP to AED, July 13, August 1, 1880, telegrams on July 22, August 14, 1880 (and several other short telegrams); AED to FDP, August 16, 1880.

79 FDP to AED, August 17, 1880, February 7, 1881; AED to FDP, August 19, 1880; Edwin Price to AED, August 24, September 17, 1880. See also Daniel Froham to AED August 21, 1880.

80 AED's copy of the script to *An American Girl* is in container #18; Stewart, "Nothing Ladylike About It," 124–47.

81 FDP to James H. Heverin, February 7, 1881, filed under Price; O. G. Bernard to AED, September 21, 1880; AED to John Habberton, [?], 1880 (draft).

82 *New York Mirror*, October 9, 1880; AED to FDP, September 27, 28, 30, 1880; FDP to AED, September 28, 30, 1880.

83 *Daily Graphic*, September 21, 1880, *Home Journal*, September 22, 1880, AED scrapbook, container #25. See also Louis O'Shaughnessy to AED, Christmas, 1880. The AEDP include several undated notes from FDP expressing her enthusiasm for the play. The critics found much to criticize in AED's script but acknowledged that the audiences were generally pleased with FDP's performance and costumes, numerous clippings, AED scrapbooks.

84 FDP to AED, December 7, 1880, (telegram) December 31, 1880; AED to FDP, December 10, 1880, (telegram) December 24, 1880.

85 FDP to James H. Heverin, February 7, 1881; George Warner to AED, January 8, 1881; AED to George Warner, January 10, 1881 (copy); *Washington Post*, January 12, 1881.

86 AED to James Heverin, April 6, May 16, 1881, container #21; *New York Times*, November 29, December 4, 17, 1881; *Washington Post*, December 4, 1881.

87 In November 1880 SED sent WR a long letter, claiming that the *Tribune*'s editor had used his newspaper, and his friendship with John McCullough, to undermine AED's career. SED to WR, November 9, 1880, WR-GC.

88 James Parton, et al., *Eminent Women of the Age; Being Narratives of the Lives and Deeds of the Most Prominent Women of the Present Generation* (Hartford: S. M. Betts & Company, 1869), 479–512; Phebe A. Hanaford, *Daughters of America; or, Women of the Century* (Augusta, ME: True & Company, 1882), 337–40.

89 "Memorandum of Agreement," March 16, 1881, container #22.

90 Dudden, *Women in the American Theater*, 92–101; Bernard Grenbanier, *Then Came Each Actor* (New York: McKay Books, 1975), 253–63; Elizabeth Reitz Mullenix, *Wearing the Breeches: Gender on the*

*Antebellum Stage* (New York: St. Martin's Press, 2000); Lillian Faderman, *Surpassing the Love of Men: Romantic Friendship and Love Between Women from the Renaissance to the Present* (1981; expanded, New York: William Morrow and Company, 1998), 220–5.

91  See *Philadelphia Evening News*, March 21, 1881, AED scrapbook, container #24.

92  AED to John Stetson, April 2, 2, 5, 6, 6 (telegram), 1881; John Stetson to AED, April 5, 6 (telegram), 7 (telegram), 11 (telegram), 1881; George K. Goodwin to AED, April 5, 5, 1881 (two telegrams on the same day); AED to J. F. Zimmerman, April 5, 1871 (telegram); SED to AED, April 11, [1871]; interview with Stetson in unidentified clipping, interview with AED, *New York Dramatic News*, May 14, 1881, AED scrapbook, container #25.

93  *Philadelphia Press*, April 7, 1881, AED scrapbook, container #25; SED to AED, April 6, 8, 1881; interview with Stetson in unidentified clipping; *Washington Post*, April 8, 1881; J. Edwin Spear to AED, April 8, 1881.

94  *Republic*, July 25, 1880, AED scrapbook, container #25; Lilian Whiting to AED, March 10, April 1, 8, 8, 1881. Ellen Everett also urged AED to tread carefully. Ellen Everett to AED, [April ?, 1881], April 10, [1881?]; Ellen Everett to SED, April 13, [1881].

95  AED to Lilian Whiting, April 26, 1881; Lilian Whiting to AED, April 29, 29 (2 notes) 1881.

96  *Washington Post*, April 21, 1881 (quoting AED's letter to the *New York Herald*), [*Philadelphia Press*?], April 26 [?], 1881, AED scrapbook, container #25.

97  See *Philadelphia Evening Bulletin*, April 21, 1881, numerous other clippings, AED scrapbook, container #25.

98  Lilian Whiting to AED, April 20, 1888; Lucy Stone to AED, April 22, 1888; *Woman's Journal*, April 22, 1881, AED scrapbook, *Boston Commonwealth*, May 14, 1881, container #25. See also Sallie White to AED, May 6, 1881.

99  *New York Dramatic News*, May 14, 1881, AED scrapbook, container #25.

100  "Memorandum of Agreement" between Anna E. Dickinson and Charles A. Mendum, July 1, 1881, container #22; *Philadelphia Press*, October 3, 1881, container #23.

101  "Receipts 1882," container #22; *New York Star*, March 21, 1882, AED scrapbook, container #25. For numerous reviews see AED scrapbook, container #25. The *Tribune*'s William Winter found AED's Hamlet so problematic (but also so significant) that 30 years later he devoted several paragraphs in a theatrical history to criticizing her performance. Winter, *Shakespeare on the Stage* (New York: Moffat, Yard and Company, 1911), 430–1. See also *New York Tribune*, March 21, 1882.

102  *Home Journal*, March 22, 1882, *Scranton Republican*, April 14, 1882, AED scrapbook, container #25. For another careful gendered analysis a year later see also *Detroit Post and Tribune*, October 12, 1883, container #23. Of course, other reviews did conclude that women simply could not pull off male parts. See the *Chicago Inter-Ocean*, February 4, 1882, container #25.

103  AED to Mr. Goodale, July 14, 1882, Schlesinger Library; William W. Kelly to AED, August 31, September 8, 1882; Joseph Waters to AED, September 9, 1882; C. R. Gardiner, November 30, 1882; J. W. Wentworth to AED, August 1, 1883; contract between Anna E. Dickinson and Jason Wentworth and Percy Hunting, June 11, 1883, container #22.

104  Numerous letters in the AEDP, including AED to SED, September 18, 19, October 2, 1883; AED to MD, September 18, October 1, 4, 1883; Caroline Nunn to AED, October 24, 1883, filed with Family Letters.

105  AED to SED, October 2, 1883; AED to MD, October 11, November 11, 1883; *Detroit Evening News*, October 22, 23, 1883, *Detroit Free Press*, October 23, 1883, *New York Clipper*, November 24, 1883, unknown newspaper, November 17, 1883, loose clippings in container #24.

## Notes to Chapter 8

1  Between November 10, 1883 and April 4, 1884 AED sent over 80 letters to MD and SED. Specific passages from AED to SED, December 4, 14, 23, 1883, January 1, 8, 12, 1884; AED to MD, January 16, 1884. See also B. W. Williams to AED, December 11, 1883. In 1884 AED kept a small notebook full of quotations, aphorisms, poems, and the like. Many stressed themes of perseverance, ignoring critics, and being bold in the face of adversity, container #17.

2 AED to SED, September 13, December 23, 1883, March 22, 1884; *New York Times*, March 17, 1884.

3 In 1878 BB bolted the Republican Party to run as the Greenback-Labor Party's candidate for governor of Massachusetts. He ended up losing to the Republican candidate after a bitter campaign. In 1879 BB again lost the state's gubernatorial election, this time as the Democrats' nominee. Howard P. Nash, Jr., *Stormy Petrel: The Life and Times of General Benjamin F. Butler, 1818–1893* (Rutherford, NJ: Fairleigh Dickinson University Press, 1969), 271–5.

4 See AED to SED, November 2, 21, 1879; AED to MD, November 6, 11, 15, 1879; BB to AED, November 12, 1879; SED to AED, November 20, 1879.

5 SED to AED, April 22, 26, 1881; BB to AED, July 15, 30, October 18, 19, 1881.

6 AED to SED, January 9, March 22, 1884.

7 AED to MD, February 22, March 9, 1884; AED to SED, March 2, 11, 16, 20, April 24, May 23 (quotation), 1884; 1884 route book, AEDP.

8 For the first six months of 1883 AED rented rooms from Ellen Everett in Philadelphia before heading west. Receipts from Ellen Everett, January 16, 1883 to June 12, 1883, container #22. AED paid Everett $150 a month, misc. family correspondence.

9 SED to AED, March 26, 1885.

10 BB to AED, January 3, 1886.

11 BB to AED, June 24, 1886. In the past, BB had written worrying that AED (as "Lizzie") had misunderstood his "motives wishes and actions." BB to AED, August 24, 1875.

12 AED to MD, February 2, 1873, December 23, 1883, January 9, March 13, 16, 21, 26, 1884; AED to SED, December 16, 23, 1883, March 16, 30, 1884, five short notes from Emily Faithfull to AED, 1884. In the late 1850s Faithfull had been involved in a famous English divorce trial, in which Admiral Henry Codrington claimed that Faithfull had had a sexual affair with his wife, Helen Smith Codrington. Martha Vicinus, *Intimate Friends: Women Who Loved Women, 1778–1928* (Chicago: University of Chicago Press, 2004), 69–82.

13 AED to MD, January 18, 22, 25, 27, February 11, March 4, 16, 30, 1884; AED to SED, November 12, 1885.

14 Mary Livermore to AED, several 1863 letters (see chapter 2), December 18, 1863 (filed under Misc. L letters).

15 AED to SED, December 27, 1883. See also AED to SED, February 24, 1884.

16 Laura E. Kellogg to AED, October 31, 1883, January 4, 1885.

17 AED to SED, January 24, 1884.

18 Frances E. Willard and Mary A. Livermore, eds., *A Woman of the Century: Fourteen Hundred-Seventy Biographical Sketches Accompanied by Portraits of Leading American Women in All Walks of Life*, 2 vols. (1893; reprinted New York: Gordon Press, 1975), 2: 767–8.

19 AED first met Whiting in 1880. The AEDP include roughly 25 letters from Whiting to AED, several from Whiting to SED, and several from AED to Whiting, all between 1881 and 1891. See also AED to SED, June 1, 1880, October 2, 1882, January 10, March 16, 30, 1884; SED to AED, March 26, 1885; AED to MD, November 1, 3, 1885.

20 [Lilian Whiting] to SED, January 7, 1884, filed with Family Letters. For one of many Whiting essays celebrating and defending AED see *Chicago Inter-Ocean*, May 10, 1885, clipping, container #24.

21 AED to SED, January 10, 1884.

22 Carol Rich to AED, 27 letters from 1879 to 1888. Quotation from April 3, 1887.

23 AED to SED, September 14, 15, October 15, 1885; SED to May 16, July 15, October 16, 1885.

24 SED to AED, May 16, November 25, December 12, 1885; Carol Rich to AED, December 14, 1885; Harriet Haines to AED, January 31, 1887. In 1865 AED injured her foot when an iron dropped on it from an upstairs window. Since then she had suffered from foot pain and sciatica. She also continued to suffer from painful hemorrhoids.

25 SED to AED, December 31, 1867, February 4, 11, 1868, January 20, 1870, December 8, 1872; AED to SED, March 18, June 13, 29, 1869; AED to MD, March 20, 1884.

26 SED to AED, November 9, 1870, April 8. 1879; *Elmira Telegram*, March 1, 1895, AED scrapbook, container #26. In 1895, AED testified that she partook of wine after baths (perhaps for rubdowns) and alcohol for medicinal purposes.

27 Carol Rich to AED, December 25, 29, 1885. The cider drink was apparently for pleasure and not medicine. During the postwar decades, it was not uncommon for women to engage in social drinking, although cultural constraints—and the power of the temperance movement—tended to make women fairly circumspect about their drinking behavior. Meanwhile, doctors commonly prescribed various alcoholic beverages for medicinal purposes, and some women used the cover of medical prescriptions for acquiring liquor for social consumption. In short, both social drinking and alcoholism among nineteenth-century women were probably more prevalent than the public evidence would indicate. See Catherine Gilbert Murdock, *Domesticating Drink: Women, Men, and Alcohol in America, 1870–1940* (Baltimore: Johns Hopkins University Press, 1998), 44–69.

28 Summaries of court testimony by AED and SED, *Elmira Telegram*, March 1, 1895. SED's testimony seemingly misdates this operation as in 1888. "Notebook of Confinement, 1893," container #21. In 1893 AED recalled that she had experienced similar symptoms in 1886 and they had been misdiagnosed as "'cirrhosis of the liver.'"

29 *Honesdale Citizen*, June 16, 1887, *New York Times*, June 17, 1887, clippings, container #22; *New York World*, June 19, 1887, *Toledo Blade*, June 2, 1887, clippings, container #23. Several of the letters from friends suggest a shared assumption that AED's illness was related to stress. See Ellen Everett to AED, June 18, 1887; Constance [Twisher?] to AED, June 19, 1887; Frank Lee Benedict to SED, June 19, 1887; Annie J. Weichman to SED, June 20, 1887; Theodore Day to SED, June 20, 1887; Fanny Earl to SED, June 20, 1887; Adelheid MacKenzie to SED, June 21, 1887; Emily Wright to AED, July 20, 1887; Charlotte Crowell to AED, January 6, 1888.

30 *Elmira Telegram*, March 1, 1895; BB to AED, October 2, November 20, 1887.

31 AED to [BB?] (draft), November 20, 1887, filed under "Unidentified Letters." In this draft AED scratched out the term "prison house." AED to BB, January 15, June 3, 1888; BB to AED, November 20, 1887, [June?] 1, 1888.

32 *Daily Graphic*, June 8, 1888, container #23; BB to AED, June 14, 1888; BB to SED, April 9, 1889; AED to BB, n.d. [April 1889?].

33 AED to SED, November 16, 1876, June 15, 1880 (quote), July 19, 1884; AED to MD, May 18, June 6, 1880, June 25, 1884.

34 At some point in the 1890s, AED drafted a lengthy document that was ostensibly an autobiography, but repeatedly the narrative returned to events surrounding the election of 1888. "Untitled Manuscript," container #10. For the election of 1888 see H. Wayne Morgan, *From Hayes to McKinley: National Party Politics, 1877–1896* (Syracuse: Syracuse University Press, 1969), 277–317; for a lively dissection of Gilded Age corruption and machine politics see Mark W. Summers, *Party Games: Getting, Keeping, and Using Power in Gilded Age Politics* (Chapel Hill: University of North Carolina Press, 2004), 3–15 and passim.

35 *New York Press*, June 17, 18, 19, July 29, 1888; *New York Mail and Express*, June 18, 1888; *Toledo Blade*, June 28, 1888; misc. clippings; *Boston Evening Traveller*, July 18, 1888; all in "Loose Clippings," container #26.

36 James S. Clarkson to AED, August 23, 1888; AED to Clarkson, November 5, 1888. There are two almost identical copies of this letter, both apparently signed by AED, in the Clarkson folder; *Washington Post*, August 3, 1888; *New York Times*, November 9, 1888; AED's testimony at the subsequent trial is summarized in the *New York Times*, May 26, 1892.

37 *Indianapolis Journal*, September 23, 1888, container #25; AED to SED, roughly 20 letters written in September and early October 1888; John I. Dille to AED, September 14, 29, 1888; Henry Payne to AED, September 23, 1888. Dille was the of the Indiana State Republican Committee; Payne was of the Wisconsin Republican State Central Committee.

38 AED to SED, September 23, 25, 1888; R. B. Harrison to AED, September 23, 1888; *Terre Haute Express*, September 25, 1888, container #25; *Indianapolis Journal*, [September 25, 1888]; *Indianapolis Sentinel*, [September 28, 1888]; *Chicago Inter-Ocean*, October 2, 1888; *Detroit Tribune*, October 4, 1888; all in "Miscellaneous Clippings," container #23. See also W. De Witt Wallace to AED, October 24, 1888.

39 *Indianapolis Sentinel*, September 25, 1888; *Daily Pharos*, September 26, 1888; *Indianapolis Journal*, September 29, 1888; *South Bend Daily Times*, October 2, 1888, all in container #25.

40 AED to SED, September 25, 1888; *Times*, September 28, 1888, container #23; numerous clippings, container #26; *Washington Post*, September 22, 1888; *New York Times*, September 30, 1888. AED noted that the New York press were picking up unfair negative reports in an unusual handwritten note in her scrapbook, container #26.

41 J. S. Clarkson to SED, October 11, 11 (telegram) 1888; AED to J. S. Clarkson, October 19 (telegram), 1888.

42 AED to J. W. Knapp, October 12, 1888 (telegram); J. W. Knapp to J. S. Clarkson, October 21, 1888 (filed with Clarkson papers); AED to General [William W.] Dudley, October 24, 1888.

43 H. S. Hull to T. S. Pritchard, October 9, 12, 1888; T. S. Pritchard to AED, October 15, 1888, all filed with T. S. Pritchard letters.

44 On the changing nature of political campaigning see Glenn C. Altschuler and Stuart M. Blumin, *Rude Republic: Americans and Their Politics in the Nineteenth Century* (Princeton: Princeton University Press, 2000).

45 Knapp to AED, October 27, 1888; AED to William C. Goodloe, October 27, 1888 (draft); Goodloe to AED, October 29, 1888; Garret A. Hobart to AED, October 30, 1888.

46 Morton Keller, *Affairs of State: Public Life in Late Nineteenth-Century America* (Cambridge, MA: Harvard University Press, 1977), 544–52.

47 AED to J. S. Clarkson, November 5, 1888. There are two very similar copies of this letter in the AEDP; *New York Times*, November 9, 1888; *Washington Post*, November 10, 17, 1888; AED to SED, November 9, 1888 (telegram); Howell & Hummel to AED, November 28, 1888, container #21; numerous clippings, container #26. On AED's lawyers see Richard H. Rovere, *Howe & Hummel: Their True and Scandalous Story* (1947; reprinted New York: Farrar, Straus and Giroux, 1985).

48 Numerous clippings, container #26.

49 "Charge of the Court, delivered by the Hon. Marcus W. Acheson, P. J. at Scranton, Pa., April 9th, 1897," Anna E. Dickinson vs. George B. Thompson, et al., in the Circuit Court of the United States: Western District. (No. 2 March Term, 1893), 9–11, copy in container #21, hereafter "Charge of the Court." For SED's description of AED's illness see SED to Rutherford B. Hayes, March 19, 1890, Rutherford B. Hayes Presidential Center, Fremond, Ohio; *Elmira Telegram*, March 1, 1895.

50 *Elmira Telegram*, March 1, 1895; BB to SED, April 9, 1889; AED to BB, copy [April 1889?] (both letters filed with Butler letters).

51 SED to Rutherford B. Hayes, March 19, 1890; Rutherford B. Hayes to Lucy Hayes, March 22, 1893, Hayes Presidential Center.

52 *Washington Post*, May 14, 1889.

53 AED to Benjamin Harrison, June 1, 1889; Benjamin Harrison to AED, June 6, 1889.

54 *Washington Post*, August 22, 30, 1889; the August 30 report quotes the *Philadelphia Press*; Howell & Hummel to AED, February 28, June 6, 1890, container #21.

55 "Charge of the Court," 11–12; "Notebook of Confinement," 99–115.

56 "Notebook of Confinement," 125 and *passim.*

57 AED to [William B, Allison], January 7, 1891; AED to J. S. Clarkson, February [7?] (telegram), 1891; AED to Allison, February 13, [1891?]; A. H. Hummel to AED, February 14, 1891; unidentified clipping, 1891, container #26.

58 A. H. Hummel to AED, January 9, 9, February 9–14, 1891, 7 telegrams; AED to Hummel, February 7–16, 1891, drafts of nine telegrams; "Charge of the Court," 17.

59 *New York Herald*, April 10, 1891, container #26; "Charge of the Court"; "Notebook of Confinement"; "Medical Certificate," February 25, 1891, container #21.

60 *New York Times*, February 27, 1891; *Washington Post*, February 27, 1891; *Brooklyn Eagle*, February 27, 1891. See also *New York Herald*, February 27, 1891; *New York World*, February 27, 1891, both in AED scrapbooks.

61 "Certificate of Lunacy," March 5, 1891, copy in container #21; *New York Herald*, April 10, 1891, AED scrapbook; "Charge of the Court." The *Herald* story includes AED's extended description of her ordeal, including excerpts from her two letters. AED's copies are in the AEDP.

62 *New York Times*, February 27, 28, 1891; *Brooklyn Eagle*, February 27, 1891; *Washington Post*, February 27, 1891.

63 *New York Times*, March 8, 15, 22,1891; *Washington Post*, March 25, April 3, 1891. On April 2, 1891, Frances Willard published a similar call for donations in the *Union Signal* (the WCTU's official organ), directing donations to be sent to Mrs. Rachel Foster Avery, the Recording Secretary of the National Council of Women, based in Philadelphia, clipping, container #23.

64 *New York Times*, April 5, 1891; *New York Herald*, April 10, 1891; *Brooklyn Eagle*, April 9, 10, 1891.

65 AED to [?], July 9, 1891.

66 *New York Herald*, April 10, 1891, AED scrapbook; *Brooklyn Eagle*, April 10, 11, 1891; *Washington Post*, April 10, 1891.

67 *New York Times*, April 11, 1891 (two stories); *Washington Post*, April 19, 1891; *Brooklyn Eagle*, April 19, 1891; *New York World*, April 11, 1891, container #24.

68 Sallie Holley to Dr. Seward, April 12, [1891]; Adelheid MacKenzie to AED, April 12, 1891; Newton Hathhorn to AED, April 13, 1891; Ellen Everett to AED, April 11, 1891; Charles MacGeachy to AED, April 18, 1891; Lilian Whiting to AED, April 13, 17, 19, 1891; *Washington Post*, April 23, 1891.

69 *Brooklyn Eagle*, April 27, 1891; *Washington Post*, April 27, 28, 1891; *New York Daily Continent*, April 28, 1891, container #23; "Personal Liberty," transcript of narrative in AED's handwriting, container #15; Frederick W. Seward, Jr., to JHY, May 14, 1941, JHYP. This letter, from Dr. Seward's son to AED's biographer includes reminiscences about AED's time at Interpines. In what must have been a particularly galling report, On April 30, 1891, the WCTU's *Union Signal*, published out of Chicago, ran a one-sentence notice reporting that AED's speech "demonstrat[ed] her insanity," container #23.

70 *New York Daily Continent*, April 29, 1891, container #23; unidentified clipping, April 1891, AED scrapbook, container #26.

71 *Washington Post*, May 4, 1891.

72 Frederick W. Seward, Jr., to JHY, May 14, 1941; AED to "Cousin Rebecca," July 1, 1891, draft.

73 Her experiences with Mitchell's rest cure were the basis for Gilman's novella *The Yellow Wallpaper* (Boston: Small, Maynard & Company, 1899).

74 *Goshen Democrat*, August 20, 1891; *New York Herald*, August 28, 1891, AED scrapbook, container #24; *Washington Post*, August 30, 1891 (quoting the *Herald*).

75 *Goshen Independent Republican*, August 21, 1891; *The Chicago Religio Philosophical Journal*, September 5, 1891, both clippings in container #23.

76 "Charge of the Jury," *Anna E. Dickinson vs. New York Press Company*, Supreme Court, County of New York, May 3, 1898, container #21; Frederick W. Seward, Jr., to JHY, May 14, 1941. Perhaps AED also objected to Seward's belief that she was drinking too much.

## Notes to Chapter 9

1 Julius Ferguson to AED, April 29, 1892; Howe and Hummel to AED, May 21, 23, 1892, container #21; *Washington Post*, May 24, 1892; *New York Times*, May 26, 27, 1892.

2 Correspondence with James Heverin, nine letters dated in 1891; correspondence with George Hart, roughly 30 letters dated in 1891; A. H. Dailey to William L. McLean, January 6, 1893, filed in Dailey, Bell, & Crane folder. Legal correspondence in container #21.

3 Mark Pomeroy to AED, July 1, 1891; AED to Pomeroy, June 28, 1891; David R. Smith to AED, August 6, 1891; David R. Smith, Jr., to AED, August 10, 31, 1891; Bachellor and Johnson to AED, November 19, 1891.

4 *New York Herald*, June 19, 1892, AED scrapbook, container #26; Julius Ferguson to AED, June 24, 1892. When the *Philadelphia Press* published an uncorrected proof of this letter without her permission, AED's lawyer threatened the newspaper with a lawsuit. Ferguson to AED, June [?], 1892; James Duffy to Ferguson, June 27, 1892.

5 W. J. Hannity to AED, October 15, 1892; AED to Josiah Quincy, October 28, 1892; AED to Hon. Thomas M. Waller, October 28, 1892; Waller to AED, October 31, 1892. For AED's earlier efforts to line up lecturing engagements see Fred M. Taylor to AED, December 18, 1891; C. Bouteson-Smith to AED, March 8, 1892. The AEDP include numerous short notices of lectures and readings in and around Goshen, Mount Vernon, and Asbury Park in the early 1890s, misc. clippings, container #23.

6  AED to BB, undated draft, April 13, 1892; BB to SED, April 9, 1889; BB to Rev. Phebe Hanaford and Ellen Miles, December 13, 1892.

7  *Washington Post*, February 6, 22, 1893; *New York Times*, February 6, 1893; McLean to Dailey, February 4, 1893; Dailey to AED, February 15, 1893.

8  Numerous notebooks in the AEDP, especially "Notebook of Confinement," container #21. For evidence of AED's extensive trial preparations see Addie W. Nash to AED, June 9, 1891, March 13, May 30, 1893; AED to Dr. H. M. Paine, December 31, 1895; AED to McLean, February 22, 1895; AED to Dailey, February 27, 1895.

9  A. H. Hummel to AED, February 14, 1891; numerous letters in the legal files, AEDP.

10  *New York Times*, March 6, 1894; Dailey to AED, February 15, 1894; McLean to Dailey, February 28, 1894.

11  McLean to Dailey, February 1, 1895; AED to Jessie Winterstein, February 27, 1895; AED to Dailey, February 27, 1895; McLean to AED, February 16, March [13?], 1895; Dailey to Jessie Winterstein, March 1, 1895. Winterstein had been Miss Jessie Gibson when AED met her in Danville.

12  Coverage of trial from *Scranton Times*, March 26, 1895; *Scranton Truth*, March 26, April 12, 1895; *Scranton Republican*, March 27, 1895; *Elmira Telegram*, March 31, April 14, 1895, all in AED scrapbook, container #23 or #31 (not microfilmed); *New York Times*, March 26, 27, 1895; *Washington Post*, March 26 (quotation), 27, April 9, 11, 1895.

13  *Washington Post*, April 11, 1895; *New York Times*, April 11, 1895.

14  M. J. McMahon to AED, April 12, 1895.

15  Dailey to AED, September 5, 1895, January 25, 1896; Dailey to McLean, January 25, February 29, 1896; Dailey to AED, September 9, 1895; AED to McLean, October 2, 1895 (draft); AED to James Shakespeare, November 12, 14, 1895; AED to Hummel, December 6, 1895 (draft); Hummel to AED, December 16, 1895, January 9, 1896.

16  *Scranton Times*, March 25, 1896, clipping, container #23; *New York Times*, March 25, 1896; McLean to AED, March 27, 1896.

17  "Charge of the Court"; *New York Times*, March 30, April 10, 1897; *Washington Post*, March 30, April 11, 1897.

18  AED to Charles Bradley, April 18, 1877 (draft); AED to McMahon, April 23, 1897 (draft); AED to Mr. Black, April 23, 1897 (draft); AED to [Don] Waters, June 7, 1897 (draft), all in AED letter book, container #18; M. J. McMahon to AED, April 7 [?], 1897; John D. France to AED, April 12, 1897. AED had originally filed three suits, including two against the doctors. One of these ended with the death of the defendant, the other—against Dr. Oglesby—was settled at some point prior to 1901. *New York World*, April 10, 1901; *Sun*, April 10, 1901, container #23. Nothing in AEDP beyond these short clippings gives any indication of what became of this case.

19  Notebooks, container #19; Julius Ferguson to AED, nine letters between October 1897 and January 1899.

20  *Scranton Tribune* March 8, 1898; *Scranton Republican*, March 8, 1898, both in container #26. According to published reports some jurors argued for a $25,000 figure.

21  This account of the *Press* trial comes from "Anna E. Dickinson vs. New York Press Company, Limited," partial trial transcript in container #21. This typescript includes AED's testimony and the judge's charge to the jury. The document was apparently prepared as part of an appeal of the original decision. The following January the *Press* settled the case for an unclear amount. Ferguson to AED, January 18, 1899; JHY, "Conversations in re: Anna E. Dickinson with Mr. George Ackley and Miss Bertha Ackley, Goshen, New York, July 29, 30, 1941," JHYP. Hereafter "Conversations."

22  *Scranton Republican*, March 8, 1898, AED scrapbook, container #28.

23  *Scranton Republican*, April 4, 1897, AED scrapbook, container #31 (not microfilmed); SED to WR, November 9, 1880, WR-GC.

24  WR's letterbooks include a few particularly personal letters that do not appear among the AEDP, but she may have destroyed them herself at WR's request years earlier.

25  "Notebook of Confinement, 1893," 40–41. A March 25, 1895, clipping from the *Scranton Truth* in the AEDP includes the handwritten notation: "this is the paper in which S. D. is engaged. John Barrett is her old friend," container #31.

26  In one of her notebooks in preparation for her trials, AED noted that SED "did not know what she had of money & valuables, nor where" and she speculated that Susan wanted to lock her away before she spent any funds she had hidden in New York. In the same notebook AED suggested that the whole "pauper-insane business" was SED's strategy "to make money out of my incarceration & to destroy my place before the public at the same time," notebook, container #19.

27  Quoted in "Judge's Charge to the Jury" in "Anna E. Dickinson vs. New York Press Company, Limited." After AED left Interpines, Seward had held her possessions against unpaid bills. This led to a long and contentious legal battle between the two. Dailey to AED, December 19, 1892, February 7, 15, 1893, October 17, 1894, February 2, 1895, container #21.

28  On Hanaford and her 44-year relationship with Miles, see Lisa M. Tetrault, "A Paper Trail: Piecing Together the Life of Phebe Hanaford," online article, Nantucket Historical Association Web site, n.d. http://www.nha.org/history/hn/HNhanaford.htm

29  "Cupid" to AED, March 11, 31, 1892, container #14 (these two letters are filed among unidentified letters, but they are almost certainly from Sallie Ackley); Ellen Miles to Sallie Ackley, February 2, 1892, January 31, February 24, 27, May 12, 1893; *Washington Post*, May 3, 1892; various receipts, container #22; *New York Herald*, May 14, 1892, AED scrapbook, container #31 (not microfilmed); Phebe Hanaford to AED, May 24, 1893; Phebe Hanaford to "Mrs. Dickinson," May 18, 1894; Phebe Hull to AED, December 9, 1891, June 19, 1892; "Nellie" Miles to AED, June 23, 1893; BB to AED, December 13, 1892. Miles's letters have the same West 12th Street address that AED used.

30  Marion Booth (Douglas) to AED, October 4, 1893 (telegram), January 8, 1895; AED to Ellen Miles, November 12, 1893 (copy); Ellen Miles to AED, January 22, [1894]; Hanaford to Mrs. Dickinson, May 18, 1894; return addresses on misc. AED correspondence. On November 15, 1894 the *Mount Vernon Chronicle* reported that AED had been living in Mount Vernon for several months, clipping, container #23.

31  Frederick W. Seward, Jr., to JHY, May 14, 1941; JHY, "Conversations in re: Anna E. Dickinson with Mr. George Ackley and Miss Bertha Ackley, Goshen, New York, July 29, 30, 1941," Ellen Miles to Sallie Ackley, January 31, 1893; Ellen Miles to AED, n.d.

32  Ellen Miles to Sallie Ackley, February 24, 1893; Frances Willard to Phebe Hanaford and Ellen Miles, December 1, 1893, Nantucket Historical Association Research Library, Nantucket, MA.

33  Ellen Miles to AED, January 22, [1894], May 15, 1895; Phebe Hanaford to Mrs. Dickinson, May 18, 1894; Ellen Miles to Sallie Ackley, October 17, 1894; Addie W. Nash to AED May 30, 1893; Phebe Hull to AED, December 9, 1894.

34  Ellen Miles to AED, two undated letters. For further evidence of conflicts and allegations see Lizzie Sargent Dickinson to AED, May 29, 1894 and Emily Dudley Wright to AED, March 24, [1894?] to AED. Both wrote harshly of the "false character" exhibited by Hanaford and Miles in their dealings with AED (quoting Wright).

35  S. May Isom to AED, September 8, 1892, June 29, 1896, October 27, November 2, 1898; Frances Adrienne Tucker to AED, March 29, 1894. There are roughly 25 letters from Isom and another three or four from Tucker in the AEDP.

36  Ann Jenness Miller to Ellen Miles, September 6, October 16, 1893, filed under Miller; *Jenness Miller Monthly*, September 1893, container #24.

37  Ellen Everett to AED, April 11, June 28, 1891, May 19, 1896. Everett wrote to AED about 20 times between 1891 and 1896, in at least six letters she answers follow-up questions about the Drexel fund.

38  AED to "My Dear Ellen" [Everett?], November 12, 1895 (draft); AED to Drexel and Company, November 12, 1895 (draft); AED to A. J. Drexel, November 25, 1895 (draft); Drexel and Company to AED, November 27, 30, 1895; AED to George C. Thomas, November 29, December 3, 1895; AED to George W. Childs, December 29, 1895 (draft). Drexel himself was deceased.

39  AED to Mrs. L. L. Blankenburg [?], December 3, 1895 (draft). This draft included handwritten notations listing the names of the signators on the circular.

40  Hon. Henry [W.?] Blair to AED, November 28, 1895; AED to Henry [W.?] Blair, November 25, December 8, 1895. Blair was probably New Hampshire Congressman Henry W. Blair. AEDP includes similar correspondence with Hon. A. K. McClure.

41  Talcott Williams to AED, December 18, 1895; AED to Talcott Williams, January 8, 1896.

42 AED to Frances Willard, December 29, 1895 (draft), January 24, 1896 (draft). Willard's letters are not in the files.

43 SBA to AED, November 5, 1895.

44 Harriet Purvis to AED, November 6, 1895; AED to Robert Purvis, November 8, 1895; AED to Harriet Purvis, December 9, 1895; AED to Charles Purvis, December 29, 1895, January 6, 1896; Charles Purvis to AED, January 3, 1896. The correspondence ends with AED's January 6 letter.

45 In 1941 George Ackley recalled that the trio moved to Goshen in 1907, but AED's correspondence includes drafts of at least five letters written in 1910 from her Bronx address, followed by letters dated September 27, 1910, and February 11, 1911, with Goshen return addresses, JHY, "Conversations."

46 For early discussions see Mark M. Pomeroy to AED, June 6, 1891; David R. Smith to AED, August 6, 1891; David R. Smith, Jr., to AED, August 31, 1891, February 7, 1892.

47 A. W. Wagnall to AED, May 27, 1893, June 4, 1897 (quotation).

48 AED to Daniel Hastings, January 14, December 23, 1898; Daniel Hastings to AED, February 14, 21, 1898. AED's January 14 letter mentions an earlier letter dated August 13, 1896.

49 AED to Senator [?], January 31, 1901. This is a draft of a long letter AED apparently wrote to all of the United States senators. In one of her scrapbooks AED included a handwritten list of senators, a published directory of federal officeholders (with checkmarks beside names), and a scrawled note that she had written to every senator, container #26. In a draft of a June 8, 1902, letter to the Senate Committee on the Philippine Archipelago, AED stated that she had written to all 88 senators on January 31, 1901.

50 Drafts of many of these letters appear in the AEDP, often referring to earlier—unanswered—letters that do not appear in the files (1901–1909). AEDP also include copies (in her handwriting) of brief responses from Senator Boise Penrose (Pennsylvania), Senator George C. Perkins (California), and Senator Nathan Scott (West Virginia). All copies are dated February 2, 1901. In writing to William Allison, AED reminded the senator of their past relationship. AED to Senator William Allison, December 10, 1907 (draft).

51 AED to Governor Charles Evan Hughes, October 2, 4, 1907; Robert H. Fuller to AED, October 3, 1907; AED to Mrs. Charles Evan Hughes, October 27, 1907.

52 AED to Josiah Quincy, April 16, 1905; Josiah Quincy to AED, April 28, 1905; AED to Henry C. Deming, September 5, 1905; William Lloyd Garrison, Jr., to AED, October 5, December 13, 1906, March 23, May 31, 1907; AED to William Lloyd Garrison, Jr., December 21, 1906, March 19 (quote), April 1, June 14, May 9, 1907 (all drafts). There are roughly 22 letters to and from Garrison in the AEDP, all dated in an eight-month period between 1906 and 1907.

53 Draft book proposal, container #20.

54 AED to Mary B. Bryan, November 25, 1906 (draft); AED to Brand Whitlock, December 22, 1907 (draft), March 13, 1908 (draft); Mary B. Bryan to AED, October 27, November 28, 1907; Brand Whitlock to AED, December 12, 1907, January 7, 1908; AED to Charles Merrill, March 12, April 8, 1908 (drafts); Hewitt Harrison Howland to AED, March 19, 1908; Charles Merrill to AED, April 10, 1908.

55 "Unidentified Manuscript," container #20. This is a roughly 350-page handwritten manuscript, in three folders.

56 AED to William Allison, May 7, 1908 (draft).

57 AED to Aggie Day Robinson, December 6, 1909; Aggie Day Robinson to AED, December 15, 1909, January 18, February 10, 1910; Edith Day Robinson to Sallie Ackley, August 8, September 27, October 20, 1909; January 14 (quotation), 17, 1910; AED to Edith Day Robinson, January 19, 1910; Edith Day Robinson to AED, January 25, 1910; Aggie Day Robinson to Sallie Ackley, March 16, 1910. EDR's first three letters to Ackley are filed with the Ackley letters, the rest are all filed under Robinson.

58 AED to Ida Tarbell, January 27, February 1, 14, 18, 1910; Ida Tarbell to AED, January 29, February 1, 1910.

59 Earle Hooker Eaton to Aggie Day Robinson, February 16, 1910. AED clipped this article from the *Sullivan County Record*, February 10, 1910. It is possible that Robinson acted on her own accord.

60 *Evening Mail*, August 11, 1910, clipping in container #23.

## Notes to Conclusion

1  *Middletown Times Herald*, October 25, 1932, container #30 (not microfilmed).
2  *New York Tribune*, February 3, 1899, container #23; *Goshen Independent Republican*, December 19, 1915, container #30; SED to AED, February 1, [1899], telegram; unidentified clipping, container #30. This clipping described SED's funeral. AED did not attend either funeral.
3  Giraud Chester, *Embattled Maiden: The Life of Anna Dickinson* (New York: G. P. Putnam's Sons, 1951), 292. Chester's biography includes no citations and he occasionally embellished or imagined scenes. His "Note on Sources" mentions an interview with Bertha Ackley, who might have been the source of this story.
4  JHY, "Conversations in re: Anna E. Dickinson with Mr. George Ackley and Miss Bertha Ackley, Goshen, New York, July 29, 30, 1941," JHYP. Hereafter JHY, "Conversations."
5  The AEDP had recently been deposited in the LC, and Young's mentor—Lincoln scholar James Randall—had steered him toward AED as a dissertation topic. Conversation with the author.
6  JHY, "Conversations." Seward also recalled that AED was going through "the change of life" and he speculated that this exacerbated her recent emotional upheavals.
7  Had AED and Ackley shared a relationship that was more balanced and intimate than that of "visiting royalty" and devoted supplicant, George Ackley would certainly have known much more than he said to JHY in 1941. But JHY might have steered clear of such topics, and Ackley might have chosen his own words carefully in front of his sister.
8  "Cupid" to AED, March 11, 1892 (this letter is from Goshen). There are roughly 20 other letters from Ackley to AED in the Ackley folder in the AEDP.
9  Phebe Hull to AED, January 8, 1893; Ellen Miles to Sallie Ackley, February 24, 27, March 3, 1893; May Isom to AED, November 2, 1898; Nellie [Miles] to AED, n.d.
10  JHY, "Conversations." It is unclear where Sallie Ackley's money came from or why it was separate from George's. In 1890 she had invested in Interpines in her own name, which suggests that she had some accumulated wealth prior to her marriage. Perhaps some of this money dated to that investment.
11  Presumably they believed that she had been drinking all along with Sallie Ackley.
12  *Middletown Times Herald*, December 30, 1932, container #30. Ackley sued AED's estate, winning $4,000 as compensation for supporting her since Sallie Ackley's death. Ackley told JHY that the compensation was for the final six years of AED's life. JHY, "Conversations."
13  The most noteworthy exception was her immensely popular "Joan of Arc." But even that lecture had a political subtext about gender roles.
14  Lyman Beecher Stowe, *Saints, Sinners and Beechers* (New York: Blue Ribbon Press, 1934 ), 346; Barbara A. White, *The Beecher Sisters* (New Haven: Yale University Press, 2003), 119–21; Ruth Bordin, *Frances Willard: A Biography* (Chapel Hill: University of North Carolina Press, 1986), 101; Laura E. Skandera-Trombley, *Mark Twain in the Company of Women* (Philadelphia: University of Pennsylvania Press, 1994), 143–50. AED met Olivia Langdon in Hartford. She would later marry Samuel Clemens (Mark Twain).
15  San Francisco *Alta California*, April 5, 1867, online at www.twainquotes.com.
16  See chapter 8.
17  As several historians have noted, Frances Willard had several intimate relationships with women, most notably Anna Gordon, but in Lillian Faderman's words she revealed "little awareness of herself as a homosexual or sexual invert." Lillian Faderman, *To Believe in Women: What Lesbians Have Done For America—A History* (Boston: Houghton Mifflin Company, 1999), 30–35; Ruth Bordin, *Frances Willard: A Biography* (Chapel Hill: University of North Carolina Press, 1986), 45–47.
18  Several female correspondents did allude to her reticence in accepting their more intimate overtures.
19  MD was not only devoutly religious, she also frequently warned her daughter about the temptations on the road. There is some evidence that she specifically disapproved of some of AED's friends.
20  For two recent studies see Glenn C. Altschuler and Stuart M. Blumin, *Rude Republic: Americans and Their Politics in the Nineteenth Century* (Princeton: Princeton University Press, 2000); Melanie Susan Gustafson, *Women and the Republican Party, 1854–1924* (Urbana: University of Illinois Press, 2001).

21 By refusing to work with Frances Willard's Women Christian Temperance Union AED lost access to some of the late nineteenth century's most enthusiastic crowds.

22 Susan A. Glenn, *Female Spectacle: The Theatrical Roots of Modern Feminism* (Cambridge, MA: Harvard University Press, 2000).

23 *Dictionary of American Biography on CD-ROM* (New York: Charles Scribner's, 1998).

24 This plaque is on display at the Slate Hill Cemetery in Goshen, New York.

## Notes to Bibliographic Essay

1 Most of the AEDP are available on 25 reels of microfilm, but the most recent acquisitions are in two unfilmed containers.

2 *New York Herald, New York World, National Anti-Slavery Standard, Providence Journal, Chicago Tribune, Peoria Morning Mail, Hartford Times, Hartford Post, Hartford Courant, Hartford Press, Middletown (CT) Constitution.* In most cases I surveyed these newspapers around the dates of Dickinson's local lectures.

3 I have acknowledged specific debts to Dr. Young's research in the notes. In one instance, Susan Dickinson's 1890 letter to Rutherford B. Hayes, Young's notes pointed me to an archive I would not otherwise have consulted.

4 The ECS-SBA Papers include documents from many archives. See Patricia G. Holland and Anna D. Gordon, eds., *The Papers of Elizabeth Cady Stanton and Susan. B. Anthony: Guide and Index to the Microfilm Edition* (Wilmington, DE: Scholarly Resources, 1992). The AEDP include over 60 letters from Anthony to Dickinson, the ECS-SBA Papers only include about a half-dozen letters from Dickinson to Anthony that had been selected for publication in Ida Husted Harper, *Life and Work of Susan B. Anthony* (Indianapolis: Bobbs-Merril, 1908), before Anthony burned her letters. Many valuable letters are reprinted in the multivolume collection, Holland and Gordon, eds., *Papers of Elizabeth Cady Stanton and Susan B. Anthony* (New Brunswick, NJ: Rutgers University Press, 1998, 2000).

# INDEX